THEORETICAL ASPECTS OF MEMORY

In recent years there have been major developments in our theoretical understanding of how our memories function. This accompanying volume to *Aspects of Memory: The Practical Aspects* is a collection of reviews of these developments by internationally recognized experts. It complements the review of the practical application of memory provided by the latter volume.

The first two chapters set past theorizing about memory in an historical context and identify the major aspects of memory to be captured by any theoretical account. Later chapters go on to discuss theoretical accounts of working memory, the development of memory and context-dependent memory. The new volume of *Theoretical Aspects of Memory* also explores major new theoretical ideas such as implicit memory and connectionism. A final section discusses the respective strengths and problems of naturalistic and laboratory research on memory.

Designed primarily with students in mind, the two volumes on aspects of memory provide an excellent authoritative textbook of current approaches to memory from both an applied and a theoretical perspective.

Peter E. Morris is Professor of Psychology at the University of Lancaster. **Michael Gruneberg** is a Senior Lecturer in Psychology at University College, Swansea.

THEORETICAL ASPECTS OF MEMORY

Second Edition

Edited by
Peter Morris
and
Michael Gruneberg

London and New York

First published in 1978
by Methuen & Co. Ltd.

Volume one of the second edition first published in 1992
by Routledge
This second edition first published in 1994
by Routledge
11 New Fetter Lane, London EC4P 4EE

Simultaneously published in the USA and Canada
by Routledge
29 West 35th Street, New York, NY 10001

Typeset in Baskerville by
Pat and Anne Murphy, Highcliffe-on-Sea, Dorset
Printed and bound in Great Britain by
Mackays of Chatham PLC, Chatham, Kent

British Library Cataloguing in Publication Data
A catalogue record for this book is available from
the British Library

Library of Congress Cataloging in Publication Data
A catalog record for this book has been requested

ISBN 0-415-06957-2 (hbk)
ISBN 0-415-06958-0 (pbk)

CONTENTS

CONTENTS

FIGURES AND TABLES

FIGURES

TABLES

CONTRIBUTORS

Mahzarin R. Banaji   Yale University, New Haven, USA.

Alan F. Collins   Lancaster University, UK.

Robert G. Crowder   Yale University, New Haven, USA.

Susan E. Gathercole   Bristol University, UK.

Michael M. Gruneberg   University College of Swansea, UK.

J. Richard Hanley   University of Liverpool, UK.

Dennis C. Hay   Lancaster University, UK.

Peter E. Morris   Lancaster University, UK.

Douglas L. Nelson   University of South Florida, Tampa, USA.

Michael Pressley   University of Maryland, College Park, USA.

Steven M. Smith   Texas A&M University, USA.

Peggy Van Meter   University of Maryland, College Park, USA.

Eugene Winograd   Emory University, USA.

Andrew W. Young   University of Durham, UK.

PREFACE

This volume represents an update of the first edition of *Aspects of Memory* (Gruneberg and Morris 1978) that was devoted to theoretical considerations. The enormous growth of research in all aspects of memory since the first edition has made it necessary to divide this edition into two volumes. The first volume on the practical aspects was published in 1992.

As with the considerable advance in the application of memory research, since the first volume was published there have been major developments in our theoretical understanding of memory. These are reflected in the many new topics covered in the current new volume that were absent in the first edition. Some issues were discussed in that edition, but have now developed into important areas with rich theoretical bases. These are represented in the present volume by the chapters on developmental aspects of strategic behaviour and meta-memory (Pressley and Van Meter), working memory (Gathercole) and context (Smith). Other areas were virtually unknown in 1978, but have come to be major influences on the theoretical thinking of researchers on memory. Two such areas represented here are implicit memory (Nelson) and connectionism (Collins and Hay).

There has also been a growing awareness that there are many ways in which memory can be studied and conceptualized that can provide competing frameworks within which research can be investigated. Connectionism is one such approach. Not only does it provide a new way of conceptualizing how information may be stored, but it also leads to the asking of novel and important questions about the processes underlying memory. At the same time, there has been a rapid growth in the study of patients with brain damage who demonstrate specific deficits in what they can remember. A whole area of cognitive neuropsychology has grown up studying individuals whose unfortunate injuries have nevertheless cast an interesting light upon the workings of the cognitive system in general and the memory system in particular (Hanley and Young).

The burgeoning activity in both practical and theoretical investigations has inevitably led to encounters with major problems. How do you capture the richness of real world remembering in your studies? How do you ensure that what you deduce can be validated and generalized to other situations? Some researchers have preferred to emphasize the value of looking at natural situations to ensure that the memory processes are recognized in their full variety (Winograd). Others have argued that there are dangers in moving away from the generalizability and control that traditional laboratory research sought to provide (Banaji and Crowder).

As in the first edition, we have tried to set the current work in an historical context by explaining how the study of memory has developed since the first speculations on the memory processes by the Greeks as early as 500 BC (Morris). Again, as in the previous edition, we have tried to survey the many factors that must be taken into account by anyone trying to understand and explain memory. Strategies, the material to be learned, metamemory, the structure of the memory system, and many other factors must be considered, and we have tried to provide the reader with a framework as an introduction to these (Morris and Gruneberg).

This and the first volume give, we believe, a major coverage of the field of memory research. They are special in that they draw upon experts who work in each area to give an introduction to their research areas. Nevertheless, the work as a whole is written with both the undergraduate and postgraduate student in mind, as well as those engaged in memory research who wish to have an up-to-date account of research in areas other than their own specific interests.

Peter E. Morris
Michael M. Gruneberg

REFERENCE

Gruneberg, M.M. and Morris, P.E. (eds) (1978) *Aspects of Memory*, London: Methuen.

1

THEORIES OF MEMORY
An historical perspective
P.E. Morris

When you have read the chapters in the two volumes of *Aspects of Memory*, you will be aware of the major current theoretical and practical issues that are being tackled by current researchers. However, to take just that snapshot of the present time and to ignore the presuppositions that have shaped the development of thinking about memory can leave the newcomer to the area with many unanswered questions and a sense of 'Yes, but why *these* questions rather than . . . ?'. Therefore, this chapter presents a brief history of the study of memory. In doing so, the hope is not only to provide a context to help explain the preconceptions and reactions of current researchers but also to highlight some of the themes that recur throughout the chapters of the two volumes. A full history of memory would require many volumes and a deeper consideration of the aims, preconceptions and world of those theorizing about memory in the past. Here, the object is to highlight some of the concepts that have shaped current theoretical ideas, many of which have a long history.

CLASSICAL ACCOUNTS OF MEMORY

The earliest consideration of the nature of memory, as with so many aspects of science and philosophy, can be found in the writings of the classical Greek and Roman philosophers and scholars. The initial reference to an observation about memory comes when the first mnemonic method was, according to tradition, invented.

Cicero, writing in 55 BC in his *De Oratore*, describes the tragedy that is supposed to have led the poet Simonides to the invention of the mnemonic *method of loci*. Simonides lived from around 556 to 468 BC and was, according to Yates (1966), 'one of the most admired lyric poets of Greece'. However, after singing a poem in honour of Scopas

1

of Thessaly, the latter gave him only half of the agreed fee because the poem had included a passage in praise of Castor and Pollux. Scopas told Simonides to obtain the rest of his fee from the twin gods. During the subsequent banquet, a message came to Simonides that two young men were outside, waiting to see him. Outside, he found no one, but while he was absent the roof of the hall fell in, mangling the bodies of all inside. The twin gods had repaid Simonides by saving him from disaster. He was able to identify the bodies for the relatives because he could remember who had been sitting in each place. According to Cicero, this experience suggested to Simonides that memory could be improved by selecting places and forming mental images of the things to be remembered in those places. This very effective mnemonic method (see e.g. Morris 1979; Higbee 1988) was taught in classical times by Cicero and others to aid orators in the recall of their speeches.

Elements of the story of Simonides with its mixture of mythology and fact may be an invention, but there is no doubt that Simonides was well known in classical times for being the inventor of the first memory aid. He is mentioned by many writers, and the Parian Chronicle (a marble tablet from Paros) refers to him as 'the inventor of the system of memory-aids' when recording his winning of a chorus prize in 477 BC (Yates 1966).

By Roman times, when Cicero was writing, memory improvement techniques were well developed, perhaps not surprisingly for a civilization that respected the orator and had less recourse to permanent means of recording information. Cicero provided an account of memory improvement for the orator, but earlier, in the mid-80s BC, a teacher of rhetoric whose name is unknown had written *Ad Herennium*, a textbook of memory techniques for the orator. The author distinguished between natural and artificial memory. The former involved the entry of information into memory simultaneously with thought; the latter was memory that was strengthened by training, which was the theme of *Ad Herennium*.

The *Ad Herennium* includes many of the traditional memory improvement techniques that were advocated and refined throughout the Middle Ages and up until the present day. The method of loci holds a central place, but other elements of the mnemonic systems also appear. So, for example, the translation of an abstract concept into an imageable form, as occurs in the keyword system (Chapter 7, Volume 1), is illustrated by recommending that an image of a ram's testicles be used to represent witnesses (*testes* in Greek).

2

By the first century AD, Quintilian in *Institutio oratoria* is casting doubt upon the more grandiose claims for the mnemonic method of loci. He points out the difficulties of forming images to abstract concepts and of remembering the words of whole speeches through the mnemonic. Rather, he advocates learning speeches by heart, with some aid from mnemonics.

This early history of memory improvement reflects the need felt then, as now, for ways of improving memory. The results were the product of intelligent study of success and failure, but were relatively little supported by theory and probably not at all by systematic experiment.

The theoretical account of memory was then, as now, heavily influenced by the available technology for recording and storing information. The most common way of making notes was to use a wax tablet that could then be cleared by either melting or scraping. This provided a very attractive metaphor for the storage of memories that recurs again and again in the accounts of the memory processes both in explaining the mnemonic systems and in the writings of philosophers when they came to consider memory.

PLATO

A famous early discussion of memory is by Plato in *Theaetetus*. Plato has Socrates introduce two metaphors of memory, one the wax tablet, the other an aviary. So, Socrates says:

> suppose for the sake of argument, that there's an imprint-receiving piece of wax in our minds: bigger in some, smaller in others; of cleaner wax in some, of dirtier wax in others; of harder wax in some, of softer in others . . .
>
> (Plato, *Theaetetus* 191c–d)

> if there is anything we want to remember . . . we hold it under the perceptions and conceptions and imprint them on it, as if we were taking impressions of signet rings. Whatever is imprinted we remember and know . . . but whatever is smudged out or proves unable to be imprinted, we've forgotten and don't know.
>
> (ibid.: 191d)

Later, Socrates gives an interpretation of a failure to recognize two friends:

I see you both some way off and not properly, and I'm eager to assign the imprint which belongs to each to the seeing which belongs to each, and to insert and fit the seeing into its own trace, so that recognition may take place. But, missing that aim, and making a transposition, I attach the seeing of each one to the imprint which belongs to the other, like people who put their shoes on the wrong feet.

(Plato, *Theaetetus* 193c)

This, then, is a template theory of memory. What is stored is an exact copy of the original and this memory trace is used by matching a new perception against the imprint.

As a starting point for the examination of memory, this is a good theory to consider, since it seems to involve the most simple technology for the recording and recognition and is the most obvious record of the past. Today we might have thought of video recordings, but the idea of memory based upon an exact record of the past and a comparison of that record with the current input is a sensible starting point for asking the question 'Is our memory system actually like that?'

Of course, it is not. We normally do not remember exact details. Our memories provide a much more complex, processed, selected and elaborated knowledge base than that of the simple copy. Template theories of perception fail to cope with the variability of stimuli that we easily process as similar (e.g. letters of the alphabet written by different people). The wax impressions would need to be the same in virtually every detail for a new perception to be reliably matched. All template theories have problems in coping with changes in the stimulus on different occasions. So, for example, seeing someone at a distance of 4 metres when we had previously seen them at only 2 metres would make recognition impossible because the image would be the wrong size. The wax tablet metaphor has no means of identifying which tablet should be examined, nor addresses how the system copes with finding one tablet among the millions that would need to exist to record all of our memories. Nor does it speak to the use of past experience as when we apply our knowledge to comprehend and predict in situations that are novel but familiar, such as eating in a new restaurant or going to a new dentist.

These criticisms of the wax tablet metaphor are not intended to denigrate Plato. He was primarily concerned with clarifying the nature of knowledge, and the metaphors were introduced to bring to the reader's attention certain aspects of remembering without implying that this was all that was involved in memorizing and recall. Nevertheless, the example does illustrate the dangers of being captured by the attraction of a metaphor. Most classical and medieval writers seem to have been satisfied with the wax tablet as a metaphor for memory. Even Marshall and Fryer (1978) in the first edition of *Aspects of Memory* describe it as a superb conceptualization of recognition memory. Yet as a theory of memory it was obviously deeply flawed. Why did it have such a hold upon the thinking of the best educated and most intelligent over hundreds of years?

There are several possible reasons. One is that there was little alternative technology of information storage to challenge the wax tablet model. Many developments in theorizing about memory have been stimulated by advances in the way that information is handled. Second, like many rich metaphors, the wax tablet is satisfying because it provides explanations for a range of phenomena. At least in that way it was a good theory. Plato could explain individual differences in memory (an issue sadly largely neglected since) in terms of the quality and amount of the wax. So, for example, if someone has 'a tiny little mind', imprints will 'have fallen on top of one another because of lack of space'. Over 2,000 years later, Freud (1924) was to be fascinated by the power of the wax tablet metaphor when he speculated on the Mystic Writing Pad as a model of the memory processes. This still popular child's toy allows writing to be erased by merely pulling free a covering sheet from another layer to which it adheres when pressed – the modern wax tablet.

However, rich metaphors may be deceptive if they are not carefully delimited and their predictions evaluated. Only some properties of the metaphor will be appropriate. Which, and how far, needs further, usually empirical, investigation. Do the individual differences in memory that occur really match those predicted by the metaphor? When should the metaphor be taken seriously and when not? For example, should one avoid getting one's head hot in case the wax melts and one's memory is erased? Obviously, this is taking seriously an irrelevant aspect of the metaphor, but which aspects are or are not relevant has to be specified and some aspects that would not be considered as relevant today once seemed so to advocates of the wax tablet metaphor. Aristotle, for example, seems to have believed that the habitual level of activity of the individual influenced the permanence of the quasi-wax encoding.

Plato was not interested in evaluating his metaphor for the very good reason that he had proposed it only as a means to helping the interpretation of the real question that interested him, namely the reliability of knowledge. The wax tablet model is propounded by Socrates only as a step in clarifying the relationship between perceiving and knowing. Elsewhere, Plato hints at other theories of memory, related to the frequency of use. So, in the *Phaedrus*, he comments that the invention of writing will produce forgetfulness because those who use it will not practise their memories. This is not, necessarily, the first reference to a common and erroneous view that non-literate societies place a higher value on memory and achieved feats of verbatim recall now lost to literate societies (Hunter 1984). Rather, Plato is concerned that without writing people have to debate to learn. Memory, then, for Plato is linked to wisdom and understanding, a view that has become important in modern work on schemas and knowledge bases (see Chapter 2).

For all the philosophers who wrote about memory prior to the nineteenth century their main preoccupation was to try to understand the status of what people claim to know and to believe about the world. Because such knowledge inevitably is based in and draws upon what we can remember and have learned from our past experience, a theory of learning and memory was required. So, philosophers from Plato through Aristotle to Hume and later found it necessary to speculate about the nature of memory. Many of these speculations were interesting. However, few of them were evaluated for their completeness and ability to capture the phenomena of memory. Nevertheless, they laid a set of presuppositions that determined the classical education of the philosophers and physicians who became the first experimental psychologists. These presuppositions became incorporated into the pre-theoretical assumptions of the early students of memory and often shaped the questions that they asked.

Plato takes the examination of memory and its implication for what we know further by imagining that what we have learned is like an aviary. Socrates remarks that:

> when we're children this receptacle [the aviary] is empty, and in place of the birds we must think of pieces of knowledge. Whatever piece of knowledge someone comes to possess and shuts up in his enclosure, we must say he has come to know.
>
> (Plato, *Theaetetus* 197d)

Plato draws the distinction between possessing knowledge and 'having' it. One may possess it as a bird enclosed within the aviary,

6

but may not be able to catch it. The same distinction was drawn again by Tulving and Pearlstone (1966) when they distinguished between information that is available (i.e. stored in memory), but which may or may not be accessible (i.e. retrieved from memory).

Plato's aviary metaphor is an early recognition that many memory phenomena result not from the failure to encode, but from a failure to retrieve. For the first time, retrieval became an issue for theorizing about memory.

ARISTOTLE

Plato's pupil, Aristotle, took a greater interest in memory than did his teacher. Aristotle appears to have been interested in memory as a phenomenon in its own right rather than merely as a factor influencing questions concerning the status of knowledge. Nevertheless, his work on memory, *De Memoria et Reminiscentia*, is an appendix to his *De Anima* which is his exposition of his theory of knowledge.

Aristotle is usually attributed with being the first person to propound the theory of the association of ideas as the basis of memory. So, for example, in *A History of Psychology* Leahey writes that 'Plato . . . hinted at laws of association, but Aristotle was the first systematically to exploit them. Aristotle discusses three laws of association – similarity, contiguity and contrast' (1987: 52).

Anyone turning to Aristotle's writings expecting to find a clear account of these laws, as they are, for example, later spelt out by the British Empiricist authors such as Hume (1739), will be disappointed. The nearest that Aristotle comes to stating the laws is when he discusses deliberately searching our memories. He has been discussing how recollection occurs through changes in the images that we experience. 'Acts of recollection happen,' he says, 'because one change is of a nature to occur after another' (Aristotle, *De Memoria et Reminiscentia* 451b10). These changes may follow each other 'out of necessity' or 'by habit'.

> When we recollect, then, we undergo one of the earlier changes, until we undergo the one after which the change in question habitually occurs. And this is exactly why we hunt for the successor, starting in our thoughts from the present or from something else, and from something similar, or opposite, or neighbouring. By this means recollection occurs.
>
> (451b16–20)

7

In the days when the theory of association was dominant, it may have been invigorating to see in this the first exposition of the theory. Now that the theory has been superseded by richer ideas about the nature of memory it may be fairer to recognize that Aristotle is not tying himself to any formal theory of the way in which images change in memory. Even the translation of *ethos* as 'habit' can be misleading, since Aristotle appears to be referring to a tendency rather than to the result of the repetition of experience. Aristotle specifically remarks that:

> It can happen that by undergoing certain changes once a person is more habituated than he is by undergoing other changes many times. And this is why after seeing some things once we remember better than we do after seeing other things many times.
>
> (451b10)

While it is reasonable to deduce from Aristotle's comments in *De Memoria et Reminiscentia* that he recognized that similar, opposite and contiguous memories may be good retrieval cues, it seems unfair to tie him too firmly to a now outmoded theory of associations. Read today, his comments seem closer to empirical observations about memory than a strong theoretical statement of associationism.

Nevertheless, Aristotle does make other strong theoretical assertions about memory. They are not about associations but about mental images. He claimed that 'it is not possible to think without an image'. This idea that remembering must be the experiencing of a mental image of something from the past was a common theme in classical accounts of memory. Furthermore, as we shall see, it continued through the thinking of the British Empiricist philosophers and found its way into the accounts of memory offered by the first experimental psychologists.

While mental images are common in some types of recall, especially autobiographical memories (see Chapter 9, Volume 1; Conway 1990), and can play important parts in memorizing and recall (see e.g. Morris 1992), a great deal of remembering takes place without such images. Moreover, the idea that images are the basis of thinking is dangerously misleading (e.g. Wittgenstein 1953). No single image, or even set of images, can capture all the meaning of a concept. For example, no image of a triangle can represent all triangles. There is much more to meaning that a mere reproduction of some copy of the thing. A swastika, for example, represents a very different dark set of meanings to someone aware of the history of the Third Reich than to a child who encounters a swastika for the first time, even though the image is the same. Image theories of memory stumble over the representation of abstract concepts, just as such concepts presented problems to orators using imagery mnemonics. Many concepts, such as Wittgenstein's famous example of 'game', cannot be defined in images any more than in lists of defining features.

Before leaving Aristotle, it is worth observing that some of what he said about memory was untrue. Here is an early illustration of the danger of accepting, as many philosophers subsequently did, the word of an authority, however famous, rather than empirically testing their claims. For example, Aristotle adopts Plato's idea of memory as an imprint and says that:

> memory does not occur in those who are subject to a lot of movement . . . just as if the change and the seal were falling on running water . . . the very quick and the very slow are also obviously neither of them good at remembering. For the former are too fluid, the latter too hard.
>
> (Aristotle, *De Memoria et Reminiscentia* 430a32)

The writings of Plato and Aristotle have been dealt with in some detail because they were so influential in defining the way memory was conceptualized prior to the advent of experimental psychology. Furthermore, the theories of Plato and Aristotle illustrate the attractions and pitfalls of a non-empirical approach to theorizing about memory. Rich metaphors may be proposed, but which are correct? The further elaboration of these metaphors normally requires taking the theories to the world to see how they cope with predicting what will and what will not be remembered.

THE BRITISH EMPIRICISTS

Through the Dark and Middle Ages memory continued to interest the well educated, and from St Augustine to Francis Bacon speculations on the organization of knowledge continued and the mnemonic systems were used and refined. A discussion of these years will be found in Yates (1966). However, our interest is in theories of memory, especially as they have influenced the development of current theorizing. We will therefore leap across 1,200 years and turn to the writings of the British Empiricist philosophers.

The British Empiricist philosophers, including Hobbes, Locke,

Berkeley and Hume, developed a theory of knowledge that rested heavily upon the association of ideas in memory. They believed that all knowledge was derived from experience – the mind of the child at birth being blank, waiting for experience of the world to 'write' upon it. While German philosophy reacted against this view that all the processes of the mind were the consequences of experience, the English-speaking philosophers remained sympathetic to these ideas and they provided the background framework for many of the first experimental psychologists.

The present discussion will concentrate upon David Hume's (1739) exposition of his view of memory in *A Treatise of Human Nature* because it represents the Empiricist view of memory in a full and clear manner. Hume begins his *Treatise* with the statement that 'All the perceptions of the human mind resolve themselves into two distinct kinds, which I shall call *impressions* and *ideas*'. Impressions are 'all our sensations, passions, and emotions, as they make their first appearance in the soul'. Ideas are 'the faint images of these in thinking and reasoning . . .'. Ideas are, therefore, memories, the re-experiencing of earlier impressions.

It is interesting to note the similarities in thinking about memory shared by Aristotle and Hume. Memory is about the re-experiencing of mental images that are copies of the original experience. Hume goes so far as to say that:

> memory preserves the original form in which its objects were presented, and that wherever we depart from it in recollecting anything, it proceeds from some defect or imperfection in that faculty.
>
> (Hume 1739: bk I, pt I, sect. I)

Hume does distinguish between memory and imagination. He asserts that the ideas of memory are more lively and strong than those of imagination. The issue of distinguishing between memories for real experiences and those that have been only imagined has returned to modern psychology under the title of 'reality monitoring' (e.g. Johnson and Raye 1981). Hume believed that all complex ideas acquired through association could be separated by the imagination. Like Aristotle, he searches for a way to characterize the link between ideas, and he describes it as 'a gentle force which commonly prevails' (bk I, pt I, sect. IV). He asserts that:

The qualities from which this association arises, and by which the mind is after this manner conveyed from one idea to another, are three, viz. *resemblance, contiguity* in time or place, and *cause* and *effect.*

So, 'our imagination runs easily from one idea to any other that *resembles* it', and:

> as the senses, in changing their objects, are necessitated to change them regularly, and take them as they lie *contiguous* to each other, the imagination must by long custom acquire the same method of thinking, and run along the parts of space and time in conceiving its objects.

As an account of free association, this would stand as a good approximation. However, Hume sees it as an account of the very basis of psychology and, through it, of epistemology. It describes for him and the other associationists the way in which the mind works, developing its concepts and its memories. As such, it is lacking in any recognition that there is much more work for a cognitive processing system to do if it is to make sense of the world and guide the comprehension, planning and acting that humans routinely demonstrate.

EBBINGHAUS

The latter half of the nineteenth century saw the development of experimental psychology, and with it the experimental study of memory. Traditionally, memory researchers have looked to Ebbinghaus' (1885) monograph *Uber das Gedachtnis* (translated into English under the title *Memory*) as the starting point of their subdiscipline. Ebbinghaus' study was, however, just one, though by far the most elaborate and controlled, study of memory in the later years of the nineteenth century. Some of these other studies will be considered shortly, but Ebbinghaus' influence upon twentieth-century memory research justifies a description of his work.

Ebbinghaus was much influenced by the history of theorizing about memory and he refers to conscious mental images and the laws of association. He was also interested in the range of memory phenomena, not just the nonsense syllable lists with which he is associated. He comments upon individual differences:

> One individual overflows with poetical reminiscences, another directs symphonies from memory, while numbers and formulae,

11

which come to a third without effort, slip away from the other two as from a polished stone.

(1885, 1913 translation: 3)

Nevertheless, he criticized the psychology of his time for being 'rich in anecdote and illustration' but unable to give detailed answers. He commented that:

we use different metaphors – stored up ideas, engraved images, well-beaten paths. There is only one thing certain about these figures of speech and that is that they are not suitable.

(1885, 1913 translation: 5)

Ebbinghaus' solution was to memorize lists of nonsense syllables (e.g. ZUD, VIW, QAR), reading and recalling the lists in order at a rate of 150 per minute. He avoided any mnemonic techniques and standardized his procedure as much as possible. In this way he was able to quantify, in terms of the time taken to relearn a list, the amount forgotten, and so study learning and retention as a function of length of list, number of repetitions, time since learning, repeated learning and the order of associations. He was able to show clear regularities – for example, in the rate of forgetting with its initial rapid loss of information, slowing exponentially over time.

The contrast to the pre-experimental speculations about memory is hard to overstate. Following the publication of Ebbinghaus' results, it was no longer satisfactory to speculate about memory but then to ignore evaluating those speculations. Ebbinghaus demonstrated what Wundt, the founder of experimental psychology, had doubted, the possibility of experimentally studying memory.

OTHER EARLY EXPERIMENTAL STUDIES OF MEMORY

Ebbinghaus himself commented that his method penetrated more deeply into memory processes 'only for a limited field'. He himself compared his method with his own learning of cantos from Byron's *Don Juan*. At virtually the same time as Ebbinghaus was reporting his studies, other psychologists were investigating a range of far more naturalistic memory phenomena.

Galton (1883) had been exploring autobiographical memories in a number of ways. He had asked eminent acquaintances, including Charles Darwin, to describe images of their breakfast tables, and he had more specifically retrieved autobiographical memories with cue words in a technique revived nearly 100 years later (see Chapter 9, Volume 1). Even earlier he had been experimenting with combining photographic images to represent compound associations in memory (Robertson 1879).

Cattell, beginning in Wundt's laboratory, had been measuring the time taken to recall in a range of conditions, such as giving category names to instances and vice versa, and recalling in one's own or a foreign language (Cattell 1887; Cattell and Bryant 1889). A little later, he had demonstrated the very poor memory that we have for familiar scenes and for the recent weather (Cattell 1895). Meanwhile, William James (1890) had been studying the possibility of improving memory for poetry through practice, using both himself and his associates as subjects. Kirkpatrick (1894) examined the effect of concreteness on recall, using word lists but also real objects by testing subjects from third grade to college. Smith (1895) showed how the recall of letters in an array was influenced by a concurrent task such as addition, saying 'la' or tapping. Colegrove (1899) collected details of the vivid memories that were retained many years after the assassination of Abraham Lincoln. In Germany, Stern (1904) was exploring distortions of eyewitness testimony in adults and children. All of these early studies opened up areas that have been studied in detail in recent years. However, at the time, while they showed the possibilities of empirical studies of memory, they were often free-standing investigations, having little theoretical grounding and not being followed up by other investigators.

Outside what was becoming 'mainstream' psychology, the psychology of memory was attracting growing attention. Amnesia was considered by Ribot (1882), while memory or its repression was central to Freud's psychoanalysis. The latter introduced the concept of repression in the mid-1890s (e.g. Freud 1896) and, of course, memory was heavily involved within other aspects of psychoanalysis, such as *The Interpretation of Dreams* (Freud 1900).

One major theoretical highlight of the late nineteenth century was the writing on memory by William James (1890). Although he collected data on remembering, James contrasted with Ebbinghaus in his concentration on theoretical rather than upon empirical questions. He distinguished between what was remembered from current consciousness, which he called primary memory, and what he called secondary memory, which involved knowledge that had been absent from consciousness. Here is the beginning of the working memory/long-term memory distinction that has been so important, especially in British psychology. James discusses many aspects of memory, but in his other writings the hints of the reinterpretation of the question to be answered by psychologists appear. James is well known for his emphasis upon the importance of habit in determining behaviour. He also discusses how the conscious experiences associated with novel actions disappear as they become habitual. Here is the basis for a psychology of what people can do, their behaviour, rather than what they consciously experience.

Even so, in the early years of the twentieth century, memory was still regarded by most psychologists as the conscious experiencing of images from the past. Nevertheless, even the structuralist Titchener attacked the simplistic theories, such as that memory involved the storing of all experiences. He stated that:

> There is no such thing as mental retention, the persistence of an idea from month to month or year to year in some mental pigeon-hole from which it can be drawn when wanted. What persists is the tendency to connection.
>
> (1899: 288)

This 'tendency to connection' refers to an association. The memory, however, according to Titchener 'is formed afresh'.

Meanwhile, the mechanization of the study of nonense syllables had begun when Muller and Schumann (1894) invented the memory drum by which the syllables were viewed through a slit as they revolved on a drum. The early years of the twentieth century saw a mixture of materials and techniques being studied under the functionalist approach. While some studied the recall of nonsense syllables or related material (e.g. Henmon 1917), others used prose passages (e.g. Lyon 1917) and even advertisements (Strong 1912).

BEHAVIOURISM AND 'VERBAL LEARNING'

However, a fundamental re-examination of the object of psychology was approaching. Some were frustrated in their search for the content of consciousness. The imageless thought controversy had brought introspection into disrepute (see Woodworth 1938 for a review by one of the protagonists). More psychologists were studying what people did rather than what they consciously experienced (see e.g. Woodworth 1931), and the philosophical climate was emphasizing positivism and the need for objective verification of scientific (or indeed any) statements (e.g. Ayer 1936; Wittgenstein 1922). Watson's advocacy of behaviour rather than consciousness as the proper subject for psychologists fell on sympathetic ears, and behaviourism became, for the middle years of the twentieth century, the dominant approach to psychology.

For the study of memory, although not of learning, this was a major set-back. It is possible to see the advent of behaviourism as the beginning of the dark ages for memory research: the vandals of behaviourism destroying the growing research base in a wide range of important areas, all of which have proved their potential since the renaissance of cognitive psychology from the late 1960s. The behaviourists regarded memory as a topic tarred with the introspectionist brush. Traditionally, it was about conscious experiences, so that the term had to be either abandoned or redefined. Watson, the founder of behaviourism, would use the term 'memory' only in inverted commas, and explained that:

> By 'memory' . . . we mean nothing except the fact that when we meet a stimulus again after an absence, we do the old habitual thing (say the old words and show the old visceral–emotional–behaviour) that we learned to do when we were in the presence of that stimulus in the first place.
>
> (1931: 237)

That this is a naive parody of what happens when we remember should be obvious. We spend much of our time in the same workplace or rooms at home with the same people, but very rarely repeat the same remarks with the tedious regularity that Watson's definition would imply.

However, if behaviourism was to suppress the study of so many aspects of memory, it did promote the study of learning. Equipped with the success of Pavlov's classical conditioning studies and Thorndike's Law of Effect, the behaviourists were able to place learning at the top of the psychological agenda. Before James (1890) *learning* in the sense of *modification of behaviour through experience* had hardly been considered by psychologists who had taken the content of consciousness as their topic. Yet, if we wish to understand what people do, it is surely more important to understand how our behaviour is shaped than to know what influences our recollections. As an agenda for research, it is hard to fault the behaviourists' emphasis upon learning. Here is not the place to discuss their failures.

The relationship between learning and memory is one that still needs considerable clarification. One major difference is that while theories of learning concern themselves with the changes that follow experience, there is no place in their theoretical descriptions for retrieval as some form of internally directed search or selection among competing alternatives. The changes that took place when the learning occurred made the state of the organism such that in a particular set of stimulus conditions a particular response will occur. The theoretical explanation has to be directed to the initial learning conditions. Perhaps more important, there is no re-experiencing of some aspect of the original conditions implied in theories of learning. On the other hand, it is the sense of re-experiencing something of the past that has been the focus of the phenomena that theories of memory have sought to explain. At its extreme this is represented by a very rich and detailed memory, as in the recall of flashbulb memories (e.g. Brown and Kulik 1977), and more commonly in a sense of familiarity and an awareness that we had encountered this in the past.

At times in the history of psychology the dominant view seems to have been that either learning or memory was subsumable into the other without need for subdivision or clarification. Until the end of the nineteenth century it was memory that held centre stage. The behaviourists reversed this and dismissed memory. Following the decline of behaviourism and the growth of cognitive psychology, memory came to the fore again. At times it looked as if phenomena best explicable in a learning framework were being forced into that of memory. Recently, perhaps for the first time, both memory and learning processes are being considered together. So, psychologists have discovered that different types of learning and remembering, generically referred to as implicit and explicit memories, are taking place at the same time with differing influences from external variables (see Chapter 5). At the same time, the study of learning has re-emerged, equipped with the very powerful simulation techniques of connectionism (see Chapter 7).

But we are getting ahead of the story of the history of memory. The years from the 1920s to the 1940s saw the term 'memory' largely disappearing from the writings of those interested in human learning. In McGeoch's (1942) classic review of *The Psychology of Human Learning* the index has no entry for memory, although there are solitary references to 'memorising, logical; memorising rote' and 'memory span'. There are, of course, no references to memory in Hull's (1943) *Principles of Behaviour*, the great attempt to systematize learning theory. Nevertheless, under the banner of 'verbal learning' the approach initiated by Ebbinghaus was being systematically developed. I will return to this major contribution shortly, but first it is worth noting that not everyone was following the behaviourist crusade.

At least two classic books from the 1930s were willing to speak of memory and remembering. One was Woodworth's *Experimental Psychology*. Woodworth chose to begin this epic review of all of experimental psychology with a chapter entitled 'Memory'. To Woodworth, a distinction between learning and memory was misleading. He wrote that:

A continuous series of cases extends from the revival of one's own experiences at one extreme to the automatic performance of a learned movement at the other, and the whole series belongs together. The difference between the extremes is a matter deserving attention, but the likeness is more fundamental.

(1938: 5)

Whether Woodworth was right still remains a major issue for theorists of memory and learning. Are the underlying processes of perceptual, motor, verbal, semantic and autobiographical memories fundamentally the same, or have we evolved mechanisms that differ radically under the demands upon these memories in serving their respective aspects of cognition? Whatever the answer, Woodworth's view allowed him to draw together the best review of research on memory up until that time. But Woodworth was already an elder statesman of psychology, and he was noted for his eclecticism. He had remarked at the end of his *Contemporary Schools of Psychology* (1931) that sitting on the fence gave you a better view.

The other classic work on memory from the 1930s was Bartlett's (1932) *Remembering*. Working in Cambridge, England, outside the behaviourist pressures in the USA, Bartlett had, nevertheless, 'As in duty bound' worked for some time in the Ebbinghaus tradition. However, in *Remembering* he presented an insightful critique of the use of nonsense syllable lists. He argued that:

(a) It is impossible to rid stimuli of meaning so long as they remain capable of arousing any human response.
(b) The effort to do this creates an atmosphere of artificiality for all memory experiments, making them rather a study of the establishment and maintenance of repetition habits.
(c) To make the explanation of the variety of recall responses

17

depend mainly upon variations of stimuli and their order, frequency and mode of presentation, is to ignore dangerously those equally important conditions of response which belong to the subjective attitude and the predetermined reaction tendencies.

(1932: 4)

Faced with the nonsense syllable list the 'organism' is forced to:

mobilise all its resources and make up, or discover, a new, complex reaction on the spot. The experimental psychologist may continue the responses until he has forced them into the mould of habit. When he has done that they have lost just that special character which initially made them the object of study.

(1932: 6)

Bartlett recognized that an understanding of remembering that would have any relevance to recall in the real world would have to allow the expertise of the individual to be brought to bear. Bartlett also recognized that schema, which he defined as 'an active organisation of past reactions, or of past experiences' (1932: 201) shapes any responding in a familiar situation. In the repeated recall of stories, Bartlett demonstrated the 'effort after meaning' that characterizes cognitive functioning when the person recalling reconstructs the original.

The Gestalt psychologists, also, carried their disagreement with behaviourism into the study of memory. Wulf (1922) had argued that memories tended to change towards good form, initiating a series of studies of the reproduction of shapes (see Woodworth 1938 for a review). Zeigarnik (1927) found that subjects remembered interrupted tasks better than those that had been completed, and interpreted this in terms of Gestalt field theory. Von Restorff (1933) demonstrated the better recall of an isolated item in an otherwise homogeneous list. Katona (1940) argued for the importance of discovery and insight rather than slow strengthening of associations as central to learning.

Despite these explorations into an expanding range of theories, the dominant direction of research was under the 'verbal learning' title, although there was little connection with normal verbal behaviour. Rather, the aim was to continue the Ebbinghaus studies, often, as he had done, using nonsense syllables in serial lists, but now sometimes introducing numbers or words, so long as they had the minimum possible initial association with any of the other material.

Paired associate learning came to replace serial learning as the preferred method, since it allowed stricter control of the stimulus and its pairing with the designated response. The typical paired associate experiment involved a list of perhaps sixteen pairs of nonsense syllables. Each pair would be separately presented for 2 seconds on a memory drum, after which the first (stimulus) item of each pair would be shown in a new order, followed after 2 seconds by the correct pairing. The subject's task was to say aloud (anticipate) the response item, with the list being repeated in a new order until every response could be correctly anticipated.

Within this constrained experimental framework a new peak of experimental rigour, analysis and often originality in testing the experimental hypothesis was achieved. McGeoch and, later, Underwood and Postman were among many psychologists who painstakingly mapped out the detailed testing of the implications of the associative theory of learning.

The students of verbal learning claimed to be interested in the establishment of empirical laws rather than in constructing formal theories. They were not offended by the epithet of 'dust-bowl empiricists' that was applied to these workers from mid-western universities in the USA. Perhaps, in comparison with the disputes over the general theories of learning developed in studying animal learning by Hull, Tolman, Spence and others, their research was less theoretical. However, in retrospect it can be seen to have been deeply influenced by a number of strong theoretical presuppositions. The associationist conception of learning was accepted without question, although applied to stimuli and responses, not to the conscious images for which the theory was originally developed. The verbal learning tradition assumed what even Ebbinghaus had not: that the learning of nonsense syllables and other novel associations in an alien context, with every effort made to suppress or avoid any benefits from mnemonics or prior experience, would contribute conclusions that could be generalized to a wider universe. The assumption was that this was basic, raw learning and, once understood, the rest of the situations in which remembering took place could be easily interpreted. This optimism over eventual generalization was part of the ethos of behaviourism. The researchers with animals were making even more sweeping claims based upon the study of rats in mazes and pigeons in Skinner boxes.

Of course, as Bartlett had warned, if you create an artificial world and rule out all the factors that determine remembering in everyday

19

life, you are in danger of leaving yourself with findings that are relevant only to your artificial world. It is not the artificiality of the tasks themselves that is the danger, since much essential research in physics and chemistry is carried out in conditions that exist only in the laboratory. The issue is whether, when you have created your laboratory task, you still retain the elements, the subject of your initial questioning. The verbal learning research was, contrary to the claim of its practitioners to be pragmatic, heavily determined by the theoretical questions generated by other researchers in the field and almost totally removed from any phenomena taking place in the real world.

From the tenets of associationism early work explored the range of associations that were formed to items further away in the lists (see Woodworth 1938 for a review). Soon, however, the two great issues of verbal learning research, transfer and interference, developed. Transfer refers to the benefits and detriments from the learning of one list for the acquisition of a new one.

In general, there was a learning to learn, so that practice on nominally unrelated lists led to quicker acquisition (e.g. Ward 1937). But the interest was in the transfer between lists under different degrees of similarity of the stimulus and response items. Osgood (1949) had produced a diagram of the 'transfer surface' predicting positive transfer (quicker learning) if the stimuli remained the same and the responses were similar, but negative transfer if they were different. In testing these predictions, it became clear that not only the associations between items but also the learning of these novel items themselves had to be taken into account in a two factor theory (Underwood and Schulz 1960). More challenging than transfer, though, was the need to explain forgetting.

Ebbinghaus had found 50 per cent forgetting in the first hour, with a steady decrease in the rate of loss thereafter. He discussed three theories for forgetting: a response competition, with images remaining unchanged but overlaid; an unlearning with the repression of ideas; and 'the crumbling into parts and the loss of separate components instead of in general obscuration' (1885: 64). McGeoch (1932, 1940) championed the importance of retroactive inhibition. This term, introduced by Muller and Pilzecker (1900), was defined by McGeoch as 'a decrement in retention resulting from activity, usually a learning activity, interpolated between an original learning and a later measurement of retention' (1942: 458).

Evidence for retroactive inhibition accumulated. Jenkins and

Dallenbach (1924) found a steady decline when recall was delayed during waking hours but none between the second and eighth hour of sleep, suggesting that the lack of activity had prevented inhibition. McGeoch and McDonald (1931) showed that learning any interpolated list was detrimental, but that the degree of interference depended upon the similarity of the interpolated material to the original.

That retroactive inhibition occurred was easily established, but its cause was less clear. Some theories favoured response competition, with associations between similar responses being difficult to discriminate (e.g. McGeoch 1936), while others argued that unlearning took place, with the interpolated list actually weakening the association between the original stimulus and response (e.g. Melton and Irwin 1940). In trying to determine between these alternatives, complex designs involving the free recall of the first stimuli's responses were developed in an attempt to discover the 'fate' of the first list associations (Barnes and Underwood 1959), but problems still remained (see Keppel 1968 for a detailed discussion).

Not all forgetting could be attributed to retroactive inhibition. As Underwood remarked on the 75 per cent forgetting of nonsense syllables observed over 24 hours:

> It seems to me an incredible stretch of an interference hypothesis to hold that this 75 per cent forgetting was caused by something which the subjects learned outside the laboratory during the 24-hour interval. Even if we agree with some educators that much of what we teach our students in college is nonsense, it does not seem to be the kind of learning that would interfere with nonsense syllables.
>
> (1957: 429–30)

Underwood (1957) demonstrated that the rate of forgetting during the 24 hours was a function of the number of similar lists that the subject had learned earlier. This proactive inhibition became a major contributor in the explanation of forgetting. However, Underwood and Postman (1960) went further and tried, unsuccessfully, to link the forgetting in the laboratory to the interference from verbal materials outside the laboratory (see Keppel 1968 for a critique).

The verbal learning researchers attempted to stay within the associationist theoretical framework, but pressure grew continuously for a richer set of explanatory concepts that would take into account the active processing and use of existing knowledge in which subjects indulged whenever possible, despite the rigours of the verbal learning experimental paradigm. As early as 1928 Glaze had published association value norms for nonsense syllables, based upon the ease of recalling or inventing a meaningful association (Glaze 1928), and researchers had found it necessary to control for these in the construction of their lists. Noble (1952) went further, measuring the number of associations that could be generated to words in 60 seconds and showing that this measure was strongly correlated with ease of learning. This measure, which Noble titled *Meaningfulness* (m), was still within the associationist tradition, but the pressures of trying to capture these influences from the everyday world within the old framework strained even the ingenuity of Underwood and Shultz (1960).

Even while the verbal learning approach was at its height, alternatives were emerging. We saw at the beginning of this chapter how the wax tablet technology for recording information influenced thinking about memory. Now, rapid developments were occurring in the handling of information. Even at a general level, academics were more aware of the problems of retrieval faced, for example, by their institution's library, and the processes of cataloguing at acquisition that had to be followed to make retrieval of books possible. Library metaphors began to appear in textbook examples. Perhaps more important was the development of information technology. At first this impinged upon psychology via information theory and the study of the transmission of information. The idea of short-term stores to hold information during processing was supported by demonstrations that there was transitory retention of a great deal of visual and acoustic information for a brief interval (Broadbent 1958; Sperling 1960).

Soon, however, the developments in computer technology brought about the idea of central processors, and the pressures created for computers by limitations in memory and memory access made the memory metaphor respectable again. Meanwhile, James' (1890) concept of a primary memory was taken up anew. Differences in processing and patterns of retention for recall of items held for only a few seconds (e.g. Peterson and Peterson 1959; Baddeley 1966) led to a widespread belief that there were separate short- and long-term memories, with the former holding a small amount of information, probably in a phonemic code that could be maintained by rehearsal, before (or during) transmission for more permanent storage in the long-term memory (Waugh and Norman 1965; Atkinson and Shiffrin 1968).

In the latter years of the 1960s the verbal learning tradition dis-integrated. Perhaps the kindest metaphor is to see the process as resembling the emergence of a butterfly from a cocoon. The bursting forth of a whole new range of experimental designs and explanatory concepts made a vivid contrast with the old shell of verbal learning that was left behind. However, perhaps without the development of rigorous methods and careful analysis in the cocoon of verbal learn-ing, the newly emerged imago would have been less attractive and successful.

Two of the first new concepts had a long history. One was the recognition of the influence of organization on recall. This included the organization that was offered by the experimenter in the new flexibility in the design of stimulus material (e.g. Bower *et al.* 1969). However, perhaps more important, given the inherently passive view of memory implicit in associationism, was the recognition of the influence of the organization that the subjects themselves could impose, drawing upon their existing knowledge (e.g. Mandler 1967).

The second escapee from the Promethean chains of behaviourism was mental imagery. For so long assumed to be the basis of memory, but then banished from the behaviourist vocabulary, it re-emerged both in demonstrations of the value of the traditional mnemonic methods (e.g. Bower 1970) and as a variable more potent than Noble's m when the image-arousing potential of words was taken into account (Paivio 1969).

The dependence of remembering upon the activities of the subject was championed by Craik and Lockhart (1972) in their levels of processing framework, which emphasized the importance of the pro-cessing task in which the subject was engaged. Massive differences in the recall and recognition of the same material could be produced by varying the processing demands (e.g. Craik and Tulving 1975). Memory was seen as being a process that depended upon both these encoding activities and the conditions at encoding and retrieval. This was summarized by Tulving in the encoding specificity principle:

> that if a stimulus in the retrieval environment renders possible or facilitates recall of the target word T, the retrieval informa-tion was appropriate to or compatible with the information contained in the episodic trace of T.

(1974: 779)

Meanwhile, the domain of memory research had been rapidly expanding. Semantic memory – our knowledge of the meaning of words and concepts, and the structure of that knowledge – was investigated by Collins and Quillian (1969), whose testing of the latency of decisions triggered a new research paradigm and a rapidly expanding theoretical structure (e.g. Collins and Loftus 1975). Attempts were made to enrich the associationist concepts by recognizing that associations could include relational information and to use the power of modern computers to develop and test large-scale models of the encoding and retrieval of meaningful prose (Anderson and Bower 1974; Kintsch 1974). Bartlett's concept of the schema was taken up, especially by the new cognitive scientists interested in computationally modelling cognition (e.g. Minsky 1975; Schank and Abelson 1977). Applied research on eyewitness testimony returned (e.g. Loftus and Palmer 1974). At the same time the study of short-term memory began to be refined as Baddeley's working memory model replaced the simple dual store by a central processor with slave articulatory and visuo-spatial scratchpads (Baddeley and Hitch 1974; see also Chapter 3).

We have reached the era covered by chapters in these two volumes of *Aspects of Memory*. In recent years there has been a growing recognition of the contribution that can be made using case studies following brain damage (see Chapter 8 of this volume). That we are not aware of having acquired much from the past has at first fascinated some researchers and then led to an exploration of the types of explicit and implicit memories (see Chapter 5). Connectionist models of learning offer a whole new opportunity for both refining associationist ideas and developing a new theoretical explanatory framework (see Chapter 7). Practical applications have been a major topic (see Volume 1), but a growth in studies of remembering in everyday contexts has stimulated controversy over the value of such research (see Chapters 9 and 10 of this volume).

There are many aspects of memory currently under intensive investigation, as these volumes describe. We have come a long way from the practical challenge of memorizing that stimulated Simonides and the theoretical speculations of Aristotle and Hume.

Nevertheless, the old adage that much further research (and theorizing) is necessary was never more true. The growing recognition of the range and complexity of memory phenomena across the years has increased our knowledge of our own ignorance. That in itself is a major achievement, since science stagnates when its practitioners are unaware of the limitations of their techniques and explanations. Hopefully, this brief history of the study of memory will help those joining this long tradition to see their place in an endeavour as old as philosophical thought. Perhaps they will have some sympathy for the oversights of those who have gone before them!

REFERENCES

Anderson, J.R. and Bower, G.M. (1972) *Human Associative Memory*, Washington, DC: Winston.

Atkinson, R.C. and Shiffrin, R.M. (1968) 'Human memory: A proposed system and its control processes', in K.W. Spence (ed.) *The Psychology of Learning and Motivation: Advances in Research and Theory*, 2, pp. 89–195, New York: Academic Press.

Aristotle, *De Memoria et Reminiscentia*. Translated by R. Sorabji (1972) *Aristotle on Memory*, London: Duckworth.

Ayer, A.J. (1936) *Language, Truth and Logic*, London: Victor Gollancz.

Baddeley, A.D. (1966) 'Short-term memory for word sequences as a function of acoustic, semantic and formal similarity', *Quarterly Journal of Experimental Psychology* 18: 362–5.

Baddeley, A.D. and Hitch, G. (1974) 'Working memory', in G.H. Bower (ed.) *Recent Advances in Learning and Motivation*, Vol. 8, New York: Academic Press.

Barnes, J.M. and Underwood, B.J. (1959) 'Fate of first list associations in transfer theory', *Journal of Experimental Psychology* 58: 97–105.

Bartlett, F.C. (1932) *Remembering*, Cambridge: Cambridge University Press.

Bower, G.H. (1970) 'Organizational factors in memory', *Cognitive Psychology* 1: 18–46.

Bower, G.H., Clark, M.C., Lesgold, A.M. and Winzenz, D. (1969) 'Hierarchical retrieval schemes in recall of categorized word lists', *Journal of Verbal Learning and Verbal Behaviour* 8: 323–43.

Broadbent, D.E. (1958) *Perception and Communication*, London: Pergamon Press.

Brown, R. and Kulik, J. (1977) 'Flashbulb memories', *Cognition* 5: 73–99.

Cattell, J.M. (1887) 'Experiments on the association of ideas', *Mind* 12: 68–74.

—— (1895) 'Measurement of the accuracy or recollection', *Science* 20: 761–76.

Cattell, J.M. and Bryant, S. (1889) 'Mental association investigated by experiment', *Mind* 14: 230–50.

Colegrove, F.W. (1899) 'Individual memories', *American Journal of Psychology* 10: 228–55.

Collins, A.M. and Loftus, E.F. (1975) 'A spreading-activation theory of semantic processing', *Psychological Review* 82: 407–28.

Collins, A.M. and Quillian, M.R. (1969) 'Retrieval from semantic memory', *Journal of Verbal Learning* 8: 240–7.

Conway, M.A. (1990) *Autobiographical Memory: An Introduction*, Milton Keynes: Open University Press.

Craik, F.I.M. and Lockhart, R.S. (1972) 'Levels of processing: A framework for memory research', *Journal of Verbal Learning and Verbal Behavior* 11: 671–84.

Craik, F.I.M. and Tulving, E. (1975) 'Depth of processing and the retention of words in episodic memory', *Journal of Experimental Psychology: General* 104: 268–94.

Ebbinghaus, H. (1885) *Uber das Gedachtnis*, Leipzig: Dunker. Translated by H. Ruyer and C.E. Bussenius (1913) *Memory*, New York: Teachers College, Columbia University.

Freud, S. (1896) 'Further remarks on the neuro-psychoses of defence', standard edition 3, p. 159, London: Hogarth Press.

—— (1900) *The Interpretation of Dreams*, standard edition, 4–5, London: Hogarth Press.

—— (1924) A note upon the 'mystic Writing-Pad', standard edition 19, pp. 227–32, London: Hogarth Press.

Galton, F. (1833) *Inquiries into Human Faculty and its Development*, London: Dent.

Glaze, J.A. (1928) 'The association value of nonsense syllables', *Journal of Genetic Psychology* 35: 255–69.

Henmon, V.A.C. (1917) 'The relation between learning and retention and amount to be learned', *Journal of Experimental Psychology* 2: 476–84.

Higbee, K.L. (1988) *Your Memory*, New York: Prentice-Hall, second edition.

Hull, C. (1943) *Principles of Behavior*, New York: Appleton-Century-Crofts.

Hume, D. (1739) *A Treatise of Human Nature*, many editions.

Hunter, I.M.L. (1984) 'Lengthy Verbatim Recall (LVR) and the mythical gift of tape-recorder memory', in K.M.J. Lagerspetz and P. Niemi (eds) *Psychology in the 1990s*, Amsterdam: Elsevier Science.

James, W. (1890) *Principles of Psychology*, New York: Holt.

Jenkins, J.G. and Dallenbach, K.M. (1924) 'Obliviscence during sleep and waking', *American Journal of Psychology* 35: 605–12.

Johnson, M.K. and Raye, C.L. (1981) 'Reality monitoring', *Psychological Review* 88: 67–85.

Katona, G. (1940) *Organizing and Memorising*, New York: Columbia University Press.

Keppel, G. (1968) 'Retroactive and proactive inhibition', in T.R. Dixon and D.L. Horton (eds) *Verbal Behavior and General Behavior Theory*, Englewood Cliffs, New Jersey: Prentice-Hall.

Kintsch, W. (1974) *The Representation of Meaning in Memory*, Hillsdale, New Jersey: Erlbaum.

Kirkpatrick, E.A. (1894) 'An experimental study of memory', *Psychological Review* 1: 602–9.

Leahey, T.H. (1987) *A History of Psychology: Main Currents in Psychological Thought*, Englewood Cliffs, New Jersey: Prentice-Hall, second edition.

Loftus, E.F. and Palmer, J.C. (1974) 'Reconstruction of automobile destruction: An example of the interaction between language and memory', *Journal of Verbal Learning and Verbal Behavior* 13: 585–9.

Lyon, D.O. (1917) *Memory and the Learning Process*, Baltimore: Warwick & York.

McGeoch, J.A. (1932) 'Forgetting and the law of disuse', *Psychological Review* 39: 352–70.

—— (1936) 'Studies in retroactive inhibition. VIII: Retroactive inhibition as a function of the length and frequency of the interpolated lists', *Journal of Experimental Psychology* 19: 674–93.

—— (1942) *The Psychology of Human Learning*, New York: Longmans, Green.

McGeoch, J.A. and McDonald, W.T. (1931) 'Meaningful relation and retroactive inhibition', *American Journal of Psychology* 43: 579–88.

Mandler, G. (1967) 'Organization and memory', in K.W. Spence and J.T. Spence (eds) *The Psychology of Learning and Motivation*, vol. 1, New York: Academic Press.

Marshall, J.C. and Fryer, D.M. (1978) 'Speak Memory! An introduction to some historic studies of remembering and forgetting', in M.M. Gruneberg and P.E. Morris (eds) *Aspects of Memory*, London: Methuen.

Melton, A.W. and Irwin, J.M. (1940) 'The influence of degree of interpolated learning on retroactive inhibition and the overt transfer of specific responses', *American Journal of Psychology* 53: 173–203.

Minsky, M.L. (1975) 'A framework for representing knowledge', in P.H. Winston (ed.) *The Psychology of Computer Vision*, New York: McGraw-Hill.

Morris, P.E. (1979) 'Strategies for learning and recall', in M.M. Gruneberg and P.E. Morris (eds) *Applied Problems in Memory*, London: Academic Press.

—— (1992) 'Cognition and consciousness', *The Psychologist* 5: 3–8.

Muller, G.E. and Pilzecker, A. (1900) 'Experimentelle Beitrage zur Lehre vom Gedachtniss', *Zeitschrift fur Psychologie*, Ergbd, 1.

Muller, G.E. and Schumann, F. (1894) 'Experimentelle Beitrage zur Untersuchung des Gedachtnisses', *Zeitschrift fur Psychologie* 6: 81–190.

Noble, C.E. (1952) 'An analysis of meaning', *Psychological Review* 59: 421–30.

Osgood, C.E. (1949) 'The similarity paradox in human learning: A resolution', *Psychological Review* 56: 132–43.

Paivio, A. (1969) 'Mental imagery in associative learning and memory', *Psychological Review* 76: 241–63.

Peterson, L.R. and Peterson, M.J. (1959) 'Short-term retention of individual items', *Journal of Experimental Psychology* 58: 193–8.

Plato, *Theaetetus*. Translated by J. McDowell (1973) Oxford: Clarendon Press.

Ribot (1882) 'Les maladies de la memoire', in W. James (1890) *The Principles of Psychology*, London: Macmillan.

Robertson, G.C. (1879) 'Mr F. Galton on generic images and automatic representation', *Mind* 4: 551–7.

Schank, R.C. and Ableson, R. (1977) *Scripts, Plans, Goals and Understanding*, Hillsdale, New Jersey: Erlbaum.

Smith, W.G. (1895) 'The relationship of attention to memory', *Mind* 4 (n.s.): 47–73.

Sperling, G. (1960) 'The information available in brief visual presentations', *Psychological Monographs General and Applied* 74: 1–29.

Stern, W. (1904) 'Wirklich keitsversuche', *Bettrago zur Psychologie der Aussage* 2: 1–31.

Strong, E.K. (1912) 'The effect of length of series upon recognition memory', *Psychological Review* 19: 447–62.

Titchener, E.B. (1899) *An Outline of Psychology*, London: Macmillan.

Tulving, E. (1974) 'Recall and recognition of semantically encoded words', *Journal of Experimental Psychology* 102: 778–87.

Tulving, E. and Pearlstone, Z. (1966) 'Availability versus accessibility of information in memory for words', *Journal of Verbal Learning and Verbal Behavior* 5: 381–91.

Underwood, B.J. (1957) 'Interference and forgetting', *Psychological review* 64: 49–60.

Underwood, B.J. and Postman, L. (1960) 'Extra-experimental sources of interference in forgetting', *Psychological Review* 67: 73–95.

Underwood, B.J. and Schulz, R.W. (1960) *Meaningfulness and Verbal Learning*, Philadelphia: Lippincott.

Von Restorff, H. (1933) 'Uber die Wirkung von Bereichsbildungen im Spurenfeld', *Psychologisch Forschung* 18: 299–342.

Ward, L.B. (1937) 'Reminiscence and rote learning', *Psychological Monographs* 49.

Watson, J.B. (1930) *Behaviorism*, New York: Norton.

Waugh, N.C. and Norman, D.A. (1965) 'Primary memory', *Psychological Review* 72: 89–104.

Wittgenstein, L. (1922) *Tractatus Logico-Philosophicus*, London: Routledge & Kegan Paul.

—— (1953) *Philosophical Investigations*, Oxford: Blackwell.

Woodworth, R.S. (1931) *Contemporary Schools of Psychology*, New York: Ronald Press.

—— (1938) *Experimental Psychology*, New York: Holt.

Wulf, F. (1992) 'Uber die Veranderung von Vorstellung (Gedachtnis und Gestalt)', *Psychologisch Forschung* 1: 333–73.

Yates, F.A. (1966) *The Art of Memory*, London: Routledge & Kegan Paul.

Zeigarnik, B. (1927) 'Das Behalten erledigter und unerledigter Handlungen', in K. Lewin (ed.) 'Untersuchungen zur Handlungs und Affekt-psychologie', *Psychologisch Forschung* 9: 1–85.

2

THE MAJOR ASPECTS OF MEMORY

P.E. Morris and M.M. Gruneberg

This chapter is intended to be an introduction to the topics that are considered in more detail in the individual chapters of this book and *Aspects of Memory: The Practical Aspects.* The philosophy of the two books is to allow experts in the leading areas of memory research to explain the theoretical and practical issues that are currently exciting the most interest. However, so that the student can see these chapters in context, it will help if we explain how these current research interests have come about within the development of memory research.

The present chapter aims to provide an introduction to the range of memory phenomena and the theoretical ideas that will allow the reader to both understand and place in context the chapters upon the more theoretical and specific aspects of memory that follow. In Chapter 1, the history of theorizing about memory was traced from around 500 BC until the 1970s. In this chapter, we introduce some of the theoretical ideas that have developed from the 1970s onwards. Some understanding of these theoretical approaches is valuable because they have often been the stimulus or the unconscious assumptions underlying the more recent theories that we present later in this text. To understand the full set of theoretical concepts that the modern memory researcher applies it is important to appreciate that there are some concepts and ideas which may not be the focus of much current theoretical attention, but which are often assumed by present-day memory researchers.

However, to evaluate any theoretical account it is necessary to have a basic awareness of the range of phenomena that theories of memory must try to explain. It is worth trying to sketch a framework of the range of memory phenomena that, ultimately, needs to be taken into account in any theory of memory.

MEMORY AND COGNITION

At first sight, perceiving, comprehending, solving problems, planning and controlling our actions might appear to be more important aspects of cognition than memory. However, without memory, intelligent behaviour becomes impossible. We use the knowledge of the past that we have retrieved to make sense of what is happening to us currently. Without that knowledge, the world becomes a terrifying and dangerous place. One example of this is the devastating consequences of the dense amnesia experienced by Clive Wearing (Baddeley 1990). Following a career as a professional musician and broadcaster, encephalitis left him with only very impaired semantic and autobiographical memories:

> He has only the haziest access to his own past, and no apparent capacity to learn anything new. In his own words, his life is 'Hell on earth – It's like being dead – all the bloody time'.
>
> (1990: 6)

Our memories allow us to make sense of the world, to plan for the future and to re-experience the past. To understand remembering, therefore, it is always necessary to bear in mind that what we remember hangs upon our current and our past cognitive processing.

Take, for example, entering a doctor's waiting room. You will draw upon your past experiences to know what, if anything, it is normal to say to the other people there. As you look around, your years of learning the language allow you to read the notices. Repetition of the context of the surgery and, perhaps, some anxiety over seeing the doctor may cue memories that you have not retrieved since your last visit. Facts you will remember from this particular moment will depend upon the way your cognitive system is currently processing the situation, and upon memories of similar situations from your past.

THE MAIN FACTORS INFLUENCING MEMORY

In this section we will try to map out the main aspects of memory that must all be taken into account if performance on any occasion is to be predicted. Potentially, there is an enormous number of variables that may influence remembering. Some have been studied in detail, but others appear to have been neglected if not forgotten (Mullin *et al.* 1993).

Your memory for any particular aspect of your environment will depend upon elements in that environment. In a controlled learning experiment, we can think of what is presented to the participants to be remembered as the experimental *materials*, and the rest of the environment as the *context*. In less formal situations, there is usually a focusing of attention upon some object, text, film or ongoing event. This, too, is the material that could be potentially remembered later, and one aspect of remembering is, therefore, the nature of such material and the context in which it is encountered.

However, remembering depends not only upon the nature of material but just as crucially upon the way that it is processed. That, in turn, will depend both upon the structures that exist within which the processing takes place and on the type of processing that is actually carried out at the particular time that a new memory is encoded. The second dimension that must, therefore, be considered is the nature of the *memory structures* that may be engaged in the processing of the material in this context. For example, what is remembered may depend upon the extent to which it is retained in the hypothesized articulatory loop of working memory rather than receiving elaborate processing in the central executive (see Chapter 3).

In processing the material and its context, the human cognitive system draws upon the benefits of its past experience. A very rich *knowledge base* interacts with the material to allow the comprehension of spoken and written messages, and the interpretation and prediction of the behaviour of people, animals and even inanimate objects. So, for example, Morris *et al.* (1985) found very high correlations between an individual's knowledge of soccer and the number of new soccer scores that they could remember after one presentation.

As a consequence of this processing, this interpretation and comprehension of the world, new memories will be encoded. But the making sense and interpretation that is carried out at any time will be a consequence of the demands of the situation in which the individual is placed. Sometimes they may be thinking deeply about what they are doing, at other times only superficial attention is required. What is encoded depends vitally upon this processing. So, for example, Craik and Tulving (1975) showed that having to answer questions about the meaning of words led to vastly better recall of the words than did merely deciding how they were printed. Similarly, Winograd (1978) showed that judging whether a face looked honest, friendly or intelligent led to better recall than asking about nose size or straightness of hair.

To understand a new instance of remembering, therefore, we would need to take into account the material to be remembered, the context, the cognitive resources represented by the different memory structures, the processing within these structures that was activated by the particular task demands of the situation, and the knowledge bases upon which the processing could draw. This, however, as a sketch covers only what is sometimes called automatic or effortless learning. For example, you almost certainly made no effort to remember what you had for breakfast this morning, but you should have no difficulty in recalling what you ate. Most of our remembering is of this form, with no deliberate effort to remember. But there are layers of further complexity once a conscious effort to learn is made, such as when trying to remember a new telephone number or points to be made in an examination essay (Hasher and Zacks 1979).

When we know that we will need to remember information, we will try to adopt strategies that will increase our performance. In choosing such strategies, we draw upon our metamemory knowledge – our beliefs about the ways in which our memories function and the ways to make the best use of them (see Chapter 4). So, when children repeat to themselves words that they need to remember, they are applying their metamemory beliefs that repeating items to oneself helps memory.

So far we have mentioned only the areas to be considered if encoding is to be fully explained. However, there remains the retention stage during which information must be stored in some way if it is to be remembered later. Finally, there are the processes of retrieval, and those associated with retrieval, such as the feeling of knowing that the information has been encoded.

The account so far is a functional one, but for remembering to occur there must be neurological activity and neurological and bio-chemical changes to record the encoded information. Such processes and the parts of the brain dedicated to the encoding and retrieval of memories can be revealed in the study of patients with neurological damage that leads to amnesia.

During this chapter we will review some of the basic findings associated with these stages in the memory processes, illustrating how they have been examined prior to the theoretical accounts given in later chapters.

MATERIALS

The early studies by Ebbinghaus (1885) and his successors were described in Chapter 1. Ebbinghaus sought to eliminate meaningful associations from the material to be memorized, and so devised the nonsense syllable. One of the main consequences of the subsequent research using nonsense material was an implication that memorizing was a slow, tedious process. For example, after 12 (4-second) presentations of a list made up of 10 nonsense syllables that elicited few associations, Cieutat *et al.* (1958) found that their subjects could recall less than 6 of the responses when shown the stimulus from the pair. Did experimenters sometimes wonder how any learning comes about under natural conditions when such frequency of repetition may be absent?

Once, however, researchers stopped trying to beat the meaningful associations that subjects so desperately sought in such experiments, and began to study them as factors leading to easier encoding, it became clear that words and concepts that were either already familiar to the subjects, or which reminded them of such words, were very much easier to learn. Various measures of the properties of words were found to predict ease of learning. These included: the number of associations that the word elicited in 30 seconds or a minute (Noble 1952); the word's frequency of use in the language (Gregg 1976); the ease with which the word elicited mental images or its concreteness (Paivio 1971); the age at which words were acquired (Morris 1981); and the strength of emotion associated with the word (Rubin 1980). Many of these variables are highly intercorrelated, making it difficult to identify reliably which are causal contributors in the learning process and which merely casual correlates. Collectively, however, they represent different measures of the general factor of the extent to which the words can make contact with existing knowledge that can then be exploited in the encoding.

There are, of course, many other types of material that may be encountered other than words. It is more common to read stories than lists of unrelated words. Here again, familiar situations will lead to different memories compared to the unfamiliar. If the familiarity aids comprehension, then better memories will follow (Bransford and Johnson 1972). However, simple generalizations are not possible, and this illustrates the need to specify carefully all the characteristics of the situation if memory performance is to be explained. Highly predictable scenarios can lead to intrusion errors in recall (Bower *et al.*

1979), while unexpectedness seems to be one of the contributors to the exceptionally detailed flashbulb memory (Conway 1990). Familiarity *can* be associated with very poor memories, such as those we have (or lack) for coins (Morris 1988a; Nickerson and Adams 1979). Can you describe in detail what is on the face of a common coin that you handle daily? Try it and see!

We depend heavily upon our eyes for information about the world, and much that we process and remember is visual. In general, pictures are better remembered than descriptions of the same scenes. One illustration of the quality of picture memory was the demonstration by Standing *et al.* (1970) of 90 per cent correct recognition after several days of 2,560 pictures presented once each for 10 seconds. A marked contrast to the difficulty of memorizing nonsense syllables! Faces present a special case, and Chapter 3 of Volume 1 describes both data and theories of face memory.

MEMORY STRUCTURES

Psychologists have hypothesized a range of separate memories that may deal in different ways with the incoming information from the external world. As was described in Chapter 1, the oldest division hypothesized is that between primary and secondary memory, proposed by James (1890). The 1960s saw this elaborated into a theory of short- and long-term memory (e.g. Atkinson and Shiffrin 1968) and modified into an influential account of the mechanisms and support systems for processing in Baddeley's working memory model (Baddeley 1986; Chapter 3). It is, however, worth noting that the interpretation of the available data as sufficient to confirm the existence of working memory has not gone unchallenged (e.g. Crowder 1993).

The working memory model introduces several subdivisions of short-term memory. There is the central executive, responsible for the main processing of the incoming information, the articulatory loop that can hold a couple of seconds of speech-like information, temporarily freeing the central executive of this load, and the visuo-spatial sketchpad that can similarly retain spatial information for a short time.

Prior even to the central executive, other very short-term, sensory memories have been postulated on the basis of the ability for apparently large amounts of visual and acoustic information to be held briefly. A visual iconic memory store was initially postulated by

Sperling (1960) and a related acoustic memory by Crowder and Morton (1969). While the demonstrations of the accessibility of much that has been presented visually or verbally for brief intervals, usually less than 1 second, are robust, there have been disputes over their interpretation (e.g. Haber 1983; Coltheart 1983).

Beyond the short intervals covered by sensory and working memories, the possible subdivisions of longer-term memory have been controversial. However, the distinction between explicit and implicit memory (Chapter 5) has been generally incorporated into the accepted conceptual anatomy of memory researchers. Explicit memories are those for which the individual can retain an awareness of the circumstances of the event recalled. Implicit memories involve no conscious awareness of the original experience but, nevertheless, changes in the performance of the subject in other ways show that the original event modified subsequent performance. In a typical experiment, for example, the completion of word fragments such as A - - A - - IN were primed by the inclusion of the target words in an earlier list. Recognition and priming appeared to be independent because the priming effect was unrelated to the individual's ability to recognize having seen the word earlier and the priming effect did not decay with the recognition performance over 7 days (Tulving *et al.* 1982).

The implicit/explicit memory distinction is justified by data that fit the defined distinction, but argument continues over whether the phenomena of implicit and explicit memory implies that there are two or more separate memory systems. Similar disputes occur over the other major divisions of longer-term memory. The terms *episodic, semantic, autobiographical, prospective, declarative, propositional and procedural memories* provide useful concepts to aid the thinking of researchers even if they do not, necessarily, represent structurally separate parts of the cognitive system.

The distinction between episodic and semantic memory was introduced by Tulving (1972). The distinction that Tulving drew was between memory for events (episodic memory) and memory for facts (semantic memory). So, for example, your memory of your first day at college is an episodic memory, while recalling the name of the capital of France draws upon semantic memory. Tulving suggested that episodic memory was a system that received and stored information about the events that happened to the individual, retaining them with information about when and where they had occurred. On the other hand, semantic memory was seen by Tulving as the memory

35

necessary for the use of language. He saw it as the organized knowledge that a person possesses about words and concepts, their meanings and the relationships between them.

This distinction between episodic and semantic memory captures two of the different aspects of memory that underlie two prototypical uses of memory. One is the recollecting of a distinctive past experience. The sensory re-experiencing of some event such as one's first day at university, with memories of details of how one felt, who one saw, etc., presents, for non-psychologists at least, a prototypical example of remembering. It is, certainly, a prototypical example of episodic memory. However, a still more fundamental use of memory is in the comprehension of language. If we fail to retain some record of the meaning of the words that we hear, our own language would be as meaningless to us as is any foreign language that we have not encountered before. The use of our memories in comprehension of language is a prototypical example of semantic memory.

These two types of remembering are clearly very different. The former is rich in re-experienced sensory information, and we are very aware of it as being an act of remembering something from our past. The use of semantic memory is, on the other hand, frequently implicit, and we are unaware of how it is taking place, or even that it is taking place at all. We will look in more detail at some of the earlier theorizing about episodic and semantic memory later in this chapter, while some of the more recent theories are discussed in Chapters 5 and 7.

Tulving (1972) believed that the very different phenomena of remembering for episodic and semantic memories implied that there were two separate memory systems. It is, however, possible to account for the differences between semantic and episodic memory within theories that assume that memory is based upon storing a record of every instance that we experience, without distinguishing between its value for episodic or semantic processing (e.g. Hintzman 1986; Logan 1988).

Tulving (1983) suggested that semantic memory was further subdivided into *procedural* and *propositional* memory systems. Procedural memory is what Ryle (1948) called 'knowing how'. We know how to tie shoelaces, use knives and forks, etc. Procedural memories retain the information underlying such skill performance. Propositional memory is for facts about the world, such as that George Bush was once a President of the USA. Ryle referred to such knowledge as 'knowing that'. The difference between 'knowing that' and 'knowing how' (propositional and procedural knowledge) is well illustrated when one comes to learn a new skill such as riding a bicycle. Acquiring the propositional knowledge that what one does is to hold the handlebars and turn the pedals is easy. Developing the appropriate procedural knowledge for doing these without falling off takes longer!

Overlapping with the concept of episodic memory is that of autobiographical memory (see Chapter 9, Volume 1). Autobiographical memory is memory about one's personal past. In many cases these are episodic memories. However, some of the knowledge that we have about ourselves is semantic knowledge, i.e. we know facts about our past without necessarily being able to remember specific memories that we can place and date.

Prospective memory is another candidate for a subdivision of longer-term memory. Remembering our plans and intentions is an important part of our control of our lives. Chapter 8 of Volume 1 reviews research on prospective memory, including some of the evidence that a separate memory system may be involved. Indeed, we should perhaps think of there being short-term prospective memories that allow us to organize and monitor our immediate intentions (see Morris 1984; Ceci *et al.* 1988).

ENCODING PROCESSES

We have already referred to the research by Craik and Tulving (1975) in which they demonstrated that processing a word for its meaning (e.g. if it will fit meaningfully into a given sentence) leads to far better retention than considering either its sound or whether it is printed in upper or lower case. The importance of the type of processing for future retention was initially highlighted by Craik and Lockhart (1972) when they put forward their *levels of processing* theory. Further research soon followed, exploring in more detail how the different types of processing can dramatically influence recall. Johnson-Laird, Gibbs and de Mowbray (1978), for example, showed that the memory for words such as *milk* or *coal* was dramatically altered depending on whether subjects were asked to classify the words in the list as 'consumable liquid' or 'unconsumable solids'. Recall was four times better for the items that shared the two properties being classified, in comparison with those that had neither property.

What is it about processing that leads to better subsequent recall? One possibility is that more elaborate and/or distinctive entries are encoded in memory. It has long been known (e.g. von Restorff 1932) that distinctive items are well remembered. For example, a number in a list of words or a word in a list of numbers will always be recalled. Distinctive faces are far easier to remember than faces with no unusual features (Valentine and Bruce 1986). The more elaborate the memory trace, the more opportunity there is for a retrieval cue to activate it later. Another important aspect of effective processing is the identification of properties that are shared by the items to be remembered. If the logical relationship between items is emphasized then far better recall can occur. For example, Bower *et al.* (1969) showed that when apparently unrelated words were restructured so that they fell into a hierarchical classification, the words could be learned four times as quickly.

Encoding depends not only upon the properties of the items to be remembered, but also upon the context in which the remembering is taking place. What is encoded is a record of the item interpreted within its context. As discussed in Chapter 6, changes in context can have big effects upon recall. It is not just the external context that is encoded, but also the current cognitive and emotional state of the individual. So, it has been found that memory is partly dependent upon the state of the individual, physically and emotionally, at the time of encoding. If the state (e.g. the mood, influence of alcohol) is repeated at encoding and retrieval then recall can be considerably higher than if the states differ (Blaney 1986).

THEORIES OF ENCODING AND RETRIEVAL

Interference theory

As was discussed in Chapter 1, the idea that forgetting takes place because of some form of interference from other memories was discussed by Ebbinghaus (1885) at the beginning of the experimental study of memory, and it continued to be a dominating theory in the study of memory until the 1960s. Any theory of memory retrieval has to take into account the issues tackled by interference theory. There are essentially two issues. One is will 'unlearning' occur? That is, will learning of new information related to the original memory in some way degrade the stored representation of that memory? The second problem is the retrieval of a specific memory from among many that may share with it a large number of similar features. In particular, the latter problem is one that is shared by all information storage and retrieval systems, whether man-made or evolved through natural selection. Indeed, interference theory identifies the fundamental issues for an explanation of recall. A failure to recall must, in some way, result either from an inadequate initial encoding or from an inadequate specification of a stored item in the information that is available to activate stored memories. A degrading of the stored record through unlearning or insufficient specification of one particular entry among competing entries are always likely bases for memory failure. However, the traditional interference theories required further elaboration and specification.

Encoding specificity and synergistic ecphory

Tulving and Osler (1968) proposed the *encoding specificity hypothesis* which Tulving (1983) developed into his theory of synergistic ecphory.

The basis of this theory is that retrieval depends upon the combination of what was stored as a consequence of the original encoding process and the cognitive activities at the time of retrieval. The original encoding will reflect the specific processing demands at the time. Retrieval will depend upon whether processing at that time involves a sufficiently similar set of processes to match those at the original encoding. This theory deals neatly with several powerful memory phenomena. One such illustration is an experiment by Barclay *et al.* (1974). They showed that words such as PIANO could have their recall considerably influenced by the aspects of a piano that were emphasized at the time of encoding. So, their subjects were given sentences such as *the man tuned the PIANO* or *the man lifted the PIANO*. When cued later with phrases such as *something melodious* or *something heavy*, recall of PIANO was much higher where the cue was *something melodious* and the original sentence was the man *tuned the piano* or where the cue was *something heavy* and the original sentence was the man *lifted the piano*. So, only specific aspects about the piano had been encoded, and the combined information of the cue and the original memory was necessary for the recall. Tulving and Thompson (1973), working within this framework, were able to show that, under certain conditions, people could fail to recognize that they had seen words earlier, but then recall them if given appropriate cues.

One of the implications of the encoding specificity research is that the context in which encoding and retrieval take place plays a central role in determining what is remembered. Context is certainly an

important factor to be considered when explaining memory performance (see Chapter 6). However, not everyone has seen the synergistic
ecphory theory as sufficiently specifying the relationship between
context and memory. Baddeley (1990), for example, argues that
context may be interactive, modifying the experience, or independent, where the context does not modify the experience itself
although it can be encoded and act as a retrieval cue.

Generate–recognize models of retrieval

Tulving's encoding specificity principle, and subsequent research,
was developed, in part, as an alternative to the generate–recognize
two-process theory of recall (Kintsch 1970; Anderson and Bower
1972). These theories assumed that recall involved first generating
possible candidate words and then a second process of recognizing if
the words had been seen earlier. Recognition memory should therefore not require the initial generation stage. This model predicted the
usual finding that recall is harder than recognition, and the so-called
frequency paradox that high frequency words are easier to recall but
harder to recognize in memory experiments. High frequency words
should be easier to generate, making recall easier. However, high
frequency words will, by definition, have been encountered by the
person on more occasions so that this may lead to confusion and
poorer recognition. Any effects, such as the organization of the
material (Kintsch 1968) or changes in the context (Chapter 6), have
much bigger effects on recall than recognition. These have been interpreted as support for the two-process account. However, recall and
generate models have difficulty in accounting for the Tulving and
Thompson (1973) demonstration that recall can sometimes be higher
than recognition.

THEORIES OF SEMANTIC MEMORY

Network theories

One development of the traditional associationist view of memory has
been network theories (e.g. Anderson and Bower 1972; Anderson
1983). Network theories assume that long-term memory storage takes
place on the basis of the formation of nodes representing concepts
connected to other concepts through relational links. The links can
specify the relationship between the concepts and other concepts.

They may, for example, indicate inclusion of a class, such as showing that a cat is a member of a class of animals. The links may show the properties of the node concept, linking, for example, 'has whiskers', 'purrs', etc. to the node for *cat*. Early models of semantic memory by Collins and Quillian (1968) were in this form, and later elaborated into more complex network models (e.g. Collins and Loftus 1975).

Not all network models are restricted to semantic memories. Anderson's models (Anderson and Bower 1972; Anderson 1983) were general models of memory where each new experience is entered as a new set of interconnections and, if necessary, nodes. These models have no separate semantic memory, but meaning is derived from the interconnections of a concept with other concepts and properties. Retrieval from the network takes place through *spreading activation*. When, at a retrieval stage, a node in the network is activated as part of processing the current incoming information, activation from that node will spread out through the associative network. Most network models assume that this activation will vary with the strength of the association between the nodes and will decline in strength the further it moves from the original node. The activated parts of the network can be used either by being retrieved or in the use of the semantic knowledge that is contained within the network.

Beyond networks

Johnson-Laird *et al.* (1984) have criticized network theories for what they call the *symbolic fallacy*. They argue that network theories can be made to account for any result and are difficult to constrain so that they have testable predictions. They argue that it is important for theories to break out from the network of interconnections and to account for the link between concepts and the real world. Most inferences that might be drawn within the network might turn out to be incorrect in a real world context. For example, use of a network would lead from the statements that A is on B's right and B is on C's right to the conclusion that A is on C's right. This might, however, be untrue if the three of them were sitting round a small circular table, such as in a café.

Some theories of memory storage have avoided the associationist/network framework. One approach, drawing upon the early work of Bartlett (1932), is seeing how our knowledge of the world is organized into packets of information known as schemas, scripts or frames

(Rumelhart and Norman 1985). Scripts or schema provide a framework that guides new processing by predicting what is to be expected and looked for, and by filling in gaps in the currently available information.

An example of the use of script knowledge would be if someone that you are eating with in a restaurant said, near the end of the meal, 'This is on me'. Without a knowledge of what happens in restaurants (e.g. that you have to pay a bill; that you pay the bill at the end of the meal; that the other person is your boss who has an expense account), you would be left wondering just what was on your companion, and why they didn't seem bothered by it!

A number of theoretical accounts based around schema and scripts were put forward during the 1970s and 1980s (see Baddeley 1990 for a review). For example, Rumelhart (1975) suggested that there was a 'story grammar' underlying most stories that helped in their comprehension. Schank and Abelson (1977) argued that we develop scripts for commonly experienced events such as going to a restaurant. Bower *et al.* (1979) suggested that people tend to reorganize what they have heard to fit with their script-based expectations, and to introduce errors into stories that would be derived from the usual script but that were not in the actual story as heard.

Schank (1982) argued that scripts are organized in a hierarchical, dynamic way. He referred to *memory organization packets* which might put together several *scenes* through these higher-level organizations. Schank was able to suggest explanations for instances of reminding. Where it was the underlying similarity at a fairly abstract level rather than the sharing of many actual physical details of the situation, that seemed to be the basis of the memory being cued. Brewer and McNamara (1984) argued that schema contribute to processing in five ways. They selectively direct attention and provide an integration of information, a framework in memory that preserves the appropriate information, a guide to retrieval and an influence on the editing of what one says or does. On the other hand, schema theories have been criticized (e.g. Alba and Hasher 1983). Schema theories tend to be lacking in precision and cannot provide the only account for the basis of encoding. For example, new information is not merely encoded into a schema with details being lost, because, in some circumstances, good verbatim recall is possible.

Hintzman (1986) has been able to illustrate how many of the phenomena associated with schema could come about on the basis of retrieving information from individual instances stored in memory rather than special frameworks. His model produces the phenomena associated with schemas, while basing the actual recall upon the processing of the collection of the instances in which the events have occurred in the past. Other alternatives to network models for semantic memory have been developed. In particular, connectionist models (see Chapter 7) have, more recently, provided a better specified approach to the way that information might be encoded in memory. Nevertheless, as discussed in Chapter 7, there are problems for connectionist models also, and many challenges remain in trying to conceptualize the processes underlying semantic memory.

STRATEGIES AND METAMEMORY

Most remembering is automatic, if not implicit. That is, we encode and retrieve information without consciously planning to do so, or trying to control the processes by which the memorizing takes place. Subsequently, we may be consciously aware of the circumstances under which the encoding took place, but we usually let the normal processes of encoding and retrieval take their course. However, memory failures are at best an irritation, at worst a disaster; they frequently involve us in embarrassment and we suspect that they lower our image in the eyes of others. It is therefore not surprising that people seek to improve their memories by adopting strategies that they believe will be beneficial.

That people can adopt different ways of processing information or of seeking to retrieve it illustrates the flexibility of our cognitive systems. We are able to consciously modify our strategies within limitations as part of the general process of controlling our actions (cf. Morris 1992). There are, however, limitations. One of these is the awareness of the possibilities for the use of such strategies. For example, as was discussed in Chapter 1, the use of mental images to provide a means of linking items together is a powerful mnemonic aid (e.g. Bower 1970; Morris and Stevens 1974). However, if you do not know this, you may resort to less successful strategies, such as repeating items over and over, or use no strategy at all. Metamemory knowledge will determine how you try to intervene to improve your memory performance, so one important aspect of the study of memory is how and in what way this metamemorial knowledge affects memory performance and is acquired from childhood onwards (see Chapter 4). The strategies that will be adopted depend upon the individual's theories about the nature of memory and its improvement.

43

However, there are at least two aspects to what we know about our memory systems. The first concerns how much knowledge we have about strategies that can be employed at both encoding and retrieval, such as the use of mental imagery for encoding and of first-letter search strategies for retrieval (Morris and Stevens 1974; Gruneberg and Monks 1976). Just as important, however, in influencing memory performance is the knowledge an individual has about what is actually stored, especially in states where retrieval is difficult. Where, for example, an individual feels he or she has an item in store even though it cannot temporarily be retrieved, the more effort is likely to be made to retrieve the missing item. This, in itself, increases the likelihood of recall (Gruneberg *et al.* 1977).

The search for ways of improving memory has a 2,500 year history, as was discussed in the first chapter. Mnemonic techniques have involved introducing meaning, organization, associations and retrieval cues into material to be remembered that is lacking in all of these features which normally aid recall. To some, the unusual techniques that this artificial imposition of such features has led to, such as the method of loci, or the conversion of foreign words into similar sounding images as in the keyword mnemonic for learning languages (Gruneberg 1992) can seem bizarre. The study of mnemonic methods was largely neglected by psychologists until the late 1960s, both because the imagery used by many common methods was ruled out as a subject for study by the dominant behaviourist orthodoxy and because so much of the history of experimental study of memory had been directed at controlling and eliminating rather than studying and developing these memory improvement strategies. Since then, the value and the limitations of such strategies have been recognized, and these were discussed in Chapters 6 and 7 of Volume 1.

During the late 1960s and 1970s many of the techniques that had been used by students and stage memory experts through the ages were investigated. Massive improvements in recall were demonstrated when subjects linked items into meaningful sentences (Bower and Clark 1969), when they organized word lists by category (Bower *et al.* 1969), or when they used the method of loci, the peg method, rhymes or, in some circumstances, first letter mnemonics (Morris and Cook 1978).

For the present chapter, the important point is that individuals can modify their memory performance by their choice of strategy. Most strategies require the investment of effort, sometimes considerable effort. Consequently, the actual adoption of strategies tends to be restricted to situations where the individual believes that the benefits of better recall will outweigh the effort involved in implementing the mnemonic technique. In much memory research, subjects do think that this is the case and will seek ways of improving their recall that they may not adopt on a day-to-day basis. When studying memory, therefore, the strategies that subjects choose to apply must be taken into account if seeking to understand performance.

INTERACTION, REALITY AND GENERALIZATION

We have considered many factors that combine to determine what will and what will not be remembered in any situation. Two key questions are: How will these factors interact and how far can research on memory produce generalizable theories and data? How will the material being experienced, the structural architecture of the memory system, the processing that is initiated, and the strategies that the individual adopts combine to produce the memory performance that psychologists can observe and test? Faced with the complexity of this challenge one approach has been to seek the maximum control over the competing factors. This was the method initiated by Ebbinghaus (1885; see Chapter 1). Its strength is the traditional strength of laboratory research – the replicability of the conditions and the opportunity to control and manipulate potential variables. It is arguable, however, that the phenomena studied by psychologists who followed in the Ebbinghaus tradition were unrepresentative of the sort of remembering that psychologists are expected to be seeking to explain, that is, the remembering that takes place in everyday life (see e.g. Neisser 1982; Morris 1988b). However, attempting to study naturally occurring phenomena brings with it the dangers of lack of control and, with that, uncertainty over the causal variables determining performance. Chapters 9 and 10 put forward the arguments in favour of these two approaches and discuss the extent to which they are incompatible.

CONCLUSION

In the first two chapters, we have tried to provide a framework for the readers of the rest of the two volumes. We have sought to show how the study of memory has developed, the theoretical developments that have guided the main streams of research, and the factors that have to be taken into account when trying to give a full description of the memory processes. In the following chapters of this volume the major current theoretical developments in studying memory are introduced, while the first volume provides a review of the major practical aspects of memory.

REFERENCES

Alba, J.W. and Hasher, L. (1983) 'Is memory schematic?', *Psychological Bulletin* 93: 203–31.

Anderson, J.R. (1983) *The Architecture of Cognition*, Cambridge, Massachusetts: Harvard University Press.

Anderson, J.R. and Bower, G.H. (1972) *Human Associative Memory*, Washington, DC: Winston.

Atkinson, R.C. and Shiffrin, R.M. (1968) 'Human memory: A proposed system and its control processes', in K.W. Spence (ed.) *The Psychology of Learning and Motivation: Advances in Research and Theory*, 2, pp. 89–195, New York: Academic Press.

Baddeley, A.D. (1986) *Working Memory*, Oxford: Oxford University Press.

—— (1990) *Human Memory: Theory and Practice*, Hove: Erlbaum.

Barclay, J.R., Bransford, J.D., Franks, J.J., McCarrell, N.S. and Nitsch, K. (1974) 'Comprehension and semantic flexibility', *Journal of Verbal Learning and Verbal Behavior* 13: 471–81.

Bartlett, F.C. (1932) *Remembering*, Cambridge: Cambridge University Press.

Blaney, P.H. (1968) 'Affect and memory: A review', *Psychological Bulletin* 99: 229–46.

Bower, G.H. (1970) 'Imagery as a relational organiser in associative learning', *Journal of Verbal Learning and Verbal Behavior* 9: 529–33.

Bower, G.H. and Clark, M.C. (1969) 'Narrative stories as mediators for serial learning', *Psychonomic Science* 14: 181–2.

Bower, G.H., Clark, M.C., Lesgold, A.M. and Winzenz, D. (1969) 'Hierarchical retrieval schemes in recall of categorized word lists', *Journal of Verbal Learning and Verbal Behavior* 8: 323–43.

Bower, G.H., Black, J.B. and Turner, T.J. (1979) 'Scripts in memory for texts', *Cognitive Psychology* 11: 177–220.

Bransford, J.D. and Johnson, M.K. (1973) 'Consideration of some problems of comprehension', in W.G. Chase (ed.) *Visual Information Processing*, New York: Academic Press.

Brewer, W.F. and McNamara, G.V. (1984) 'The nature and functions of schemas', in R.S. Wyer and T.K. Srull (eds) *Handbook of Social Cognition*, vol. 1, Hillsdale, New Jersey: Erlbaum.

Ceci, S.J., Baker, J.E. and Bronfenbrenner, U. (1988) 'Prospective remembering, temporal calibration, and context', in M.M. Gruneberg, P.E. Morris and R.N. Sykes (eds) *Practical Aspects of Memory: Current Research and Issues*, vol. 1, *Memory in Everyday Life*, Chichester: Wiley.

Cieutat, V.J., Stockwell, F.E. and Noble, C.E. (1958) 'The interaction of ability and amount of practice with stimulus and response meaningfulness (m, m') in paired associate learning', *Journal of Experimental Psychology* 56: 193–202.

Collins, A.M. and Loftus, E.F. (1975) 'A spreading-activation theory of semantic processing', *Psychological Review* 82: 407–28.

Collins, A.M. and Quillian, M.R. (1969) 'Retrieval from semantic memory', *Journal of Verbal Learning and Verbal Behavior* 8: 240–7.

Coltheart, M. (1983) 'Iconic memory', *Philosophical Transactions of the Royal Society, London B* 302: 283–94.

Conway, M.A. (1990) *Autobiographical Memory: An Introduction*, Milton Keynes: Open University Press.

Craik, F.I.M. and Lockheart, R.S. (1972) 'Levels of processing: A framework for memory research', *Journal of Verbal Learning and Verbal Behavior* 11: 671–84.

Craik, F.I.M. and Tulving, E. (1975) 'Depth of processing and the retention of words in episodic memory', *Journal of Experimental Psychology: General* 104: 268–94.

Crowder, R. (1993) 'Short-term memory: where do we stand?', *Memory and Cognition* 21: 142–45.

Crowder, R.G. and Morton, J. (1969) 'Precategorical Acoustic Storage (PAS)', *Perception and Psychophysics* 5: 365–73.

Ebbinghaus, H. (1885) *Uber das Gedachtnis*, Leipzig: Dunker. Translated by H. Ruyer and C.E. Bussenius (1913) *Memory*, New York: Teachers College, Columbia University.

Gregg, V. (1976) 'Word frequency, recognition and recall', in J. Brown (ed.) *Recognition and Recall*, Chichester: Wiley.

Gruneberg, M.M. (1992) 'The practical application of memory aids: Knowing how, knowing when and knowing when not', in M.M. Gruneberg and P.E. Morris (eds) *Aspects of Memory*, vol. 1, *The Practical Aspects*, London: Routledge.

Gruneberg, M.M. and Monks, J. (1976) 'The first letter strategy', *IRCS Medical Science: Psychology and Psychiatry* 4: 307.

Gruneberg, M.M., Monks, J. and Sykes, R.N. (1977) 'The first letter mnemonic aid', *IRCS Medical Science: Psychology and Psychiatry* 5: 304.

Haber, R.N. (1983) 'The impending demise of the icon: A critique of the concept of iconic storage in visual information processing', *Behavioral and Brain Sciences* 6: 1–11.

Hasher, L. and Zacks, R.T. (1979) 'Automatic and effortful processing in memory', *Journal of Experimental Psychology: General* 108: 356–88.

Hintzman, D.L. (1986) ' "Schema Abstraction" in a multiple-trace memory model', *Psychological Review* 93: 411–28.

James, W. (1890) *Principles of Psychology*, New York: Holt.

Johnson-Laird, P.N., Gibbs, G. and de Mowbray, J. (1978) 'Meaning, amount of processing, and memory for words', *Memory and Cognition* 6: 372–5.

Johnson-Laird, P.N., Hermann, D.J. and Chaffin, R. (1984) 'Only connections: A critique of semantic networks', *Psychological Bulletin* 96: 292–315.

Kintsch, W. (1968) 'Recognition and free recall of organized lists', *Journal of Experimental Psychology* 78: 481–7.

―――― (1970) *Learning, Memory and Conceptual Processes*, New York: Wiley.

Logan, G.D. (1988) 'Toward an instance theory of automatization', *Psychological Review* 95: 492–527.

Morris, P.E. (1981) 'Age of acquisition, imagery, recall and the limitations of multiple-regression analysis', *Memory and Cognition* 9: 277–82.

—— (1988a) 'Expertise and everyday memory', in M.M. Gruneberg, P.E. Morris and R.N. Sykes (eds) *Practical Aspects of Memory: Current Research and Issues*, vol. 1, *Memory in Everyday Life*, Chichester: Wiley.

—— (1988b) 'Memory research: Past mistakes and future prospects', in G. Claxton (ed.) *Growth Points in Cognition*, London: Routledge.

—— (1992) 'Cognition and consciousness', *The Psychologist* 5: 3–8.

Morris, P.E. and Cook, N. (1978) 'When do first letter mnemonics aid recall?', *British Journal of Educational Psychology* 48: 22–8.

Morris, P.E. and Stevens, R. (1974) 'Linking images and free recall', *Journal of Verbal Learning and Verbal Behavior* 13: 310–15.

Morris, P.E., Tweedy, M. and Gruneberg, M.M. (1985) 'Interest, knowledge and the memorising of soccer scores', *British Journal of Psychology* 76: 417–25.

Mullin, P.A., Herrman, D.J. and Searleman, A. (1993) 'Forgotten variables in memory theory and research', *Memory* 1: 43–64.

Neisser, U. (1982) *Memory Observed*, San Francisco: Freeman.

Nickerson, R.S. and Adams, M.J., (1979) 'Long-term memory for a common object', *Cognitive Psychology* 11: 287–307.

Noble, C.E. (1952) 'An analysis of meaning', *Psychological Review* 59: 421–30.

Paivio, A. (1971) *Imagery and Verbal Processes*, New York: Holt, Rinehart & Winston.

Rubin, D.C. (1980) '51 properties of 125 words: A unit of analysis of verbal behavior', *Journal of Verbal Learning and Verbal Behavior* 19: 736–55.

Rumelhart, D.E. (1975) 'Notes on a schema for stories', in D.G. Bobrow and A. Collins (eds) *Representation and Understanding*, New York: Academic Press.

Rumelhart, D.E. and Norman, D.A. (1985) 'Representation of knowledge', in A.M. Aitkenfead and J.M. Slack (eds) *Issues in Cognitive Modelling*, London: Erlbaum.

Ryle, G. (1949) *The Concept of Mind*, London: Hutchinson.

Schank, R.C. (1982) *Dynamic Memory*, New York: Cambridge University Press.

Schank, R.C. and Abelson, R. (1977) *Scripts, Plans, Goals and Understanding*, Hillsdale, New Jersey: Erlbaum.

Sperling, G. (1960) 'The information available in brief visual presentations', *Psychological Monographs: General and Applied* 74: 1–29.

Standing, L.G., Cornezio, J. and Haber, N. (1970) 'Perception and memory for pictures: Single-trial learning of 2,500 visual stimuli', *Psychonomic Science* 19: 73–4.

Tulving, E. (1972) 'Episodic and semantic memory', in E. Tulving and W. Donaldson (eds) *The Organization of Memory*, New York: Academic Press.

—— (1983) *Elements of Episodic Memory*, Oxford: Oxford University Press.

Tulving, E. and Osler, S. (1968) 'Effectiveness of retrieval cues in memory for words', *Journal of Experimental Psychology* 77: 593–601.

Tulving, E. and Thomson, D.M. (1973) 'Encoding specificity and retrieval processes in episodic memory', *Psychological Review* 80: 353–73.

Tulving, E., Schacter, D.L. and Stark, H.A. (1982) 'Priming effects in word-fragment completion are independent of recognition memory', *Journal of Experimental Psychology: Learning, Memory and Cognition* 8: 336–42.

Valentine, T. and Bruce, V. (1986) 'The effects of distinctiveness in recognising and classifying faces', *Perception* 15: 525–35.

Von Restorff, H. (1932) 'Uber die Wirkung von Bereichsbildungen im Spurenfled', *Psychologische Forschung* 18: 299–342.

Winograd, E. (1978) 'Encoding operations which facilitate memory for faces across the life span', in M.M. Gruneberg, P.E. Morris and R.N. Sykes (eds) *Practical Aspects of Memory*, London: Academic Press.

3

THE NATURE AND USES OF WORKING MEMORY

S. E. Gathercole

One of the most important developments within cognitive psychology over the past 20 years has been the shift away from viewing short-term memory as a receptacle for lists of unrelated items, and towards seeing it as a dynamic system that plays a critical role in a wide range of complex cognitive activities. Increasingly, short-term memory is characterized as a flexible system which can satisfy a wide range of different information-processing needs. An index of this developing emphasis on the active rather than passive functions of short-term memory is provided by the increasing use of the term 'working memory' to refer to this system. Working memory appears to be central to aspects of human behaviour as important and diverse as vocabulary acquisition, learning new faces and consciousness. The aim of this chapter is to provide an introduction to both the nature and uses of this vital memory system.

AN OVERVIEW OF THE WORKING MEMORY MODEL

The widespread acceptance of the central role played by working memory in cognition has its roots in the highly successful model of working memory introduced originally by Baddeley and Hitch in 1974, and revised by Baddeley in 1986. One of the reasons that this model has made such a significant impact is that it offers a far more flexible characterization of short-term memory than earlier theories such as those of Waugh and Norman (1965) and Atkinson and Shiffrin (1968). These theories were developed primarily to account for the short-term retention of verbal information only, and they offered an essentially static view of short-term memory. According to both, memory items are represented in phonological form in a temporary store of limited capacity where they can be lost as a consequence of either decay or interference. Through rehearsal, it was suggested that items could be maintained in the temporary store, and could also be successfully transferred into a more durable semantically based memory system.

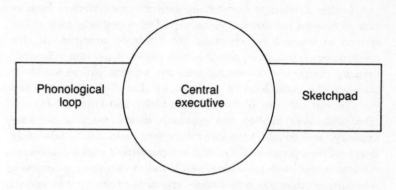

Figure 3.1 A schematic representation of the general structure of the working memory model.

The architecture of the working memory model is very different, and is depicted in simplified form in Figure 3.1. The main component is termed the 'central executive'. This component has flexible processing resources that are limited in capacity, and can be used both to regulate and coordinate the flow of information within working memory, and to perform processing and storage operations. The central executive is supplemented by two *slave systems* that are specialized for the processing and maintenance of material in particular domains. The *phonological loop* retains verbal material in terms of its speech-based characteristics. The second slave system is the *visuo-spatial sketchpad*, and this is specialized for processing material that can be represented in terms of either its visual or spatial characteristics.

A number of features have contributed to the enduring success of the working memory model. The first feature is its *flexibility*. The combination of the general purpose resources provided by the central executive and the more specialized processing and storage functions fulfilled by the phonological loop and sketchpad results in an efficient and coordinated system that is able to respond to a wide range of cognitive demands. The slave systems can handle memory tasks requiring the maintenance of restricted amounts of either verbal or visuo-spatial information, leaving the valuable limited-capacity resources of the central executive free to support a range of higher-level cognitive activities. The high degree of flexibility of this system stands in clear contrast with the rigid structure and predominantly verbal nature of earlier models of short-term memory.

A further strength of the working memory model derives from its close links with the *dual-task methodology*. Developed originally in the context of research on attention, the rationale underpinning this methodology is that if two activities both call upon a common limited-capacity component of working memory, subjects will be unable to maintain the same level of performance that they achieved when carrying out only one of the tasks. Baddeley and Hitch (1974) and other colleagues applied this approach to the study of working memory, and sought to devise concurrent tasks which selectively disrupted the operation of the three components of working memory. A number of suitable tasks have been found. Articulatory suppression – requiring subjects to continuously articulate irrelevant information such as 'the, the, the' during a memory task – appears to block the operation of the phonological loop (Baddeley *et al*. 1975b). Use of the sketchpad is disrupted when subjects concurrently track a moving visual target (Baddeley and Lieberman 1980; Baddeley *et al*. 1975a). Finding a concurrent task that places significant demands upon the central executive has proved more problematic, but activities which appear to place significant burdens on this component include asking subjects to remember a lengthy sequence of random digits (Baddeley and Hitch 1974) and generating sequences of random letters (Baddeley 1986). Using this range of tasks, researchers have been able to isolate with considerable precision exactly which component of working memory – the central executive, the phonological loop or the sketchpad – contributes to performance on particular tasks.

A third feature of the working memory model that has contributed significantly to its enduring success is its *adaptability*. A consequence of the model's essentially modular nature is that it has the capacity to preserve its general structure while more local aspects of the model are undergoing revision. This combination of adaptability and stability is clearly illustrated by the development of the phonological loop model. The nature of this system has undergone considerable change in recent years. Baddeley and Hitch (1974) originally termed this component the *articulatory loop*, and characterized it as a tape-like loop of articulatory information which has a maximum temporal capacity of just over 2 seconds. Findings over the subsequent years identified a number of shortcomings of this simple view which were resolved by splitting the loop system into the two components described in the next section (Salame and Baddeley 1982). Later still, Baddeley (1986) renamed the system the *phonological* loop in response to accumulating evidence indicating that articulatory processes *per se* may not be critical to the operation of the system. This gradual process of differentiation and refinement of the phonological loop model represents the cumulative achievements of many years of research, and as a consequence the present model (although still by no means perfect as we shall see later) readily accommodates an extensive body of empirical findings. And because of the independence of the three components of working memory from one another, scientific progress in one aspect of the model does not have disturbing repercussions for the other components. So, theory and research relating to the central executive and sketchpad during this period were able to progress independently of the gradual evolution of the phonological loop.

Finally, the working memory model has proved to have remarkable *generality*. The current model has been achieved by drawing upon evidence from a wide range of subject populations: most notably, this has included neuropsychological cases suffering from accidental brain damage and children throughout all stages of development, as well as the more traditional subject group sampled in short-term memory research, normal adults. The current strength of the model and of the approach it embodies owes much to this convergence of evidence across subject populations. One benefit is of course that this increases the potential research community for whom the model may provide a useful theoretical and empirical tool. Even more importantly, the convergence of results across experimental, neuropsychological and developmental populations lends considerable weight to the resulting model.

THE PHONOLOGICAL LOOP

The phonological loop has been extensively investigated in recent years. A range of empirical phenomena have been found to be systematically related in a way that appears to be most parsimoniously explained in terms of a loop system comprising two separable components: a phonological store and subvocal rehearsal process. The current model of the phonological loop (cf. Baddeley 1986) is shown in Figure 3.2. It comprises two related but separable components: the phonological short-term store and an articulatory rehearsal process. Phonological representations of items are held in the store, where they will eventually decay unless reactivated by rehearsal. The rehearsal process is believed to consist of subvocal articulation; more specifically, it is suggested that the articulatory gestures involved in saying aloud an item are activated at a high level, but are not actually executed. Thus, when we rehearse, we are able to choose not to move our lips or any other parts of the articulatory apparatus.

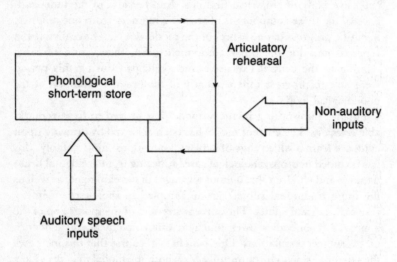

Figure 3.2 The phonological loop model.

Note that auditory and non-auditory verbal information gain access to the phonological loop in different ways. Spoken items are automatically represented in the phonological store, where they may be prevented from decaying by subvocal rehearsal. Non-auditory verbal material, though, such as printed words or pictures of name-able objects, can be represented in the phonological store only if it is first subvocally articulated, via the rehearsal process. Once in the store, though, non-auditory inputs behave in the same way as spoken items. This two-component model has proved capable of accounting for many key findings in short-term memory research.

The rehearsal process

The standard working memory position is that rehearsal involves the subvocal articulation of verbal memory items, and that it operates in real time. To illustrate in more detail how the process is believed to work, two short-term memory phenomena which have been intimately linked with the rehearsal component of the phonological loop are considered here. The first phenomenon is the articulatory suppression effect. It has been known for many years that requiring subjects to repeatedly say an irrelevant item during a memory test greatly impairs immediate verbal memory performance (e.g. Murray 1967). Detailed investigations of the characteristics of the articulatory suppression effect indicate that its disruptive influence on recall occurs as a consequence of engaging subjects in an articulatory activity which prevents them from simultaneously subvocally articulating the memory items. It appears that subjects cannot choose to overtly articulate one item and covertly articulate another at the same time.

The second memory phenomenon attributed to the articulatory rehearsal process is the word length effect. In the first report of the word length effect, Baddeley *et al.* (1975a) compared recall of visually presented lists containing 1-syllable words (such as *sum*, *wit*, *hate*) with lists containing 5-syllable items (such as *university*, *aluminium*, *opportunity*). The task required the subjects to recall the words in a list in the correct sequence. Recall accuracy was much higher for the lists containing short words than those containing long words, even though the words of different lengths were matched for variables such as their frequency of occurrence within the language, and their abstractness. A further experiment demonstrated that it was not the number of syllables in the word *per se* that was critical, but rather how long it takes to pronounce them. Thus, memory span was better for lists of 2-syllable words such as *pewter* and *wicket* that have relatively short articulatory durations than lengthier items such as *harpoon* and *Friday*.

Most importantly, the differences in memory scores across lists containing words of different lengths have been shown to be entirely predictable from the amount of time it takes subjects to either read aloud the memory stimuli (Baddeley *et al.* 1975a) or repeat them as fast as possible (Hulme *et al.* 1984). Thus the longer it takes subjects to articulate a particular set of words, the poorer will be their memory spans for those items. The working memory explanation for this linear relationship is simple. Because this rehearsal process is believed to involve subvocal articulation, items that take a relatively long time to articulate explicitly also take a relatively long time to articulate subvocally. A consequence of this is that lengthy multisyllabic items receive less frequent rehearsals than short items, and so are more likely to decay to an indiscriminable level in the phonological store.

Consistent with the notion that both the articulatory suppression and word length effects share common origins in subvocal rehearsal, the two phenomena have been found to interact with one another. Baddeley *et al* (1975a) found that for visually presented memory lists, the word length effect *disappeared* when subjects had to engage in articulatory suppression during the presentation of the memory items. Recall performance was generally lower under the articulatory suppression condition than in the control condition where subjects had no concurrent task. In addition, the advantage to short over long items was lost with suppression. For auditory lists too, articulatory suppression during the memory tasks has been found to remove the word length effect, provided that suppression activity continues during recall as well as list presentation (Baddeley *et al*. 1984). The standard explanation for this interaction between these two effects is that as articulatory suppression prevents the subjects from rehearsing the memory lists items, there will be no difference in recall performance attributable to the differential efficiency of the rehearsal process with short and long items. In other words, it does not matter much how quickly the items are not being rehearsed!

Recent findings have, however, identified some shortcomings of the working memory account of rehearsal. One problem concerns the proposed *articulatory* nature of the rehearsal process. Bishop and Robson (1989) investigated the short-term memory abilities of a group of individuals born with cerebral palsy who had never been able to speak. They therefore had no opportunity to develop normal articulatory skills. If subvocal rehearsal does involve activating articulatory codes, these individuals should not be able to rehearse. An immediate memory task was designed to test this hypothesis. Recall was measured in terms of the direction and sequence of subjects' eye gazes at an array of pictures which corresponded to the set of memory items, in order to overcome the output difficulties of this special group. The surprising finding was that their serial recall accuracy measured in this way showed a normal sensitivity to word length.

This finding indicates that articulatory skills are *not* critical to the word length effect in serial recall, and so to rehearsal. Is rehearsal articulatory at all, then? The answer appears to be that articulatory activity is indeed involved in rehearsal, but that its involvement is at the level of abstract articulatory plans, rather than of explicit gestures. Waters *et al.* (1992) investigated the memory characteristics of a group of patients with deficits in high-level articulatory planning. This group showed no sensitivity to word length, indicating that they were failing to rehearse the memory items. The result is important, as it indicates that the rehearsal normally involves a process of serially activating high-level articulatory plans which is impaired in this particular class of neuropsychological patient.

A further problem with the rehearsal component of the current phonological loop model concerns accumulating evidence that word length effects may arise for reasons other than subvocal rehearsal. Findings reported by Cowan *et al.* (1992) indicate that the poorer recall of lists of long than short words is a consequence of the fact that it takes longer to recall a sequence of lengthy items than a sequence of short ones. Consistent with this result, Burgess and Hitch (1992) constructed a connectionist model of the phonological loop which produced a clear word length effect in the absence of a rehearsal mechanism. The basis for the word length effect in this model was simply that recalling long words takes more time, and so allows more decay than recalling short words. This evidence favours the view that the word length effect may arise either at the stage of planning speech-motor output (Gathercole and Hitch, in press) or in the act of explicit spoken output (Cowan *et al.* 1992). Whether these represent alternative or additional sources of word length effects in memory to the rehearsal-based mechanisms is a matter which can be resolved only by further research. It does, however, seem clear that the role assigned to rehearsal in the present model is incomplete and will probably require further revision in the near future.

The phonological store

The phonological store holds the phonological features of verbal material. Without rehearsal, the phonological representations decay with time. One robust short-term memory phenomenon that has been attributed to the story is the *phonological similarity effect* (Conrad and Hull 1964). This refers to the finding that recall of memory lists in which the items all sound very similar to one another (such as *bat*, *can*, or *B, C, T*) is typically much poorer than recall lists where the items are very distinctive from one another in terms of their sound structure (such as *cat*, *egg*, *sun*, or *R*, *W*, *H*). The effect occurs with visually as well as auditorily presented memory lists, and therefore cannot simply be explained in terms of perceptual confusion between the sounds of the items at input.

Salame and Baddeley (1982) suggested that the similarity effect arises from the phonological store component of the phonological loop in the following way. As phonological representations of items in the store are liable to partial loss of information due to decay, the disruptive consequences of this degradation will increase in severity as the phonological similarity between list items increases. The reason for this is that the probability of losing a phonological feature necessary to discriminate an item from the rest of the restricted memory set will increase with the degree of phonological similarity of the set. Thus, the loss of the first phoneme of the sound corresponding to the letter *C* will make it indiscriminable from *B* and *D* in a list of phonologically similar items, but nonetheless be distinct from *R* and *W* in a phonologically distinct list. Thus loss of the same information will be much more disruptive for memory performance for lists that are high in phonological similarity.

Articulatory suppression has been found to interact with the phonological similarity effect in a highly selective manner which is entirely consistent with the phonological loop model shown in Figure 3.2 (Baddeley *et al.* 1984; Levy 1971; Peterson and Johnson 1971). With visually presented lists, the phonological similarity effect in recall is abolished by articulatory suppression. Suppression reduces the level of performance for all lists, but its influence is greatest for the phonologically distinct lists so that, under suppression, there is no longer any advantage to recall distinct over similar lists. The explanation for this is that articulatory suppression prevents any visual material from being recoded via subvocal rehearsal into a phonological form suitable for the phonological store. And without access to the phonological store, the phonological similarity effect cannot occur.

A different pattern of results is found when the memory lists are presented auditorily. Although once again performance is lower when subjects engage in articulatory suppression, the advantage in recall for distinct over similar lists is preserved under the conditions of suppression. This result is once again in line with the phonological loop model, because auditory material is believed to gain entry to the phonological store *without* rehearsal. Thus, preventing rehearsal via articulatory suppression will not stop the similarity effect arising with auditory material.

Current debate is centring on the nature of the psychological mechanism controlling access to the store. Salame and Baddeley (1989) have suggested that a filter specialized to detect the physical characteristics of speech governs entry of auditory information into the phonological store, although more recent work indicates that this view needs substantial revision (Jones *et al.* 1992). So, although useful, the present characterization of the phonological store requires further development in order to provide a comprehensive account of the data.

Uses of the phonological loop

An important feature of the working memory approach, and one which distinguishes it from previous approaches, is the emphasis it places on the flexible contribution of short-term memory to cognitive activities which do not necessarily have an explicit memory component. This section considers some of the cognitive skills which have been found to depend heavily on the phonological loop (see Gathercole and Baddeley 1993 for review).

Vocabulary acquisition

One cognitive activity which appears to place significant demands on the phonological loop is vocabulary acquisition. Learning new words is a particularly important process during childhood; it is estimated that during the first 5 years of life alone, the average child learns over 2,000 words (Smith 1926). Peak rates of vocabulary growth occur during the school years; recent estimates are that, between the ages of 7 and 16, children typically acquire 3,000 new words every year (Nagy and Herman 1987). And even during adulthood, vocabulary acquisition continues at a more sedate pace, unless a new language is learned when, once again, rate of learning new words can be very high.

Studies of both children and adults have established a close link between the phonological loop and word learning. Children's phonological working memory skills have been found to be very effective predictors of their natural acquisition of vocabulary. We studied 80 children from school entry at age 4 at intervals through to age 8 (Gathercole and Baddeley 1989; Gathercole *et al.* 1992). At each age, measures were taken of the child's phonological memory skills and their vocabulary knowledge, as well as a range of other factors. The principal phonological memory taken in this study involved the child repeating non-words spoken by the experimenter. The number of non-words correctly repeated were scored.

Between the ages of 4 and 7 years, there was a close relationship between the non-word repetition measure and the children's scores of the vocabulary test (Gathercole *et al.* 1992). The correlations between the two measures were .559 at age 4, .524 at age 5, and .562 at age 6. Each of these correlations was highly significant even after other factors such as the children's ages, non-verbal intelligence scores and reading abilities had been controlled. Similarly, Service (1992) studied older Finnish children initially as they were about to embark on an English language learning programme. The children's scores on a task involving the repetition of unfamiliar sound sequences before starting English provided an extremely good predictor of their class grades in English (with a correlation of .650), tested principally by vocabulary tests, over two years later. So, in both of these studies, the adequacy of children's phonological memory skills appears to have placed a significant constraint on their abilities to learn novel words.

The relationship between phonological working memory and word learning has also been demonstrated experimentally. Gathercole and Baddeley (1990) compared the rate at which 5-year-old children of low and high phonological memory skills learned novel names such as 'Pimas' and 'Sommel' for toy monsters. Consistent with the view that phonological memory skills influence ease of vocabulary acquisition, the fastest rates of learning were obtained for the high memory group.

Papagno *et al.* (1991) explored phonological involvement in vocabulary learning with adult subjects. They found that subjects were impaired at learning associations between visually presented pairs of familiar words and novel words (e.g. 'thread-paglir') when they were simultaneously engaged in articulatory suppression. This result clearly fits well with the view that the phonological loop mediates the long-term learning of new words, as blocking the contribution of the loop system by articulatory suppression should prevent this system from being used in the learning task. Interestingly, though, Papagno *et al.* found that articulatory suppression did not disrupt long-term learning when subjects were able to use semantic information to mediate the links between the familiar and novel word pairs (see also

Papagno and Vallar 1992). It therefore appears that phonological memory demands can be bypassed if alternative forms of representation, such as the semantic associations between two words, are available to mediate learning.

Very similar conclusions were reached on the basis of detailed investigations of the vocabulary learning abilities of a neuropsychological patient (Baddeley *et al.* 1988). P.V. suffered a cerebro-vascular accident (a stroke) which resulted in localized damage to the left hemisphere and a short-term memory deficit. Earlier work with P.V. established that this deficit corresponded to a highly specific impairment of the phonological loop (Vallar and Baddeley 1984). The question was: would she show a corresponding deficit in the long-term learning of new words? If the phonological loop is critical to long-term phonological learning, she should. And she did: P.V. proved completely unable to learn the associations between any familiar word–non-word pairs (as in 'thread-netka'), although she did learn associations between pairs of familiar words (as in 'rose-sky'). Once again, this result indicates that the phonological loop is important for long-term phonological learning, although when new words can be learned by other means such as constructing semantic relationships between familiar words, loop involvement can be avoided.

In summary, evidence from studies of children, adults and neuropsychological patients converges on the view that the phonological loop is critically involved in learning novel phonological structures. The process of constructing stable representations of the sound structures of new words in long-term memory apparently depends on the presence of a temporary representation of the novel phonological structure in the phonological loop. The precise mechanisms controlling this transfer of information from short-term storage into long-term memory are as yet not fully understood. It does, however, seem clear that good phonological memory skills are needed for learning new words. Given the present emphasis attached to vocabulary knowledge within current educational practice, with vocabulary tests providing one of the most widely used indices of verbal intelligence in popular IQ test batteries such as the WISC-R (Wechsler 1974), the adequacy of children's memory skills is likely to be an important influence on their education attainments.

Language comprehension

The phonological loop has also been linked with language comprehension. Although the meaning of individual words and simple phrases can be accessed without involvement of the phonological loop (Baddeley 1978; Kleiman 1975), it does appear to play an important role when an individual is attempting to understand the meaning of a complex clause or sentence. Evidence for this view comes from both experimental studies of normal adult subjects, and single case investigations of patients with highly specific phonological loop deficits.

Baddeley *et al.* (1981) asked subjects to make decisions about whether lengthy sentences were semantically anomalous or not. On half of the trials subjects engaged in articulatory suppression whilst reading the sentences. An example of an anomalous sentence is 'She doesn't mind going to the dentist to have fillings, but she doesn't like the *rent* when he gives her an injection in the beginning'. Accuracy of detecting anomalous sentences decreased significantly under suppression. A similar result was obtained by Waters *et al.* (1987). Once again, subjects were required to make semantic acceptability decisions about printed sentences in different concurrent conditions. Articulatory suppression increased both the speed and accuracy with which subjects responded to the most syntactically complex sentences (such as 'The man hit the landlord that requested the money'). Moreover, Waters *et al.* found that performance was unaffected by a concurrent tapping task, thus ruling out the possibility that the decline in performance was just due to the general difficulty of completing two tasks at once.

These results provide direct support for the notion that the phonological loop does contribute to the comprehension of complex sentences. Neuropsychological patients with severe phonological memory deficits also provide a fruitful source of 'natural' data on this issue. Numerous single cases have been reported in recent years in which a memory deficit corresponding to a selective impairment of the phonological loop has been accompanied by comprehension deficits for linguistically complex materials. The specific types of linguistic construction which patients have been found to have difficulties understanding vary from case to case, and include semantically passive verb constructions such as 'The boy was pushed by the girl' (Caramazza *et al.* 1981; Friedrich *et al.* 1985), centre-embedded clauses such as 'The man the boy hit carried the box' (Saffran and Marin 1975), and lengthy sentences such as 'The equator divides the world into two halves, the northern and the southern' (Baddeley *et al.* 1987; Martin and Feher 1990).

On the basis of evidence showing that the phonological loop constrains the comprehension of complex sentence structures, Baddeley *et al.* (1987) suggested that the loop acts as a *mnemonic window* during sentence processing, providing a phonological representation of the incoming messages. For most sentences, the linguistic structures will be processed 'on-line' as the words are presented, and there will be no need to consult the phonological loop representation. For syntactically complex or lengthy sentences, however, linguistic analysis may lag behind the input, and so take place 'off-line'. In these situations, the comprehender may need to check the order of the wording in the phonological loop representation in order to complete full syntactic analysis. Baddeley *et al.*'s idea is that the size of the chunk that needs to be retained in the mnemonic window varies with the structure of the material. Only when the size of the chunk needed to support accurate interpretation of a sentence or passage exceeds the available capacity of an individual's phonological loop would comprehension problems be expected to arise. Examples of linguistic situations in which the critical chunk size would be large would include lengthy sentences, and sentences containing embedded clauses. The mnemonic window view readily explains why comprehension of these kinds of sentences is sensitive to reduced phonological loop capacity as a consequence of either brain damage or experimental manipulations such as articulatory suppression.

Summary

Abilities to readily learn new words and to understand language are critical to any individual's capacity to communicate, and both abilities appear to depend on the phonological loop. Poor phonological loop skills may also compromise children's success at developing a strategy of phonologically recoding print into sound during the early stages of reading development (Gathercole and Baddeley 1993), and also their acquisition of arithmetic expertise (Hitch and McAuley 1991). Together, these finds lend considerable weight to the working memory premise that, far from being a passive storage system, short-term memory has an active and flexible nature.

THE SKETCHPAD

The sketchpad is a slave system or working memory that is specialized for the processing and storage of visual and spatial information. Although theoretical development of a detailed model of the sketchpad is less advanced as yet than that of the sister phonological loop system, a number of important characteristics of visual working memory have now been established.

The first systematic study of the sketchpad was carried out by Baddeley *et al.* (1975b). Across a number of experiments, a task was used which requires the storage of an imagined spatial sequence. Subjects are shown a 4 × 4 matrix of empty cells, except one cell marked as the starting square. In one version of the task, the experimenter reads out a list of instructions which enable subjects to mentally 'fill' cells of the matrix. For example, the instructions might be: 'In the starting square put a 1. In the next square to the right put a 2. In the next square up put a 3 . . .' and so on, typically up to the number 8. Recall was tested by asking subjects to repeat back the sentences in the order presented. Most subjects report that the way they do the task involves encoding the sentences as a path through the matrix, and that at recall the sentences are reconstructed from this stored image.

Baddeley *et al.*'s idea was that the image may be constructed and maintained in the sketchpad. In order to test this possibility, they devised a concurrent task which they considered may block or disrupt use of the sketchpad, in a way analogous to the way that articulatory suppression impairs the phonological loop. The concurrent task they chose involved the subjects tracking the trajectory of a visual signal with a stylus. The findings were clear. Errors on the spatial memory task increased dramatically when subjects simultaneously carried out the tracking test, relative to the control condition of no concurrent task. A further version of the matrix task was also included. In this task, subjects again had to retain a series of sentences, but no spatial relationship between the items was given to allow the construction of an image. So, the instructions might be: 'In the starting square put a 1. In the next square to the quick put a 2. In the next square good put a 3 . . .' and so on. To recall the sentences, subjects were forced to verbally encode and maintain the sentences, and performance was much lower than in the spatial version of the task. And, importantly, performance in the verbal vision was unaffected by concurrent visuo-spatial tracking. Together, these results are consistent with the view that there is a component of working memory specialized for processing and maintaining visuo-spatial information.

Another paradigm that has been employed to explore the sketchpad involves the use of imagery mnemonics. The beneficial consequences of using imagery as opposed to rote verbal learning to support the retention of verbal material have been well established by researchers such as Bower (1970) and Paivio (1971). One attractive possibility is that the sketchpad may provide the medium for generating and storing images. Baddeley and Lieberman (1980) tested this hypothesis. They asked subjects to remember lists of unrelated words either by using rote repetition or by using a technique known as the 'pegword' mnemonic. This mnemonic involves teaching subjects to associate each of the numbers between 1 and 10 with a highly imageable word that rhymes with the digit name. For example, the number 1 is associated with an image of a bun, 2 with a shoe, 3 with a tree, and so on. Subjects are then trained to use the images as a way of remembering a series of items by linking each memory item with the image associated with the word's position in the list. So, if the first two words in the memory list were *table* and *glass*, the subject would attempt to generate an image incorporating a table with a bun, and another image involving both a glass and a shoe. Once learned, this technique has proved an extremely effective means of enhancing memory for unrelated sequences of words.

Whether the pegword mnemonic uses the sketchpad or not was investigated by observing the consequences of concurrent visuo-spatial tracking whilst using the mnemonic device. Baddeley *et al.* (1975a) had found clear evidence that this concurrent task does selectively impair the functioning of the sketchpad. If the imagery mnemonic also uses this component of working memory, its effectiveness should be reduced when subjects are simultaneously tracking. The prediction was supported. Baddeley and Lieberman found that pursuit rotor tracking impaired recall of lists in the imagery condition, but not when subjects were using the rote repetition strategy. In further experiments, this pattern of selective interference between the use of imagery and an irrelevant visuo-spatial activity has been generalized to imagery techniques other than the pegword mnemonic.

There are, however, difficulties with simply interpreting memory performance on tasks using spatial and imagery materials in terms of the sketchpad. One particular area of difficulty arises from evidence for central executive contribution to performance on such tasks. Phillips and Christie (1977) asked subjects to recall sequences of 3 × 3 matrices in which the cells were randomly filled. The task was very hard, but subjects were much better at remembering the last matrix in the list than preceding ones. It seems plausible that this one-item recency effect arises because the last item was represented in the sketchpad. However, the recency effect was abolished when subjects performed mental arithmetic tasks after the end of the list and prior to recall. It is not clear how the sketchpad could contribute to mental arithmetic, and other work points to this task being served primarily by the central executive and phonological loop components of working memory (Hitch 1980). Phillips and Christie's findings therefore indicate that performance on spatial memory tasks may be mediated by the general purpose resources of the central executive rather than a specialized visuo-spatial slave system such as the sketchpad.

Another area of difficulty concerns whether the sketchpad system should be characterized as spatial, visual or both. Early findings favoured the view that the sketchpad was primarily spatial in nature. Using their matrix task described earlier, Baddeley et al. (1975b) found that although performance was disrupted by concurrent visuo-spatial tracking, it was quite unaffected by a more visual concurrent task involving making judgements about the brightness of a patch of light. Findings reported by Logie (1986), however, conflicted with the conclusion that the sketchpad was more spatial than visual in character. Logie devised a concurrent task in which subjects had to judge whether a plain coloured square was either the same or different in colour to the one preceding it. A highly selective pattern of interference occurred. The presence of squares disrupted recall of unrelated word lists using the pegword mnemonic, but not when a rote repetition strategy was employed. The lack of spatial pattern in a plain coloured square provides a relatively minor spatial component, and so suggests that concurrent visual as well as spatial processing can disrupt the use of an imagery mnemonic. The result indicates that a heavy spatial component is not essential for use of the sketchpad.

One possibility is that the simple distinction between visual and spatial dimensions is in fact an artificial one: most natural events have both visual and spatial features which cannot readily be separable. Distinguishing the functioning of the sketchpad at this level of fine-grained detail may therefore be inappropriate and yield results that are not readily interpretable. Certainly, research focusing on more global properties of the sketchpad has successfully and clearly established that the verbal and visuo-spatial capacities of working memory are dissociable. In particular, recent work by Brandimonte *et al.* (1992) has shown that performance on an imagery task can significantly *improve* under conditions of articulatory suppression. Brandimonte *et al.* convincingly argue that this counter-intuitive result of enhanced recall in a concurrent task condition arises because suppression prevents the subjects from attempting to use a less effective strategy of verbal mediation in the imagery task. As a consequence, suppression forces subjects to utilize the more effective visual codes as a basis for memory performance.

In summary, there is clear evidence that the working memory system has the capacity for processing and maintaining information in a non-verbal form that preserves its visual and spatial features. The resources supporting performance on visuo-spatial tasks appear to be readily distinguishable from the sister phonological loop system. As yet, however, identifying whether performance on a particular task reflects the specialized resources of the sketchpad slave system or the more general purpose central executive component is proving to be less than straightforward. More detailed exploration of the empirical phenomena related to the sketchpad is needed before a well-specified model with the same explanatory power as the corresponding model of the phonological loop can be plausibly constructed.

Uses of the sketchpad

Most research on the sketchpad has used tasks in which subjects either have to use a constrained imagery mnemonic to remember memory items, or are asked to remember meaningless non-verbal material, such as matrices with cells filled at random. Although useful for exploring the theoretical nature of this memory system, such tasks do not readily strike chords with everyday cognitive activity. For most individuals, the occasions on which we consciously use imagery seem rather rare, and the need to retain meaningless visuo-spatial patterns for short periods is also thankfully infrequent.

Does this mean that the sketchpad does not provide a useful resource to support complex cognitive activities? Not at all. Although the contributions of the sketchpad to non-memory cognitive tasks have yet to be investigated systematically, there are clear indications that this component may satisfy some important information-processing demands. An illustration of the potential contributions of the sketchpad to everyday cognitive functioning is provided by a case study of a neuropsychological patient with right hemisphere damage. E.L.D., studied by Hanley *et al.* (1991), appeared to have an impairment of the sketchpad. Her performance on the matrix task used by Baddeley *et al.* (1975b) was exceptionally poor; whereas normal subjects were able to perform reasonably with sets of 8 sentences, E.L.D. made many errors on sequences containing 6 sentences. She also showed a notable deficit on another test of non-verbal short-term memory, known as Corsi blocks. This test is in wide clinical use, and involves a board containing nine randomly located blocks being placed in front of the subject. The experimenter taps a sequence of the blocks, and the subject is required to reproduce the sequence immediately. E.L.D. made far more errors than control subjects on sequences containing 4, 5, 6 and 7 items.

So, on standard tests of visuo-spatial memory, the patient performed at a very low level. In contrast, immediate verbal memory tests revealed normal phonological loop function. One of the interesting aspects of this patient is that her original complaint did not relate directly to this highly specific short-term memory deficit. Her more pressing problem was that she found it extremely difficult to recognize the faces of people that she had met subsequent to her illness, and also encountered problems in learning routes in unfamiliar territories, such as the way back to her new flat. These problems proved easy to demonstrate in the laboratory, too (Hanley *et al.* 1990). Across a series of tests, E.L.D.'s recognition memory for unfamiliar faces and objects was well below the normal range. She also was very poor at identifying the faces of celebrities who had become famous prior to the onset of her brain damage, but was as good at controls at faces famous prior to the trauma.

The clear implication of this profile of cognitive deficits is that E.L.D.'s impaired sketchpad has prevented her from being able to learn novel visual information, such as faces, spatial layouts and objects. It therefore appears that adequate short-term visuo-spatial memory skills must be necessary in order to construct stable long-term memory representations of that information. This seems quite plausible. If someone cannot remember an unfamiliar face after a few seconds, we would not expect them to be able to recognize it days and weeks later. It is notable that the consequences of the sketchpad deficit in this patient are directly analogous to the results of the phonological loop impairment suffered by P.V. (Baddeley *et al.* 1988). P.V. was unable to retain unfamiliar phonological material even temporarily, and so proved completely unable to learn new words. Once again, a short-term memory deficit resulted in a corresponding impairment of long-term learning for that domain of information.

The case of E.L.D. is an important one. It provides a clear demonstration that, despite theoretical debates and uncertainties about how best to characterize the mechanisms and processes embodied in the sketchpad, it is a component of working memory which fulfils many useful functions in everyday life. Learning about new visual events is an ability which makes the human race particularly responsive to changes in the environment. The present evidence suggests that, without the sketchpad, our adaptability would be significantly reduced.

THE CENTRAL EXECUTIVE

Since Baddeley and Hitch (1974) first introduced the concept of the central executive, many different functions have been ascribed to the most complex and powerful component of the working memory model. It has been suggested that the central executive is involved in *regulatory and control* activities. Amongst these activities feature the control of attention and action, the regulation of the flow of information through components of the working memory system, and the retrieval of information from long-term memory. More generally, the central executive has been suggested to house consciousness. The central executive is also believed to possess both *storage and processing* capabilities that are fuelled by limited capacity processing resources. These resources are general purpose in nature, and so can be flexibly deployed in order to respond to a wide range of different information-processing requirements. It has even been suggested that individual differences in available resources may be the roots of variation in intelligence.

As yet, there is no single model of the central executive that integrates both regulatory and its processing functions, although more specific models characterizing the separate functions are available. Here, we focus on one particular model that has already proved to be a useful basis for developing experimental methodologies to explore the nature of the central executive.

The central executive as a supervisory attentional system

Shallice (1982, 1988; Norman and Shallice 1980) has developed a model of the psychological control of action which Baddeley (1986) has adopted as a characterization of the regulatory functions of the central executive. The model is represented schematically in Figure 3.3, and distinguishes between two levels of the control of action.

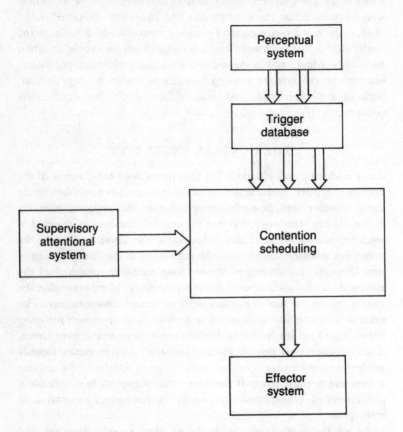

Figure 3.3   A simplified version of the model of action control.

At the lower level, a system of *contention scheduling* operates. This consists of the routine activation of specialized and hierarchically organized schemas that govern behaviour in specific ways. For example, there may be a *driving schema* that activates subroutines such as steering, gear-changing and braking schemas. Each schema is activated by specific inputs that may occur either externally or internally to the system, although activation for a particular schema has to exceed a critical threshold before it is triggered. Thus, the sight of red lights at the rear of the car ahead may be sufficient to activate the *braking* schema. Once a schema has been triggered, it inhibits other incompatible schemas. For example, activation of the braking schema would presumably (hopefully!) inhibit the accelerating schema.

The contention scheduling system controls the occurrence of routine actions. However, there are many times when our actions seem to be *consciously* controlled rather than the products of automatic behavioural routines. For example, although most aspects of driving behaviour can be performed apparently without effort, the same behaviours are exceptionally effortful during the early stages of learning to drive. And even when we have become skilled drivers, some driving-related activities still require conscious effort. One example occurs when we decide to take a different route home from work, perhaps in order to drop a letter off at a postbox which is not on the usual route. Choosing not to follow the usual route is a difficult and attention-demanding process, and one that has a high probability of failure unless the new goal (to choose the different route) is being actively rehearsed at the critical choice point in the route.

Shallice proposed that actions such as these that require conscious control involve the operation of the high-level control mechanism, the *supervisory attentional system (SAS)*. The SAS is a limited-capacity system that can activate or inhibit schemas directly, and so can over-ride the routine process of contention scheduling. By combining the powerful but resource-demanding SAS and the autonomous process of contention scheduling, human action is controlled by an efficient and responsive system.

One of the strengths of the model is that it readily accounts for a pattern of behavioural deficits associated with damage to the frontal lobes which Baddeley (1986) has termed the *dysexecutive syndrome*. It has long been known that damage to these cortical areas leads to disturb-ances in the conscious control of behaviour. The suggestion is that the SAS (or the central executive) is impaired or completely absent in such patients (Baddeley 1986; Shallice 1988). Two behavioural dis-turbances that are frequently observed in patients with frontal lobe damage can be readily explained by this theory. The first is their excessive *distractibility*. It is frequently observed that patients cannot concentrate on a particular task, and become repeatedly side-tracked by irrelevant features of the environment. For example, they may move around the room continuously touching and adjusting objects. Shallice (1988) suggests that this behaviour occurs when actions are controlled only by the contention scheduling system. In the absence of strong activation of a single schema which will inhibit other incompatible schemas, schemas are continuously triggered by external stimuli. In other words, the attentional system becomes dominated by environmental stimuli.

The other behavioural disturbance is termed *perseveration*, and involves excessive rigidity of behaviour. Patients will repeatedly perform the same activity, in an apparently inappropriate manner. For example, a simple task such as naming the object depicted in a line drawing may be completed correctly on the first trial. On subsequent trials, though, the patient will often continue to respond with the name of the original picture, even though this response is now incorrect. The suggestion is that perseverative behaviour of this kind arises when the patient's contention scheduling system is dominated by the high level of activation of one particular schema within the contention scheduling system. As the SAS is believed to be impaired in such patients, there is no opportunity for it to intervene and damp down the schema. In the absence of this high-level restraint, it continues to dominate.

It has also been suggested that the SAS is critically involved in planning future actions. In order to test this hypothesis, Shallice and Burgess (1991) systematically investigated the planning abilities of three patients with frontal lobe deficits. Clinical descriptions of their behaviour were certainly consistent with a planning deficit. Each patient appeared to be unable to concentrate on any tasks other than the most simple activities, and was notably untidy. On one occasion, for example, the patient A.P. was discovered at the local golf course after leaving the therapy room to get some coffee. Another case, F.S., almost never spontaneously initiated activities, and shopped every day to buy a few necessary items only. There was no indication of planning ahead.

Shallice and Burgess asked the patients to complete a task involving multiple subgoals in a nearby pedestrian precinct. A card was given to the patients which listed eight tasks. These included simple activities such as buying a brown loaf and a packet of throat pastilles, and obtaining information about, for example, the name of the coldest place in Britain the previous day, and the rate of exchange of the French franc. In addition, a list of rules was given. For example, the patients were asked to spend as little money as possible and not to enter a shop unless with the intention of making a purchase.

All of the frontal lobe patients made many more errors on this multiple errand task than control subjects. On the basis of a detailed analysis of their errors, Shallice and Burgess identified four different processes that are deficient in frontal lobe patients. These were the articulation of goals (e.g. aiming to buy a loaf of bread), the formulation of provisional plans (e.g. deciding to go to the bakers to get the loaf), the creation of marker cues which trigger planned actions (e.g. planning to post a letter [the planned action] on the way out of the bakers [the trigger cue]), and the actual triggering of actions by cues (e.g. remembering to go to the postbox when leaving the bakers). Each of these critical components of planning behaviour, Shallice and Burgess suggest, is controlled by the SAS.

In order to effectively incorporate the model developed by Shallice within the working memory framework, it is necessary to identify experimental activities that place significant demands on the SAS. Baddeley (1986) suggested that attempting to generate random sequences of letters may constitute one such activity. Subjects are asked to produce a paced sequence of letters of the alphabet, in an unsystematic sequence. Typically, the task is initially fairly easy, but becomes progressively more difficult, with subjects showing an increasing tendency to produce unsystematic sequences such as 'ABCD', 'TV' and 'GB'. Research with this task carried out many years previously (Baddeley 1966) had demonstrated that the randomness of the sequence increased with the amount of time that the subject has available between items. Baddeley suggested that in order to successfully complete the task, the SAS is needed to overrule the routine letter-producing processes that are likely to generate stereotyped sequences such as those mentioned above. By increasing the pace at which the letters have to be generated by the subject, available resources are reduced and so the lower-level system starts to make an increasing contribution to the task.

Using the random letter generation task as a means of occupying the central executive, Baddeley (1993) has started to explore the links between consciousness and the central executive. The initial results look promising. Work with Teasdale used a situation in which subjects were left in an experimental room without any task to complete, and asked from time to time whether their thoughts had wandered from the immediate situation (Teasdale *et al.* in preparation). The incidence of 'mind-wandering' decreased when the subjects were required to randomly generate letter sequences rather than do nothing. Furthermore, on those occasions when mind-wandering did occur in the random generation condition, subjects

73

were more likely to have produced a stereotypical letter sequence just previously. These results are consistent with a view that occupying the central executive with a task prevents other mental activities – such as thinking about task-unrelated matters – from capturing the limited resources of the system. By this account, the central executive may indeed be viewed as the seat of consciousness.

This recent work on the central executive represents an interesting and challenging development of the working memory approach. It looks as though relatively simple tasks can be used to explore possible functions of the central executive, such as planning and consciousness, that once would have been considered experimentally intractable. In parellel with neuropsychological evidence, experimental studies of the central executive are likely to lead to important advances in our understanding of the nature of this central component of working memory.

Different approaches have yielded theoretical models which may be useful for characterizing the way in which the central executive performs other types of functions. The work by Daneman, Carpenter and their North American colleagues on the processing and storage capacities of a general working memory system akin to the central executive has led to a particularly relevant theoretical perspective. Daneman and Carpenter (1980) demonstrated that individual differences in the comprehension of spoken and written language are highly correlated with subjects' performance on a verbal memory span task that places significant demands on both processing and storage (see also Daneman and Carpenter 1983; King and Just 1991; MacDonald *et al.* 1992). On the basis of these findings, this group have proposed that individuals have at their disposal a pool of limited-capacity resources that can be used to serve both processing operations and the storage of information. One consequence of this is that a trade-off between processing and storage activities is necessary whenever a langauge processing task exceeds the limited resources available to the comprehender. A further suggestion is that individuals differ in the size of the total pool of resources available to them, and that this variation is the basis for individual differences in demanding tasks such as the comprehension of language.

In summary, it appears that both research and theory on the central executive component of working memory are very much alive and kicking. Although an adequate integrated model of the component has yet to be produced, there are already well-developed theoretical perspectives with associated empirical traditions which look set to greatly advance our understanding of this important cognitive system in the near future.

CONCLUSION

The strengths of the working memory approach lie in the breadth of its impact on understanding cognition. The specific working memory model is a well-elaborated theoretical structure which readily caters both for specialized processing activities carried out at a minimum cost to limited capacity resources (via the two slave systems, the phonological loop and the sketchpad) and for more open-ended regulatory and processing types of function (mediated by the central executive). The two types of mechanism in combination give rise to a flexible short-term memory system that contributes to cognitive activities as complex and diverse as vocabulary acquisition, learning to read, mental arithmetic, language comprehension, the learning of spatial routes and of new faces, planning, and the control of action. The implication is clear: working memory is an important and hard-working system that is central to many everyday cognitive activities.

REFERENCES

Atkinson, R.C. and Shiffrin, R.M. (1968) 'The control of short-term memory', *Scientific American* 225: 82–90.

Baddeley, A.D. (1966) 'The capacity for generating information by randomization', *Quarterly Journal of Experimental Psychology* 18: 119–29.

—— (1978) 'Working memory and reading', in P.A. Kolers, M.E. Wrolstad and H. Bouma (eds) *Processing of Visible Language*, vol. 1, pp. 355–70, New York: Plenum Press.

—— (1986) *Working Memory*, Oxford: Oxford University Press.

—— (1993) 'Working memory and consciousness', in A. Collins, S.E. Gathercole, M.A. Conway and P.E. Morris (eds) *Theories of Memory*, pp. 11–28, Hove: Erlbaum.

Baddeley, A.D. and Hitch, G.J. (1974) 'Working memory', in G. Bower (ed.) *The Psychology of Learning and Motivation*, vol. 8, pp. 47–90, New York: Academic Press.

Baddeley, A.D. and Lieberman, K. (1980) 'Spatial working memory', in R. Nickerson (ed.) *Attention and Performance*, VIII, pp. 521–39, Hillsdale, New Jersey: Erlbaum.

Baddeley, A.D., Eldridge, M. and Lewis, V. (1981) 'The role of subvocalisation in reading', *Quarterly Journal of Experimental Psychology* 33A: 439–54.

Baddeley, A.D., Lewis, V.J. and Vallar, G. (1984) 'Exploring the articulatory loop', *Quarterly Journal of Experimental Psychology* 36: 233–52.

Baddeley, A.D., Vallar, G. and Wilson, B. (1987) 'Sentence comprehension and phonological memory: Some neuropsychological evidence', in M.

Coltheart (ed.) *Attention and Performance*, XII, London: Erlbaum.

Baddeley, A.D., Papagno, C. and Vallar, G. (1988) 'When long-term learning depends on short-term storage', *Journal of Memory and Language* 27: 586–96.

Baddeley, A.D., Thomson, N. and Buchanan, M. (1975a) 'Word length and the structure of short-term memory', *Journal of Verbal Learning and Verbal Behavior*, 14: 575–89.

Baddeley, A.D., Grant, S., Wight, E. and Thomson, N. (1975b) 'Imagery and visual working memory', in P.M.A. Rabbitt and S. Dornic (eds) *Attention and Performance*, V, pp. 205–17, London: Academic Press.

Bishop, D.V.M. and Robson, J. (1989) 'Unimpaired short-term memory and rhyme judgement in congenitally speechless individuals: Implications for the notion of "Articulatory Coding"', *Quarterly Journal of Experimental Psychology* 41A: 123–40.

Bower, G.H. (1970) 'Analysis of a mnemonic device', *American Scientist* 58: 496–510.

Brandimonte, M.A., Hitch, G.J. and Bishop, D.V.M. (1992) 'Influence of short-term memory codes on visual image processing: Evidence from image transformation tasks', *Journal of Experimental Psychology: Learning, Memory and Cognition* 18: 157–65.

Burgess, N. and Hitch, G.J. (1992) 'Towards a network model of the articulatory loop', *Journal of Memory and Language* 31: 429–60.

Caramazza, A., Berndt, R.S., Basili, A.G. and Koller, J.J. (1981) 'Syntactic processing deficits in aphasia', *Cortex* 17: 333–48.

Conrad, R. and Hull, A.J. (1964) 'Information, acoustic confusion, and memory span', *British Journal of Psychology* 55: 429–32.

Cowan, N., Day, L., Saults, J.S., Keller, T.A., Johnson, T. and Flores, L. (1992) 'The role of verbal output time in the effects of word length on immediate memory', *Journal of Memory and Language* 31: 1–17.

Daneman, M. and Carpenter, P.A. (1980) 'Individual differences in working memory and reading', *Journal of Verbal Learning and Verbal Behavior* 19: 450–66.

—— (1983) 'Individual differences in integrating information within and between sentences', *Journal of Experimental Psychology: Learning, Memory and Cognition* 9: 561–84.

Friedrich, F.J., Martin, R. and Kemper, S.J. (1985) 'Consequences of a phonological coding deficit on sentence processing', *Cognitive Neuropsychology* 2: 385–412.

Gathercole, S.E. and Baddeley, A.D. (1989) 'Evaluation of the role of phonological STM in the development of vocabulary in children: A longitudinal study', *Journal of Memory and Language* 28: 200–13.

—— (1990) 'The role of phonological memory in vocabulary acquisition: A study of young children learning arbitrary names of toys', *British Journal of Psychology* 81: 439–54.

—— (1993) *Working Memory and Language Processing*, Hove: Erlbaum.

Gathercole, S.E. and Hitch, G.J. (1993) 'The development of rehearsal: A revised working memory perspective', in A. Collins, S.E. Gathercole, M.A. Conway and P.E. Morris (eds) *Theories of Memory*, pp. 189–210, Hove: Erlbaum.

Gathercole, S.E., Willis, C., Emslie, H. and Baddeley, A. (1992) 'Phonological memory and vocabulary development during the early school years: A longitudinal study', *Developmental Psychology* 28: 887–98.

Hanley, J.R., Pearson, N.A. and Young, A.W. (1990) 'Impaired memory for new visual forms', *Brain* 113: 1131–48.

Hanley, J.R., Young, A.W. and Pearson, N.A. (1991) 'Impairment of the visuo-spatial sketchpad', *Quarterly Journal of Experimental Psychology* 43A: 101–23.

Hitch, G.J. (1980) 'Developing the concept of working memory', in G. Claxton (ed.), *Cognitive Psychology: New Directions*, pp. 156–96, London: Routledge & Kegan Paul.

Hitch, G.J. and McAuley, E. (1991) 'Working memory in children with specific arithmetical learning difficulties', *British Journal of Psychology* 82: 375–86.

Hulme, C., Thomson, N., Muir, C. and Lawrence, A. (1984) 'Speech rate and the development of short-term memory span', *Journal of Experimental Child Psychology* 38: 241–53.

Jones, D., Madden, C. and Miles, C. (1992) 'Privileged access by speech to short-term memory: The role of changing state', *Quarterly Journal of Experimental Psychology* 44A: 645–70.

King, J. and Just, M.A. (1991) 'Individual differences in syntactic processing: The role of working memory', *Journal of Memory and Language* 30: 580–602.

Kleiman, G.M. (1975) 'Speech recoding in reading', *Journal of Verbal Learning and Verbal Behavior* 14: 323–39.

Levy, B.A. (1971) 'The role of articulation in auditory and visual short-term memory', *Journal of Verbal Learning and Verbal Behavior* 10: 123–32.

Logie, R.H. (1986) 'Visuo-spatial processes in working memory', *Quarterly Journal of Experimental Psychology* 38A: 229–47.

MacDonald, M.C., Just, M.A. and Carpenter, P.A. (1992) 'Working memory constraints on the processing of sentence ambiguity', *Cognitive Psychology* 24: 56–98.

Martin, R.C. and Feher, E. (1990) 'The consequences of reduced memory span for the comprehension of semantic versus syntactic information', *Brain and Language* 38: 1–20.

Murray, D.J. (1967) 'The role of speech responses in short-term memory', *Canadian Journal of Psychology* 21: 263–76.

Nagy, W.E. and Herman, P.A. (1987) 'Breadth and depth of vocabulary knowledge: Implications for acquisition and instruction', in M.G. McKeown and M.E. Curtis (eds) *The Nature of Vocabulary Acquisition*, pp. 19–35, Hillsdale, New Jersey: Erlbaum.

Norman, D.A. and Shallice, T. (1980) 'Attention to action: Willed and automatic control of behavior', University of San Diego CHIP report 99.

Paivio, A. (1971) *Imagery and Verbal Processes*, New York: Holt, Rinehart & Winston.

Papagno, C. and Vallar, G. (1992) 'Phonological short-term memory and the learning of novel words: The effects of phonological similarity and item length', *Quarterly Journal of Experimental Psychology* 44A: 47–67.

Papagno, C., Valentine, T. and Baddeley, A. (1991) 'Phonological short-

77

term memory and foreign-language vocabulary learning', *Journal of Memory and Language* 30: 331–47.

Peterson, L.R. and Johnson, S.T. (1971) 'Some effects of minimizing articulation on short-term retention', *Journal of Verbal Learning and Verbal Behavior* 10: 346–54.

Phillips, W.A. and Christie, D.F.M. (1977) 'Interference with visualization', *Quarterly Journal of Experimental Psychology* 29: 637–50.

Saffran, E.M. and Marin, O.S.M. (1975) 'Immediate memory for word lists and sentences in a patient with deficient auditory short-term memory', *Brain and Language* 2: 420–33.

Salame, P. and Baddeley, A.D. (1982) 'Disruption of memory by unattended speech: Implications for the structure of working memory', *Journal of Verbal Learning and Verbal Behavior* 21: 150–64.

—— (1989) 'Effects of background music on phonological short-term memory', *Quarterly Journal of Experimental Psychology* 41A: 107–22.

Service, L. (1992) 'Phonology, working memory, and foreign-language learning', *Quarterly Journal of Experimental Psychology* 45A: 21–50.

Shallice, T. (1982) 'Specific impairments of planning', *Philosophical Transactions of the Royal Society of London* B298: 199–209.

—— (1988) *From Neuropsychology to Mental Structure*, Cambridge: Cambridge University Press.

Shallice, T. and Burgess, P. (1991) 'Deficits in strategy application following frontal lobe damage in man', *Brain* 114: 727–41.

Smith, M.E. (1926) 'An investigation of the development of the sentence and the extent of vocabulary in young children', *University of Iowa Studies in Child Welfare* 3 (5).

Teasdale, J.D., Proctor, L. and Baddeley, A.D. (in preparation) 'Working memory and stimulus-independent thought', cited in Baddeley, A.D. (in press) 'Working memory and consciousness', in A. Collins, S.E. Gathercole, M.A. Conway and P.E. Morris (eds) *Theories of Memory*, Hove: Erlbaum.

Vallar, G. and Baddeley, A.D. (1984) 'Fractionation of working memory: Neuropsychological evidence for a short-term store', *Journal of Verbal Learning and Verbal Behavior* 23: 151–61.

Waters, G.S., Caplan, D. and Hildebrandt, N. (1987) 'Working memory and written sentence comprehension', in M. Coltheart (ed.) *Attention and Performance*, XII, Hillsdale, New Jersey: Erlbaum.

Waters, G.S., Rochon, E. and Caplan, D. (1992) 'The role of high-level planning in rehearsal: Evidence from patients with apraxia of speech', *Journal of Memory and Language* 31: 54–73.

Waugh, N.C. and Norman, D.A. (1965) 'Primary memory', *Psychological Review* 72: 89–104.

Wechsler, D. (1974) *Manual for the Wechsler Intelligence Scale for Children – Revised*, New York: Psychological Corporation.

4

WHAT IS MEMORY DEVELOPMENT THE DEVELOPMENT OF?

A 1990s theory of memory and cognitive development 'twixt 2 and 20

M. Pressley and P. Van Meter

When the above question was first posed by Flavell in 1971, the answer reflected the research community's then predominate focus on strategies. Despite the attention paid to strategies in the late 1960s and early 1970s, the participants in the published symposium for which John Flavell served as a discussant provided some hints that other factors such as metamemory and knowledge would prove important in the studies of the 1970s. We doubt, however, they were aware then just how much effort in later years would be devoted to understanding how strategies, metacognition, knowledge (as well as a few other interesting theoretical variables, in particular, motivation and cognitive capacity) act and interact to effect memory development.

We have answered the question 'What is memory development the development of?' many times in lectures, informal discussions and publications. The answer varies from the relatively simple 'It involves the complex interactions of strategies, knowledge, metacognition, motivation and capacity' to the more complex answer provided in the 200 pages of Schneider and Pressley (1989), *Memory Development 2 to 20*.

To aid understanding of the simpler answer, the first author sometimes adds an anecdote about a middle-aged professor who uses mnemonic strategies to remember the names of students in his class. His metacognition about the strategy is well developed: he knows how the strategy can be contorted to remember those dreaded hyphenated names – including the hyphen – and how it can be adapted so that it can be remembered that Pierre LeBlanc really is a native French speaker whereas Pierre Charday is not. His application of it is facilitated by a well-developed knowledge base. Thus, when he had to remember Patty Sikorski's name, he saw her flying a Sikorsky helicopter over rice paddies, an association permitted only by knowledge of aircraft and places where helicopters have provided a lot of service in US history. His motivation to use the strategy is great, for students are impressed when he rattles off every name the second day of class. Additionally, there is the positive intrinsic feeling associated with transforming those student faces in the crowd into faces with names. Although this professor knows that mnemonic image construction requires a great deal of working memory capacity, he also recognizes that he is able to construct memorable mnemonic images for most names.

As this anecdote proceeds, listeners often ask, 'But what happened to memory development? We asked about memory development!' The story continues. There once was a time when this now middle-aged professor did not possess such a mnemonic strategy and could not have executed it consistently even if someone had clued him into the existence of the strategy: as a preschooler and elementary-age student, he had neither the capacity nor the prior knowledge to execute such a procedure. Because his grade school neither taught nor emphasized the utility of strategies, there was little motivation to learn or use strategies. Somehow, between preschool and mid-life, much has changed with respect to memory. It is all very complicated with strategy use possible because of his knowledge base and motivation and metacognition and capacity. For some who ask about memory development, this is all they need to know, although they also do not need the detail developed by Schneider and Pressley (1989).

We provide here a chapter-length, contemporary answer to Flavell's question by addressing what we view as the five most important components in memory development, highlighting important and recent evidence bearing on them, framing our discussion within the traditional themes and conclusions offered in the memory development literature. Although some of our colleagues might quibble with our selection of components, the following factors are common in contemporary theories of memory and cognitive development:

- *Capacity* is loosely defined as the amount of information that can be maintained and worked on in consciousness at any instant.

Functional capacity may increase as components of memory tasks become automatized or as knowledge increases and reorganizes (and, thus, permits 'chunking' of to-be-learned content into larger meaningful units).

- *Strategies* are sequences of operations that are matched to task requirements. A strategic sequence can always be carried out consciously and controlled, although sometimes it occurs unconsciously and automatically (e.g. when a strategy is required to do a familiar task in a familiar situation, the strategy is so well known that it can be executed automatically).

- *Knowledge* is the voluminous content of long-term memory, with much of it well organized and easily accessible and other knowledge more scattered and retrievable given specific cues or stimulation (e.g. a grown man reminded of his fifth birthday party when he finds the fire engine he received as a present in a corner of his parents' attic).

- *Metacognition* is long-term knowledge of variables affecting thinking as well as current awareness of the state of cognition. Metamemory is a specific form of metacognition, including both long-term knowledge of factors affecting memory and memory processes and awareness of the current state of memory. Knowledge of where and when particular strategies can be applied is an especially important type of metamemory.

- *Motivational beliefs* are understandings that affect the likelihood of a person using the strategies and knowledge they have acquired to mediate new learning.

Although the discussion that follows is organized around these individual components, many of the interactions between components will also be covered: memory development reflects not only the growth of single competencies but also the interplay of multiple expanding competencies that support and advance one another. This modern perspective is placed in historical perspective, for the richness of the interactions is better appreciated when contrasted with simpler hypotheses that once were the state-of-the-field thinking.

CAPACITY

A common assumption in information-processing theories is that there is a short-term memory capacity that differs from long-term memory (e.g. Atkinson and Shiffrin 1968; Baddeley 1986). Long-term capacity is apparently unlimited, with very little that is in long-term memory activated at any given moment. Short-term memory, on the other hand, is limited in capacity (e.g. 7 ± 2 chunks of information; Miller 1956), and necessitates that information held there be continuously, actively processed (e.g. rehearsed) lest it be forgotten. Theorists have tagged a variety of labels to this ability which enables humans to both hold information in mind and mentally work with it (i.e. attention, Kahnemann 1973; and M-space, Case 1985; especially Pascual-Leone 1970). Baddeley (1986), for example, has argued that the term short-term memory refers only to the ability to store information whereas working memory permits both the storage and the manipulation of information. In this chapter, the terms short-term and working memory will be used interchangeably to refer to the capacity that permits conscious processing of information.

There is increasingly better recall with increasing age from 2 years to adulthood on a variety of memory span tasks (see Schneider and Pressley 1989, Chapter 2). Thus, the conclusion has been drawn that short-term capacity increases with age. There has been a fierce debate, however, over whether capacity increases or only seems to increase (e.g. Dempster 1981, 1985) because of maturation and improvement of other skills and abilities. Most evidence supports the view that developmental increases in short-term memory span tasks are due more to non-capacity, rather than capacity, shifts. For example, increases in speed of information processing between childhood and adulthood decreases the capacity demand and, thus, account for at least some of the developmental increases in memory span. When children recognize a to-be-learned picture faster or rehearse items more quickly, these processes place less demand on the capacity that does exist, leaving more capacity for the processing of additional information and, thus, increasing memory performance. That is, the functional short-term capacity (e.g. Case 1985) is increased even if actual capacity as determined by neurological structures might remain constant. This possibility is supported by strong correlations between memory span measures and speed-of-information-processing measures (e.g. Case *et al.* 1982). This conclusion is also supported by manipulations intended to reduce the effects of processing speeds, such as providing adults half as much time to process each picture as children in a short-term span test of memory for pictures (e.g. Chi 1977) or by constructing short-term memory lists that were named at the same rate by adults and children (i.e. lists in a foreign language for adults but the native language for children; e.g. Case *et al.* 1982). Such manipulations result in children and adults remembering comparable amounts on span tests, in contrast to typical adult advantages in memory.

Developmental increases in functional short-term memory lead to improved memory performance not only by increasing the number of to-be-remembered items which can be processed simultaneously but also through interactions with strategy use. With greater functional capacity, more capacity is left for the processing of memory strategies in addition to the to-be-remembered items. A number of developmental researchers have succeeded in producing evidence that a variety of memory strategies decrease in difficulty with increasing age, substantiating that younger learners use a greater proportion of their functional capacity to carry out strategies than do older students and young adults.

Dual-task methodology has proven useful in this area of research. The subject in such a study carries out a non-memory, secondary task (e.g. tapping a telegraph key or pushing a button in response to a tone), first as a single task and then while doing a primary memory task. The degree to which the memory task interferes with performance on the non-memory task is an indication of the amount of short-term capacity involved in performing the memory task. If more tones are missed or responded to more slowly after the memory task is introduced, the conclusion is drawn that the memory task requires a high proportion of the subject's short-term capacity; if responding to tones is not affected by the memory task, the inference is that the memory task is not pushing the limits of the subject's short-term capacity – there is enough functional capacity to do the secondary task and the primary memory task at the same time. An important finding in this context is that the execution of various strategies, such as rehearsal, memory-for-location and elaboration, produce more disruption of non-memory task performance in younger compared to older subjects (e.g. Guttentag 1984; Kee and Davies 1988, 1990, 1991; Miller *et al.* 1991). The general argument is that, with development, these strategies are more automatically executed. Thus, the proportion of the total functional short-term capacity needed to carry them out is reduced.

Several studies have been particularly informative about the interaction between strategy use and capacity limitations. For example, in Pressley *et al.* (1987a) and Cariglia-Bull and Pressley (1990), children's short-term capacity proved to be an important predictor of memory performance in conditions involving the instructed use of a complex strategy (i.e. construction of mental images representing prose content), but not in control conditions when children were left to their own devices. (The control children seemed to choose less capacity-demanding strategies, such as rehearsal of the sentences.) The outcomes in these studies were consistent with the conclusion that children who cannot hold and manipulate several pieces of information in mind simultaneously cannot use strategies that require such processing (i.e. they cannot hold a sentence in short-term memory while constructing an image that captures the meaning of the sentence).

Another telling experimental manipulation in documenting the role of short-term capacity in use of strategy is known as the 'reduction of demands' approach: children often can perform a capacity-demanding strategy more certainly or capably when efforts are made to reduce the capacity demanded by the strategy. One example was Miller et al.'s (1991) demonstration that children's use of a memory-for-location strategy is more effective when the task is modified so as to reduce the number of procedures children must execute simultaneously; Pressley and Levin (1978) demonstrated that the effectiveness of a mnemonic imagery strategy with children co-varied inversely with the number of steps required for the subjects to carry out the strategy.

Capacity limitations may also affect the person's willingness to carry out a strategy which is highly effortful (i.e. one requiring a large portion of capacity). Even if a person can carry out a capacity-demanding strategy, people perceive they are exerting higher effort when a strategy stretches the limits of capacity than when it does not. Thus, for any given strategy, it will seem easier to a person who is high in capacity to carry out the strategy than it will seem to a low capacity person; in other words, strategy execution will be more of a mental hassle for the low capacity compared to the high capacity individual. Thus, when given a choice, the low capacity individual is less likely to use strategies he or she knows than is the high capacity student (see Guttentag et al. 1987).

With the introduction of knowledge base considerations, it becomes clear that memory capacity is also involved in a three-way interaction with strategies and the knowledge base. More specifically, as the total knowledge possessed by a learner increases, many strategies are easier to carry out because knowledge that is used as part of the strategic process (e.g. semantic relationships that can be used as elaborative links for paired associates; Kee and Davies 1988, 1990,

1991) is more available and easier to access (e.g. Bjorklund and Buchanen 1989). This ease in access and retrieval further decreases the capacity demands during processing of to-be-remembered items.

In summary, although there are large individual differences in the rate of development, there are functional increases in memory capacity with development. These functional capacities affect not only the number of to-be-remembered items which can be processed at a time but also the strategies which can and are executed.

STRATEGIES

There are many dated discussions of memory strategy development which present the conclusion that preschoolers are not strategic, that memory strategies do not develop until the elementary-school years. This conclusion was based on a few early studies of children's rehearsal behaviours during list learning. In those studies, students were presented lists of items to learn, for example, a row of cards which was turned over one card at a time during a study trial to reveal a series of unrelated pictures. Participants in such studies were then required to recall the items on the list, often including their order of presentation. Typically, there were both primacy and recency effects: 10- to 12-year-old students were more likely to recall the first item on a list than the second item which was more recallable than the third item, and so on until near the end of the list (i.e. there was a primacy effect). Additionally, the last, or most recent, item on the list was very likely to be recalled (i.e. there was a recency effect). In contrast, not only was the overall recall of 5- or 6-year-olds typically not nearly as high as the recall of 10- to 12-year-olds, there was either a much less pronounced primacy effect or none at all. There often was a recency effect with 5- and 6-year-olds, however. The absence of a primacy effect suggested that these children were not using the time from the presentation of the first item to the last to rehearse the to-be-remembered items, or at least not cumulatively rehearse them. The primacy effect depends on cumulative rehearsal which moves the items from short-term into long-term memory, with the order to the items coded by rehearsing the items in their sequence of presentation (e.g. 'apple, frog, table, nail . . .', 'apple, frog, table, nail, paper . . .', etc.; e.g. Barclay 1979; Flavell *et al.* 1966; Hagen and Kingsley 1968; Ornstein *et al.* 1975). Recency effects occur because the final item is still in short-term memory (Atkinson and Shiffrin 1968) and, thus, may be easily recalled; if short-term memory does not expand with

increasing age after 3, then recency would be expected at all developmental levels after age 3, with that outcome obtained in a number of
the same studies reporting developmental increases in the likelihood
of primacy effects.

Other evidence also supported the perspective that rehearsal
strategies during list learning develop between 5 and 11 years of age.
Flavell *et al.* (1966), for example, observed a developmental increase
in lip movement during list learning between 5 and 10 years of age.
Such data are complemented by outcomes in studies requiring
children to overtly rehearse to-be-remembered list items. Overt
rehearsal of individual items (i.e. the item currently being presented)
by young grade-school children evolves into much more complex,
cumulative rehearsal over the course of the grade-school years (e.g.
Cuvo 1975; Kellas *et al.* 1973; Naus and Ornstein 1983; Ornstein and
Naus 1978, 1985; Ornstein *et al.* 1975). Elegant analysis of children's
pause times as they examine list items were conducted. In these
studies, subjects could pace themselves as they turned over cards to
reveal items on a to-be-learned list. Older children were more likely
to pause longer with successive list items than younger children (e.g.
Ashcroft and Kellas 1974; Belmont and Butterfield 1969, 1971). That
is, for older children, more time was spent on the second than the first
item, since cumulative rehearsal of 2 items takes longer than
rehearsal of 1 item; more time for the third item than the second item
reflected cumulative rehearsal of 3 items versus 2 items.

Much evidence was generated in diverse studies to support the conclusion that, by the late grade-school years, children use rehearsal
strategies not produced by younger children who, thus, were referred
to as *production deficient* (i.e. they did not produce and use the strategies
used by older children; e.g. Flavell 1970). If measurement is sensitive
enough, as it has been in more recent research, strategy use by preschoolers during list learning can be detected. For example, Baker-
Ward *et al.* (1984) presented preschool children with sets of toys. In
one condition, the children were told to play with the toys. In a
second condition, a memory demand was made, with the children
asked to remember a subset of the toys. The addition of this memory
demand dramatically changed how children reacted to the toys.
Those given the memory demand played less with the toys and spent
more time looking at and saying the names of the to-be-remembered
items.

Newman (1990), using a similar experimental design, obtained a
similar outcome. Lange *et al.* (1989) were also able to document

simple list-learning strategies in preschoolers, such as differential attention to to-be-learned items. What was striking in all three of these investigations, however, was that the strategies deployed by the preschoolers did not increase learning. Thus, although preschoolers may employ strategies to learn a list, these strategies may not always be effective. Still, characterizing strategy development as a 5- to 11-year-old 'thing' does not do justice to the clear differences in behaviour of preschoolers faced with memory demands versus other demands (e.g. to play).

Indeed, preschool youngsters can be very strategic when presented with a familiar type of memory problem in a familiar setting. One of the best-known demonstrations was provided by DeLoache et al. (1985), using the familiar setting of the child's living room and the familiar task of retrieving a toy. In some conditions in this research, the adult hid the toy (e.g. a Big Bird doll under a pillow on the couch) with the child watching and aware that retrieval would be required later. In this situation, even 2-year-olds are strategic. Although pre-schoolers played in the living room during the retention interval (i.e. the period of time between when the object was hidden and when retrieval was attempted), they often looked at the place where the toy was hidden, sometimes even pointing to the location and saying the name of the object. DeLoache et al. (1985) were certain that these were memory strategies because preschoolers in comparison conditions did not exhibit them. That is, if Big Bird was placed on the sofa in view, no checking back or verbal rehearsal occurred. Pre-schoolers used memory strategies only when there was a memory demand.

That strategy development is not a 5- to 11-year-old development is also made clear by considering the different strategies employed by adolescents. For example, Barclay (1979) demonstrated that grade-school children do not recognize during list learning that as the end of a list is approaching, a smart approach is to fast-finish (i.e. maximize the number of end-of-the-list items retained in short-term memory by studying them quickly). In contrast, some university students use a cumulative rehearsal, fast-finish strategy. That is, there is refinement of list-learning strategies between adolescence and young adulthood. Another example of development of list-learning strategies beyond the grade-school years was provided by Ornstein et al. (1975), who studied the increasing complexity of overt cumulative rehearsal into the middle-school years. Ornstein et al. (1975) observed that the size of rehearsed portions of the list increased from the early grade-school years through grade 8. In addition, some extremely powerful strategies for serial list learning, which are employed by at least some sophisticated adult memorizers, such as use of the one-is-a-bun, two-is-a-shoe mnemonic (e.g. Miller *et al.* 1960), are never observed in children. In summary, the 5- to 11-/12-year-old interval is a period of great change in use of rehearsal by students in Western schools, but it is not the only time when development of list-learning strategies occurs.

Another strategy which has been especially well documented as increasing in use during adolescence is elaboration of to-be-associated materials. Since Rohwer and Bean's (1973; see also Rohwer 1973, 1980) study suggesting that at least some students acquire elaboration strategies during the high school years, there have been reports converging on the conclusion that when given arbitrarily related paired items, adolescents are more likely than younger students to use an elaboration strategy to learn these pairs (e.g. Beuhring and Kee 1987a, b; Kennedy and Suzuki 1977; Pressley and Levin 1977; Waters 1982). Thus, given a long list of pairs such as turkey-rock, high school students are more likely to encode the pair with verbal mediators such as 'Turkeys have rocks in their gizzards' or interactive images (e.g. a turkey pecking at a rock) than are elementary students, giving older students a higher rate of recall.

We must emphasize that when studies of memory development were initiated in the mid-1960s, it was expected that they would be revealing about development *per se*. The problem, of course, was that so long as the studies were conducted in Western cultures, developmental level and educational attainment would be inevitably confounded (i.e. the grade-5 student differs from the grade-1 student in terms of both the number of years lived and the number of years in school). Thus, a number of researchers set out for various outposts in the Third World, seeking comparisons of same-aged schooled and non-schooled populations. These researchers laboured hard to provide 'clean' comparisons and eventually succeeded in doing so. What they discovered from this research, however, was that use of memory strategies had little to do with development and much to do with education. For example, because list learning was a popular paradigm at the time these cross-cultural studies were conducted, such memory tasks were exported to study strategy development in other lands. Thus, in Morocco, primacy was observed for students who had Western schooling but not for other Moroccans (Wagner 1974, 1978). In contrast, when Western and non-Western students were compared on tasks for which there was equal involvement in the cultures (e.g. recall of well-structured stories by Liberian tribesmen and American grade-school students), there was little difference in performance of Western and non-Western participants (e.g. Mandler *et al.* 1980). On those occasions when non-Western people have been tested on memory tasks well matched to their cultures relative to Western culture, their memories have sometimes proven superior to that of Western children (e.g. Kearins 1981; Wagner 1978).

Recent cross-cultural research has made even clearer that use of Western memory strategies depends more on experience than development. Not all Western, industrialized cultures encourage to the same degree the use of the strategies studied by American researchers, with differences in the amount of environmental support for memory strategies relating to children's use of strategies (see Kurtz 1990 for an exceptionally thorough discussion). For example, Carr *et al.* (1989) determined that German parents teach memory strategies at home more than do American parents. They also observed greater use of a memory strategy (i.e. sorting of to-be-recalled items into semantic categories at study) by German compared to American children, replicating Schneider *et al.* (1986).

Within-culture experiential differences have also been linked to differences in use of memory strategies, bolstering the case that experience counts more than development in the determination of strategy use. Bebko (1979, 1984) observed that elementary-age deaf children were less likely to rehearse during list learning than same-age children with normal hearing. Bebko and McKinnon (1990) replicated this finding and demonstrated that the apparent differences in use of rehearsal evaporated if an adjustment was made that took into account the number of years the child had experienced language. Thus, a non-handicapped 7-year-old would have 7 years of language experience; so would an 11-year-old deaf child of deaf parents first enrolled in sign language instruction at age 4. Children equal in years of language experience rehearsed about the same amount, regardless of hearing experience.

In summary, memory strategy development is a long-term affair, with different strategies developing at different rates and at different times. Whether a child manifests Western-style memory strategies is associated with whether they experience Western-style education, language and life. Within Western culture, a number of specific home and schooling influences probably contribute to strategy use. Strategy instruction is one type of experience which has been studied more than others, however. There have been many demonstrations that people can be taught different memory strategies (Pressley *et al.* 1982b), including the ones studied extensively by developmental psychologists, such as rehearsal, categorization and elaboration. This large body of research on strategy instruction, most of which was experimental in design, complements demonstrations that the extent of strategy use and environmental experiences co-vary. The correlational studies suggest that natural variation in experiences could be determinants of differences in strategy use; the experimental studies establish that differences in experiences can cause differences in strategy use. Much of memory development is development of strategic competence with the use of strategies depending greatly on other components, including knowledge, metamemory, motivational beliefs and capacity.

KNOWLEDGE

A possibility raised in the late 1970s and early 1980s was that too many of the developmental increases in memory competence were being attributed to the development of strategies. The argument was that some of the learning presumably mediated by use of strategies was actually due to automatic activation of prior knowledge related to to-be-learned content. Such activation of prior knowledge presumably permits elaboration and organization of new material so that it is meaningful and memorable.

Much of the strategies versus knowledge debate focused on list learning, particularly lists composed of categorized items (e.g. car, potato, rabbit, beans, truck, bicycle, onion, squirrel and mouse). With increasing age, not only are more items recalled from such lists, but also the organization of recall changes, with greater evidence of category structure being used to mediate recall with increasing age. The use of category structure was inferred to the extent that items from the same category were recalled together. The 'strategic' interpretation of these developments was that with increasing age students were using their knowledge of categories to encode information at study as it was presented (e.g. Moely 1977). The 'knowledge base' interpretation was that, with increasing age, the knowledge base expands and is better organized. This larger, better organized knowledge base is more accessible and, thus, when an older child encounters a categorizable list, the list items are automatically related to the knowledge base resulting in the list being organized by category of recall (e.g. Lange 1973, 1978).

Expertise and memory

The knowledge base interpretation was appealing for several reasons. First of all, a prominent 'strategies' hypothesis in the problem-solving literature – which was a popular arena for information processors studying the nature of mind and thinking – had fallen (e.g. see Perkins and Salomon 1989). That is, the possibility that there were a few general problem-solving strategies that, when learned and applied, would permit dramatic improvements in thinking (e.g. Newell and Simon 1972; Polya 1954, 1957) had been evaluated and found wanting: little was gained by teaching general problem-solving strategies if students did not possess large amounts of prior knowledge in the domain in which the strategies were to be applied.

As the general strategies hypothesis fell, cognitive psychologists in the late 1970s (e.g. Chase and Simon 1973) were able to provide dramatic evidence of the potency of the knowledge base in mediating memory. Without a doubt, Chi (1978) conducted the study in this genre that had the greatest impact on students of memory development. This study included 10-year-old chess experts and adult chess novices. When subjects were presented with chess boards with pieces in meaningful positions, the children recalled more than the adults. This contrasted with the adult–child memory difference, favouring adults, on a traditional digit span test. Chi's (1978) conclusion that knowledge can play a large role in mediating memory has been strengthened by constructive replications of the expert–novice differences observed in her original study (e.g. Horgan and Morgan 1990; Schneider et al. 1992).

Other theory and research appearing in the late 1970s (e.g. see Anderson and Pearson 1984; Mandler 1984) was consistent with the position that new learning can be largely determined by prior knowledge, with more knowledgeable people often able to learn well because they can relate new information to prior knowledge (i.e. assimilate new information, consistent with the use of the term by many knowledge theorists, including Piaget [1970] and Rumelhart [1980]). This led to the intellectual impetus for taking the knowledge base hypothesis seriously, with many studies of expertise reported for diverse domains. The consistent finding was that well-developed knowledge in a domain was associated with rapid recognition of meaningful patterns and, thus, efficient processing in the domain (see Chi *et al.* 1988).

The large role of knowledge in children's memory

No one pushed harder the possibility that the effects of strategies on memory development had been overestimated – and the role of knowledge ignored – than did David Bjorklund (e.g. 1985, 1987). To support this position, Bjorklund conducted many studies of children's learning of categorizable lists, believing such work could be revealing about the relative roles of strategies and prior knowledge in mediating new learning. Our perspective, however, is that such studies cannot provide information about whether developmental increases and changes in the organization of memory are due to age-related increases in the knowledge base or the use of strategies. The knowledge hypothesis attributes these changes to automatic activation of the well-structured knowledge base in which items are stored according to categories; the strategy hypothesis would predict that strategic processing would lead to the grouping of items by category at study and retrieval. Thus, both the strategy and the knowledge hypotheses lead to the same prediction: the level and organization of serial recall should shift with increasing age. This is, in fact, the empirical outcome that was known even before Bjorklund conducted his studies. Nonetheless, Bjorklund claims that strategic use of categorizing would be implicated if after studying a randomly ordered list of categorizable words, words from the same categories were recalled together with brief latency between items compared to the latency between categories of items (i.e. items A1, A2, A3 and A4 from the same category are recalled together with little time between items, followed by a pause before recall of items from the B category which are also recalled quickly once the category is entered). We can see no reason not to expect this pattern even if the reorganization of the words had been an automatic reaction stimulated by associations between the list and the knowledge base. Thus, we do not put much weight on one of the largest bodies of evidence cited to support the conclusion that much of memory depends on prior knowledge, reflecting associations to prior knowledge.

Even when the categorizable-list data are ignored, however, the evidence is overwhelming that the knowledge base has a huge effect on children's memory. The short list that follows contains some of our favourite examples of knowledge-based mediation of memory, listed from the most basic, laboratory effects to outcomes that are more ecologically valid in that the materials and tasks are consistent with real-world memory demands:

- Paired associates that are related via prior knowledge (e.g. ranch–cowboy) are easier to learn than arbitrary paired associates (e.g. ranch–floor), with a number of researchers demonstrating this phenomenon over the years (e.g. Kee and Davies 1988, 1990; Rohwer *et al*. 1982).

- People (including children) recall more information from text if they are high in prior knowledge pertaining to the text (e.g. Chiesi *et al*. 1979), with such knowledge permitting elaboration of meanings expressed in the prose (e.g. Brown *et al*. 1977) supporting inferential processing (Pearson *et al*. 1979) and awareness of when information in the text has been comprehended versus when its significance remains obscure.

- The degree of prior knowledge pertaining to text content is a much better predictor of comprehension and memory of text than are measures of general intelligence (e.g. Schneider and Körkel 1989; Schneider *et al*. 1989, 1990).

One way to interpret these outcomes is that prior knowledge is a causal variable, which is a distinct possibility given repeated observations of co-variations between prior knowledge and memory. As every introductory psychology student knows, however, even repeated correlations do not imply causation. The only way to make a causal case would be through manipulation of prior knowledge, through building prior knowledge in learners and then determining whether the knowledge had an effect on subsequent learning and memory.

DeMarie-Dreblow (1991) attempted just that. The criterion task was recall of a list of birds. Before presentation of this list, children (grades 2 through 5) in a knowledge condition received a great deal of instruction intended to increase their 'prior' knowledge about some of the birds that appeared on the subsequently presented list. This was accomplished via videotapes and experimenter explanations about attributes characterizing birds (e.g. type of feet, diet, nesting, migration patterns). This instruction, in fact, did increase subjects' knowledge of the birds taught.

What this knowledge did not do, however, was to affect subsequent learning of lists of birds. That is, recall was not affected by the knowledge manipulation. The experimenter monitored whether subjects overtly rehearsed during list presentation, moved the presentation cards around (e.g. to form and use categories), or self-tested. Use of these strategies also was not affected by the knowledge manipulation.

Suggesting that the knowledge manipulation may have been too difficult for young children, DeMarie-Dreblow (1991) replicated the most important features of her study with adults, producing the same results: the knowledge instruction manipulation increased knowledge but did not affect list learning.

On the face of it, DeMarie-Dreblow's (1991) study might be seen as damaging to the theoretical position that high prior knowledge mediates memory, either through automatic associations to the knowledge base or by enabling the use of strategies (e.g. use of categorizing strategies is only possible if subjects know or can devise categories that differentiate to-be-learned content). Fortunately, for knowledge theorists, there are alternative interpretations of the data. In order for knowledge related to listed items to make an impact on list learning, that knowledge may need to be learned to a very high degree, sufficient so that associations to the prior knowledge occur automatically rather than with conscious effort. When knowledge has just been acquired, as was the case in DeMarie-Dreblow, it may have been that the connections between the newly established knowledge and the birds' names was not so automatic. Second, it may be that the particular information taught to the subjects was not seen as useful by subjects in classifying birds or in restructuring rehearsal patterns (e.g. rehearsing birds clustered according to characteristics such as type of feet, nesting, diet, migration patterns, etc.). Thus, subjects may have used more personally salient dimensions to classify the birds other than those characteristics which were taught (e.g. colourful v. drab birds, birds of prey v. other birds, and so on). In short, although we believe that the problem DeMarie-Dreblow chose to study is important and explores methodology useful in understanding how the knowledge base develops to mediate memory, there are alternative interpretations of her null results that mandate caution in interpreting the outcomes as damaging to the position that prior knowledge plays or can play a causal role in determining memory. Studies examining the progression of knowledge acquisition from initial teaching to the point at which this knowledge begins mediating memory performance would aid in understanding how the knowledge base develops to the extent that it enables memory performance.

There are other ways to think about knowledge and strategies simultaneously than in the either/or fashion emphasized thus far in this section. One possibility briefly alluded to in the discussion of the DeMarie-Dreblow (1991) study is that prior knowledge sometimes can enable use of strategies. In order to illuminate such a possibility, it is necessary to use experimental designs that permit separation of the effects of prior knowledge alone, the strategy in question alone, and prior knowledge and the target strategy operating together. Pressley and Brewster (1990) generated such a study, one providing evidence that teaching prior knowledge that can enable use of a strategy can certainly have a causal effect on memory.

Pressley and Brewster asked Canadian middle-school students to learn some facts about Canadian provinces (e.g. Canada's first museum was in Ontario), with half of the subjects in the study instructed to use an imagery strategy and the other half left to their own devices to learn the facts. The imagery instruction was to imagine the fact occurring in a setting unique to the province in question. Thus, for the previous example, imagining a museum in the midst of downtown Toronto would be appropriate. With most of the students lacking prior knowledge of geographical features distinguishing the Canadian provinces, it was necessary to provide instructional support before students were able to construct useful images. Only half of the students were provided this instruction, however, resulting in a 2 (imagery instruction) × 2 (prior knowledge images provided v. not provided) design. The subjects receiving prior knowledge instruction were presented 12 pictures, 1 for each of the 10 Canadian provinces and 2 for the territories, with each picture a stereotypical representation of some prominent setting in the province (e.g. a picture of a wheat field for Saskatchewan, a photograph of Peggy's Cove and its lighthouse for Nova Scotia, and so on). The prior knowledge subjects studied these picture–province associations until they knew them all, with test trials involving presentation of the pictures one at a time and recall of the province name continuing until performance on the task was perfect.

Neither the strategy instruction nor the picture learning manipulation alone increased learning much over what was obtained in the control condition. The best performance, which was clearly better than recall in the control and comparison conditions, was in the condition in which subjects had been taught the prior knowledge images before being asked to use the associative imagery strategy. Possessing an image of Nova Scotia permits the construction of an image of some fact occuring in Nova Scotia. That is, prior knowledge enabled the use of a strategy that could not be executed profitably in the absence of prior knowledge.

Much of good thinking involves the coordinated use of strategies and prior knowledge rather than the isolated effects produced by one or the other (e.g. Pressley *et al*. 1989a). In particular, the operations that define many strategies often specify ways that prior knowledge can be used in the service of learning. That is, strategies often encourage people to use prior knowledge more completely than they would otherwise. Elaborative interrogation is such a strategy and one which has received a great deal of attention from our research group (for a review see Pressley *et al*. 1992b).

Our studies of elaborative interrogation have involved learning of facts, sometimes presented singly as in the Pressley and Brewster (1990) study, discussed a few paragraphs back, and sometimes embedded in extended texts. When we designed elaborative interrogation, our assumption was that people often do not relate to-be-learned content to their prior knowledge to the extent that they could. We hypothesized that if people were led to think more fully about to-be-learned facts, they would activate substantial prior knowledge. Thus, when presented new facts to learn, such as 'The first museum in Canada was in Ontario', subjects in our elaborative interrogation conditions have been asked why-questions – they have been asked to explain why each fact made sense.

One elaborative interrogation study conducted by Martin and Pressley (1991) demonstrated that it is the orientation to supporting prior knowledge which promotes the learning of facts with elaboration studies. Martin and Pressley demonstrated that not just any type of why-questioning promotes learning of facts. In doing so, they effectively eliminated many other potential explanations of elaborative interrogation effectiveness, including that such questioning increases time on task, arousal, semantic orientation to the facts, and so on. If such general factors were responsible for elaborative interrogation effects, they would be expected to boost performance regardless of whether the question being answered by the learner affected activation of prior knowledge supportive of the fact being learned. Only why-questions leading to recall specifically of long-term knowledge supportive of the province–fact association increased recall. That is, questions of the form 'Why would this fact be true of this province?' increased learning, whereas questions such as 'Why would this fact be surprising for this province?' and 'Why would this fact have made more sense for other provinces?' had no significant impact on memory.

Researchers studying the elaborative interrogation strategy believe they are teaching people a strategy that leads them to access and use their prior knowledge to mediate learning. Dramatic evidence in support of this position came in a study by Woloshyn *et al.* (1992). Their experiment included Canadian and German college students who were asked to learn facts about Canadian provinces and German states. They did so either using elaborative interrogation or by rereading the facts. First, there was a huge effect for prior knowledge, with learning of homeland facts much better than learning of facts about the foreign land. There was also a clear effect of the strategy. Most critically, however, the best performance was obtained when elaborative interrogation was used to learn facts from one's homeland. Thus, for German students, performance was best when learning facts about Germany via elaborative interrogation; for Canadian students, performance was best when learning facts about Canada via elaborative interrogation. Extensive prior knowledge used in conjunction with strategies that encourage the effective use of prior knowledge is a winning combination if the goal is to maximize learning.

In sum, elaborative interrogation consistently produces substantially increased learning with adult learners. Although the effects have not been as large or consistent with children, there is more evidence in favour of such effects, at least by the end of the elementary-grade years, than there is contrary evidence. The research has been analytical enough so that it is possible to conclude the effects are probably due to greater prior knowledge activation occurring for subjects in elaborative interrogation compared to control conditions. Our view is that one of the most profitable directions for researchers interested in knowledge effects is to explore the intellectual power of knowledge when it is coordinated with strategies well matched to some task. This is an especially attractive possibility given the increasing recognition that extensive, well-organized prior knowledge is available beginning with the preschool years. Old views of knowledge that suggested preschoolers' knowledge was either poorly developed or organized in ways not well matched to mature strategies are yielding to evidence that preschoolers' representations are structurally more similar to adult representations than they are different.

Children's representation of knowledge and development of such representations

A recurring speculation in the memory development literature has been that young children's representations of knowledge are different from the representations of older children. Prominent among these theories was Bruner *et al.*'s (1966) conception that the representations of preschoolers are more motoric and imaginal than the representations of slightly older children. According to this point of view, older children's more highly developed verbal capacities result in representations that are verbally richer than the representations of younger children. This theory was strained, however, by demonstrations that, if anything, younger children have more difficulty representing information imaginally than do grade-school children (see Pressley 1977 for a review).

Other memory development researchers and theorists proposed that grade-school children were more likely to represent categorical relationships between concepts held in memory than were preschoolers (e.g. Denney 1972; McCauley *et al.* 1976), an hypothesis consistent with classic Piagetian theory (e.g. Piaget 1970). Attempts at generating data consistent with this possibility (e.g. Denney and Ziobrowski 1972; Worden 1976) produced mixed evidence at best (see Ornstein and Corsale 1979 for commentary). Subsequent demonstrations of sensitivity to categorical structure by 2-year-olds in memory situations killed this hypothesis entirely (e.g. Faulkender *et al.* 1974; Goldberg *et al.* 1974; see Mandler 1979 for commentary), with these data complemented by demonstrations that even 2- and 3-year-olds can sort familiar objects into appropriate categories (for data and reviews see Carey 1985; Gelman and Baillargeon 1983; Horton 1982; Markman and Callahan 1984; Sugarman 1983).

We know now that children's knowledge is often extremely complex and well organized. During the late 1970s and in the 1980s, researchers provided massive evidence that adults store large amounts of information in schematic form (e.g. Anderson and Pearson 1984), for example, coding all of the information that occurs in familiar types of episodes, such as going to a restaurant (Schank and Abelson 1977). During this same period of time, demonstrations of schematic memory in older preschoolers (i.e. 4- to 5-year-olds) began to appear. For example, it was shown that children coded the temporal and spatial characteristics of recurring events such as going to McDonald's, eating meals at home, bedtime, making cookies, attending a birthday party and going to museums (e.g. Hudson and Nelson 1983; Hudson and Shapiro 1991; McCarthy and Nelson 1981; Nelson 1978; Nelson and Gruendel 1981). These schemata make a difference, greatly affecting memory when children are presented new information that can be processed and organized via the schemata. Examinations of children's inference generation have demonstrated such schematic effects on memory. Thus, consider what happens when a child is questioned about the following short story:

> Johnny and his mom and dad were going to McDonald's. Johnny's father told him he could have dessert if he ate all his dinner. They waited in line. They ate their hamburgers. And they had ice cream.

> (Hudson and Slackman 1990: 378)

Can a 4- to 7-year-old answer the question 'Why did they stand in line?' even though there is nothing in the paragraph about standing in line? As the parent of any fast-food-fed 4-year-old knows, children have no difficulty with such a question. Their well-developed schemata permit inferences that affect long-term memory of what went on at a restaurant.

The power of schemata is particularly obvious when young children are presented stories not quite consistent with their schematic knowledge of their world. Consider, for example, this not-quite-right story that Hudson and Nelson (1983, adapted from Table 1: 628) presented to 4- to 7-year-olds:

> One day it was Sally's birthday and Sally had a birthday party.
> Sally's friends all came to her house.
> Sally opened her presents and found lots of new toys.
> Everybody played pin the tail on the donkey.
> Then Sally and her friends ate the cake.
> They had some chocolate and vanilla ice cream.
> Everybody had peppermint candy, too.
> Sally blew out all the candles on the cake.
> Sally's friends brought presents with them.
> Then it was time for Sally's friends to go home.

Most readers of this volume probably recognized that the presents were opened before it was specified that the friends had brought them, and the cake was eaten before the candles were blown out. The use of a birthday-party schema to comprehend and remember this story was apparent when the children in Hudson and Nelson (1983) recalled it: sometimes the story was repaired during recall by not mentioning either one or both of the misordered elements. Alternatively, when the misordered acts were reported, they tended to be placed in schematically correct order rather than as specified in the story. In short, recall of the story was consistent with the schema for the birthday party even though the original presentation of the story was not. Although the children in Hudson and Nelson (1983) tended not to recall many inferences, the inferences that did occur were consistent with what usually happens at birthday parties.

Hudson (1988) also demonstrated that children are often willing to accept that some schema-relevant events occurred in a story even though they did not. The 4- to 7-year-olds in Hudson (1988) heard stories about going to McDonald's and going grocery shopping. They were then given a recognition test and asked to discriminate between sentences they had heard before and those they had not. The most important finding was that the children were quite willing to accept script-relevant sentences that had not been presented in the story as if they had been presented.

One of the most important assumptions of schema theory (e.g. Anderson and Pearson 1984) is that schemata are built up through many encounters with events. That probably holds much of the time, although recent evidence makes clear that even preschoolers acquire a large amount of extremely durable knowledge about complex situations from single experiences.

Fivush et al. (1984) examined kindergarten children's memories for a specific trip to a museum of archaeology versus their general memories for museums. Memories of the archaeology museum were tapped immediately after the trip occurred, 6 weeks following the trip, and 1 year later. Memory for this specific museum proved to be very good with few intrusions from children's general 'museum-trip' script. The potential for a single episode having long-term impact on knowledge was bolstered by evidence that the archaeology trip was remembered well 1 year later. In a follow-up investigation, Hudson and Fivush (1991) determined that the event was remembered even 6 years after the trip occurred.

Hudson (1990) further contrasted memory of a specific event, attendance at one session of a creative movement workshop, with memory of repeated workshop sessions. The participants in the study were nursery school and kindergarten children. Memory of details was better for the workshop immediately preceding the test trial, if only 1 workshop had been attended rather than 4 workshops. When 4 workshops had been attended, the children tended to recall the entire sequence of events during the workshop better than when only 1 workshop had been attended. That is, with repeated encounters of the workshop, some general knowledge of relationship between activities during the workshop had been built up, information critical to a schematic representation of such workshops. One cost of this improved memory for sequence with repeated visits to the workshop was that details from workshops 1, 2 and 3 were misremembered as having occurred during workshop 4. Once a schema is formed, memory of specific details declines, with an increase in the possibility of interference due to memory of specific happenings during sessions other than the session that is to be remembered in detail.

What Nelson, Hudson, Fivush and their associates have demonstrated is that even young children's knowledge is organized schematically, with the development of a schema beginning with the first instance of an event. The evidence they have produced about the development and functions of schemata in memory suggest that these powerful representations of knowledge are similar both structurally and functionally to the schematic representations of adults.

Summary

The early studies of expertise, such as Chi's (1978), provided evidence of the power of knowledge other than strategic knowledge. Moreover, knowledge was able to account for learning of more complex phenomena (e.g. what was recalled from trips to museums, restaurants and skills classes) than the list-learning situations studied by the strategy researchers. Since then, a variety of strategies that can increase memory of more complex materials, such as text, have been validated (e.g. Pearson and Dole 1987; Pressley et al. 1989b), providing new interest in strategies as aids to learning.

Strategies and other knowledge complement one another in skilled thinking. Thus, strategies to elaborate paired associates, messages in texts or to-be-learned facts often work only if there is an extensive knowledge base containing information that can be related to the to-be-learned content. For example, categorization strategies can only be applied if the learner has knowledge of the categories represented by list items. It is also true, however, that sometimes a person with extensive prior knowledge will make automatic associations to new input that will render such input memorable without intentional strategic efforts on the part of the learner. Thus, if presented paired-associates that are strongly associated (e.g. needle–balloon), elaborations may occur automatically (e.g. Guttentag 1989). More often, however, people fail to relate to-be-learned content to their knowledge base as extensively as they could. In those cases, encouraging strategic processing, like elaborative interrogation, can boost performance. If the learner lacks the prior knowledge required to enable such strategies, then application of a strategy that does not require extensive prior knowledge may be what is required. Thus, if one is learning vocabulary items in a language so foreign to the learner that no cognates are known by the student, then use of strategies that do not rely so much on prior knowledge of cognates is justified and necessary (e.g. keyword mnemonics for learning completely foreign items; see Pressley *et al.* 1982a). In brief, which memory strategy is useful for a task often varies with the learner's prior knowledge that can be related to the task situation. Good memory is based not on knowledge or strategies but on recursive interaction between strategic plans, other knowledge and a few other factors.

METACOGNITION (METAMEMORY)

Many of the early investigations of metamemory were concerned with determining functional relationships between metamemory and memory. For example, did long-term knowledge of when and where a strategy could be applied determine whether a person used a strategy appropriately? Did awareness of how well learning was proceeding (i.e. monitoring) affect decisions about continuing a current strategy or changing to a new one?

However, initial investigations, aimed at identification of meta-memory–memory connections, failed to find such connections (e.g. Kelly *et al.* 1976; Salatas and Flavell 1976), with failures to identify memory–metamemory connections prominently cited as evidence that such connections might be inconsequential, if they existed at all (e.g. Cavanaugh and Perlmutter 1982). As these views predominated into the early 1980s, critics began to point out problems with the reliability of many metacognitive measures (e.g. Cavanaugh and Perlmutter 1982). Such criticism resulted in the development of more defensible measurement of metamemory and more precise hypotheses in the 1980s.

By 1988, there were more than sixty empirically based publications examining potential metamemory–memory connections (Schneider and Pressley 1989, Chapter 5). A meta-analysis conducted by Wolfgang Schneider and reported by Schneider and Pressley (1989, Chapter 5) permitted the unambiguous conclusion that there are statistical associations between various types of metamemory and memory (overall r based on 123 correlations was 0.41). Furthermore, retrospective analyses usually turned up operational characteristics in the earlier negative studies that could have artefactually reduced the metamemory–memory associations (e.g. a ceiling effect in Kelly *et al.* 1976; procedural aspects that made use of an optimal strategy especially difficult in Salatas and Flavell 1976). Thus, the current perspective, based on recent, more methodologically sound studies, is that memory and metamemory connections contribute to memory performance.

Although there have been many attempts to catalogue the various types of metacognition (see Schneider and Pressley 1989, Chapter 5), the two types of information alluded to in the introductory paragraph of this section are a valid breakdown, as far as strategies are concerned: (a) long-term knowledge of effective and ineffective cognitive procedures and when they are applicable, and (b) monitoring of one's memory and readiness for a memory test. In general, Schneider's meta-analysis produced evidence of metamemory–memory relationships for both of these types of metacognition, although monitoring-memory relationships tended to be slightly higher than relationships between long-term knowledge of/about strategies and memory. Brief, additional consideration of these two types of metamemory will provide a flavour of some of the most important contemporary thinking about metamemory and its role in regulating memory strategies and use of knowledge.

Monitoring

Monitoring of one's memory requires the person to determine if they have successfully memorized the to-be-learned material and to base subsequent study strategies on this determination. If, for example, a learner senses the material has not been adequately memorized, he or she may study more or change strategies. Thus, a person who monitors well knows when they do and do not know the material, with this awareness gleaned from self-monitoring presumed critical in cognitive decision-making, a conclusion supported by monitoring-memory performance correlations such as the ones summarised in Schneider and Pressley (1989, Chapter 5).

A hypothesis dating back to the early thinking on metacognition (e.g. Flavell 1977) is that monitoring in young children is particularly deficient, accounting in part for the relatively poor executive control (e.g. election of effective memory strategies) by preschoolers and children in the early elementary grades compared to older students. A number of studies of awareness have been conducted in reaction to this developmental hypothesis, with some clear findings emerging from this database.

One consistent observation is that if 4- to 8-year-olds are asked whether they are ready to be tested on content, they are overtly optimistic. Overconfidence occurs regardless of whether the tested content was just studied in preparation for the test or is stored in long-term memory (e.g. Clifford 1975, 1978; Entwisle and Hayduk 1978; Flavell et al. 1970; Levin et al. 1977; Parsons and Ruble 1977; Phillips 1963; Pressley and Ghatala 1989; Stipek 1983; Stipek and Hoffman 1980; Yussen and Berman 1981; Yussen and Levy 1975). Children in this age range believe they will perform at ceiling on whatever test they face (i.e. if told there were 30 items on the list, they assert that they will remember all 30 items). Even after taking a test on the material and performing well below ceiling, 4- to 8-year-olds continue to believe they will have very good memory of the material – next time (e.g. Clifford 1978; Levin et al. 1977; Parsons and Ruble 1977; Pressley and Ghatala 1989; Stipek and Hoffman 1980). One reason this is so is that young children believe they have done much better on tests than they actually did. That is, if asked immediately after taking a test about their level of performance, children overestimate how well they did (Berch and Evans 1973; Bisanz et al. 1978; Kelly et al. 1976; Masur et al. 1973; Pressley and Ghatala 1989; Pressley et al. 1987b). In short, young children, on average, overestimate how ready they are to remember something and how well they have remembered once tested. (We emphasize, however, that these conclusions apply on average because of an observation made by Pressley and Ghatala (1989) and confirmed by inspection of the distributions of data in Clifford (1975), Entwisle and Hayduk (1978), Flavell et al. (1970), Levin et al. (1977) and Pressley et al. (1987b): although most young children overestimate, a small number greatly underestimate their memory.)

A major developmental finding with respect to monitoring is that slightly older children are substantially more accurate than 4- to 8-year-olds in both their predictions of memory performances and their awareness of how they did on a recently completed test. One of the more complete of the developmental studies was Pressley and Ghatala (1989), which spanned grades 1 to 8. In that study, there was collection of prediction data before taking a practice test, postdiction data (i.e. awareness of performance on the practice test), and predictions about performance on a future test after taking a practice test. In general, there was increased accuracy on all three measures of awareness with increasing age. What was also striking, however, was that even the oldest participants in the study were not perfectly aware of either how they would do on an upcoming test or how they did on a recently completed test.

What has become extremely clear in recent studies, especially ones tapping learning from text, is that even adults are often completely unaware of how much or exactly what they have learned from text. For example, adult subjects in Pressley *et al.* (1987c) read a chapter in their introductory psychology text in preparation for a quiz that was familiar in format. Their predictions of performances on the quiz were 80 per cent off on average (i.e. often offering estimates of anticipated test performance that were $3\frac{1}{2}$ or more items higher or lower than actual test performance of $4\frac{1}{2}$ items out of 15). Glenberg and his colleagues (Glenberg and Epstein 1985, 1987; Glenberg *et al.* 1982) have reported that adults are extremely inaccurate in pinpointing which parts of a text will be remembered later. Perhaps most shocking of all, adults often believe they have extracted and remembered the main idea from text, when in fact they have completely missed the point of a reading (Pressey and Ghatala 1988; Pressley *et al.* 1990a, b). That adults often fail to use efficient strategies when attempting to learn text may be in part explicable by failures to monitor. For example, appropriate activation of restudy strategies depends on awareness that material has not yet been learned (see Pressley *et al.* 1992a).

In concluding this subsection, we emphasize the difference in outlook about monitoring compared to a decade ago. Early studies of monitoring (Markman 1977, 1979, 1981), which relied on detection of inconsistencies in text, concluded that upper-level elementary children could detect inconsistencies and monitor their comprehension of text even if primary children experienced difficulties doing so: Markman's conclusions about monitoring of text processing seemed sensible given that primary children monitored so poorly on traditional memory tasks, with memory monitoring much improved by the end of the grade-school years. The early work on monitoring converged to suggest monitoring developed to a high level of proficiency by the end of childhood. What has become clear since then, however, with more direct measures of monitoring (i.e. failure to monitor was inferred from failures to detect inconsistencies in the Markman work) and assessment of monitoring in more realistic and demanding situations, is that even adults fail to monitor accurately much of the time.

A final detail not mentioned until this point, but one that is important, is that whenever there are sex differences in monitoring, they are in the direction of boys being more confident than girls about their memory (see Pressley and Ghatala 1989 for a review of the relevant studies). With young children especially, the net effect of the lower confidence for girls is that they are more accurate than boys in their estimations of their memory.

Long-term knowledge about memory (including strategies)

The first substantial metamemory finding reported in the research literature was that long-term knowledge of factors affecting memory increases with development during the elementary-school years (Kreutzer et al. 1975). Kreutzer et al. (1975) asked children questions such as whether the colour of a set of pictures would affect learning of the pictures, if more learning occurs when someone studies for 5 minutes versus 1 minute, how they would attempt to learn a set of pictures, and what could be done to assure a child would remember to take ice skates to school the next morning.

That there were many items on the Kreutzer et al. (1975) inventory that grade-5 children could not answer suggested that long-term knowledge of the variables which affect memory may continue to develop into adolescence and adulthood. There were also clear individual differences in what the children knew, with some children knowing more and some less, and with none of the children necessarily being able to answer the same questions as other children.

John Borkowski recognized that such individual differences with respect to what people knew about memory and cognition might be telling with respect to cognitive control. At a 1979 conference, Borkowski (subsequently published as Borkowski 1985) made the point that metacognition was critical to executive control of strategies and, in particular, to generalization of strategies, a perspective that would be embraced by many other investigators in the first half of the 1980s (e.g. Brown et al. 1983). This was an eminently reasonable hypothesis, given that generalization requires recognizing when there is a need to use a strategy, how strategies that are known might be related to such needs, and how strategies that are known can be flexibly adapted to new situations – in short, a lot must be known about memory in order to generalize strategies.

Borkowski's hypothesis (1985) had been informed by reading Belmont, Butterfield and Ferretti's (1982) analyses of the cognitive training literature with mentally retarded students. Belmont *et al.* (1982) had analysed all of the published studies documenting generalization by retarded children of strategy training from one task to another, noting that, in all of the successful studies, participants had been provided a substantial amount of metamemorial information. Subjects in these studies had been made aware of the need to design strategies matched to the demands of memory tasks, take into account how they might perform without a strategy, and monitor their ongoing learning. As a long-time student of learning in retarded populations, Borkowski understood the many conceptual similarities between teaching and learning in retarded and normal children and, thus, advanced the hypothesis that the strong co-variation in the literature on mental retardation between metacognitive input during training and generalization augured such relationships with normal functioning students.

Consistent with the hypothesis that metamemory plays a critical role in generalization of newly acquired strategies, Borkowski and his colleagues set out to determine if differences in what an individual knows about memory-predicted generalization and long-term use of memory strategies, and if interventions designed to increase such metamemory would enhance transfer and maintenance of newly learned strategies.

Kurtz and Borkowski (1984) produced evidence consistent with both of these possibilities. They first assessed the long-term knowledge of factors affecting memory of their grade-1 and grade-3 subjects. The children in the study responded to items from Kreutzer *et al.*'s (1975) original metamemory scale, items tapping knowledge of strategies, the usefulness of planning, differential task difficulty and monitoring. Competence on some basic memory tasks (categorizable list learning and paired-associate learning) was also assessed in order to provide an estimate of baseline performance before training.

Following the initial assessments, children were divided into three groups. Two of the groups received metamemory training including information about how the mind works and how memory could be improved by use of strategies well matched to memory task requirements. Some demonstrations of the potential effects of strategies (not ones subsequently trained in the study) were included in this meta-memory instruction. In short, children in the two metamemory-trained conditions received a great deal of information about the role of strategies in cognition. Children in the third condition interacted with the experimenters but did not receive metamemory instruction. Then, one of the metamemory-trained groups and the control group were taught how to use categorization to learn categorizable lists. These same subjects were taught an elaboration strategy for learning of paired associates. No instruction in these strategies was provided to the children in the second metamemory group.

In the final session, all participants were asked to perform memory tasks that could be mediated by categorization and elaboration strategies, although these test tasks were not identical in structure to the tasks presented during training (i.e. they were transfer tasks). The most dramatic outcome was that generalization of the strategies to the new tasks was greatest in the metamemory-strategy-trained condition for those participants who had good metamemory at the beginning of the study. What Kurtz and Borkowski (1984) concluded was that individual differences in metamemorial competence produced dif-ferences in the sensitivity to new metacognitive information, with the combined effect of the individual differences in metamemorial competence and the metacognitive producing generalization.

Since that early work, Borkowski, Kurtz and their colleagues have continued to explore individual differences in long-term knowledge about memory as a determinant of strategy generalization. Meta-memory status has proven to be a powerful predictor of transfer and long-term use of trained strategies, better than other predictors such as psychometric intelligence (Kurtz and Borkowski 1987; Kurtz et al. 1988) and cognitive tempo (i.e. impulsivity or reflectivity; e.g. Borkowski et al. 1983). General awareness of cognition, as measured by metamemory scales, is associated with effective use of cognitive resources such as newly learned strategies.

Experimental manipulation of long-term metamemory has not been explored as thoroughly as naturally occurring individual dif-ferences in knowledge about memory. This is unfortunate since such experimental research has great potential for providing convincing validation of the metamemory construct as a causal variable in memory; it is puzzling, because, to the extent such information has been manipulated, it has been possible to produce striking relation-ships between provision of information about memory variables and long-term use of strategies.

For example, O'Sullivan and Pressley (1984) taught grade-5 and grade-6 students in four different conditions about an imagery-based procedure for learning associations between cities and the products produced in those cities. The four imagery-strategy training conditions varied with respect to the amount of information provided about where and when the imagery strategy could be applied (i.e. information about structural characteristics of to-be-learned materials that permit flexible application of the strategy). Transfer of the imagery-based strategy to a Latin-vocabulary learning task varied between these imagery training conditions, such that greater transfer was obtained in conditions that more completely specified the structural parameters permitting adaptation of the strategy. Outcomes like this one (also Kurtz and Borkowski 1984, described earlier) provide support for the position that some types of metacognitive information can be supplied to children via direct instruction, with the children then able to use the knowledge to guide subsequent processing.

One type of metacognitive information manipulated more than any other in studies to date has been the utility of strategies being taught. These studies are especially important because information about the gains provided by a strategy can provide incentive to use a strategy. Thus, studies examining the effect of strategy utility instruction on subsequent use of a strategy provide a bridge between the metacognitive and motivational literatures.

MOTIVATIONAL BELIEFS AND KNOWLEDGE

Some beliefs and knowledge motivate use of cognition. Most of these beliefs and knowledge are really a form of metamemory or metacognition in that they constitute knowledge about memory or thinking. They are covered in this separate section on motivation, however, because these forms of metacognition fuel cognitive efforts, with the efforts most typically studied being strategies.

Knowledge of strategy utility

One of the earliest hypotheses to be invested in the metacognitive literature was that informing students about the usefulness, or utility, of strategies they were learning would increase continued use, or maintenance, of these trained strategies. Thus, a number of studies appeared during the 1970s and early 1980s in which one group of subjects was taught a strategy and informed about its utility and

109

another group was simply taught how to use the strategy. The consistent finding was that providing utility information did, in fact, increase strategy maintenance (e.g. Black and Rollins 1982; Borkowski *et al.* 1976; Cavanaugh and Borkowski 1979; Kennedy and Miller 1976; Lawson and Fuelop 1980; Paris *et al.* 1982; Ringel and Springer 1980; see Pressley *et al.* 1984a, 1985). In short, knowledge that a strategy improves performance motivates long-term use of the strategy.

Referring back to our discussion on monitoring deficiencies even in adults, it becomes clear that, left on their own, people may not be able to determine the utility of newly taught strategies (e.g. Pressley *et al.* 1984b). A conclusion that emerged from a number of studies conducted in the 1980s was that the utility of a strategy was often missed unless the learner used the strategy and was *tested* over the material studied with the strategy, tested in a way that made salient that more was learned using the strategy than by using other approaches.

Consider what happened in one study of adult vocabulary learning (Pressley *et al.* 1988). Subjects in the study learned foreign vocabulary words on two occasions, separated by a 2-week interval. In five of the conditions of the study, subjects were taught an imagery-based mnemonic method for learning foreign words, one that produced much better learning than strategies used spontaneously by the subjects in the study such as rehearsal of the words and definitions. The five conditions varied with respect to how much opportunity subjects had to observe the positive difference that the imagery-based mnemonic method made. In the most complete condition, subjects first tried learning a list of vocabulary using their own methods, followed by a test on the items. Then, they learned another list of vocabulary, half of which was learned with the efficient mnemonic method and half with rehearsal followed by a subsequent test for memory of definitions. Thus, these subjects could compare test performance using the imagery-based strategy with both rehearsal and their own approach. In a second condition, subjects studied and were tested on the baseline list and then learned and were tested on an entire list studied with the imagery method, permitting a direct comparison of test performance following both their own method and the imagery method. In a comparably complete third condition, subjects used the imagery method to learn half the items on a list and rehearsal to learn the remaining items, followed by the test. A fourth condition afforded no explicit opportunity to compare the imagery method with other methods, with subjects simply learning a list of words using the imagery method and receiving a test on the words studied. The fifth and least opportune condition involved simply telling students about the imagery method without permitting them to practise using it. Control subjects were provided no information about the imagery or rehearsal strategies during this first session and were given no practice opportunities.

Two weeks later all subjects returned to meet with the same experimenter again in the same room. This time, they were presented with a list of new foreign vocabulary items and asked to study them, instructed to do whatever they wanted to learn the words, except they had to do it aloud. There was a linear increase in evidence of imagery-strategy maintenance from conditions in which imagery practice occurred without an opportunity to compare imagery-mediated performance with other performances to the condition in which there were two sources of comparison (i.e. with their own approach and with rehearsal). In fact, there was no evidence of maintenance when participants had simply been taught the imagery strategy and practised it with subsequent testing on items studied with imagery. This is a particularly noteworthy outcome, since this condition most resembled many strategy training conditions with the target strategy taught, practised and memory tested. Maintenance is more likely when people have opportunities to see that their strategic efforts are paying off. Many times, however, such as when people are taught a single new strategy and practise it in isolation, strategy instruction is not structured so as to make salient the effects produced by the new strategy, with the result being an incomplete understanding of the efficacy of the newly learned approach.

With children, however, more is required than with adults for them to understand the benefits of a newly learned strategy and to use that knowledge to affect subsequent strategy use. Thus, in Pressley *et al.* (1984c), 10- to 13-year-olds who tried both an effective vocabulary strategy and a less effective one and were tested over items studied with these strategies failed to apply the more effective strategy to a new vocabulary task unless they were explicitly prompted to consider strategy utility information as they made their subsequent strategy decision. Ghatala *et al.* (1986) demonstrated that 7-year-olds would not maintain a more effective strategy unless they were taught to (a) attend to and assess performances using the more effective and a less effective strategies, (b) attribute performance increases produced by the more effective strategy as due to use of the more potent approach, and (c) use the information gained from practice and testing to make future strategy decisions.

A coherent pattern emerges from these studies illustrating that young children can attend to and use strategy utility information when prompted to do so, but such attention and use of utility information in decision-making is anything but automatic. By the middle-grade-school and middle-school years, simply providing such information (if subjects have not had a chance to compare effective-strategy-mediated performances with other performances) or gently prompting attention to utility information (if subjects did have opportunity to compare effective and ineffective strategies through practice and tests over practised items) promotes long-term use of strategies that are taught. By adulthood, opportunities to compare effective and ineffective strategies during study and testing produce clear understanding of relative utility, with utility information a clear determinant of whether a strategy is used in the future. (One possible reason for children requiring more prompting than adults in order for them to make use of strategy utility information is that their perceptions of the relative effectiveness of strategies mediating test performances are not as accurate as the perceptions of adults after they have been tested [see especially Pressley *et al.* 1984c]). A final twist, not covered until this point because it is tangential to the focus in this chapter on memory development in the first two decades of life, is that reliance on utility to guide strategy seems to peak during young adulthood and dissipate in later years: when retirement-age adults practise strategies and experience tests over practice-list items, they discern the relative utility of the strategies used. Even so, when they make decisions about future use of strategies, other criteria prevail, such as the familiarity of the strategy and the effort required to use it (Brigham and Pressley 1988).

Effort attributions

According to Weiner's (1979) motivational framework, how people explain their performance on a task has important consequences for future behaviours. When performing a given task, the outcome may be attributed to the effort expended, ability, task difficulty or luck. Attributions to any of the latter three factors of ability, task difficulty or luck has the potential for undermining performance, for such attributions reflect beliefs that performance is out of personal control (see Deci and Ryan 1985), the product of an inherent unchangeable factor, test characteristics controlled by others, or the fates. Only attributing prior success or failure to effort motivates future efforts.

This analysis is certainly incomplete, however. Some strategies – namely, those mismatched to the current memory task – can require enormous effort and not produce good learning. Thus, suppose you try hard to learn a serial list of concrete nouns by making a mental picture of each item as it is revealed on the list. Thus, if the experimenter says wolf, you imagine a wolf. If the experimenter says car, you imagine a car, and so on for the forty or so items on this list. Will this strategy help at recall, especially recall of the items in the order presented? Not much, if at all. Perhaps you make the effort attribution, concluding your poor performance on this first attempt was because you did not try hard enough to make a good picture for each one. Thus, the second time through you really concentrate, making certain every image is complete and detailed. Will this do much good will respect to recalling the items in order? No. Effort alone is not what makes memories. Effort expended through task-appropriate processes is what is required (e.g. Morris *et al.* 1977). A strategy matched to the task of learning a list of concrete nouns in the above described case would be a variation of the one-is-a-bun procedure extended for forty items. The strategy of simply imagining each object as named, however, would mediate recognition memory for the list of forty items (e.g. being able to decide whether 'car' or 'truck' was on the list; e.g. Ghatala and Levin 1976).

Margaret Clifford (1984) offered a modified effort-attribution analysis, pointing out that motivation to expend cognitive effort on strategies should be high if instruction makes salient the connections between performance outcomes and effort deployment through strategies. Borkowski and his colleagues have explicitly investigated this possibility. For example, Reid and Borkowski (1987) included three conditions: a self-control strategy training condition, a self-control strategy training plus attribution training condition, and a strategy-training control condition. All of the hyperactive and learning disabled participants in the study were required to learn paired-associate lists. The strategy taught in all three conditions was a form of elaboration known to improve paired-associate learning. The self-control part of the training in the two more complete conditions involved a self-instruction regimen designed to inhibit impulsive reactions and increase the likelihood that the elaboration strategy would be executed in an orderly fashion at a reasonable pace. The critical difference between the self-control strategy instruction and the self-control strategy instruction plus attribution condition was the addition of information in the latter condition about how beliefs about success and failure can make a difference in cognition. In addition, the plus-attribution subjects were shown how individual items were either correct or incorrect on the post-test depending on whether the strategy had been executed at study. In short, the plus-attribution condition was filled with prompts designed to assure that strategy-performance linkages were salient and that students would attribute correct recall to strategy use and incorrect recall to failures to carry out the strategy. The results were dramatic: even 10 months later, the self-control strategy instruction plus attribution subjects continued to use the strategy.

Borkowski *et al.* (1988) and Carr and Borkowski (1989) also obtained increases in the durable and general use of summarization strategies (for learning of text) by low achieving children when explicit feedback about the importance of effort in strategy use was added to instruction. In addition, Carr *et al.* (1989) determined that if parents communicate to their children that efforts expended in using strategies will pay off, children are more open to learn and use new strategies. When all of the data across the Borkowski studies is considered, there is reason for high confidence that increasing the likelihood that students attribute their strategy-mediated successes to the use of strategies increases long-term use of strategies.

Possible selves

It is not uncommon for an 11- or 12-year-old student who has a history of learning failures to believe that it is impossible for him or her to learn well, often attributing past failures to low ability and, thus, believing there is little reason to try hard. The alternative perspective is that it is possible to do well by learning strategies and acquiring knowledge well matched to current schools demands. These successes then prepare for tomorrow's challenges, which can be met by learning new strategies and acquiring additional knowledge.

Borkowski *et al.* (1990) proposed that what needs to be done in the short-term for such students is to teach them strategies that will help them meet the challenges they are facing now and convince them that they are capable of doing well if they learn and apply task-appropriate strategies. Such students need to understand that it is possible for them to do well – that being a good student is a *possible self* for them (e.g. Markus and Nurius 1986). Beyond that, such students need to be convinced that success in life is possible for them, that a possible eventual self is a literate, intellectually able adult. In short, the diagnosis was that students who are doing poorly relative to peers require both strategy training and massive doses of motivational supplement. They require specific utility information about the strategies they are learning and substantial encouragement to attribute learning gains to acquisition of strategies. But they also require more, which is instruction aimed at changing their self-perceptions and perceptions about what it is possible for them to become. Years of failure have led them to believe they are failures; a great deal of success embellished with instruction that makes salient how they can be successful both now and in the future is required.

Again, Borkowski and his colleagues are on the cutting edge, currently formulating instruction designed to improve student's possible selves (Borkowski *et al*. 1992; Day *et al*. 1992). Preliminary results are promising, encouraging a perspective on motivation that is much broader than has traditionally been evaluated in studies of memory or memory strategy instruction. The certain linkages between utility information and effort-through-strategies attributions that were obtained in basic research fuel optimism that larger-scale motivational interventions that stimulate long-term use of entire repertoires of cognitive skills and strategies will be developed and validated.

CONCLUSION

That the five components considered here are interactive should be obvious from the interactions considered throughout the chapter. Thinking of memory development in terms of strategy development alone is an obsolete perspective: use of strategies does increase with development – because of increases in knowledge and capacity, because of expanding metamemory and because of increasing under-standing of the utility of strategies. In turn, when strategies are carried out, there are opportunities for the general knowledge base to expand (e.g. strategies that increase learning from text increase the extent of a learner's knowledge), metamemory to increase (e.g. increased understanding that the strategy works in settings and with tasks associated with strategy practice), and motivational beliefs to shift (e.g. understanding that the pay-offs provided by the strategy come at a great cost of effort). There is even the possibility that functional capacity will increase, at least for the strategy being used: with practice, strategies are carried out more automatically; with increased automaticity, less effort is required for a strategy to be carried out. We could go on and on, detailing many potential inter-active relationships between these five factors. That interactions between factors are being validated inspires confidence that the 'theory' of memory development offered here is valid. More ambitious tests are now being carried out, however.

One well-respected approach to theory validation is the 'instruc-tional study' (e.g. Belmont and Butterfield 1977). If a factor is a causal factor with respect to memory, memory should improve if people who do not use the component are instructed to use it. For the five-factor theory presented here, it is a little more complicated, however: the theory is that effective memory is produced by a repertoire of strategies well matched to important task demands, extensive knowledge of the world that can be and is used in conjunction with strategies, extensive metamemory detailing when and where to use strategies and other knowledge to mediate learning and cognition, supportive motiva-tional beliefs and knowledge, and high functional capacity (which is made possible in part by high knowledge of the world and extensive practice of strategies that are known). An instructional study matched to the present theory would require simultaneous coordination of strategy instruction with enhancement of metamemory about strategies and motivational beliefs about strategy effects on per-formance. Students would have to be taught how to articulate the newly learned procedures with other knowledge. Instruction would have to be designed to maximize functional capacity.

We (and our colleagues) are now conducting studies tapping simultaneous enhancement of repertoires of strategies, knowledge, metacognition, motivation and functional capacity. The aim is to understand the effects of teaching strategies designed to enhance ecologically valid learning. First, we identified school settings where effective strategy instruction was ongoing. In particular, some schools are now teaching students a variety of strategies for increasing memory of text, with students commonly taught to make images as they read, ask themselves questions about the content of text, summarize and reread when confused. We have focused our attention on schools where teaching such packages of strategies appears to produce exceptionally high achievement to what would be expected for the population or high test scores relative to otherwise comparable students. That is, consistent with much of the 'effective schools' literature, we have used an 'outlier school' methodology (see Firestone 1991).

What we have found to date is completely consistent with the theoretical perspective offered in this chapter. At the heart of this instruction are extensive direct explanations and modelling of strategies by adult teachers, with these teachers encouraging strategy application and adaptation over the course of the year. The students practise use of strategies as part of reading in groups. Strategies are taught over long periods of time in these schools, permitting long-term practice in executing the strategies themselves (and hence increases in automaticity) and in identifying situations that call for the strategies (and hence in metacognition about the strategies). Teachers also provide some metacognitive information, especially emphasizing the advantages conferred by strategies. Students are explicitly taught to coordinate their extensive knowledge of the world with use of strategies. See Pressley *et al.* (1992c) for detailed coverage of such instruction, which is substantially more flexible and multi-faceted than predecessor strategies instruction packages designed by cognitive psychologists to enhance learning from text (e.g. reciprocal teaching, Palincsar and Brown 1984; informed strategies for learning, Paris and Oka 1986).

Brown *et al.* (in preparation) have recently performed a quasi-experimental evaluation of such instruction. Lower-achieving grade-2 students in five classes received a year of strategy instruction as described in the last paragraph. Controls in five other classes received conventional instruction. Although the strategy-instructed and control subjects performed comparably during the first semester of the study on a variety of measures tapping memory for text material, by the end of the second semester there were clear and large advantages for the strategy-instructed subjects over the controls.

Although the Brown *et al.* (in preparation) outcomes fuel enthusiasm for long-term strategy instruction which is rich in metamemory and motivational enhancement, we recognize that rich strategy instruction is not common in schools (see Moely *et al.* 1992). If such instruction is ever to become more widespread, it is essential that the nature of such teaching does not seem overwhelming to teachers. One way to increase understanding of such teaching is to increase understanding of the conceptual foundations of effective learning. We hope that this chapter advances that cause, making obvious that good thinking and learning is very complicated but that much of it can be understood in terms of capacity, strategies, other knowledge, metacognition and motivational beliefs. That is our current perspective about what memory development, and cognitive development in general, is the development of.

REFERENCES

Anderson, R.C. and Pearson, P.D. (1984) 'A schema-theoretic view of basic processes in reading comprehension', in P.D. Pearson, M. Kamil, R. Barr and P. Mosenthal (eds) *Handbook of Reading Research*, pp. 255–91, New York: Longman.

Ashcraft, M.A. and Kellas, G. (1974) 'Organization in normal and retarded children: Temporal aspects of storage and retrieval', *Journal of Experimental Psychology* 103: 502–8.

Atkinson, R.C. and Shiffrin, R.M. (1968) 'Human memory: A proposed system and its control processes', in K.W. Spence and J.T. Spence (eds) *The Psychology of Learning and Motivation*, vol. 2, pp. 90–197, New York: Academic Press.

Baddeley, A. (1986) *Working Memory*, New York: Oxford University Press.

Baker-Ward, L., Ornstein, P.A. and Holden, D.J. (1984) 'The expression of memorization in early childhood', *Journal of Experimental Child Psychology* 37: 555–75.

Barclay, C.R. (1979) 'The executive control of mnemonic activity', *Journal of Experimental Child Psychology* 27: 262–76.

Bebko, J. (1979) 'Can recall differences among children be attributed to rehearsal effects?', *Canadian Journal of Psychology* 33: 96–105.

—— (1984) 'Memory and rehearsal characteristics of profoundly deaf children', *Journal of Experimental Child Psychology* 38: 415–28.

Bebko, J.M. and McKinnon, E.E. (1990) 'The language experience of deaf children: The relation to spontaneous rehearsal in a memory task', *Child Development* 61: 1744–52.

Belmont, J.M. and Butterfield, E.C. (1969) 'The relations of short-term memory to development and intelligence', in L.P. Lipsitt and H.W. Reese (eds) *Advances in Child Development and Behavior*, vol. 4, pp. 30–83, New York: Academic Press.

—— (1971) 'What the development of short-term memory is', *Human Development* 14: 236–48.

—— (1977) 'The instructional approach to developmental cognitive research', in R.V. Krail, Jr, and J.W. Hagen (eds) *Perspectives on the Development of Memory and Cognition*, pp. 437–81, Hillsdale, New Jersey: Erlbaum.

Belmont, J.M., Buttefield, E.C. and Ferretti, R.P. (1982) 'To secure transfer of training increase self-management skills', in D.K. Detterman (ed.) *How and How Much can Intelligence be Increased?*, pp. 147–54, Norwood, New Jersey: Ablex.

Berch, D.B. and Evans, R.C. (1973) 'Decision processes in children's recognition memory', *Journal of Experimental Child Psychology* 16: 148–64.

Beuhring, T. and Kee, D.W. (1987a) 'Developmental relationships among metamemory, elaborative strategy use, and associative memory', *Journal of Experimental Child Psychology* 44: 377–400.

—— (1987b) 'Elaboration and associative memory development: The metamemory link', in M.A. McDaniel and M. Pressley (eds) *Imagery and Related Mnemonic Processes: Theories and Applications*, pp. 257–73, New York: Springer-Verlag.

Bisanz, G.L., Vesonder, G.T. and Voss, J.F. (1978) 'Knowledge of one's own responding and the relation of such knowledge to learning', *Journal of Experimental Child Psychology* 25: 116–28.

Bjorklund, D.F. (1985) 'The role of conceptual knowledge in the development of organization in children's memory', in C.J. Brainerd and M. Pressley (eds) *Basic Processes in Memory Development: Progress in Cognitive Development Research*, pp. 103–42, New York: Springer.

—— (1987) 'How age changes in knowledge base contribute to the development of children's memory: An interpretive review', *Developmental Review* 7: 93–130.

Bjorklund, D.F. and Buchanen, J.J. (1989) 'Developmental and knowledge base differences in the acquisition and extension of a memory strategy', *Journal of Experimental Child Psychology* 48: 451–71.

Black, M.M. and Rollins, H.A. (1982) 'The effects of instructional variables on young children's organization and free recall', *Journal of Experimental Child Psychology* 33: 1–19.

Borkowski, J.G. (1985) 'Signs of intelligence: Strategy, generalization, and metacognition', in S.R. Yussen (ed.) *The Growth of Reflection in Children*, pp. 105–44, Orlando, Florida: Academic Press.

Borkowski, J.G., Levers, S. and Gruenenfelder, T.M. (1976) 'Transfer of mediational strategies in children: The role of activity and awareness during strategy acquisition', *Child Development* 47: 779–86.

Borkowski, J.G., Weyhing, R.S. and Carr, M. (1988) 'Effects of attributional retraining on strategy based reading comprehension in LD children', *Journal of Educational Psychology* 80: 46–53.

Borkowski, J.G., Carr, M., Rellinger, E. and Pressley, M. (1990) 'Self-regulated cognition: Interdependence of metacognition, attributions, and self-esteem', in B.F. Jones and L. Idol (eds) *Dimensions of Thinking and Cognitive Instruction*, pp. 53–92, Hillsdale, New Jersey: Erlbaum.

Borkowski, J.G., Peck, V., Reid, M. and Kurtz, B. (1983) 'Impulsivity and strategy transfer: Metamemory as mediator', *Child Development* 54: 459–73.

Borkowski, J.G., Day, J.D., Saenz, D.S., Dietmeyer, D., Estrada, T. and Groteluschen, A. (1992) 'Expanding the boundaries of cognitive interventions', in B. Wong (ed.) *Intervention Research with Students with Learning Disabilities*, pp. 1–21, New York: Springer-Verlag.

Brigham, M.C. and Pressley, M. (1988) 'Cognitive monitoring and strategy choice in younger and older adults', *Psychology and Aging* 3: 249–57.

Brown, A.L., Bransford, J.D., Ferrara, R.A. and Campione, J.C. (1983) 'Learning, remembering, and understanding', in J.H. Flavell and E.M. Markman (eds) *Handbook of Child Psychology*, vol. III, *Cognitive Development*, pp. 77–166, New York: Wiley.

Brown, A.L., Smiley, S.S., Day, J.D., Townsend, M.A.R. and Lawton, S.C. (1977) 'Intrusion of a thematic idea in children's comprehension and retention of stories', *Child Development* 48: 1454–66.

Brown, R., Pressley, M. and Schuder, T. (in preparation) *Quasi-Experimental*

Evaluation of Transactional Strategies Instruction at the Grade-2 Level, College Park, Maryland: University of Maryland, National Reading Research Center.

Bruner, J.S., Olver, R.R. and Greenfield, P.M. (1966) *Studies in Cognitive Growth*, New York: Wiley.

Carey, S. (1985) *Conceptual Change in Childhood*, Cambridge, Massachusetts: MIT Press.

Cariglia-Bull, T. and Pressley, M. (1990) 'Short-term memory differences between children predict imagery effects when sentences are read', *Journal of Experimental Child Psychology* 49: 384–98.

Carr, M. and Borkowski, J.G. (1989) 'Attributional training and the generalization of reading strategies with underachieving children', *Learning and Individual Differences* 1: 327–41.

Carr, M., Kurtz, B.E., Schneider, W., Turner, L.A. and Borkowski, J.G. (1989) 'Strategy acquisition and transfer: Environmental influences on metacognitive development', *Developmental Psychology* 25: 765–71.

Case, R. (1985) *Intellectual Development: Birth to Adulthood*, Orlando, Florida: Academic Press.

Case, R., Kurland, D.M. and Goldberg, J. (1982) 'Operational efficiency and the growth of short-term memory span', *Journal of Experimental Child Psychology* 33: 386–404.

Cavanaugh, J.C. and Borkowski, J.G. (1979) 'The metamemory–memory "connection": Effects of strategy training and maintenance', *Journal of General Psychology* 101: 161–74.

Cavanaugh, J.C. and Perlmutter, M. (1982) 'Metamemory: A critical examination', *Child Development* 53: 11–28.

Chase, W.G. and Simon, H.A. (1973) 'Perception in chess', *Cognitive Psychology* 4: 55–81.

Chi, M.T.H. (1977) 'Age differences in memory span', *Journal of Experimental Child Psychology* 23: 266–81.

—— (1978) 'Knowledge structure and memory development', in R.S. Siegler (ed.) *Children's Thinking: What Develops?*, pp. 73–96, Hillsdale, New Jersey: Erlbaum.

Chi, M.T.H., Glaser, R. and Farr, M.J. (1988) *The Nature of Expertise*, Hillsdale, New Jersey: Erlbaum.

Chiesi, L., Spilich, G.J. and Voss, J.F. (1979) 'Acquisition of domain-related information in relation to high and low domain knowledge', *Journal of Verbal Learning and Verbal Behavior* 18: 257–73.

Clifford, M.M. (1975) 'Validity of expectation: A developmental function', *Alberta Journal of Educational Research* 21: 11–17.

—— (1978) 'The effects of quantitative feedback on children's expectation of success', *British Journal of Educational Psychology* 48: 220–6.

—— (1984) 'Thoughts on a theory of constructive failure', *Educational Psychologist* 19: 108–20.

Cuvo, A.J. (1975) 'Developmental differences in rehearsal and free recall', *Journal of Experimental Child Psychology* 19: 265–78.

Day, J.D., Borkowski, J.G., Dietmeyer, D., Howsepian, B.A. and Saenz, D.S. (1992) 'Possible selves and academic achievement', in L. Winegar and J. Valsiner (eds) *Children's Development within Social Contexts: Metatheoretical,*

Theoretical, and Methodological Issues, Hillsdale, New Jersey: Erlbaum.

Deci, E.L. and Ryan, R.M. (1985) *Intrinsic Motivation and Self-Determination in Human Behavior*, New York: Plenum.

DeLoache, J.S., Cassidy, D.J. and Brown, A.L. (1985) 'Precursors of mnemonic strategies in very young children's memory', *Child Development* 56: 125–37.

DeMarie-Dreblow, D. (1991) 'Relation between knowledge and memory: A reminder that correlation does not imply causation', *Child Development* 62: 484–98.

Dempster, F.N. (1981) 'Memory span: Sources of individual and developmental differences', *Psychological Bulletin* 89: 63–100.

—— (1985) 'Short-term memory development in childhood and adolescence', in C.J. Brainerd and M. Pressley (eds) *Basic Processes in Memory Development: Progress in Cognitive Development Research*, pp. 209–48, New York: Springer-Verlag.

Denney, N.W. (1972) 'A developmental study of free classification in children', *Child Development* 43: 221–32.

Denney, N. and Ziobrowski, M. (1972) 'Developmental changes in clustering criteria', *Journal of Experimental Child Psychology* 13: 275–82.

Entwisle, D. and Hayduk, L. (1978) *Too Great Expectations: The Academic Outlook of Young Children*, Baltimore, Maryland: Johns Hopkins Press.

Faulkender, P.J., Wright, J.C. and Waldron, A. (1974) 'Generalized habituation of concept stimuli in toddlers', *Child Development* 45: 1002–10.

Firestone, W.A. (1991) 'Educators, researchers, and the effective schools movement', in J.R. Bliss, W.A. Firestone and C.E. Richards (eds) *Rethinking Effective Schools Research and Practice*, pp. 12–27, Englewood Cliffs, New Jersey: Prentice-Hall.

Fivush, R., Hudson, J. and Nelson, K. (1984) 'Children's long-term memory for a novel event: An exploratory study', *Merrill-Palmer Quarterly* 30: 303–16.

Flavell, J.H. (1970) 'Developmental studies of mediated memory', in H.W. Reese and L.P. Lipsitt (eds) *Advances in Child Development and Behavior*, pp. 181–211, New York: Academic Press.

—— (1971) 'First discussant's comments: What is memory development the development of?', *Human Development* 14: 272–8.

—— (1977) *Cognitive Development*, Englewood Cliffs, New Jersey: Prentice-Hall.

Flavell, J.H., Beach, D.H. and Chinsky, J.M. (1966) 'Spontaneous verbal rehearsal in a memory task as a function of age', *Child Development* 37: 283–99.

Flavell, J.H., Friedrichs, A.G. and Hoyt, J.D. (1970) 'Developmental changes in memorization processes', *Cognitive Psychology* 1: 324–40.

Gelman, R. and Baillargeon, R. (1983) 'A review of Piagetian concepts', in J.H. Flavell and E.M. Markman (eds) *Handbook of Child Psychology: Cognitive Development*, vol. 3, New York: Wiley.

Ghatala, E.S. and Levin, J.R. (1976) 'Children's recognition memory processes', in J.R. Levin and V.L. Allen (eds) *Cognitive Learning in Children*, pp. 135–62, New York: Academic Press.

Ghatala, E.S., Levin, J.R., Pressley, M. and Goodwin, D. (1986) 'A componential analysis of the effects of derived and supplied strategy-utility information on children's strategy selections', *Journal of Experimental Child Psychology* 41: 76–92.

Glenberg, A.M. and Epstein, W. (1985) 'Calibration of comprehension', *Journal of Experimental Psychology: Learning, Memory and Cognition* 11: 702–18.

—— (1987) 'Inexpert calibration of comprehension', *Memory and Cognition* 15: 84–93.

Glenberg, A.M., Wilkinson, A.C. and Epstein, W. (1982) 'The illusion of knowing: Failure in the self-assessment of comprehension', *Memory and Cognition* 10: 597–602.

Goldberg, S., Perlmutter, M. and Meyers, N. (1974) 'Recall of related and unrelated lists by 2-year-olds', *Journal of Experimental Child Psychology* 18: 1–8.

Guttentag, R.E. (1984) 'The mental effort requirement of cumulative rehearsal: A developmental study', *Journal of Experimental Child Psychology* 37: 92–106.

—— (1989) 'Age differences in associative learning: Strategic propensity and knowledge access effects', presented at the biennial meeting of the Society for Research in Child Development, Kansay City.

Guttentag, R.E., Ornstein, P.A. and Siemens, L. (1987) 'Children's spontaneous rehearsal: Transitions in strategy acquisition', *Cognitive Development* 2: 307–26.

Hagen, J.W. and Kingsley, P.R. (1986) 'Labelling effects in short-term memory', *Child Development* 39: 113–21.

Horgan, D.D. and Morgan, D. (1990) 'Chess expertise in children', *Applied Cognitive Psychology* 4: 109–28.

Horton, M.S. (1982) 'Category familiarity and taxonomic organization in young children', unpublished doctoral dissertation, Stanford University.

Hudson, J.A. (1988) 'Children's memory for atypical actions in script-based stories: Evidence for a disruption effect', *Journal of Experimental Child Psychology* 46: 159–73.

—— (1990) 'The emergence of autobiographical memory in mother–child conversation', in R. Fivush and J.A. Hudson (eds) *Knowing and Remembering in Young Children*, pp. 166–96, New York: Cambridge University Press.

Hudson, J.A. and Fivush, R. (1991) 'As time goes by: Sixth graders remember a kindergarten experience', *Applied Cognitive Psychology* 5: 347–60.

Hudson, J. and Nelson, K. (1983) 'Effect of script structure on children's story recall', *Developmental Psychology* 19: 625–35.

Hudson, J.A. and Shapiro, L.R. (1991) 'From knowing to telling: The development of children's scripts, stories, and personal narratives', in A. McCabe and C. Peterson (eds) *Developing Narrative Structure*, pp. 89–136, Hillsdale, New Jersey: Erlbaum.

Hudson, J.A. and Slackman, E.A. (1990) 'Children's use of scripts in inferential text processing', *Discourse Processes* 13: 375–85.

Kahnemann, D. (1973) *Attention and Effort*, Englewood Cliffs, New Jersey: Prentice-Hall.

Kearins, J.M. (1981) 'Visual spatial memory in Australian aboriginal children of desert regions', *Cognitive Psychology* 13: 434–60.

Kee, D.W. and Davies, L. (1988) 'Mental effort and elaboration: A developmental analysis', *Contemporary Educational Psychology* 13: 221–8.

—— (1990) 'Mental effort and elaboration: Effects of accessibility and instruction', *Journal of Experimental Child Psychology* 49: 264–74.

—— (1991) 'Mental effort and elaboration: A developmental analysis of accessibility effects', *Journal of Experimental Child Psychology* 52: 1–10.

Kellas, G., Ashcroft, M.H. and Johnson, N.S. (1973) 'Rehearsal processes in the short-term memory performance of mildly retarded adolescents', *American Journal of Mental Deficiency* 77: 670–9.

Kelly, M., Scholnick, E.K., Travers, S.H. and Johnson, J.W. (1976) 'Relations among memory, memory appraisal, and memory strategies', *Child Development* 47: 648–59.

Kennedy, B.A. and Miller, D.J. (1976) 'Persistent use of verbal rehearsal as a function of information about its value', *Child Development* 47: 566–9.

Kennedy, S.P. and Suzuki, N.S. (1977) 'Spontaneous elaboration in Mexican-American and Anglo-American high school seniors', *American Educational Research Journal* 14: 383–8.

Kreutzer, M.A., Leonard, C. and Flavell, J.H. (1975) 'An interview study of children's knowledge about memory', *Monographs of the Society for Research in Child Development* 40 (1, serial no. 159).

Kurtz, B.E. (1990) 'Cultural influences on children's cognitive and metacognitive development', in Wo. Schneider and F.E. Weinert (eds) *Interactions among Aptitudes, Strategies, and Knowledge in Cognitive Performance*, pp. 177–99, New York: Springer-Verlag.

Kurtz, B.E. and Borkowski, J.G. (1984) 'Children's metacognition: Exploring relations among knowledge, process, and motivational variables', *Journal of Experimental Child Psychology* 37: 335–54.

—— (1987) 'Development of strategic skills in impulsive and reflective children: A developmental study of metacognition', *Journal of Experimental Child Psychology* 43: 129–48.

Kurtz, B.E., Borkowski, J.G. and Deshmukh, K. (1988) 'Metamemory development in Maharashtrian children: Influences from home and school', *Journal of Genetic Psychology* 149: 363–76.

Lange, G. (1973) 'The development of conceptual and rote recall skills among school age children', *Journal of Experimental Child Psychology* 15: 394–406.

—— (1978) 'Organization-related processes in children's recall', in P.A. Ornstein (ed.) *Memory Organization in Children*, pp. 101–28, Hillsdale, New Jersey: Erlbaum.

Lange, G., MacKinnon, C.E. and Nida, R.E. (1989) 'Knowledge, strategy, and motivational contributions to preschool children's object recall', *Developmental Psychology* 25: 772–9.

Lawson, M.H. and Fuelop, S. (1980) 'Understanding the purpose of strategy training', *British Journal of Educational Psychology* 50: 175–80.

Levin, J.R., Yussen, S.R., DeRose, T.M. and Pressley, M. (1977) 'Developmental changes in assessing recall and recognition memory capacity', *Developmental Psychology* 13: 608–15.

McCarthy, K.A. and Nelson, K. (1981) 'Children's use of scripts in story recall', *Discourse Processes* 4: 59–70.

McCauley, C., Weil, C.M. and Sperber, R.D. (1976) 'The development of memory structure as reflected by semantic-priming effects', *Journal of Experimental Child Psychology* 22: 511–18.

Mandler, J.M. (1979) 'Categorical and schematic organization in memory', in C.R. Puff (ed.) *Memory, Organization, and Structure*, pp. 259–99, New York: Academic Press.

—— (1984) *Stories, Scripts, and Scenes: Aspects of Schema Theory*, Hillsdale, New Jersey: Erlbaum.

Mandler, J.M., Scribner, S., Cole, M. and DeForest, M. (1980) 'Cross-cultural invariance in story recall', *Child Development* 51: 19–26.

Markman, E.M. (1977) 'Realizing that you don't understand: A preliminary investigation', *Child Development* 48: 986–92.

—— (1979) 'Realizing that you don't understand: Elementary school children's awareness of inconsistencies', *Child Development* 50: 643–55.

—— (1981) 'Comprehension monitoring', in W.P. Dickson (ed.) *Children's Oral Communication Skills*, pp. 61–84, New York: Academic Press.

Markman, E.M. and Callahan, M. (1984) 'An analysis of hierarchical classification', in R. Sternberg (ed.) *Advances in the Psychology of Human Intelligence*, pp. 325–66, Hillsdale, New Jersey: Erlbaum.

Markus, H. and Nurius, P. (1986) 'Possible selves', *American Psychologist* 41: 954–69.

Martin, V.L. and Pressley, M. (1991) 'Elaborative interrogation effects depend on the nature of the question', *Journal of Educational Psychology* 83: 113–19.

Masur, E.F., McIntyre, C.W. and Flavell, J.H. (1973) 'Developmental change in apportionment of study time among items in a multitrial free recall task', *Journal of Experimental Child Psychology* 15: 237–46.

Miller, G.A. (1956) 'The magical number seven, plus or minus two: Some limits on our capacity for processing information', *Psychological Review* 63: 81–97.

Miller, G.A., Galanter, E. and Pribram, K. (1960) *Plans and the Structure of Behavior*, New York: Holt, Rinehart & Winston.

Miller, P.H., Wood-Ramsey, J. and Aloise, P.A. (1991) 'The role of strategy effortfulness in strategy effectiveness', *Developmental Psychology* 27: 738–45.

Miller, P.H., Seier, W.L., Probert, J.S. and Aloise, P.A. (1991) 'Age differences in the capacity demands of a strategy among spontaneously strategic children', *Journal of Experimental Child Psychology* 52: 149–65.

Moely, B.E. (1977) 'Organizational factors in the development of memory', in R.V. Kail and J.W. Hagen (eds) *Perspectives on the Development of Memory and Cognition*, pp. 203–36, Hillsdale, New Jersey: Erlbaum.

Moely, B.E., Hart, S.S., Leal, L., Santulli, K.A., Rao, N., Johnston, T. and Hamilton, L.B. (1992) 'The teacher's role in facilitating memory and study strategy development in the elementary school classroom', *Child Development* 63: 653–72.

Morris, C.D., Bransford, J.D. and Franks, J.J. (1977) 'Levels of processing versus transfer appropriate processing', *Journal of Verbal Learning and Verbal Behavior* 16: 519–33.

Naus, M.J. and Ornstein, P.A. (1983) 'Development of memory strategies: Analysis, questions, and issues', in M.T.H. Chi (ed.) *Trends in Memory*

Development Research, vol. 9, pp. 1–30, Basel: Karger.

Nelson, K. (1978) 'How young children represent knowledge of their world in and out of language', in R. Siegler (ed.) *Children's Thinking: What Develops?*, pp. 255–73, Hillsdale, New Jersey: Erlbaum.

Nelson, K. and Gründel, J. (1981) 'Generalized event representations: Basic building blocks of cognitive development', in M.E. Lamb and A.L. Brown (eds) *Advances in Developmental Psychology*, vol. 1, pp. 131–58, Hillsdale, New Jersey: Erlbaum.

Newell, A. and Simon, H.A. (1972) *Human Problem Solving*, Englewood Cliffs, New Jersey: Prentice-Hall.

Newman, L.S. (1990) 'Intentional and unintentional memory in young children: Remembering vs. playing', *Journal of Experimental Child Psychology* 50: 243–58.

Ornstein, P.A. and Corsale, K. (1979) 'Organizational factors in children's memory', in C.R. Puff (ed.) *Memory, Organization, and Structure*, pp. 219–57, New York: Academic Press.

Ornstein, P.A. and Naus, M.J. (1978) 'Rehearsal processes in children's memory', in P.A. Ornstein (ed.) *Memory Development in Children*, pp. 69–99, Hillsdale, New Jersey: Erlbaum.

Ornstein, P.A. and Naus, M.J. (1985) 'Effects of knowledge base on children's memory strategies', in H.W. Reese (ed.) *Advances in Child Development and Behavior*, vol. 19, pp. 113–48, New York: Academic Press.

Ornstein, P.A., Naus, M.J. and Liberty, C. (1975) 'Rehearsal and organizational processes in children's memory', *Child Development* 46: 818–30.

O'Sullivan, J.T. and Pressley, M. (1984) 'Completeness of instruction and strategy transfer', *Journal of Experimental Child Psychology* 38: 275–88.

Palincsar, A.S. and Brown, A.L. (1984) 'Reciprocal teaching of comprehension-fostering and comprehension-monitoring activities', *Cognition and Instruction* 1: 117–75.

Paris, S.G. and Oka, E.R. (1986) 'Children's reading strategies, metacognition and motivation', *Developmental Review* 6: 25–66.

Paris, S.G., Newman, R.S. and McVey, K.A. (1982) 'Learning the functional significance of mnemonic actions: A microgenetic study of strategy acquisition', *Journal of Experimental Child Psychology* 34: 490–509.

Parsons, J. and Ruble, D. (1977) 'The development of achievement-related expectations', *Child Development* 48: 1075–9.

Pascual-Leone, J. (1970) 'A mathematical model for the transition rule in Piaget's developmental stages', *Acta Psychologica* 32: 310–45.

Pearson, P.D. and Dole, J.A. (1987) 'Explicit comprehension instruction: A review of research and a new conceptualization of instruction', *Elementary School Journal* 88: 151–65.

Pearson, P.D., Hansen, J. and Gordon, C. (1979) 'The effect of background knowledge on young children's comprehension of explicit and implicit information', *Journal of Reading Behavior* 11: 201–9.

Perkins, D.N. and Salomon, G. (1989) 'Are cognitive skills context bound?', *Educational Researcher* 18: 16–25.

Phillips, B.N. (1963) 'Age changes in accuracy of self-perceptions', *Child Development* 34: 1041–6.

Piaget, J. (1970) 'Piaget's theory', in P.H. Mussen (ed.) *Carmichael's*

Manual of Child Psychology, vol. 1, pp. 703–32, New York: Wiley, third edition.

Polya, G. (1954) *Mathematics and Plausible Reasoning*, vol. I, *Induction and Analogy in Mathematics* and vol. II, *Patterns of Plausible Inference*, Princeton, New Jersey: Princeton University Press.

—— (1957) *How to Solve It*, Garden City, New York: Doubleday Anchor Books, second edition.

Pressley, M. (1977) 'Imagery and children's learning: Putting the picture in developmental perspective', *Review of Educational Research* 47: 586–622.

Pressley, M. and Brewster, M.E. (1990) 'Cognitive elaboration of illustrations to facilitate acquisition of facts: Memories of Prince Edward Island', *Applied Cognitive Psychology* 4: 359–69.

Pressley, M. and Ghatala, E.S. (1988) 'Delusions about performance on multiple-choice comprehension tests', *Reading Research Quarterly* 23: 454–64.

—— (1989) 'Metacognitive benefits of taking a test for children and young adolescents', *Journal of Experimental Child Psychology* 47: 430–50.

Pressley, M. and Levin, J.R. (1977) 'Developmental differences in subjects' associative learning strategies and performance: Assessing a hypothesis', *Journal of Experimental Child Psychology* 24: 431–9.

—— (1978) 'Developmental constraints associated with children's use of the keyword method for foreign language vocabulary learning', *Journal of Experimental Child Psychology* 26: 359–72.

Pressley, M., Borkowski, J.G. and O'Sullivan, J.T. (1984a) 'Memory strategy instruction is made of this: Metamemory and durable strategy use', *Educational Psychology* 19: 94–107.

—— (1985) 'Children's metamemory and the teaching of memory strategies', in D.L. Forrest-Pressley, G.E. MacKinnon and T.G. Waller (eds) *Metacognition, Cognition, and Human Performance*, pp. 111–53, Orlando, Florida: Academic Press.

Pressley, M., Borkowski, J.G. and Schneider, Wo. (1989a) 'Good information processing: What it is and what education can do to promote it', *International Journal of Educational Research* 13: 668–78.

Pressley, M., El-Dinary, P.B. and Brown, R. (1992a) 'Skilled and not-so-skilled reading: Good information processing and not-so-good information processing', in M. Pressley, K.R. Harris and J.T. Guthrie (eds) *Promoting Academic Competence and Literacy in School*, pp. 91–127, San Diego, California: Academic Press.

Pressley, M., Levin, J.R. and Delaney, H.D. (1982a) 'The mnemonic keyword method', *Review of Educational Research* 56: 61–92.

Pressley, M., Levin, J.R. and Ghatala, E.S. (1984b) 'Memory strategy monitoring in adults and children', *Journal of Verbal Learning and Verbal Behaviour* 23: 270–88.

—— (1988) 'Strategy-comparison opportunities promote long-term strategy use', *Contemporary Educational Psychology* 13: 157–68.

Pressley, M., Cariglia-Bull, T., Deane, S. and Schneider, Wo. (1987a) 'Short-term memory, verbal competence, and age as predictors of imagery instructional effectiveness', *Journal of Experimental Child Psychology* 43: 194–211.

Pressley, M., Ghatala, E.S., Woloshyn, V. and Pirie, J. (1990a) 'Being really, really certain you know the main idea doesn't mean you do', *Yearbook of the National Reading Conference* 39: 249–56.

—— (1990b) 'Sometimes adults miss the main ideas in text and do not realize it: Confidence in responses to short-answer and multiple-choice comprehension items', *Reading Research Quarterly* 25: 232–49.

Pressley, M., Heisel, B.E., McCormick, C.G. and Nakamura, G.V. (1982b) 'Memory strategy instruction with children', in C.J. Brainerd and M. Pressley (eds) *Progress in Cognitive Development Research*, vol. 2, *Verbal Processes in Children*, pp. 125–59, New York: Springer-Verlag.

Pressley, M., Levin, J.R., Ghatala, E.S. and Ahmad, M. (1987b) 'Test monitoring in young grade school children', *Journal of Experimental Child Psychology* 43: 96–111.

Pressley, M., Ross, K.A., Levin, J.R. and Ghatala, E.S. (1984c) 'The role of strategy utility knowledge in children's strategy decision making', *Journal of Experimental Child Psychology* 38: 491–504.

Pressley, M., Johnson, C.J., Symons, S., McGoldrick, J.A. and Kurita, J.A. (1989b) 'Strategies that improve memory and comprehension of what is read', *Elementary School Journal* 90: 3–32.

Pressley, M., Snyder, B.L., Levin, J.R., Murray, H.G. and Ghatala, E.S. (1987c) 'Perceived readiness for examination performance (PREP) produced by initial reading of text and text containing adjunct questions', *Reading Research Quarterly* 22: 219–36.

Pressley, M., Wood, E., Woloshyn, V.E., Martin, V.L., King, A. and Menke, D. (1992b) 'Encouraging mindful use of prior knowledge: Attempting to construct explanatory answers facilitates learning', *Educational Psychologist* 27: 91–110.

Pressley, M., El-Dinary, P.B., Gaskins, I.W., Schuder, T.L., Bergman, J., Almasi, J. and Brown, R. (1992c) 'Beyond direct explanation: Transactional instruction of reading comprehension strategies', *Elementary School Journal* 92: 513–55.

Reid, M. and Norkowski, J.G. (1987) 'Causal attributions of hyperactive children: Implications for training strategies and self-control', *Journal of Educational Psychology* 79: 296–307.

Ringel, B.A. and Springer, C.J. (1980) 'On knowing how well one is remembering: The persistence of strategy use during transfer', *Journal of Experimental Child Psychology* 29: 322–33.

Rohwer, W.D., Jr (1973) 'Elaboration and learning in childhood and adolescence', in H.W. Reese (ed.) *Advances in Child Development and Behavior*, vol. 8, pp. 1–57, New York: Academic Press.

—— (1980) 'An elaborative conception of learner differences', in R.E. Snow, P.A. Federico and W.E. Montague (eds) *Aptitude, Learning, and Instruction*, vol. 2, *Cognitive Process Analysis of Learning and Problem Solving*, pp. 23–46, Hillsdale, New Jersey: Erlbaum.

Rohwer, W.D., Jr and Bean, J.P. (1973) 'Sentence effects and noun-pair learning: A developmental interaction during adolescence', *Journal of Experimental Child Psychology* 15: 521–33.

Rohwer, W.D., Jr, Rabinowitz, M. and Dronkers, N.F. (1982) 'Event knowledge, elaborative propensity, and the development of learning proficiency', *Journal of Experimental Child Psychology* 33: 492–503.

Rumelhart, D.E. (1980) 'Schemata: The building blocks of cognition', in R. Spiro, B. Bruce and W. Brewer (eds) *Theoretical Issues in Reading Comprehension*, pp. 35–58, Hillsdale, New Jersey: Erlbaum.

Salatas, H. and Flavell, J.H. (1976) 'Behavioral and metamnemonic indicators of strategic behaviors under remember instructions in first grade', *Child Development* 47: 81–9.

Schank, R.C. and Abelson, R. (1977) *Scripts, Plans, Goals, and Understanding*, Hillsdale, New Jersey: Erlbaum.

Schneider, Wo. and Körkel, J. (1989) 'The knowledge base and text recall: Evidence from a short-term longitudinal study', *Contemporary Educational Psychology* 14: 382–93.

Schneider, Wo. and Pressley, M. (1989) *Memory Development between Two and Twenty*, New York: Springer-Verlag.

Schneider, Wo., Körkel, J. and Weinert, F.E. (1989) 'Domain-specific knowledge and memory performance: A comparison of high- and low-aptitude children', *Journal of Educational Psychology* 81: 306–12.

—— (1990) 'Expert knowledge, general abilities, and text processing', in Wo. Schneider and F.E. Weinert (eds) *Interactions among Aptitudes, Strategies, and Knowledge in Cognitive Performance*, pp. 235–51, New York: Springer-Verlag.

Schneider, Wo., Borkowski, J.G., Kurtz, B.E. and Kerwin, K. (1986) 'Metamemory and motivation: A comparison of strategy use and performance in German and American children', *Journal of Cross-Cultural Psychology* 17: 315–36.

Schneider, W., Gruber, H., Gold, A. and Opwis, K. (1992) 'Chess expertise and memory for chess positions in children and adults', presented at the annual meeting of the American Educational Research Association, San Francisco.

Stipek, D. (1983) 'Young children's performance expectations: Logical analysis or wishful thinking?', in J. Nicholls (ed.) *The Development of Achievement Motivation*, pp. 33–56, Greenwich, Connecticut: JAI Press.

Stipek, D. and Hoffman, J. (1980) 'Development of children's performance-related judgments', *Child Development* 51: 912–14.

Sugarman, S. (1983) *Children's Early Thought*, Cambridge, Massachusetts: Cambridge University Press.

Wagner, D.A. (1974) 'The development of short-term and incidental memory: A cross-cultural study', *Child Development* 45: 389–96.

—— (1978) 'Memories of Morocco: The influence of age, schooling, and environment on memory', *Cognitive Psychology* 10: 1–28.

Waters, H.S. (1982) 'Memory development in adolescence: Relationships between metamemory, strategy use, and performance', *Journal of Experimental Child Psychology* 33: 183–95.

Weiner, B. (1979) 'A theory of motivation for some classroom experiences', *Journal of Experimental Child Psychology* 71: 3–25.

Woloshyn, V.E., Pressley, M. and Schneider, W. (1992) 'A researcher-educator collaborative interview study of transactional comprehension strategies instruction', *Journal of Educational Psychology* 48: 231–46.

Worden, P.E. (1976) 'The effects of classification structure on organized free recall in children', *Journal of Experimental Child Psychology* 22: 519–29.

Yussen, S.R. and Berman, L. (1981) 'Memory predictions for recall and recognition in first-, third-, and fifth-grade children', *Developmental Psychology* 17: 224–9.

Yussen, S.R. and Levy, V.M. (1975) 'Developmental changes in predicting one's own span of short-term memory', *Journal of Experimental Child Psychology* 19: 502–8.

5

IMPLICIT MEMORY

D. L. Nelson

Most people believe that *remembering* consists of recalling information to report it or to think about it. When we are asked, we can usually report what we ate for breakfast, the latest hit tune or movie, or the result of taking the square root of 4. We can divulge this information or we can think about related information that we know about eating breakfast, pursuing entertainment or doing mathematical problems. The common understanding of remembering is that this process involves a conscious act of recalling what we have just experienced or previously learned. Just as we might look for a book in the library, we look inside our minds for information with our success depending upon whether the information is known or, analogously, by whether the book is in the library. However, this view of remembering is far too simple. Remembering consists of a variety of complex processes that sometimes involve conscious intent and sometimes do not.

In his classic treatise on memory, Ebbinghaus (1885/1964) distinguished between memories produced by conscious acts of recall and memories that affect performance without becoming conscious. He noted that, in some cases, we intentionally and purposefully call information back into consciousness out of a desire to remember, and that, in many other cases, the effects of accumulated experience implicitly influence performance without our being aware of it. This implicit influence is typified in the performance of skills as varied as pole vaulting, typing and reading. The trained pole vaulter is unlikely to pause momentarily before the jump while consciously retrieving the purpose of holding the pole, nor is the skilled typist likely to be conscious of finger movements, nor the experienced reader of accessing memorial representations of the words in a text. These are all examples of highly skilled activities in which previously acquired memories play a fundamental but implicit role in the performance of the skill.

Psychologists have been interested in unconscious processes throughout the history of the field and this interest has recently focused on the role of such processes in memory (e.g. for reviews see Richardson-Klavehn and Bjork 1988; Roediger 1990a; Schacter 1987; Shimamura 1986). The purpose of this chapter is to provide a selective review of two different but related approaches to the study of implicit memory. The first approach involves attempts to manipulate awareness of the relationship between some recent experience and the memory test by varying the nature of the test task, the test instructions, or both (e.g. Tulving *et al.* 1982; Warrington and Weiskrantz 1970). In the typical experiment, all subjects are exposed to the same information during a study episode and the important manipulations are made during testing. On *explicit* tests of memory, subjects are told to remember the studied information. The relationship between what was studied and the nature of the test task is made explicit, with subjects directly told to recover the studied information. Memory researchers have traditionally relied on using explicit tasks to explore issues in memory. More recently, they have been using both explicit and implicit tasks and the contrast between the two means for testing memory has led to a number of exciting new findings. On *implicit* tests, memory is assessed using testing procedures that make no reference to the information presented during the study episode (Graf and Schacter 1985; Roediger 1990a; Schacter 1987). If anything, attempts are made to disguise the importance of the prior study experience to ensure that any effects related to that experience arise from unintentional processes and not from deliberate attempts to remember (Schacter *et al.* 1989).

The second approach to studying implicit memory involves estimating what subjects know about familiar words before they participate in an experiment and then showing that what they know influences their ability to remember (e.g. Anisfeld and Knapp 1968; Nelson *et al.* 1992a). We accumulate hundreds of experiences with the same words in various contexts over our lifetimes and, as a result of this accumulation, words become associated or linked with other words in memory. Because of such links, experiencing a familiar word unconsciously activates or primes the representations of associatively related words, e.g. reading the word DINNER activates *supper, eat, lunch*, and so on (e.g. Collins and Loftus 1975). The function of this activation is to promote comprehension by providing access to what is known about the word so that it can be comprehended. The individual associates linked to a given word can be brought to the level of conscious awareness as when subjects are asked to produce the first word that comes to mind but, under most conditions (e.g. reading), subjects are not likely to be aware of this activation, nor do they seem to be aware of how many associates a word has or how they are interconnected. Nevertheless, these characteristics can be measured and then manipulated under various experimental conditions, and the results of such manipulations indicate that the implicit activation of related words can have substantial effects on the ability to remember what was experienced.

These approaches to studying implicit memory will be described in the next two sections of this chapter. The first section describes attempts to understand implicit memory by manipulating awareness of the relationship between the retention test and the prior study episode, and the following section examines findings showing that implicitly activated information affects performance in both explicit and implicit memory tasks. The final section compares the two approaches.

MANIPULATIONS OF AWARENESS

Task dissociations

Warrington and Weiskrantz (1970) made an important discovery that was interpreted much later as an early demonstration of implicit memory (Roediger 1990a). Researchers had known for a long time that the brain damage resulting from head trauma in the temporal area or from long years of vitamin-deficient alcoholism produced very forgetful individuals while leaving perceptual and other cognitive functions relatively intact. Even after hundreds of meetings amnesic individuals were often unable to learn the names of the people directly responsible for their care. A name was likely to be forgotten just minutes after being introduced. Researchers concluded that such individuals were incapable of transferring verbal information from short-term memory to long-term memory (e.g. Baddeley and Warrington 1970). However, the results of the Warrington and Weiskrantz experiments challenged this interpretation. In one of these studies, they presented amnesics and control subjects with words to remember, and then they measured memory for the words using four different retention tests. Two of these tests conformed to what are now called explicit tests and two conformed to what are now called implicit tests.

The two explicit tests involved free recall and recognition. These tests can be classified as explicit because the test instructions made direct references to the study episode and subjects were deliberately attempting to remember their recent experience. In the free recall test, the subjects were asked to write down as many words from the studied list as they could recall in any order on a blank sheet of paper. In the recognition test, the studied words were randomly mixed with new words and subjects were asked to indicate which words appeared on the study list and which words did not. The two implicit tests required subjects to generate words from letter cues, and these tests can be classified as implicit because the test instructions made no reference to the words presented in the prior study episode. In one test, the subjects were asked to identify each fragmented word and, in the other, they were asked to think of a word that had the same beginning letters as the stem cue. The subjects were told simply that any word was acceptable but, of course, the experimenters were interested in the number of words recovered from the study list. For current perspectives, the recovery of a list word could arise because its representation was activated or primed during the study episode and this priming should elevate the probability of implicitly recovering the word on the test.

The results of this experiment are presented in Figure 5.1 (Warrington and Weiskrantz 1970, Experiment 2). As shown in the upper portion of the figure, performance on the explicit tests conformed to what researchers have come to expect from brain-damaged individuals. Their free recall and recognition test scores were substantially lower than the scores for the control subjects. The lower portion of the figure shows the relative performance of the two groups of subjects on the implicit tests, and these results indicate equivalent levels of performance for brain-damaged and control subjects. Brain damage of this type appeared to impair memory performance selectively, causing deficits on explicit tests while leaving performance on implicit tests unaffected. In current terminology, brain injury and performance on the two types of test are said to be *dissociated*. This dissociation indicated that some types of memory may be preserved after particular types of brain damage, and that it is inappropriate to assume that memory failure in amnesics is due solely to problems associated with transferring information from short-term memory to long-term memory. In the more recent memory literature, the results have been used to support the conclusion that implicit tests measure the results of unconscious learning (e.g. Roediger 1990a; Shimamura

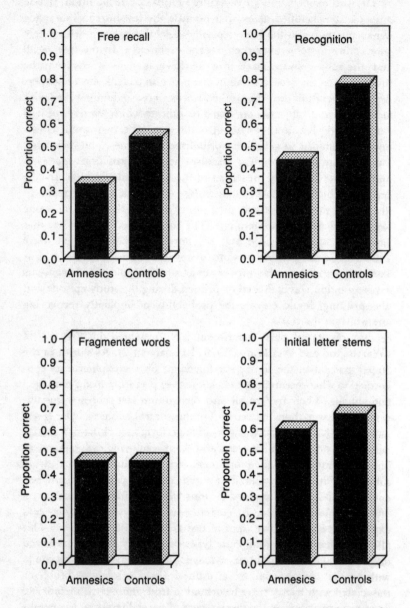

Figure 5.1 Performance on explicit tests (free recall and recognition) and implicit tests (fragmented words and initial letter stems) for amnesic and control subjects.

1986). Amnesic individuals do not remember studying the word list and are typically unaware that they know anything about the materials. As a result, they perform poorly in comparison with the controls when the retention test directly refers to the study materials and they perform at equivalent levels when the test is implicit. The findings suggest that alcoholic-induced amnesia may selectively destroy the areas of the brain involved in conscious retrieval while leaving areas involved in unconscious retrieval relatively intact.

Similar explicit–implicit task dissociations have been obtained by other researchers using memory-disordered subjects (e.g. Graf *et al.* 1984; Jacoby and Witherspoon 1982) and elderly subjects (e.g. Light and Singh 1987). Such dissociations, however, are not limited to special populations. There are now numerous demonstrations of task dissociations in normal, young adult subjects, and much of the early work on this problem can be credited to Jacoby and his colleagues (e.g. Jacoby 1983; Jacoby and Dallas 1981; Jacoby and Witherspoon 1982). In his experiments, the subjects studied a list of words and then were given an explicit or an implicit test. The explicit test required subjects to recognize the studied words embedded in a list of new words serving as distractors or lures. In contrast, the implicit test required subjects to identify and name words presented under perceptually difficult conditions. The studied words and the new words were intermixed and presented under perceptually clear conditions for 30 minutes each, followed by a masking stimulus consisting of ampersands. The mask made it difficult for subjects to see the words easily, but many of them could be named anyway. Note that naming the words did not require any reference to the prior study list. Furthermore, the experimenters were careful not to mention the relationship between the study list and the words presented in the perceptual identification test. Implicit memory is implicated to the extent that subjects identify more studied words than new words, and the difference between the two types of words is called the *priming effect*.

Rather than comparing the performance of two types of subjects on explicit and implicit tasks as did Warrington and Weiskrantz, Jacoby (1983) used college age subjects and had them study the words in different ways. In one condition, they read the critical words aloud without context (e.g. xxx–COLD). In another condition, they read the critical words aloud in the presence of meaningfully related words (e.g. hot–COLD) and, in the third condition, they had to guess or generate the critical words from the meaningfully related words (e.g. hot–???). In the generation condition, subjects never saw the critical words but they could easily generate them from the meaningfully related words provided by the experimenter. The purpose of manipulating study conditions was to exploit a result known as the generation effect. Previous work using explicit tasks had shown that recall and recognition are facilitated when subjects generate words from memory in response to cues as compared to merely reading them (e.g. Slamecka and Graf 1978). The expectation was that similar results would be obtained in the recognition task used in this experiment, and the question focused on what would happen in the implicit perceptual identification task. If the manner of study was all-important, then the study condition variable should have the same effects on both tests. Alternatively, if the manner of testing subjects provides access to different kinds of information, then the results could be different for the explicit recognition task compared to the implicit identification task. The findings are shown in Figure 5.2, and as the upper panel shows, the expected results were obtained on the explicit recognition test. The probability of correct recognition (hits) was highest in the generation condition, lowest in the read condition, and intermediate in the meaningful context condition. In sharp contrast, the lower panel shows that exactly the opposite results were obtained on the implicit identification test. Although performance was better for study words than for new words in all three study conditions (the priming effect), identifying and naming the studied words was most likely when subjects had read the words and least likely when they had generated them without having seen them. These findings indicated that dissociative effects for implicit and explicit tests could be found for normal subjects and, most importantly, it helped to strengthen the hypothesis that the two types of tests tap into fundamentally different types of information.

Dissociative effects for explicit and implicit tasks have since been demonstrated from a number of other variables. Changes in the physical format of the stimuli from study to test have a greater effect in implicit than in explicit tasks (Kirsner and Dunn 1985; Richardson-Klavehn and Bjork 1988; Weldon 1991). For example, hearing the study words instead of seeing them substantially reduces performance on perceptual identification but has only small effects on recognition (Jacoby and Dallas 1981). Similar effects are evident in the fragment completion task in which subjects are given letters and spaces as test cues and are asked to produce a word, e.g. completing PE–C–L to make PENCIL (Blaxton 1989; Roediger and Blaxton 1987). Studying pictures as compared to words (the names of the pictures)

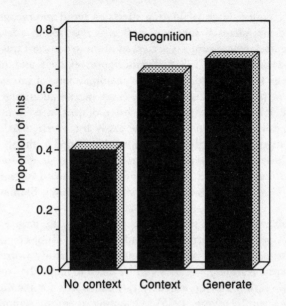

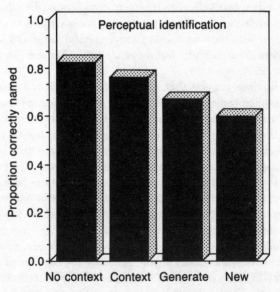

Figure 5.2 Comparative results of the explicit recognition test and the implicit perceptual identification test.

normally produces large facilitating effects on recall and recognition, but the normal pictorial superiority effect is reversed in a fragment completion task where subjects are asked to complete word fragments (Weldon and Roediger 1987). Furthermore, explicit and implicit tasks appear to respond differently to manipulations of interference and level of processing during study. Studying an additional list of words either before or after a study list produces interference that reduces recall and recognition for the study list words, particularly when the interfering words are meaningfully related to the study list words. However, this type of interference effect is substantially reduced on implicit tests involving word stems or word fragments as test cues (Graf and Schacter 1987; Nelson *et al.* 1989; Sloman *et al.* 1988).

Level of processing is manipulated by varying the nature of the encoding operations during the study episode. Subjects can be required to orient to the physical features of the study words or to their semantic features, e.g. they can be asked to name the vowels in each word or they can be asked to rate the words for pleasantness (e.g. Craik and Tulving 1975). Orienting them to semantic as opposed to physical features has a large facilitating effect on explicit free recall and recognition tests. However, level of processing during study has only a small effect on fragment completion when that task is completed under implicit test instructions asking subjects to complete the fragment with the first word to come to mind (Graf and Mandler 1984; Nelson *et al.* 1992b; Squire *et al.* 1985; but see Challis and Brodbeck 1992).

These findings suggest that, compared to explicit tasks, performance on implicit tasks is affected more by study-to-test mismatches in physical format than by semantic factors related to interference and to how well the study list has been encoded. However, not all variables have dissociative effects on explicit and implicit tasks. Other variables have similar effects on performance in the two tasks. For example, studying the words of the list more than once facilitates performance in both types of task as long as the practice is spread out over time (Feustal *et al.* 1983; Jacoby and Dallas 1981; Perruchet 1989). Introducing a delay between the study list and the test reduces performance in both tasks (e.g. Sloman *et al.* 1988). Furthermore, given word fragment or word stem cues at test, reducing the number of possible words that fit the cue increases the probability of recovering the studied word. This increase is found regardless of whether subjects are given explicit instructions to use the cues to recall study list words or implicit test instructions to produce the first word to come to mind that shares the same letters as the cue (e.g. Nelson *et al.* 1987; Nelson *et al.* 1989).

Theoretical interpretations of task dissociations

The findings produced by manipulations of explicit and implicit tests of memory show that some variables produce dissociative effects whereas other variables have similar effects on performance in the two types of tests. Theoretical interpretations of the findings, how-ever, have been focused on the dissociative effects. Dissociative or interactive effects are particularly useful for theory development because they emphasize differences in performance resulting from differences in subjects or experimental conditions. Such discrepancies pose a particular challenge to theories of memory based solely on the results of explicit tests of memory and therefore the challenge applies to most theories developed before the mid-1980s. These theories must be able to explain dissociative effects based on task differences or risk oblivion.

At present, dissociative effects related to explicit and implicit tests have been explained from two different points of view. Some researchers have concluded that these effects reflect the action of different memory systems (e.g. Cave and Squire 1992; Cohen and Squire 1980; Hayman and Tulving 1989; Schacter 1989, 1992; Squire 1986; Tulving and Schacter 1990). Generally speaking, system theorists assume that explicit tests tap into one memory system whereas implicit tests rely on a different system. Alternatively, other researchers argue that memory is a unitary system and that these dissociative effects are produced by different processes operating in the two tasks (e.g. Graf and Mandler 1984; Jacoby 1983, 1991; Mason and MacLeod 1992; Nelson *et al.* 1992a; Roediger 1990a). Process theorists assume that the mental steps involved in accessing memories differ for the two types of tasks, and that assump-tions about memory systems are unwarranted, particularly when only behavioural data are in evidence. Important differences are expressed within systems and within process views, but these differences will be neglected in order to focus on the main characteristics and criticisms associated with each point of view.

Memory systems explanations

Researchers favouring a multiple-systems interpretation of explicit–implicit dissociations often point to research with brain-injured individuals on the assumption that the damage selectively interferes with the ability to consciously recollect information while leaving other systems intact. In these terms, amnesics perform more poorly on explicit memory tasks than normals because the damage interferes with the memory system underlying the conscious processing associated with semantic elaboration (e.g. Graf *et al.* 1985; Squire 1987). Amnesics do about as well as normals on implicit memory tasks because the system underlying well-learned automatic skills is preserved by the disorder. Other evidence favouring the multiple systems view comes from studies using positron emission tomography (PET) to measure changes in the brain while processing a word. These studies suggest that semantic information and visual information are processed by different brain regions (e.g. Peterson *et al.* 1988).

These theorists can also explain dissociative effects obtained with normal subjects. Their explanation requires the assumption that performance on explicit tests such as recall is more dependent on the system involving the recollection of semantically elaborated events, whereas performance on implicit tasks such as fragment completion is more dependent on the system underlying perceptual skills. With this assumption, they can explain why levels of processing manipulations tend to have larger effects on explicit tests and why changes in perceptually related information between study and test have larger effects on implicit tests. Different brain structures are presumably more or less involved in the performance of each task.

Schacter and his colleagues have been among the strongest advocates of the multiple systems explanation (Cooper *et al.* 1992; Schacter 1992; Schacter *et al.* 1990; Schacter *et al.* 1991a; Schacter *et al.* 1991b). They conducted a series of experiments in which subjects studied line drawings of novel objects before being given either an explicit recognition test or an implicit memory task. In the implicit memory task, the drawings were presented rapidly (e.g. 50 minutes) and subjects had to make decisions about whether the object was possible or impossible. As illustrated in Figure 5.3, half of the objects presented in the experiment were structurally possible (upper panel) and half were structurally impossible (lower panel). Structurally possible objects could be built in a wood shop, but structurally impossible objects could not be constructed because they contain flaws produced by ambiguous lines. Both studied and non-studied objects were presented during testing so the magnitude of priming effects could be measured, but no references to the study episode were made. As far as the subjects were concerned, the object decision task required them to make object decisions and was unrelated to the study episode.

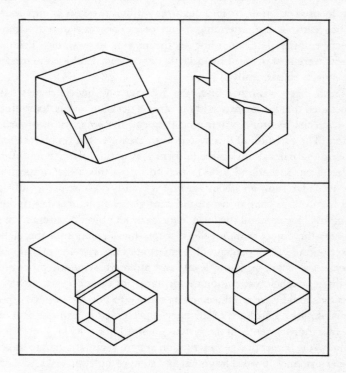

Figure 5.3 Possible objects (upper panel) and impossible objects (lower panel).

Several important findings emerged from this series of studies. First, for structurally possible objects, subjects made more accurate decisions for studied than for unstudied objects, that is, a priming effect was observed. Studying the possible objects primed the object decision even though the test made no reference to the prior study episode. However, a priming effect was not obtained for structurally

141

impossible objects. Decisions for impossible objects were no more accurate for studied objects than for unstudied objects, and this was true even after the impossible objects had been studied several times and subjects could recognize them with a high level of accuracy. Second, similar results were obtained for memory-disordered patients suggesting that the system responsible for producing the priming effect for possible objects was preserved in these subjects. Third, priming effects for possible objects were reduced following study tasks that focused attention on local features within the object as opposed to global features, e.g. attending to one of its corners reduced priming effects compared to attending to the objects as a whole. Priming effects were also reduced by tasks that encouraged subjects to process the objects semantically.

From these and other findings, Schacter and his colleagues have concluded that performance in the objects decision task is determined by a special memory system that they call the *perceptual representation system*. The function of this system is to create global representations among the parts of an object to form a structural description of the object (see Sutherland 1968). According to this view, impossible objects fail to show an advantage of prior study because of the difficulties involved in computing a consistent global structural description. Similarly, focusing on the local features of an object or attempting to process the object semantically disrupts the formation of the global description. The perceptual representation system presumably operates at a pre-semantic level, and although semantic processing facilitates explicit recognition performance for these objects, such processing should have a reduced effect or no effect on the implicit object decision task. This form of memory is preserved in amnesia and can operate independently of the system involved in conscious processing. Finally, the perceptual representation system is also thought to underlie performance in word fragment and stem completion tasks (Tulving and Schacter 1990). According to Schacter's multiple system theory, priming effects in the object decision, word fragment and stem completion tasks reflect an unconscious form of memory concerned with the perceptual identification of words and objects.

Processing explanations

Schacter's and other multiple system theories can explain explicit–implicit task dissociations, but these theories have not gone unchallenged. Many psychologists have argued that the same dissociations can be explained without resorting to assumptions about different brain systems being involved in implicit and explicit tasks. The crux of the argument put forth by advocates of the processing explanation is that the dissociations are the result of different processes being involved in explicit and implicit tasks. The mental operations engaged when subjects are consciously recollecting an experience are presumably different at least in some respects from the operations engendered in implicit tasks (e.g. Blaxton 1989; Jacoby 1983; Mason and MacLeod 1992; Roediger 1990a; Roediger et al. 1989; Tenpenny and Shoben 1992). In this view, memory tests involve a variety of different processes, including those linked to perceptual information, semantic information and those related to activation, search, matching, decision, and so on, and some of these processes presumably assume varying degrees of importance in different retention tasks.

Roediger and his colleagues have advocated the processing approach and have emphasized the importance of two general assumptions in their attempt to explain dissociations between explicit and implicit tests. The first assumption is that cognitive operations can be divided into two types: data-driven processes and conceptually driven processes. Data-driven processes emphasize the physical and perceptual features of a stimulus, whereas conceptually driven processes emphasize its meaning. The second assumption is that test performance will benefit to the extent that the cognitive operations performed during testing match those performed during the study episode. This idea is generally known in the literature as *transfer appropriate processing* (e.g. Morris et al. 1977).

In applying these assumptions, Roediger and his colleagues have suggested that explicit and implicit tests encompass both data-driven and conceptually driven processes. However, they have also argued that explicit tests tend to be more conceptually driven and implicit tests tend to be more data driven. For example, word stem completion, fragment completion and perceptual identification tasks rely primarily on data-driven processes, whereas recall and recognition are more dependent on conceptually driven processes. In this approach, dissociations between explicit and implicit tests of memory are then attributed to differential emphases on the two types of processes. For example, in the fragment completion task, changes in modality from study to test are disruptive because performance in this task is highly dependent on data-driven processes that are mismatched as a result of the change in modality. When the subject hears the study words or experiences them as pictures, performance on a fragment completion test is disrupted because performance on this test depends heavily upon having *seen* the words during study (e.g. Roediger and Blaxton 1987; Weldon and Roediger 1987; Weldon 1991). In this task, transfer-appropriate processing operations are more compatible when the words have been seen rather than heard because the test cue is seen and the match between the encoding and retrieval operations should be greater.

Roediger's process approach explains the dissociation results without making any assumptions about the existence of multiple memory systems. Nevertheless, the usefulness of the transfer-appropriate assumption and the distinction between data-driven and conceptually driven processing have been disputed (e.g. Masson and MacLeod 1992; Nelson *et al.* 1992b; Schacter 1992; Tenpenny and Shoben 1992). One difficulty with the transfer-appropriate processing idea arises from its circularity. Decisions concerning the degree of transfer-appropriate processing are completely tied to experimental outcomes. For example, if type font is changed from study to test and this change produces a reduction in perceptual identification performance, the researcher can conclude that the change reduced the match of encoding and retrieval operations. Alternatively, if the font change had no effect, the researcher can conclude that type font is irrelevant in the perceptual identification task. The assumption of transfer-appropriate processing survives the test in either case. Without independent means of measuring the degrees of transfer-appropriate processing involved when study-to-test changes are made in different tasks, the validity of this assumption cannot be tested and the concept can be used only after the data have been collected.

A similar problem has arisen for the distinction between data-driven and conceptually driven processing. For example, dissociations have been demonstrated *within* implicit tests that supposedly measure the same type of processing (Masson and MacLeod 1992; Schwartz 1989; Weldon 1991; Witherspoon and Moscovitch 1989). Both word fragment completion and perceptual identification are considered to be data-driven tests and the same variable should have similar effects in both tasks. However, Witherspoon and Moscovitch (1989) discovered that the processes underlying perceptual identification and fragment completion for the same words were statistically independent. Knowing that a particular word is easy in one task tells us nothing about how easy or hard it will be on the other task. Schwartz (1989) found that generating the study words from semantic cues during the study episode reduced perceptual identification performance compared to reading the same words, but had no effect on word fragment completion. Semantic processing during the study episode produced as much priming in the fragment completion task as reading the word. Similarly, Weldon (1991) had subjects study word compounds that either preserved the meaning of the target word (e.g. *Scotch* bottle) or altered its meaning (e.g. *Scotch* tape), and then tested implicit memory for the target word (e.g. Scotch) using perceptual identification and word fragment completion tasks. Encoded meaning affected the amount of priming observed in word fragment completion, but did not effect perceptual identification.

The theoretical framework proposed by Roediger and his colleagues can explain these findings, by assuming that the fragment completion task involves a conceptually driven component whereas the perceptual identification task does not. Given the differences between these tasks this assumption may seem reasonable, but accepting it makes the distinction between data-driven and conceptually driven processing as circular as the transfer-appropriate processing assumption. The distinction is defined by the experimental outcome. Furthermore, accepting this assumption immediately produces another problem. Under certain conditions, generating the study words produces as much priming in the perceptual identification task as seeing and reading them even though the generated words have *never been seen*. Masson and MacLeod (1992) showed that priming effects were more apparent for read than for generated items when the generated words were highly integrated in the encoding context, as occurred in the Jacoby (1983) and Schwartz (1989) studies. In contrast, when the generated words were poorly integrated into the encoding context, priming was just as high for generated words that had not been seen as for read words. These findings indicate that the perceptual identification task also involves a conceptually driven component.

The assumption that implicit tests are more data driven than explicit tests may be correct despite these findings, but it is now very clear that the idea of *data-driven tests* is an oversimplified misnomer (Weldon 1991). Performance on tasks such as word fragment completion, word stem completion and perceptual identification is clearly affected by the modality of the study experience. Seeing the study words as compared to hearing them clearly influences priming in these tasks. However, it is now equally clear that some aspect of meaning encoded during the study experience can affect performance in these tasks. It is also clear that this aspect of meaning is different from the meaning encoded when subjects engage in the elaborative semantic processing likely to be involved in levels of processing manipulations (e.g. rating words for pleasantness, concreteness, using them in a sentence, and so on). The problem lies in conceptualizing the differences between these two kinds of meaning. The likely possibility is that seeing or hearing a familiar word activates its meaning and related meanings automatically as part of the comprehension process (e.g. Masson and MacLeod 1992; Nelson and Friedrich 1980; Nelson and McEvoy 1979; Nelson *et al.* 1992a; Simpson and Burgess 1985). Automatically activated meaning involves the activation of a word's most closely related associates, e.g. the word BUTTER activates *bread*, *toast*, and so on. Such activation provides rapid access to information previously linked to the word and this type of meaning is likely to be free of the particular context in which the word appears (Barsalou 1982). Once the word has been comprehended, its meaning can be elaborated using consciously controlled encoding processes such as those involved in rating pleasantness or creating a sentence that uses the word. Given the distinction between the *automatic* and *consciously controlled* aspects of meaning, it is possible to conclude that the more automatic aspects of meaning involved in word comprehension can play an important role in determining performance in perceptual identification, fragment completion and stem completion tasks. These tasks are not purely data driven, nor can they be described as relying exclusively on a single memory system such as the perceptual representation system (Tulving and Schacter 1990). However, more elaborative aspects of meaning appear to play a lesser role or no role at all in these tasks as long as subjects are operating under the influence of implicit testing instructions that make no reference to the study episode (e.g. Nelson *et al.* 1992b).

The difficulties involved in being able to predetermine the relative amounts of data-driven and conceptually driven processing for any test under any particular set of encoding conditions pose serious problems for the framework proposed by Roediger and his colleagues. Nevertheless, this framework has served a useful purpose in drawing attention to the role that data-driven processing plays in most implicit tests, and it has been invaluable in promoting processing explanations for implicit test findings. The more recent results concerning the importance of the more automatic aspects of meaning simply extend our understanding of the processes involved in explicit and implicit tasks. There appear to be two types of automatic processes when familiar stimuli are encountered, one type linked to the physical characteristics of the stimuli and another type linked to the more immediate aspects of its meaning. In addition, there appears to be another general type of process involved in consciously controlled learning activities and this process is involved in elaborating meaning. These processes contribute to performance on both explicit and implicit tasks, but to varying degrees depending on the specific task and the nature of the conditions prevailing during the study episode. In general, all three processes appear to contribute to performance in explicit tasks, whereas only the more automatic aspects of processing appear to make substantial contributions to performance in implicit tasks (Nelson *et al.* 1992a). Although this interpretation of the findings does not conform to the letter of Roediger's proposal, it is consistent with the spirit of his ideas and it serves to maintain the integrity of the processing explanation as well.

Are the systems and process approaches compatible?

The multiple system and process frameworks developed in the attempt to understand dissociations between explicit and implicit memory describe the findings from fundamentally different perspectives. One approach relies heavily on a metaphor grounded in the language of brain structures, and the other relies heavily on a metaphor founded on hypothetical mental steps. These differences are important because each framework is likely to lead to research that would not be generated from the perspective of the other framework.

At another level, however, the views are eminently compatible. Brain structures certainly underlie all mental processing, and differences in processing provide the necessary behavioural evidence for forming conclusions about the functions of different brain structures. This commonality implies that work inspired from one perspective can serve to constrain work done from another perspective. Schachter (1992) has made a strong case for what he calls a cognitive-neuroscience approach and suggests that research findings developed in one domain should be used to constrain the theorizing in the other and that hypotheses generated in one domain should also be tested in the other. For example, some of the findings reviewed above suggest that it would be useful to postulate a process involving the more automatic aspects of meaning to understand performance in some implicit tasks. These findings should stimulate attempts by researchers

147

who prefer the brain metaphor to search for evidence of brain structures responsible for mediating the more automatic aspects of meaning that are different from the structures that ostensibly involve consciously controlled elaborative processing. For example, what enables amnesics to perform as well as normals in the fragment completion task: mechanisms underlying the data-driven processing component or mechanisms underlying the more automatic aspects of meaning, or both?

The argument that such an approach will quickly add too many brain structures to memory (e.g. Roediger 1990b) loses some of its appeal when we consider that no one has proposed a limit on the number of hypothetical processes. Data-driven processes, for example, consist of a fairly large number of potentially independent subprocesses, including those associated with analysing the visual features of the words, those responsible for translating the visual features into letters, those required to turn the letters into phonemic features, and so on (e.g. McClelland and Rumelhart 1981). Just as these steps to word recognition can be conceptualized as constituting different mental processes, they can be conceptualized as involving different brain structures and, in either case, the number of separable entities involved is likely to be large but finite.

A more serious problem for both of these approaches concerns the assumption that subjects performing implicit tasks are unaware of the relationship between the information encoded during the study episode and the test task. Past research on unconscious learning has floundered on the issue of awareness (Dulany et al. 1984; Holender 1986), and this may be the issue that halts progress on this topic again. The problem with the current procedures for investigating implicit memory is that most researchers assume that subjects are unaware of the study–test relationship because it is never mentioned. Given the interest level of many of the participating subjects this assumption is often reasonable, but an assumption is no guarantee. For example, after completing several fragments or after naming several words presented in perceptual identification, some of the subjects may notice that some of the words appearing on the test were presented during the study episode. Thereafter, these subjects may self-instruct themselves to produce more list words as responses to improve their level of performance. As a result, implicit tasks may involve some unknown combination of both conscious and unconscious processes.

Jacoby (1991) addressed this problem directly and proposed an interesting solution. He argued that the differences between explicit and implicit tests will best be understood by focusing on the distinction between *automatic* and *intentional* processes, and he proposed a methodology for estimating the separate contributions of each of these processes. For example, in a fragment completion task, some of the test cues are designated by the experimenter as 'inclusion' cues to be used by the subjects to recall list words, or when recall fails, to produce the first appropriate word that comes to mind. Other fragment cues are designated as 'exclusion' cues that are to be used to exclude any list words that might occur to the subjects while in the process of completing the cue. The rationale underlying this manipulation is that inclusion cues provide an estimate of both intentional and automatic contributions to recall. With this instruction, subjects recall some words because of active attempts to produce words from the study episode and they recall other words as a result of processes that occur automatically and without conscious awareness. In contrast, the exclusion cues provide an estimate of the automatic component. If a subject knowingly recalls a list word to a particular test cue, this word must be excluded, leaving only the automatically recalled words that the subject fails to recognize as list words. By applying simple algebra to the recall scores produced under each instructional set, separate estimates can be determined for the contribution of each hypothetical process. Jacoby's technique offers a promising new method for separating the relative contributions of conscious and unconscious processes in both explicit and implicit tests.

IMPLICITLY ACTIVATED ASSOCIATES AND MEMORY

Measuring long-term associations

The second approach to the study of implicit memory involves a technique that takes advantage of the automatic aspects of meaning mentioned earlier (e.g. Nelson and Friedrich 1980; Nelson and McEvoy 1979; Nelson *et al.* 1990; Nelson *et al.* 1992a). Instead of varying the task and test instructions and looking for dissociations among the manipulated variables, the number of associates linked to words in long-term memory are manipulated. If the number of associates connected to a word in long-term memory affects performance in some task, the inference that implicitly activated memories have played a role in that task can be made. In this approach to studying implicit memory, what people know about a familiar word is measured beforehand to determine whether memory for a recently experienced word is influenced by what has become connected to it. People have countless experiences with the same word in many different contexts and as a result familiar words become connected to related words to the point that 'the mind may run from almost anything to anything' (Hobbes 1839: 15).

The first problem for an investigator using this technique is to measure the connected associates for a large sample of words, and the most commonly used procedure requires the collection of association norms (for a review of such procedures see Cramer 1968). Such norms are often collected by giving approximately 150 people the same set of 100 words with a blank next to each word. They are asked to write the first word that comes to mind that means the same thing or that is strongly related to the word provided by the investigator. The results of this procedure indicate that all words have two interesting characteristics. First, for a given word, 150 people do not produce 150 different response words. There is often a high level of agreement among the subjects in that some response words are given more frequently than others, i.e. 60 subjects may give the same word, 40 another word, 20 another, and so on. This characteristic is often called dominance or *strength*. Second, the number of words linked to a given word varies continuously. Some words have only 2 or 3 different associates whereas other words reliably elicit more than 25 associates. This characteristic will be called *set* size. For example, as shown in Figure 5.4, the word BIBLE has only 8 associates including God, book, church, and so on, whereas the word HAM has 18 associates, including pig, eggs, meat, and so on. Words are connected to other words because of learning that occurs throughout our lifetimes and these connections vary in both relative strength and number. The associates produced by this means are highly reliable (Cramer 1968; Nelson and Schreiber 1992), and it is assumed that the associates provided by a group of subjects provide a reliable and valid measure of the associates of an individual subject (Cochran and Wickens 1963).

General procedures

Once a large sample of items has been normed, words presented during study and testing episodes can be preselected to have either small or large sets of associates. Words with small sets are defined as those with 1–8 associates and those with large sets typically have

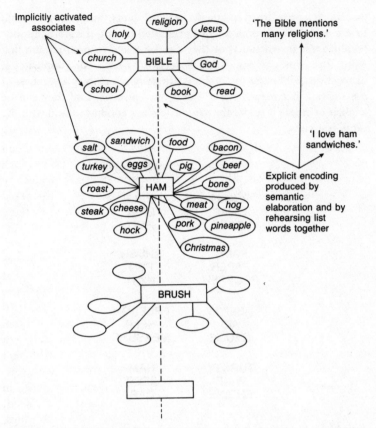

Figure 5.4 Implicitly activated associates of the words BIBLE and HAM as each word is read off the screen in a hypothetical experiment.

16–25 associates. In the standard procedure, subjects are presented with a list of briefly exposed words and they are asked to process them in some specified manner. For example, as illustrated in Figure 5.4, they could be asked to create a sentence for each word shown or to rehearse the words of the list together. Words with small associative sets such as BIBLE and words with large associative sets such as HAM might be presented along with other words that differ in set size in the study list. This study episode is followed by a test trial during which the test cues are shown one at a time with each cue related to one of the words appearing in the study list. Test cues serve as clues that help subjects recover study words and they consist of associated words, word fragments or word stems. Subjects can be told to use each cue to recall a word presented during the study episode (explicit test instructions) or they can be asked to produce the first word that comes to mind that is related to each cue (implicit test instructions). The test instructions are designed to vary awareness of the relation between the study and test episodes, and they can be explicit or implicit under the same encoding conditions and with the same test cues.

Test cues	Studied targets
PSALM	BIBLE
FINAL	LAST
QUICK	FAST
PAINT	BRUSH
PAPER	PEN
PROSPER	RICH
LIBERTY	FREEDOM
AID	HELP
GAUGE	MEASURE
TURKEY	HAM
WINE	BEER
ENGINE	CAR

Figure 5.5 Example of words used to study cue and target set size effects.

When words with different set sizes are used as cues during the test trial, *cue set size* is manipulated; when these words are presented as the items to be learned, *target set size* is being manipulated. To illustrate these manipulations, Figure 5.5. presents a list of target words and test cues in which both cue and target set size have been varied so that all combinations of small and large cue and target set size are represented. If performance on some test varies with either cue or target manipulations, set size effects have been demonstrated, e.g. set size effects are demonstrated when studied target words with smallet sets of associates (e.g. BIBLE) are easier to recall than those with larger sets of associates (e.g. HAM). Note that such effects reflect an implicit or unconscious influence because associates of the physically presented words used as targets or as test cues are never presented during the task. An important assumption of this approach is that when a familiar word is experienced either as a study word or as a test cue, it implicitly activates its related associates. Such activation corresponds to the early and automatic stages of the processing of meaning and is critical to comprehension because it provides rapid access to information about the stimulus beyond what is physically present in the word itself.

Cue set size effects

In experiments on cue set size, subjects usually study about 2 dozen unrelated words presented 1 word at a time for 3 seconds. This study is followed by a test in which subjects are given related words, word stems or word fragments as cues to help them remember the study words (e.g. the words PSALM and PAINT might be used as test cues for the study words BIBLE and BRUSH, respectively). This procedure is known as an extralist cueing task because the test cues are not present during the study trial and are in essence 'extra' or outside the study list.

The variable of main interest in these experiments is the set size defined by the test cues. In the usual experiment, one-half of the test cues are connected to their target words and to a few other associates in long-term memory, and the remaining one-half are connected to their target words and many other associates in long-term memory. The strength of the pre-existing connection between each test cue and its target is carefully equated in these experiments within each level of cue set size because cue-to-target strength has a large effect on recall. Equating strength ensures the equivalence of the probability of guessing the target in each set size condition.

The results of experiments on cue set size indicate that this variable exerts a consistent effect on the probability of recalling the studied words (for a review see Nelson et al. 1992a). Test cues having smaller sets of connected associates produce higher levels of recall, by about 13–15 per cent, than those having larger sets of associates. Recall is more likely when the test cue is related to fewer competing associates in long-term memory. This effect appears to be a very general phenomenon because it is obtained for both young and elderly adults and is produced by a large variety of different types of test cues, including associatively related words, category names, pictures, word stems and word fragment cues. Interestingly, cue set size effects do not vary with how well the words of the study list have been encoded. The magnitude of the effect is about the same regardless of whether the study list is short or long, presented for two trials or for one trial before the test, studied for 6 seconds per word as opposed to 1.5 seconds, or studied with an effective or a poor learning strategy. The effect is also nearly the same regardless of whether the test instructions are explicit or implicit or whether the test trial is administered immediately or after a delay. All of these variables affect the number of words recalled from the study list without affecting the magnitude of the cue set size effect.

Target set size effects

Experiments on target set size are conducted under essentially the same extralist cueing conditions as those that manipulate cue set size, except that the manipulation is made within the list of studied words rather than among the test cues (e.g. BIBLE and HAM appear in the study list). These experiments show essentially the same results as the experiments on cue set size: words with smaller sets of associates are more likely to be recalled than those with larger sets of associates (Nelson et al. 1992). As with manipulations of cue set size, the recall advantage for target words having small associative sets averages about 13–15 per cent across many comparisons.

Most importantly, target set size effects do not vary appreciably with how well the targets have been encoded or whether the test instructions are explicit or implicit (Nelson et al. 1992a; Nelson et al. 1992b). As shown in Figure 5.6, target set size effects are equally apparent when subjects rate the words for concreteness or name their vowels during the study episode. Rating concreteness increases the probability of recall compared to naming vowels, but has no influence on the magnitude of the target set size effect. Similarly, studying the words for 6 seconds instead of 1.5 seconds or studying concrete instead of abstract words improves recall without changing the magnitude of the effect. Finally, as shown in the lower right panel of Figure 5.6, target set size effects are essentially the same regardless of whether the test instructions are explicit (direct) or implicit (indirect). Automatically activated associates affect target recovery on both types of test (Nelson et al. 1992b; and see Besson et al. 1992 for related results). Like the cue set size effect, the target set size effect is a robust phenomenon that appears to be unaffected by how well the target has been encoded and by whether or not the test instructions refer to the study episode.

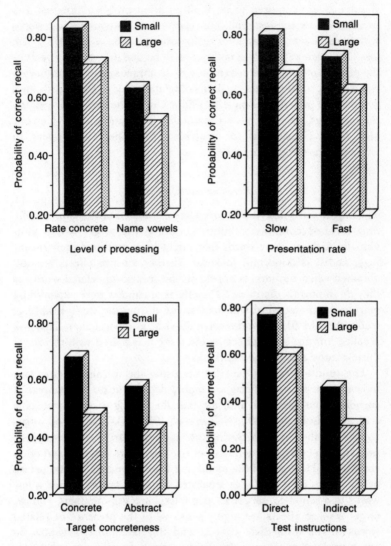

Figure 5.6 Target set size effects as a function of level of processing and presentation rate during study, as a function of concreteness of the study words, and as a function of test instructions.

The target set size effect, however, is influenced by distracting subjects just before testing them. In all the experiments mentioned so far, the test trial was administered immediately after the study trial.

If subjects are required to do multiplication problems for just 4–5 minutes before the test trial, the relative recall advantage for words with smaller sets of associates melts away (Nelson *et al.* 1985). The loss of this advantage does not appear to be due only to the effects of the passage of time. The magnitude of the target set size is unaffected when subjects study additional lists of related or unrelated words for a comparable period (Nelson *et al.* 1993). Unlike the cue set size effect, the target set size depends on maintaining attention to the memory task itself. Distractions to completely different tasks appear to eliminate the effect altogether.

Encoding context effects

The experiments described above were conducted under contextually impoverished conditions. Subjects studied the target words individually without other words that might have modified their meanings, and it is important to know whether set size effects are still obtained when the targets appear in the context of related words as they do in normal discourse. The effects of context were explored by pairing the target word with its test cue during the study trial (e.g. study PSALM BIBLE and receive PSALM as the test cue). This task is called intralist cueing because the test cue is paired with the target during study and appears *in* the list.

The results of many experiments using the intralist cueing task indicate that set size effects are highly dependent on the context of encoding, but they also indicate that the timing of that context is critical (Nelson *et al.* 1992; Nelson *et al.* 1992b). When related words appear together as pairs during the study trial or when they appear next to each other in sentences, set size effects are reduced and often eliminated. However, if the modifying word appears 1 second before or after the target or if it is separated from the target by just a few words in a sentence, target set size effects are still obtained. Hence, target set size effects are highly sensitive to the presence of related words in the immediate context and this fact must somehow be accommodated by theory. Implicitly activated memories sometimes do and sometimes do not affect recall and it is important to understand why this is so.

Theoretical interpretation of set size effects

Set size effects are important for three reasons. First, the presence of such effects indicates that previously acquired connections to related words in long-term memory can influence recall. Recall is not only a function of explicitly engaged processing operations such as rehearsing words or generating sentences or images. Set size effects indicate that the recall of a recently studied word in the presence of an extralist cue is a function of the number of associates linked to the test cue and to the studied word through learning that took place long before the laboratory episode. The smaller the number of implicitly activated associates, the more likely recall will be. Second, such effects indicate that unconsciously activated information can affect memory for consciously experienced events. Memory for a recent experience apparently can be influenced by previously acquired information even though that information may never have been brought to the level of conscious awareness. The magnitude of set size effects is uninfluenced by the nature of the explicit encoding activities and by whether explicit or implicit instructions are given to the subjects during the test trial. Set size effects apparently have little or nothing to do with how well the intentional or conscious processing aspects of the task are performed and are presumably related to automatic and implicit processing activities. Finally, set size effects will help us better understand processes associated with comprehension. Target set size effects are highly sensitive to distractions to other tasks and to the presence of meaningfully related words in the immediate context. This sensitivity is consistent with the assumption that set size effects reflect the action of a basic mechanism concerned with comprehension. One function of the memory system is to provide rapid access to related information, and while the activation of such information can support recall under limited conditions, there would be little need to sustain such activation over long periods, nor would there be a need to sustain such information when it is no longer relevant in the current context.

A model has been proposed by Nelson and his colleagues for explaining set size effects and other findings (Nelson *et al.* 1992a). The model is called PIER because it assumes that target recovery in both implicit and explicit tests is a function of the *processing of implicit and explicit representations*. PIER incorporates separate assumptions concerning encoding and retrieval because target recovery is thought to be a function of the nature of the encoding experience and the nature of the conditions prevailing during test.

157

Encoding assumptions

As illustrated in Figure 5.4, encoding involves an implicit processing component concerned with the automatic activation of related information and an explicit processing component related to intentional processing activities executed by the subject (e.g. Hasher and Zacks 1979; Nelson *et al.* 1992a; Shiffrin and Schneider 1977). The implicit component involves the activation of meaningfully related associates directly connected to each studied word (e.g. reading HAM activates *pig*, *eggs*, *meat*, and so on). These associates can be brought to the level of awareness, as when asked to free associate to a given stimulus, but this activation is normally implicit and occurs without awareness. These associates vary in strength and in number for different words, and their activation is automatic and represents an important step in the comprehension process that produces a representation that can be used to support later recall.

The nature of this representation is presumed to be highly sensitive to the encoding context provided by the surrounding words. When the immediate context fails to specify the meaning of a study word, its associates are activated and remain activated until attention is distracted to another cognitive task. In contrast, when the immediate context presents another word that is meaningfully related to the study word, associates of the studied word are activated but are then rapidly inhibited (e.g. Gernsbacher and Faust 1991; Kintsch 1988; Tipper 1985). In the absence of context, the memory system in essence activates what it knows about the stimulus and, in the presence of a meaningfully related context, largely irrelevant associates are selectively inhibited as attention is focused on comprehending the relationship between the words. The representation created during the study episode incorporates associates related to the study word. The activation status of these associates depends on the presence and the immediacy of meaningfully related context words. Associates are included in the representation in an activated state when the context fails to specify the meaning of the study word, and they are included in an inhibited state when the context specifies its meaning.

At the same time that the implicit processing component is doing its job, subjects are engaged in explicit processing activities. These activities may include merely reading the words, rehearsing the words of the list, generating them from cues, naming their vowels, rating them for pleasantness, making images, and so on. Such activities involve conscious controlled encoding operations usually suggested by the experimenter in the instructions to subjects. According to PIER, these activities produce representations that vary in encoding strength with the nature of the conditions of practice (e.g. presentation rate, number of study trials) and the strategies (e.g. rehearsal, imagery) applied during the learning process. For example, a slower presentation rate, more study trials and a better encoding strategy all increase the strength of the explicit encoding of the studied target word.

Retrieval assumptions

The operation of implicit and explicit processing components during the study episode produces independent memory representations, each of which can be searched during the test trial. Given a cue at test, PIER assumes that a studied word can be recovered either by searching through explicit representations produced by conscious processing operations or by searching through implicit representations activated by the test cue and the studied word. For example, given TURKEY as a cue for HAM, the search can be directed to the representations of the list words produced as a result of consciously controlled processing activities until a word that is related to the test cue is produced (e.g. by searching through representations of list words such as BIBLE, FREEDOM, END, HAM, and so on). The search can also be directed to the representations activated by the test cue in long-term memory (e.g. TURKEY activates *thanksgiving, ham, chicken, bird*, and so on). PIER assumes that each search is conducted independently of the other and that each process has an additive effect on the level of observed recall. This means that variables that increase the strength of the explicit encoding such as number of study trials will increase the probability of recovering the target but will not influence the magnitude of set size effects.

The explicit search involves sampling representations created by explicit encoding processes and the success of this search is governed by the encoding strength of the studied word (Raaijmakers and Shiffrin 1981). In contrast, as illustrated in the upper panel of Figure 5.7, the implicit search process involves sampling associates activated by the test cue and by the studied word. The likelihood of sampling the target is greater when fewer competing associates are activated, and this sampling algorithm is what produces both cue and target set size effects. The associates of the test cue are activated by the cue, and if the target is sampled as a member of this set, it activates associates

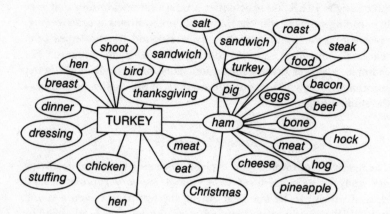

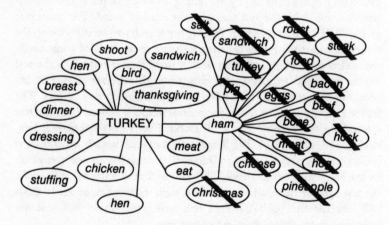

Figure 5.7 The numbers of associates theoretically activated by the test cue and by the target effect recall.

functionally linked to it during the study episode. As suggested in the upper panel of Figure 5.7, if the associates of *ham* are still in a state of activation, then they will be reactivated during the test trial and set size effects linked to the target will be observed. Alternatively, as suggested in the lower panel of Figure 5.7, if none of its associates are in a state of activation because of distractions produced by attention shifts or because of context-induced inhibition effects, then set size effects linked to the targets will not be found. In this model, cue set size effects will be apparent whenever some extralist cues activate more information than others as long as these cues provide only partial information about the target, e.g. some of its letters or a meaning-related word. Target set size effects in contrast depend on the number of implicitly activated associates and on conditions prevailing before and after the study episode.

MANIPULATIONS OF AWARENESS AND PIER

PIER provides a straightforward means for understanding the set size findings and constitutes a fairly detailed model for understanding the relationship between explicitly and implicitly created memories. Although omitted here, the model also provides an explanation for set size effects related to the physical features of words (e.g. rhyme), and for predicting the effects of set size in different types of retention tests such as perceptual identification, word fragment completion, free recall and recognition. With its assumptions concerning the activation of associates, the model also implies that the connectivity among these associates could represent another important facet of implicit memory that is yet unexplored.

PIER differs in several important ways from other approaches to studying implicit memory. First, PIER is designed to investigate the effects of implicitly activated memories in a variety of tasks. Set size effects are directly tied to implicit memories. In contrast, researchers bent on manipulating test awareness are attempting to investigate the systems or processes underlying implicit memory by varying the task and the test instructions. Given implicit test instructions, performance on a task presumably provides an indication of the systems or processes mediating implicit memory. Second, set size can be manipulated separately during the encoding and retrieval phases of a task and can be combined with the manipulation of other variables known to affect explicit encoding. This flexibility allows researchers to link effects of implicit memory to encoding, retrieval, or both processes. To the contrary, manipulations of test awareness are confined to the test trial itself and therefore it is difficult to determine whether the effects emerge only during retrieval or are controlled by encoding processes as well. Finally, PIER assumes that performance in both explicit and implicit tests reflects the results of memories created as a result of both conscious and automatic processing activities, and PIER offers some suggestions for evaluating and separating the two components. Researchers manipulating awareness by varying test instructions tend to assume that the test itself reflects the action of one process or the other (for a similar suggestion see Jacoby 1991).

Despite these differences, the two approaches are compatible in many respects. Both approaches recognize the importance of implicit memory, and as was suggested earlier, manipulations of test awareness can easily be combined with manipulations of set size. The combination possesses the strength of each approach because the effects of implicit memory can be more specifically linked to encoding or retrieval processes involved in the performance of both explicit and implicit tests. The advantages of the combined approach are apparent, but even if the two approaches continue on separate paths, what is really important is that Ebbinghaus' 1885 suggestion that accumulated experience unconsciously affects performance is again being taken seriously by scientists all over the world.

ACKNOWLEDGEMENTS

Work on this chapter was supported by grant MH 16360 from the National Institute of Mental Health. My special thanks go to Cathy McEvoy and Vanesa McKinney for their comments on an earlier draft of this chapter.

REFERENCES

Anisfeld, M. and Knapp, M.E. (1968) 'Association, synonymity, and directionality in false recognition', *Journal of Experimental Psychology* 5: 132–41.

Baddeley, A. and Warrington, E.K. (1970) 'Amnesia and the distinction between long- and short-term memory' *Journal of Verbal Learning and Verbal Behavior* 9: 176–89.

Barsalou, L.W. (1982) 'Context-independent and context-dependent information in concepts', *Memory and Cognition* 11: 211–27.

Besson, M., Fischler, I., Boaz, T. and Raney, G. (1992) 'Effects of automatic associative activation on explicit and implicit tests', *Journal of Experimental Psychology: Learning, Memory and Cognition* 18: 89–105.

Blaxton, T.A. (1989) 'Investigating dissociations among memory measures: Support for a transfer appropriate processing framework', *Journal of Experimental Psychology: Learning, Memory and Cognition* 15: 657–68.

Cave, C.B. and Squire, L.R. (1992) 'Intact and long-lasting repetition priming in amnesia', *Journal of Experimental Psychology: Learning, Memory and Cognition* 18: 509–20.

Challis, B.H. and Brodbeck, D.R. (1992) 'Level of processing affects priming in word fragment completion', *Journal of Experimental Psychology: Learning, Memory and Cognition* 18: 595–607.

Cochran, S.W. and Wickens, D.D. (1963) 'Prediction of learning by group-rated association values versus individual-rated association values', *Journal of Verbal Learning and Verbal Behavior* 2: 509–12.

Cohen, N. and Squire, L.R. (1980) 'Preserved learning and retention of pattern analyzing skills in amnesia: Dissociation of knowing how and knowing that', *Science* 210: 207–10.

Collins, A.M. and Loftus, E.F. (1975) 'A spreading-activation theory of semantic processing', *Psychological Review* 82: 407–28.

Cooper, L.A., Schacter, D.L., Ballesteros, S. and Moore, C. (1992) 'Priming and recognition of transformed three-dimensional objects: Effects of size and reflection', *Journal of Experimental Psychology: Learning, Memory and Cognition* 18: 43–57.

Craik, F.I.M. and Tulving, E. (1975) 'Depth of processing and the retention of words in episodic memory', *Journal of Experimental Psychology: General* 104: 268–94.

Cramer, P. (1968) *Word Association*, New York: Academic Press.

Dulany, D.E., Carlson, R.A. and Dewey, G.I. (1984) 'A case of syntactical learning and judgement: How conscious and how abstract?', *Journal of Experimental Psychology: General* 113: 541–55.

Ebbinghaus, H. (1885/1964) *Memory: A Contribution to Experimental Psychology*, New York: Dover.

Feustal, T.C., Shiffrin, R.M. and Salasoo, A. (1983) 'Episodic and lexical contributions to the repetition effect in word identification', *Journal of Experimental Psychology: General* 112: 309–46.

Gernsbacher, M.A. and Faust, M.E. (1991) 'The mechanisms of suppression: A component of general comprehension skill', *Journal of Experimental Psychology: Learning, Memory and Cognition* 17: 245–62.

Graf, P. and Mandler, G. (1984) 'Activation makes words more accessible, but not necessarily more retrievable', *Journal of Verbal Learning and Verbal Behavior* 23: 553–68.

Graf, P. and Schacter, D.A. (1985) 'Implicit and explicit memory for new associations in normal and amnesic subjects', *Journal of Experimental Psychology: Learning, Memory and Cognition* 11: 501–18.

Graf, P., Shimamura, A.P. and Squire, L.R. (1985) 'Priming across modalities and priming across category levels', *Journal of Experimental Psychology: Learning, Memory and Cognition* 11: 385–95.

Graf, P., Squire, L.R. and Mandler, G. (1984) 'The information that amnesic patients do not forget', *Journal of Experimental Psychology: Learning, Memory and Cognition* 10: 164–78.

Hasher, L. and Zacks, R.T. (1979) 'Automatic and effortful processes in memory', *Journal of Experimental Psychology: General* 108: 356–88.

Hayman, C.A. and Tulving, E. (1989) 'Is priming in fragment completion based on a "traceless" memory system?', *Journal of Experimental Psychology: Learning, Memory and Cognition* 15: 941–56.

Hobbes, T. (1839) *Human Nature*, London: John Bohn.

Holender, D. (1986) 'Semantic activation without conscious identification in dichotic listening, parfoveal vision, and visual masking: A survey and appraisal', *The Behavioral and Brain Sciences* 9: 1–66.

Jacoby, L.L. (1983) 'Remembering the data: Analyzing interactive processes in reading', *Journal of Verbal Learning and Verbal Behavior* 22: 485–508.

—— (1991) 'A process dissociation framework: Separating automatic from intentional uses of memory', *Journal of Memory and Language* 30: 513–41.

Jacoby, L.L. and Dallas, M. (1981) 'On the relationship between auto-biographical memory and perceptual learning', *Journal of Experimental Psychology: General* 110: 306–40.

Jacoby, L.L. and Witherspoon, D. (1982) 'Remembering without aware-ness', *Canadian Journal of Psychology* 2: 300–42.

Kintsch, W. (1988) 'The role of knowledge in discourse comprehension: A construction–integration model', *Psychological Review* 95: 163–82.

Kirsner, K. and Dunn, J.C. (1985) 'The perceptual record: A common factor in repetition priming and attribute retention', in M.I. Posner and O.S.M. Martin (eds) *Mechanisms of Attention: Attention and Performance*, XI, pp. 547–66, Hillsdale, New Jersey: Erlbaum.

Light, L.L. and Singh, A. (1987) 'Implicit and explicit memory in young and older adults', *Journal of Experimental Psychology: Learning, Memory and Cognition* 13: 531–41.

McClelland, J.L. and Rumelhart, D.E. (1981) 'An interactive activation model of context effects in letter perception: Part 1. An account of basic findings', *Psychological Review* 88: 375–407.

Masson, M.E. and MacLeod, C.M. (1992) 'Reenacting the route to inter-pretation: Enhanced perceptual identification without prior perception', *Journal of Experimental Psychology: General* 121: 145–76.

Morris, C.D., Bransford, J.D. and Franks, J.J. (1977) 'Levels of processing versus transfer appropriate processing', *Journal of Verbal Learning and Verbal Behavior* 16: 519–33.

Nelson, D.L. and Friedrich, M.A. (1980) 'Encoding and cuing sounds and senses', *Journal of Experimental Psychology: Learning, Memory and Cognition* 6: 717–31.

Nelson, D.L. and McEvoy, C.L. (1979) 'Encoding context and set size', *Journal of Experimental Psychology: Learning, Memory and Cognition* 5: 292–314.

Nelson, D.L. and Schreiber, T.A. (1992) 'Word concreteness and word structure as independent determinants of recall', *Journal of Memory and Language* 31: 237–60.

Nelson, D.L., Bajo, M.T. and Casanueva, D. (1985) 'Prior knowledge and memory: The influence of natural category size as a function of intention and distraction', *Journal of Experimental Psychology: Learning, Memory and Cognition* 11: 94–105.

Nelson, D.L., Gee, N.R. and Schreiber, T.A. (1992b) 'Sentence encoding and implicitly activated memories', *Memory and Cognition* 20: 643–54.

Nelson, D.L., Keelean, P.D. and Negrao, M. (1989) 'Word-fragment cuing:

The lexical search hypothesis', *Journal of Experimental Psychology: Learning, Memory and Cognition* 15: 388–97.

Nelson, D.L., McEvoy, C.L. and Schreiber, T.A. (1990) 'Encoding context and retrieval conditions as determinants of the effects of natural category size', *Journal of Experimental Psychology: Learning, Memory and Cognition* 16: 31–41.

Nelson, D.L., Schreiber, T.A. and Holley, P.E. (1992a) 'The retrieval of controlled and automatic aspects of meaning on direct and indirect tests', *Memory and Cognition* 20: 671–84.

Nelson, D.L., Canas, J., Bajo, M.T. and Keelean, P.D. (1987) 'Comparing word fragment completion and cued recall with letter cues', *Journal of Experimental Psychology: Learning, Memory and Cognition* 13: 542–52.

Nelson, D.L., McEvoy, C.L., Janczura, G.A. and Xu, J. (1993) 'The relationship between implicit and explicit memories', *Journal of Memory and Language* 32: 667–91.

Perruchet, P. (1989) 'The effect of spaced practice on explicit and implicit memory', *British Journal of Psychology* 80: 113–30.

Peterson, S.E., Fox, P.T., Posner, M.I., Mintun, M. and Raichle, M.E. (1988) 'Positron emission tomographic studies of the cortical anatomy of single-word processing', *Nature* 331: 585–9.

Raaijmakers, J.G.W. and Shiffrin, A.M. (1981) 'Search of associative memory', *Psychological Review* 88: 93–134.

Richardson-Klavehn, A. and Bjork, R.A. (1988) 'Measures of memory', *Annual Review of Psychology* 39: 475–543.

Roediger, H.L. (1990a) 'Implicit memory: Retention without remembering', *American Psychologist* 45: 1043–56.

—— (1990b) 'Implicit memory: A commentary', *Bulletin of the Psychonomic Society* 28: 373–80.

Roediger, H.L. and Blaxton, T.A. (1987) 'Effects of varying modality, surface features, and retention interval on priming in word fragment completion', *Memory and Cognition* 15: 379–88.

Roediger, H.L., Weldon, M.S. and Challis, B.H. (1989) 'Explaining dissociations between explicit and implicit measures of retention: A processing account', in H.L. Roediger and F.I.M. Craik (eds) *Varieties of Memory and Consciousness: Essays in Honor of Endel Tulving*, pp. 3–41, Hillsdale, New Jersey: Erlbaum.

Schacter, D.L. (1987) 'Implicit memory: History and current status', *Journal of Experimental Psychology: Learning, Memory and Cognition* 13: 501–18.

—— (1989) 'On the relation between memory and consciousness: Dissociable interactions and conscious experience', in H.L. Roediger and F.I.M. Craik (eds) *Varieties of Memory and Consciousness: Essays in Honor of Endel Tulving*, pp. 3–41, Hillsdale, New Jersey: Erlbaum.

—— (1992) 'Understanding implicit memory: A cognitive neuroscience aproach', *American Psychologist* 47: 559–69.

Schacter, D.L., Bowers, J. and Booker, J. (1989) 'Intention, awareness, and implicit memory: The retrieval intentionality criterion', in S. Lewandowsky, J.C. Dunn and K. Kirsner (eds) *Implicit Memory: Theoretical Issues*, pp. 47–65, Hillsdale, New Jersey: Erlbaum.

Schacter, D.L., Cooper, L.A. and Delaney, S.M. (1990) 'Implicit memory for unfamiliar objects depends on access to structural descriptions', *Journal of Experimental Psychology: General* 119: 5–24.

Schacter, D.L., Cooper, L.A., Tharan, M. and Rubens, A.B. (1991a) 'Preserved priming of novel objects in patients with memory disorders', *Journal of Cognitive Neuroscience* 3: 118–31.

Schacter, D.L., Cooper, L.A., Delaney, S.M., Peterson, M.A. and Tharan, M. (1991b) 'Implicit memory for possible and impossible objects: Constraints on the construction of structural descriptions', *Journal of Experimental Psychology: Learning, Memory and Cognition* 17: 3–19.

Schwartz, B.L. (1989) 'Effects of generation on indirect measures of memory', *Journal of Experimental Psychology: Learning, Memory and Cognition* 15: 1119–28.

Shiffrin, R.M. and Schneider, W. (1977) 'Controlled and automatic information processing: II. Perceptual learning, automatic attending, and a general theory', *Psychological Review* 84: 127–90.

Shimamura, A.P. (1986) 'Priming effects in amnesia: Evidence for a dissociable memory', *Quarterly Journal of Experimental Psychology* 38A: 619–44.

Simpson, G.B. and Burgess, C. (1985) 'Activation and selection processes in the recognition of ambiguous words', *Journal of Experimental Psychology: Human Performance and Perception* 11: 28–39.

Slamecka, N.J. and Graf, P. (1978) 'The generation effect: Delineation of a phenomenon', *Journal of Experimental Psychology: Human Learning and Memory* 4: 592–604.

Sloman, S.A., Hayman, C.A.G., Ohta, N., Law, J. and Tulving, E. (1988) 'Forgetting in primed fragment completion', *Journal of Experimental Psychology: Learning, Memory and Cognition* 14: 223–39.

Squire, L.R. (1986) 'Mechanisms of memory', *Science* 232: 1612–19.

—— (1987) *Memory and Brain*, New York: Oxford University Press.

Squire, L.R., Shimamura, A.P. and Graf, P. (1985) 'Independence of recognition memory and priming effects: A neuropsychological analysis', *Journal of Experimental Psychology: Learning, Memory and Cognition* 11: 37–44.

Sutherland, N.S. (1968) 'Outline of a theory of pattern recognition in animal and man', *Proceedings of the Royal Society, London* B 171: 297–317.

Tenpenny, P.L. and Shoben, E.J. (1992) 'Component processes and the utility of the conceptually-driven/data-driven distinction', *Journal of Experimental Psychology: Learning, Memory and Cognition* 18: 25–42.

Tipper, S.P. (1985) 'The negative priming effect: Inhibitory priming by ignored objects', *Quarterly Journal of Experimental Psychology* 37A: 571–90.

Tulving, E. and Schacter, D.L. (1990) 'Priming and human memory systems', *Science* 247: 301–6.

Tulving, E., Schacter, D.L. and Stark, H.A. (1982) 'Priming effects in word-fragment completion are independent of recognition memory', *Journal of Experimental Psychology: Learning, Memory and Cognition* 8: 336–42.

Warrington, E.K. and Weiskrantz, L. (1970) 'Amnesic syndrome: Consolidation or retrieval?', *Nature* 228: 628–30.

Weldon, M.S. (1991) 'Mechanisms underlying priming on perceptual tests', *Journal of Experimental Psychology: Learning, Memory and Cognition* 17: 526–41.

Weldon, M.S. and Roediger, H.L. (1987) 'Altering retrieval demands reverses the picture superiority effect', *Memory and Cognition* 15: 269–80.

Witherspoon, D. and Moscovitch, M. (1989) 'Stochastic independence between two implicit memory tests', *Journal of Experimental Psychology: Learning, Memory and Cognition* 15: 22–30.

6

THEORETICAL PRINCIPLES OF CONTEXT-DEPENDENT MEMORY

S.M. Smith

INTRODUCTION

When contextual cues affect remembering, memory is said to be context-dependent. Along with memory's dependence upon practice, similarity and temporal factors, contextual cueing represents one of the basic mechanisms used in theories of memory (e.g. Anderson and Bower 1973; Glenberg 1979; Hintzman 1988; Kintsch 1974; Raaijmakers and Shiffrin 1980; Thomson and Davies 1988). Context-dependent memory implies that when events are represented in memory, contextual information is stored along with memory targets; the context can therefore cue memories containing that contextual information.

There are many different operational definitions of context. 'Context' refers to that which surrounds a target, whether the surrounding is spatial, temporal or meaningful in nature. The present chapter will be limited to considerations of *incidental* context – that is, spatial and temporal contexts that are not obviously related to the targets on a memory test. The literature on meaningful contexts encompasses many research domains, including encoding specificity (e.g. Tulving and Thompson 1973), depth and spread of processing (e.g. Craik and Tulving 1975), and complex representational structures, such as scripts (e.g. Schank and Abelson 1977), schemata (e.g. Thorndyke 1977) or mental models (e.g. Glenberg *et al*. 1987). Although meaningful contexts may adhere to the same principles as those that apply to incidental contexts, they may also give rise to other meaning-driven phenomena that are beyond the scope of the present chapter.

This chapter will first briefly review empirical evidence related to incidental and context-dependent memory, including environmental context- and state-dependent memory. These two research domains have found parallel patterns of results, implying that there are similar mechanisms at work. The empirical overview will be followed by a discussion of a set of principles for theories that deal with context-dependent memory.

SUMMARY OF EMPIRICAL FINDINGS

Environmental context

The incidental background surrounding a target refers to its environmental context. Although some have challenged the reliability of environmental context-dependent memory findings (e.g. Eich 1985; Fernandez and Glenberg 1985), the preponderance of empirical results shows that environmental context effects are found reliably (for reviews see Smith 1988; Vela and Smith 1992). A meta-analytic review of studies of environmental context-dependent memory in humans found that, across all published studies, context manipulations have reliably affected memory (Vela and Smith 1992). Not all effect sizes, however, are equal; variations can be found as a function of the memory paradigm used, the type of input processing given to the targets, and the type of test used to assess memory. Evidence related to these factors will now be briefly reviewed, and their theoretical significance will be discussed later.

Paradigms

The most popular memory paradigm used to assess incidental context-dependent memory has been reinstatement (e.g. Godden and Baddeley 1975; Smith 1979, 1985a). Reinstatement paradigms typically arrange for memory testing to occur either in the context in which target events were experienced, or in another context. Evidence of contextual cueing, then, is the finding that events are remembered better when the original context is reinstated, presumably due to the cues provided by the context. Effect sizes in reinstatement studies are reliably greater than zero, relatively small, on the average, and depend upon other factors to be discussed.

An early context reinstatement study used rats as subjects (Carr 1917). Carr found that if a rat learned to run a maze that was oriented in a particular way towards the overhead room lights, performance was better if the lighting arrangement was reinstated, rather than

169

altered. Animal learning and memory studies of context effects now constitute a sizeable literature composed of highly reliable findings (Balsam and Tomie 1985).

Studies examining incidental contextual reinstatement effects on humans were reported by S. Smith and Guthrie (1927), in which verbal targets were used, and context was operationally defined as indoors v. outdoors, and presence v. absence of the odour of oil of wintergreen. As with the animal studies, people recalled more when the incidental environment was reinstated. Since the time of that report, many other incidental contextual manipulations have resulted in reinstatement effects, including under water (with scuba gear) v. on dry land (Godden and Baddeley 1975), with Beethoven v. jazz music playing (Smith 1985a), in a sensory deprivation flotation tank v. a lounge (Smith and Sinha 1985) and, most commonly, in one laboratory room v. another (e.g. Smith 1979; Smith *et al.* 1978; Smith *et al.* 1990).

Physical reinstatement of incidental environmental contexts is not always necessary to achieve contextual cueing effects. Subjects tested in an altered context who are instructed to imagine the learning context recall as much as those who are physically returned to the learning environment (Smith 1979, 1984). Imagined context reinstatement instructions have also proven to be effective recall aids in situations involving eyewitness memory (e.g. Malpass and Devine 1981). Such instructions constitute an important component of 'guided memory' methods, which have been shown to improve eyewitness memory in a number of studies (e.g. Fisher *et al.* 1984; Geiselman 1988). Theoretical implications of the findings that subjects can imaginally generate their own context cues will be considered later in this chapter.

The interference reduction paradigm (e.g. Bilodeau and Schlosberg 1951; Greenspoon and Ranyard 1957) uses a target list and an interfering list that are learned either in the same environments or in different environments (Table 6.1). When interference effects are reduced because the lists are learned in different environments, that is taken as evidence of context-dependent memory. If contextual cues are associated with only the target list rather than with both the target and interfering lists, then the contextual information used in recall should cue fewer interfering memories.

Incidental context effects have been more robust with interference reduction than with physical reinstatement paradigms (Smith 1988; Vela and Smith 1992). The most cogent explanation of this pattern

Table 6.1 Retroactive interference reduction paradigm

	Control group	Interference reduction
1. Original list learning	Context A	Context A
	.	.
	.	.
	.	.
2. Interpolated list learning	Context A	Context B
	.	.
	.	.
	.	.
3. Recall test for first list	Context A	Context A

relates to the idea expressed earlier that subjects can generate their own imagined context clues from memory. Bjork and Richardson-Klavehn (1989) suggested that subjects in the interference reduction group have no reason to mentally reinstate the interpolated list context, as it should not cue memory for the initial list, and it would be counterproductive because it would revive interfering memories. Those subjects in the control group cannot use context cues to differentiate the two learned lists, and therefore suffer from interference. In contrast, subjects in physical reinstatement studies can imaginally generate their own context cues if they are tested in an altered context. To the extent that subjects spontaneously use imagined context to cue memory in reinstatement paradigms, the observed differences between physically challenged v. reinstated contexts will be reduced.

Although relatively few studies using the multiple input context paradigm have been reported, it has proven a reliable method for observing context-dependent memory (Smith 1982, 1984, 1985b; Smith and Rothkopf 1984). In this paradigm a target set is studied repeatedly and tested with a free recall test. The study sessions are conducted either all within a single context or each in a different context. Recall is typically tested in a new unfamiliar context in all conditions. The usual result is that material is recalled better if the input contexts are varied rather than kept constant. This effect differs from the more common reinstatement findings because it examines context-dependence (and independence) as a function of input conditions, independent of retrieval conditions.

Type of test

The type of memory test given to the subject is influential in determining whether or not incidental context-dependent memory is found (Smith 1988; Smith *et al*. 1978; Vela and Smith 1992). The rule that appears to apply most generally among context-dependent memory studies will be referred to as the 'outshining' principle (Smith 1986, 1988; Vela and Smith 1992), which states that tests that provide non-contextual cues, or that encourage subjects to generate such cues from memory, are the *least* likely to find context-dependence. The outshining principle will be briefly discussed in relation to test type and type of input processing, in addition to theoretical implications of the principle.

Because memory tests cue subjects, they must provide the subject with memory cues of one type or another. Tests differ in terms of the cues they provide; cues can vary in terms of their number, strength of association with targets, specificity (number of targets associated with a cue), and a variety of other dimensions. Cues on a free recall test, for example, are few, weakly associated with targets and general (non-specific). Free recall instructions typically provide little, instructing subjects simply to recall items from a list in any order. In contrast, recognition tests provide many specific cues that are strongly associated with memory targets; the targets, themselves, are supplied on the test. Consistent with the outshining principle, contextual reinstatement effects are likely to occur on a free recall test, in which few non-contextual cues are provided (e.g. Godden and Baddeley 1975; Smith 1979, 1985a; Smith *et al*. 1978), but they are not likely to occur on a recognition test, when many strong cues are given (e.g. Godden and Baddeley 1980; Jacoby 1983; Smith *et al*. 1978).

The outshining principle also indicates that tests that encourage subjects to use non-contextual cues, even those generated imaginally from the subjects' own memories, are less likely to find effects of incidental contextual manipulations than tests that do not encourage the use of non-contextual cues. Traditional tests of memory, such as recall and recognition, are known as *direct* memory tests because they explicitly direct the subject to remember the target events in question (Richardson-Klavehn and Bjork 1988). In the course of intentionally trying to remember target events the subject may feel encouraged to use any cues that are provided or that can be generated from memory, including non-contextual cues. Therefore, direct memory tests may encourage the use of non-contextual cues, which would diminish findings of context-dependent memory.

Indirect memory tests, on the other hand, are tasks that do not direct the subject to the memories in question, but that are sensitive to memories nonetheless (Richardson-Klavehn and Bjork 1988). The most commonly reported indirect memory test is the word completion task, in which the subject sees a fragment or a stem of a word, and must complete the word by providing the remaining letters (e.g. Tulving *et al.* 1982). Results typically show that completion of word fragments is better for words recently presented than for words not recently studied (e.g. Tulving *et al.* 1982). Another indirect memory test is spelling of spoken homophones (e.g. BARE/BEAR, GROWN/ GROAN). If subjects study a set of homophones on a list, memory is indicated when subjects spell homophones consistent with the studied set, rather than giving alternate spellings (e.g. Jacoby and Wither-spoon 1981). A third indirect test is the general knowledge test. On this test subjects may be biased to give previously studied words as answers when they guess at general knowledge questions. Indirect memory tests focus subjects' attention on tasks other than memory for a studied list; thus, observed remembering is unintentional.

Because they do not encourage the use of cues for remembering event memories, indirect measures should be ideal for observing context-dependence. Although relatively few such studies have been reported, those reported have shown robust effects of context-dependence. Smith *et al.* (1990) found effects of context manipulations using a homophone spelling test, and Vela (1991) found effects on both fragment completion and general knowledge tests. These results are consistent with the outshining principle.

Associative processing at input

Vela and Smith's (1992) meta-analysis also found that incidental context effects are modulated by the type of input processing used when targets are learned. Specifically, they noted that in the reported literature context effects have been most likely to occur when learning instructions prevented associative processing among the targets, and least likely when associative input processing was encouraged. For example, Smith (1986) presented target words incidentally, on trials of a short-term memory (STM) task, a task that would discourage associative input processing. In that study context-dependence was observed even though a recognition memory test was used. In contrast, Fernandez and Glenberg (1985) had subjects construct sentences with target words in several experiments, thus requiring associative input processing, and failed to observe context-dependence even using a free recall test.

Although subjects can use many different sources of cues to aid memory, associative cues are especially helpful, particularly when words are used as memory targets. Because cues can be generated from memory even when they are not explicitly provided by the memory test, associative cues can be used as long as they have been established at input. Therefore, associative processing at input encourages the use of non-contextual cues at test, thus minimizing the effects of incidental context cues in accordance with the outshining principle.

Intrinsic context

Geiselman and Bjork (1980) distinguished between contextual information which is extrinsic to the memory targets that are under scrutiny, and that which is intrinsic to the targets. The incidental contextual cues referred to above represent extrinsic context cues because they are not actually part of the verbal memory targets used in those studies. An intrinsic context cue, in contrast, is an incidental characteristic of the target itself, such as the voice in which a target is spoken, or the type font or colour of a printed stimulus. For example, Dulsky (1935) manipulated the colour backgrounds of paired associates that were presented and tested on coloured cards, and found a context-dependent effect: memory was best when the colour backgrounds at input and test matched.

The voice contexts of word targets were manipulated along with rehearsal type (elaborative v. rote rehearsal) and rehearsal duration by Geiselman and Bjork (1980), who used a recognition test to assess memory. When subjects studied the words by using elaborative rehearsal, no effect of reinstating v. altering the speaker's voice at test was found. With rote rehearsal, however, voice context-dependence was observed, with the effect getting stronger for longer rehearsal durations. Geiselman and Bjork (1980) and Baddeley (1982) suggested that intrinsic context cues may affect recognition memory, in contrast to extrinsic context cues, which often do not appear to affect recognition (e.g. Godden and Baddeley 1980; Smith *et al.* 1978). Since the Geiselman and Bjork (1980) study, however, findings of recognition affected by extrinsic context have been reported (e.g.

Canas and Nelson 1986; Smith 1986; Smith and Vela, in press).

Another study of intrinsic context effects (Wright and Shea 1991) manipulated features of computer displays, examining the context-dependence of typing brief practised sequences. Subjects practised typing 3- and 4-key sequences which were cued by 3 or 4 corresponding digits displayed on a computer screen. Each of 3 sequences practised was always presented in a characteristic position on the screen (top, middle or bottom), in a particular colour (blue, red or yellow), with a specific shape outline around the digits on the screen, and with a particular accompanying tone. No mention was made of these incidental stimuli to the subjects. Wright and Shea found that for the more difficult 4-key sequences subjects were more prone to errors when context cues were suddenly switched or removed than when they were reinstated.

In general, it can be concluded that intrinsic context cues function in much the same way as extrinsic cues. Whether their effects are more reliable than those of extrinsic cues may depend upon other factors, such as how overloaded the cues are, whether they are over-shadowed at input, or outshone at test. These issues will be discussed in a later section.

State-dependent memory

When memory depends upon manipulations of internal states rather than external stimuli, it is said to be state-dependent. Internal states refer to drug-induced or pharmacological states and mood states. As with incidental environmental context effects, state-dependent memory studies show that reinstatement of learning conditions optimizes recall. Most state-dependent studies have used a reinstatement paradigm (see Eich 1980 and 1989 for reviews).

State-dependent memory results are often 'asymmetric', a term used to indicate a particular configuration of results when an experimental design uses two drug states at input and at test, referred to as 'drug' and 'placebo'. The two reinstated conditions are those with input and test both in the drug condition, or both in the placebo condition. The altered state conditions are those having input in a placebo state and test in a drug state, and those with input in drug and test in placebo states.

If the drug had no main effect on either learning or recall, then an input state by test state interaction would be symmetric; having input and test both in the drug state would be equally as beneficial to memory as having input and test both in the placebo condition. Both of the altered state conditions would also perform equally well, both at a lower level than the two reinstated conditions. An asymmetric result, on the other hand, would be a main effect of drug and a state-dependent interaction. For example, if alcohol impairs recall but shows a state-dependent effect, then the pattern of results is asymmetric (e.g. Eich 1989). The asymmetric result is particularly fascinating because a drug that typically impairs long-term memory (i.e. alcohol) can actually enhance memory if the target material was learned while in that drug state (e.g. Stillman et al. 1974).

Although state-dependent memory effects have at times been criticized as unreliable, Eich and others (Eich 1980, 1989; Eich and Metcalfe 1989) have shown that state-dependent effects depend upon the cues that are present at test, and that the effects require a reliable manipulation of internal states. When these factors are taken into account, reliable state-dependent effects are found.

When memory tests that provide good memory cues are used to assess state-dependent memory, the effects are small or non-existent, as is the case with environmental contextual cues. For example, recall of a categorized word list tested using marijuana-induced states was found to be state-dependent if a free recall test was used, but not if recall was cued with category cues (Eich et al. 1975). Furthermore, Eich (1980) showed that cued recall and recognition tests, which provide specific memory cues, were less likely than free recall tests to show state-dependent effects.

A second necessity that is critical for observing state-dependent memory effects is a reliable manipulation of internal states. For example, Eich (1980) concluded that drug state-dependent effects required effective doses of drugs, noting that studies whose drug treatments did not cause main effects on acquisition or retention usually did not observe state-dependence. Observations of mood-dependent memory may also depend upon the reliability of mood manipulations. Mood induction techniques that use hypnosis or thinking of affectively valenced memories may place too much reliance on the subject's willingness and ability to cooperate. One method that looks promising for reliably inducing mood states combines a continuous self-report procedure with listening to affectively valenced music (Eich and Metcalfe 1989). Studying and testing of targets are undertaken only after the subject's self-reports indicate a sufficient mood change.

Mood-dependent memory must be distinguished from mood-congruent memory (e.g. Blaney 1987). Mood congruence is the finding that emotionally laden stimuli are learned and remembered best when their affective valence matches the subject's mood. For example, in a depressed mood, a subject might learn and remember negatively valenced words, such as 'funeral' or 'sorrow', better than positively valenced words, such as 'funny' or 'carnival'. Although mood congruent effects resemble mood-dependent memory effects, they are not the same. Mood-dependence is a principle that relates study and test moods to each other, whereas mood congruence describes a relation between subjective moods and target stimuli.

THEORETICAL PRINCIPLES

A number of basic principles can be induced from the empirical studies reviewed above. Although these principles are intended to explain contextual dependence, they do not necessarily imply specific theoretical mechanisms. Principles such as cue overload, outshining or decontextualization can be implemented with different theoretical mechanisms in different theories. Any memory theory, however, that involves context-dependent memory should incorporate these basic principles.

The principles to be considered here will include cue-dependence, overshadowing, contextual fluctuation, cue overload, memory probe, outshining and decontextualization.

Cue-dependent memory

The principle of cue-dependent memory is simply that performance on memory tasks is influenced by associated memory cues. If contextual information is associated with target material, then contextual cues should stimulate memory for associated material.

There are many theoretical mechanisms that can explain context-dependent memory, and a few will be described here. These include activation of a set of information in memory, direct context-to-item associations, mediation by internal states, and activation of cognitive operations.

Activation of a search set

Shiffrin (1970) described retrieval as a probabilistic iterative process involving sampling-with-replacement from a delimited set of information in memory. The delimited set was referred to as a 'search set', or the set of information in memory that was to be deliberately searched. By keeping memory searches within this set, one's retrieval efforts could be more efficient than if all of memory were searched.

Smith *et al.* (1978) hypothesized that incidental environmental contexts may cue memory by helping to delimit such a search set. In terms of Shiffrin's (1970) memory search model, this might mean that only memories with contextual associations are included in the search set. This search set hypothesis is consistent with findings in both environmental context- and state-dependent studies that recall is more likely than recognition to be affected by context manipulations (e.g. Eich 1980; Godden and Baddeley 1975, 1980; Smith *et al.* 1978). Although retrieval is of fundamental importance in free recall, in which the subject must search memory to find targets, it is not as important a process in recognition memory tasks, in which targets are supplied by the experimental task. Thus, contextual delimitation of a search set would be less likely to affect recognition memory.

Context-to-item associations

The exact nature of context-to-item associations depends upon whether one conceives of contexts and items as unitary or multi-componential. A unitary context or components of a context can be associated with clusters of targets, individual targets or components of targets. There are many possible conceptions of contextual associations, but all involve direct associations of contextual information with target information. An example is SAM (e.g. Raaijmakers and Shiffrin 1980), in which each word in long-term store is associated to some varying degree with a representation of the context.

Theories that employ direct context-to-item associations would all appear to predict that item familiarity should be increased when input and text contexts match. For example, Kintsch (1974) described a matching process in which a cue, containing perceptual, contextual and semantic information, is matched with episodic memory codes. The greater the overlap of contextual elements in the cue and memory codes, the likelier it is that the match will be successful. This matching process, for example, is the basis of Kintsch's description of recognition memory judgements.

The evidence that incidental context affects performance on familiarity-based memory tasks is inconclusive. Recognition memory tasks have been found to be less sensitive than recall to incidental context manipulations. Several studies using incidental contexts have failed to show context-dependent recognition, even under the same conditions that produce context-dependent recall (e.g. Godden and Baddeley 1975, 1980; Smith *et al.* 1978). On the other hand, other studies *have* found incidental context-dependent recognition effects (e.g. Canas and Nelson 1986; Leight and Ellis 1981; Smith 1986; Smith and Vela, in press). Furthermore, indirect memory measures that furnish target items for subjects (thus limiting the need for retrieval) have been found to be sensitive to context-manipulations (e.g. Smith *et al.* 1990; Vela 1991). These results support the notion of direct context-to-item associations.

Mediation by internal states

Results of state-dependent memory studies show that memory is modulated by relations between internal states at input and at test. Eich (1989) has hypothesized that the mechanisms responsible for internal state-dependent memory are also the ones involved in external context-dependent memory. If configurations of external stimuli help cue internal states, then reinstatement of external contextual stimuli could reinstate the internal state that was present at input. Thus, observations of external context-dependent memory could be mediated by internal states.

Logically, one must have an internal representation of an input context if reinstatement of that context is to cue associated memories. An external context can therefore affect memory only by mediation of an internal representation of the context. Whether a representation of a context is a mood or some other form of internal state must depend upon one's definition of an internal state. The state-mediation hypothesis, however, implies that an internal *response* to an environmental context, not a representation of it, leads to reinstatement of memories. That internal response might be labelled an affect, a mood or some other type of state.

One implication of the state-mediation hypothesis is that there are stimuli that reliably induce the same mood. In support of this notion, Eich and Metcalfe (1989) have found that certain musical selections consistently induce the same mood across subjects. Another implication of the state-mediation hypothesis is that environmental contextual changes that result in context-dependent memory should also induce consistent internal states. In separate studies, music backgrounds have been used to observe context-dependent memory (Balch *et al.*

1992; Smith 1985a) and mood states (Eich and Metcalfe 1989). If a single study manipulated external contexts and measured internal states, it would be expected that internal states would be better predictors of memory performance than environmental contexts. At this time, such tests have not been conducted.

Activation of cognitive operations

Stillman *et al.* (1974) proposed a fascinating hypothesis in relation to state-dependent memory. Using the analogy of memory as a set of storage files, they proposed that, rather than conceiving of different internal states as separate file drawers, one could think of each state as using its own distinct filing system. In cognitive terms, different cognitive operations would be used for different classifying systems. At input a particular set of cognitive operations would be cued by the prevailing state, and those operations would be used to classify the studied material. At test, if the same operations were cued by a reinstatement of the input state, then the same classifying system could be effectively used to retrieve information. Altering the state at test would cue different cognitive operations, resulting in the use of an inappropriate classifying system for searching memory.

The notion of context as an activated set of cognitive operations was also discussed by Bower (1972), who elaborated ideas proposed by Estes (1955). Those ideas will be discussed briefly in a later section on contextual fluctuation.

Overshadowing

Not all information in the stimulus environment is necessarily encoded and stored in memory. A feature may not be stored when other more salient features are present in the environment because of a limited attentional capacity to encode and store features of stimuli.

Overshadowing and blocking are well-known phenomena in the domain of animal learning and cognition, both of which essentially show that a stimulus that can be learned when presented in isolation might not be learned when another stimulus is present. For example, a thirsty animal can be trained to suppress licking when a tone (Cue 1) is used as the conditioned stimulus, or trained with a light (Cue 2), but when both tone and light are used as a composite conditioned stimulus, the subject shows learning only for the tone (e.g. Matzel *et al.* 1985). This situation is depicted in Table 6.2, and is referred to as 'overshadowing'.

Table 6.2 Overshadowing

	Learning	*Test cue*	*Mean log latency (sec)*
Cue 2 Learning	Pair Cue 2 with target	Cue 2	2.0
Cue 1 and 2 (Composite) learning	Pair Cue 1 plus Cue 2 with target	Cue 1	2.3
		Cue 2	1.2 (overshadowing)

Note: Cue 1 is a strong cue, and Cue 2 is a weak cue. Sample data are from Matzel *et al.* (1985). Higher scores indicate better memory performance. Overshadowing is found: Cue 2 is ineffective if learned simultaneously with Cue 1 as part of a compound stimulus.

Overshadowing has usually been attributed to a failure in learning the weaker cue (Cue 2, the light). Although various mechanisms have been proposed for this storage failure, one that is relevant to the present topic is that the subject's limited attentional capacity becomes taken up by the more salient cue, preventing attention, and therefore learning, of the weaker cue (e.g. Mackintosh 1975).

Geiselman and Bjork (1980) gave essentially the same explanation for their findings that recognition memory was context-dependent following primary rehearsal, but not after secondary rehearsal at input. They proposed that, with secondary rehearsal, inter-item associations occupied the subject's attentional capacity, reducing the amount of attention that could be used to store contextual information. Primary rehearsal occupies far less attentional capacity, allowing more resources to be devoted to learning contextual cues. In terms of overshadowing, context-dependent memory was not observed following associative rehearsal because learning of the weaker context cue was diminished owing to attentional resource limitations. This learning-based explanation of why context effects are sometimes not observed contrasts with the outshining hypothesis, which focuses more on retrieval explanations. Outshining will be considered in a later section of this chapter.

Contextual fluctuation

William James' (1890) idea of the 'stream of consciousness' indicated that the thoughts with which one apprehends the world fluctuate over time, changing, while remaining related to what has gone before. Because of this fluctuation of consciousness, James also pointed out the idea that a thought cannot be re-experienced in exactly the same way twice, because the consciousness in which it appears has flowed and changed from the previous occasion.

Contextual fluctuation theory (e.g. Bower 1972; Estes 1955) can be considered an approach to the study of the stream of consciousness. The theory uses a statistical analysis of fluctuations in thinking, applying this analysis to the issue of how a stimulus is apprehended on different occasions. Estes (1955) noted that, in a given stimulus environment, only a subset of the stimulus elements are conditioned on any learning trial. For example, if the word 'MOUSE' were given as a to-be-learned target in a memory experiment, it could be encoded in several different ways, such as 'a small animal', a word that rhymes with 'house', a computer peripheral device or a noun beginning with the letter 'm'. Bower (1972) postulated that each target is encoded by an active encoding operator, and that the set of operators active at any given moment is smaller than the entire set of possible operators.

Bower (1972) defined context as the sum of external and inter-operative stimuli that accompany a target stimulus, placing particular emphasis on 'mental set', a product of the stream of consciousness. Furthermore, he stated that the active set of encoding operators was influenced by the prevailing context (this notion of context-dependence was previously referred to as 'activated cognitive opera-tions' [Stillman *et al.* 1974]). Bower formulated the 'contextual drift' hypothesis, which states that, in lieu of systematic changes in context, there will be a gradual fluctuation of external events as well as internal mental events that increases contextual changes over time. Therefore, the probability that the same encoding operators are active on two occasions decreases with greater time owing to greater contextual drift (Figure 6.1).

The contextual drift hypothesis represents an alternative to theories based on the passage of time. Because time passage correlates with contextual drift, according to this view, context-dependent phe-nomena may seem to be time-dependent. Systematic manipulation of contextual cues, however, supersedes temporal changes because the critical determinant of the active set of cognitive operators is context.

Mensink and Raaijmakers (1988, 1989) have formally incorpor-ated a temporally determined mechanism for contextual fluctuation in the SAM memory model proposed by Raaijmakers and Shiffrin (1980). Following from Estes (1955) and Bower (1972), they have proposed that fluctuation between the active and inactive sets of contextual elements is a stochastic time-dependent process. The model simulates and predicts several phenomena related to interference, such as spontaneous recovery and proactive interference.

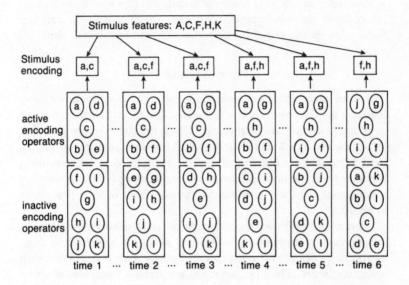

Figure 6.1 Fluctuation between the sets of active and inactive encoding operators yields cognitive contexts that differ more as more time passes.

Glenberg's (1979) component-levels theory took an important step beyond earlier formulations, of contextual fluctuation, because it noted that environmental fluctuation is not random in most memory experimental contexts; faster changing cues are likely to be more specific than slower changing cues. The fastest changing cues in a typical list-learning memory experiment are those that represent and distinguish the separate items studied on a target list. These are called *descriptive* components because they describe characteristics of a target item, such as its spelling, phonology and meaning. The next fastest changing components are called *structural* because they represent an item's associative or categorical structure. Several items, each with different descriptive components, may all belong to the same associative structure. The slowest changing components are *contextual*, because all of the items are studied within the same general context. Contextual components are the most general because essentially all of the target traces contain the same contextual information. Descriptive components are the most specific because no two items contain the same descriptive information. It will presently be shown how a cue's specificity determines the cue's strength; for the moment, however, it is most relevant to note that contextual, structural and descriptive information do not typically fluctuate in a completely random fashion, as characterized by earlier accounts of contextual 'drift'.

Cue overload

The more targets that are associated with a cue (i.e. the more overloaded it is), the less likely it is that a specified target will be generated in recall, given the cue in question. This is the cue overload principle (Watkins and Watkins 1970). Although cue overload was originally used to explain the build-up of proactive interference on short-term memory tests, the principle has considerable value for understanding a variety of cognitive phenomena, among them context-dependent memory.

Glenberg (1979) used the principle of cue overload to explain the differential effectiveness of descriptive, structural and context cues. Descriptive cues are the most specific because each is associated with a distinct target. Their cue strengths are greater than those of structural cues, which have more associated targets, and are thus more overloaded. Context cues are the most overloaded, being associated with all targets, and are therefore the weakest cues.

Poorer recall has been found for list learning that occurs all in a single context than when parts are learned in different contexts (Smith 1982, 1984; Smith and Rothkopf 1984). This supports the notion of cue overload in contextual cueing. The context cue in the single context condition is more overloaded than the cues in the multiple input context condition, and is therefore a weaker cue.

Memory probe

A memory probe is a theoretical mechanism that assembles information for searching memory. According to the principle of cue-dependence, information included in the memory probe elicits retrieval of memory traces that contain that information. Many theories use the device of a memory probe, including SAM (e.g. Raaijmakers and Shiffrin 1980), CHARM (J.M. Eich 1982) and MINERVA 2 (Hintzman 1986). For example, SAM is endowed with a short-term memory store in which cues are assembled and used to probe long-term store. Governed by a recovery rule, the probe samples information in memory that is then accessed and evaluated.

Similarly, MINERVA 2 uses a probe that activates information in long-term (secondary) memory. The information that is activated is referred to as the 'echo', which is placed in short-term (primary) memory. This echo has an intensity, which is used as an indication of familiarity, and a content, which refers to the set of information coded in the echo. The term 'echo' will be borrowed for the remainder of this chapter to refer not only to Hintzman's MINERVA 2 model, but more generically, to any model that uses the idea of a set of information that results from the process of probing long-term memory.

What information is included in a probe when memory is searched? There must be a system for determining the contents of the memory probe. For most models the information included in a probe consists primarily of representations of the cues provided by the memory test, as well as cues resulting from a previous probe of memory (e.g. Hintzman 1986; Metcalfe 1982). If no cues are formally provided, the SAM model begins probing memory with only a context cue until initial retrievals provide more cues to be included in subsequent probes.

Unfortunately, such probe composition systems do not adequately characterize the multiplicity of methods that subjects may use to search memory; one may recall a list from beginning to end, in alphabetical order, in terms of a story or link mnemonic, or in a variety of other ways. Critical to the issue of context-dependence is the finding that subjects can generate their own context cues from memory, although they may not do so spontaneously (Smith 1979). A subject is therefore able to voluntarily include a context cue that is not physically present in a memory probe.

It is proposed that both an expert system that generates cues for a given task and a default system are needed to create a policy for determining the contents of a memory probe. By default, a memory probe will include representations of provided cues, recently revived memories and ambient contextual information. Therefore, on an implicit memory test the incidental test context can be expected to affect memory because the subject is not motivated to include non-ambient contextual information in the memory probe (Smith *et al.* 1990). On an explicit test, however, if testing occurs in an altered context, an expert system can include relevant non-ambient contextual information in a memory probe owing to instructions or prior experience with such self-generated cues.

Outshining: Hidden context effects

The idea of outshining uses a psychophysical metaphor; a dim light, such as the light one sees from a star, is more difficult to detect when there is more background light, as compared with the same light when the surroundings are darker (Smith 1988). Although the outshining principle can be formulated as a mechanism that obeys psychophysical laws, it can be supported by several other mechanisms as well.

To determine whether or not a particular cue, such as a context cue, has been learned, one should test memory with the cue present v. absent. This assumes that subjects do not generate the cue from memory, as previously discussed. If memory is enhanced by providing the cue, this result is taken as evidence that the cue was learned. Would an absence of an effect indicate that a cue was not learned? Such could be the case, but there are alternative possibilities as well, even if the cue was successfully stored in memory. For example, there may be questions about the sensitivities of various memory tests for detecting the cues in question, and statistical power concerns. It may also be that learning was not detected because the subject used other cues to guide memory. Such a case, in which the learning of a cue is not detected because subjects use alternate cues, is referred to as outshining. Outshining (Table 6.3) differs from overshadowing (Table 6.2) in that outshining occurs not because of a learning failure, but rather because test cues prevent detection of the learned cue. Several theoretical mechanisms that could account for outshining will now be briefly described.

Subadditive cueing

When two (or more) cues are provided by the test or the experimenter, their combined effectiveness (relative to testing with neither cue provided) may be equal to the sum of their independent cue strengths (additivity), greater than the added strengths (configural or superadditivity), or less than the added strengths (subadditivity). Of interest here is the subadditive case, in which the combined effectiveness of two cues is less than the sum of the effectiveness of the two cues measured independently.

Table 6.3 Outshining

	Learning	Test cues	d'	
Same context; no strong cue	Pair Cue 1 plus Cue 2 with target	Cue 2	1.5	Context dependence; no outshining from strong cue at test
Different context; no strong cue	Pair Cue 1 plus Cue 2 with target	No cue	1.1	
Same context with strong cue	Pair Cue 1 plus Cue 2 with target	Cue 1 and Cue 2	1.8	No context dependence; outshining from strong cue at test
Different context with strong cue	Pair Cue 1 plus Cue 2 with target	Cue 1 alone	1.8	

Note: Cue 1 is a strong cue, and Cue 2 is a weak context clue. Sample data are from Smith and Vela (1986). Higher scores indicate better memory performance.

Subadditivity has been used to infer that cues contain redundant information; a second cue only benefits memory to the extent that it adds new information to a memory probe not provided by the first cue. For example, Tulving and Watkins (1975) proposed that memory traces consist of many components, each of which can be cued by related information in a memory probe. The power of each cue for evoking a memory refers to the cue's valence. If a combination of two cues produced as much memory cueing as the sum of the cue valences, the two stimuli would be considered to cue non-redundant components of the target trace. On the other hand, if components of the trace are cued by both stimuli, the cues would be said to contain redundant information.

For example, as illustrated in Figure 6.2, a memory trace representing the studied word 'CHAIR' might contain both phonological and semantic components. A memory probe containing the retrieval cue 'BEAR' might overlap with only the phonological component, whereas the cue 'STOOL' might coincide with only the semantic component. As such, the two cues would be said to be non-redundant, and memory cueing would be an additive function of the two cue valences. On the other hand, the cue 'BEAR' and the cue 'FARE' both coincide with a phonological component of the target trace; thus, a combination of the two cues might produce a cueing effect equal to less than the sum of the two cue valences.

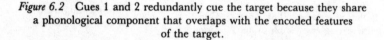

Encoded word	Cue 1	Cue 2 (redundant)	Cue 3 (non-redundant)
CHAIR	BEAR	FARE	STOOL

Phonological codes:	'ch' 'är'	'b' 'är'	'f' 'är'	's''t' 'ɒl'
Semantic codes:	4-legs for sitting	furry fierce	money fee	3-legs for sitting

Figure 6.2 Cues 1 and 2 redundantly cue the target because they share a phonological component that overlaps with the encoded features of the target.

A memory cueing technique called the reduction method (Tulving and Watkins 1975) consists of probing a memory trace with two different cues in succession to determine the overlap among cues with respect to a given memory trace. This is based on the idea that each cue may be associated with a set of the components of a target memory trace. If two cues are associated with completely redundant components of the target memory trace, then a composite of the two cues will provide no greater access to the target trace than would either cue individually. Only if the cues are completely non-redundant should a composite of the two give additive cueing effects.

Signal detection approach

A signal detection approach to outshining might use a monitoring system that detects the information activated when a memory probe addresses long-term memory (i.e. the echo). Adding relevant cues to the memory probe should increase the echo intensity by increasing the similarity between the probe and the material stored in memory. A system that monitors the echo's intensity should therefore be sensitive to the effects of adding memory cues to a test situation.

Figure 6.3 shows strength distributions for studied and non-studied items. The top distribution shows strengths for items cued by a weak cue (e.g. a context cue), and the middle distribution corresponds to memory strengths elicited by a strong cue (e.g. an associative cue).

Assuming that adding a cue to the probe shifts the stronger distribution a fixed amount (related to the cue's *strength*), the amount of the distribution that *surpasses* the memory criterion as a result of the cue is indicated by the shaded area. The shaded areas will be referred to as the *cueing effects* of the cues. Of particular relevance is the effect of the weak context cue (darker shading) when the strong cue is absent (top) v. present (bottom) in the probe. The same cue can be seen to have a much smaller effect when the strong cue is present as compared to the effect when the strong cue is missing. Thus, in this signal detection analysis, outshining is represented by the smaller effect that a weak context cue has when a strong cue is present.

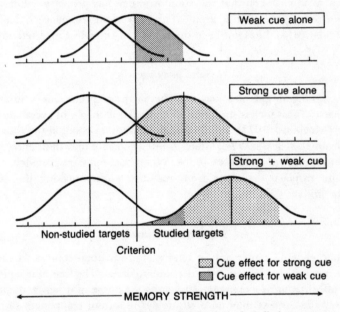

Figure 6.3 Adding a cue shifts the distribution of studied targets past the criterion.

It should be noted, however, that the same signal detection analysis predicts outshining (subadditivity) only when the strong cue exceeds a particular strength. If the cues are weak enough, their combined effects can be superadditive, just as can be demonstrated with psychophysical power functions. Of relevance to the present chapter, however, is that when the strong cue is strong enough, a signal detection analysis can explain findings in which contextual cueing effects are not detected owing to the presence of strong cues.

Submergence

Another hypothetical mechanism responsible for outshining will be referred to as 'submergence'. Submergence refers to cases in which a combination of cues in a probe alters or masks features of the cues that would otherwise overlap with information encoded in the target memory trace. This is suggested as the opposite of emergent or configural properties that might produce superadditive cueing effects. Submergence might occur when cues are processed differently at test than at input, such that the composite cue has properties different from those processed at input. The idea of submergence is highly speculative, and has not been the subject of empirical investigations.

Limited probe capacity

Outshining might also occur if the memory probe has a limited capacity. This idea is similar to the attentional theory of overshadowing (Macintosh 1975), except that the limitation is not at the time of learning but at test. The probe's limited capacity may limit encoding (or assembly) of a memory probe. When both cues are provided, one might displace the other from memory probe, making the cues subadditive.

Decontextualization

When evoking a memory no longer depends upon contextual cues, the memory can be said to be decontextualized. The first time a piece of information is experienced, such as the name of a new acquaintance, the context may be a relatively important component of the name's representation in memory. Alternately, a piece of information that is experienced in many contexts, such as a close friend's name, is more likely to be decontextualized. The difference between context-dependent knowledge is essentially the difference between episodic and semantic memories (Tulving 1972).

Hintzman's MINERVA 2 model of memory (e.g. 1986) provides a mechanism for decontextualization of items that are experienced multiple times. Each different experience of an item is represented as a separate memory trace. Although the contexts in which an item is experienced may vary, there must be some information in each trace that is consistent; otherwise the different memory traces would not be considered to represent the same item. When MINERVA 2 searches memory using a probe in which a target item is represented, the echo that is returned contains a summation of all memory traces in which the item is encoded. The content of that echo will reveal primarily the features common to all or most of the traces. Contextual information, however, may vary greatly among the traces summed in the echo. Thus, no one particular context is clearly specified in the echo, whereas one prototype represented by the common features of the target item is clearly delineated. Because memory of the prototype is not dependent upon any one context cue, the memory can be considered to be decontextualized.

Of course, if an item is consistently associated with a particular context, then even a large number of memory traces would be context-dependent, because that context would be as consistently represented in an echo as the other consistent features of an item. In effect, the context would appear to be a defining feature of the item, and the item would remain context-dependent. This pattern is supported by empirical evidence that shows that memory of target items repeated in the same context are more context-dependent than items repeated in different contexts (Glenberg 1979; Smith *et al.* 1978). Therefore, both theory and empirical evidence suggest that practice in varied contexts enhances decontextualization.

SUMMARY

Incidental background contexts, such as environmental settings, moods and drug states, have been found to reliably affect memory. Regardless of the physical test context, subjects can sometimes imaginally reinstate their input context. Therefore, tests that do not encourage the use of self-generated context cues, such as indirect tests and interference reduction paradigms, are most likely to find context effects. Overshadowing by more salient cues at input can prevent storage of context cues, thus diminishing context effects. Even when context cues are stored, context-dependent effects can be diminished by outshining, when non-contextual cues are used to probe memory. Therefore, tests that provide cues (e.g. recognition) are more likely than tests with few cues (e.g. free recall) to find context effects. The principles of contextual fluctuation, cue overload and decontextualization are also important theoretical principles.

ACKNOWLEDGEMENT

This work was supported by National Institute of Mental Health grant R01 MH4473001 awarded to Steven Smith.

REFERENCES

Anderson, J.R. and Bower, G.H. (1973) *Human Associative Memory*, Washington, DC: Winston.

Baddeley, A.D. (1982) 'Domains of recollection', *Psychological Review* 89: 708–29.

Balsam, P.D. and Tomie, A. (1985) *Context and Learning*, Hillsdale, New Jersey: Erlbaum.

Baltsch, W.R., Bowman, K. and Mohler, L.A. (1992) 'Music-dependent memory in immediate and delayed word recall', *Memory and Cognition* 20: 21–28.

Bilodeau, I.M. and Schlosberg, H. (1951) 'Similarity in stimulating conditions as a variable in retroactive inhibition', *Journal of Experimental Psychology* 41: 199–204.

Bjork, R.A. and Richardson-Klavehn, A. (1989) 'On the puzzling relationship between environmental context and human memory', in C. Izawa (ed.) *Current Issues in Cognitive Processes: The Tulane Floweree Symposium on Cognition*, pp. 313–44, Hillsdale, New Jersey: Erlbaum.

Blaney, P.H. (1987) 'Affect and memory: A review', *Psychological Bulletin* 99: 229–46.

Bower, G.H. (1972) 'Stimulus-sampling theory of encoding variability', in A.W. Melton and E. Martin (eds) *Coding Processes in Human Memory*, pp. 85–124, Washington, DC: Winston.

Canas, J.J. and Nelson, D.L. (1986) 'Recognition and environmental context: The effect of testing by phone', *Bulletin of the Psychonomic Society* 24: 407–9.

Carr, H.A. (1917) 'Maze studies with the white rat: I. Normal animals; II. Blind animals; III. Anosmic animals', *Journal of Animal Behavior* 7: 259–306.

Craik, F.I.M. and Tulving, E. (1975) 'Depth of processing and the retention of words in episodic memory', *Journal of Experimental Psychology: General* 104: 268–94.

Dulsky, S.G. (1935) 'The effect of a change of background on recall and relearning', *Journal of Experimental Psychology* 18: 725–40.

Eich, J.E. (1980) 'The cue-dependent nature of state-dependent retrieval', *Memory and Cognition* 8: 157–73.

—— (1985) 'Context, memory, and integrated item/context imagery', *Journal of Experimental Psychology: Learning, Memory and Cognition* 11: 764–70.

—— (1989) 'Theoretical issues in state-dependent memory', in H.L. Roediger and F.I.M. Craik (eds) *Varieties of Memory and Consciousness: Essays in Honor of Endel Tulving*, pp. 331–54, Hillsdale, New Jersey: Erlbaum.

Eich, J.E. and Metcalfe, J. (1989) 'Mood-dependent memory for internal versus external events', *Journal of Experimental Psychology: Learning, Memory and Cognition* 15: 443–55.

Eich, J.E., Weingartner, H., Stillman, R.C. and Gillin, J.C. (1975) 'State-dependent accessibility of retrieval cues in the retention of a categorized list', *Journal of Verbal Learning and Verbal Behavior* 14: 408–17.

Eich, J.M. (1982) 'A composite, holographic, associative recall model', *Psychological Review* 89: 627–61.

Estes, W.K. (1955) 'Statistical theory of spontaneous recovery and regression', *Psychological Review* 62: 145–54.

Fernandez, A. and Glenberg, A.M. (1985) 'Changing environmental context does not reliably affect memory', *Memory and Cognition* 13: 333–45.

Fisher, R.P., Geiselman, R.E., Holland, H.L. and MacKinnon, D.P. (1984) 'Hypnotic and cognitive interviews to enhance the memory of eyewitnesses to crime', *International Journal of Investigative and Forensic Hypnosis* 7: 28–31.

Geiselman, R.E. (1988) 'Improving eyewitness memory through mental reinstatement of context', in G.M. Davies and D.M. Thomson (eds) *Memory in Context: Context in Memory*, pp. 245–66, New York: Wiley.

Geiselman, R.E. and Bjork, R.A. (1980) 'Primary versus secondary rehearsal in imagined voices: Differential effects on recognition', *Cognitive Psychology* 12: 188–205.

Glenberg, A.M. (1979) 'Component-levels theory of the effects of spacing of repetitions on recall and recognition', *Memory and Cognition* 7: 95–112.

Glenberg, A.M., Meyer, M. and Lindem, K. (1987) 'Mental models contribute to foregrounding during text comprehension', *Journal of Memory and Language* 26: 69–83.

Godden, D.R. and Baddeley, A.D. (1975) 'Context-dependent memory in two natural environments: On land and under water', *British Journal of Psychology* 66: 325–32.

—— (1980) 'When does context influence recognition memory?', *British Journal of Psychology* 71: 99–104.

Greenspoon, J. and Ranyard, R. (1957) 'Stimulus conditions and retroactive inhibition', *Journal of Experimental Psychology* 53: 55–9.

Hintzman, D.L. (1986) ' "Schema abstraction" in a multiple-trace memory model', *Psychological Review* 93: 411–28.

—— (1988) 'Judgments of frequency and recognition memory in a multiple trace memory model', *Psychological Review* 95: 528–51.

Jacoby, L.L. (1983) 'Perceptual enhancement: Persistent effects of an experience', *Journal of Experimental Psychology: Learning, Memory and Cognition* 9: 21–38.

Jacoby, L.L. and Witherspoon, D. (1981) 'Remembering without awareness', *Canadian Journal of Psychology* 36: 300–24.

James, W. (1890) *The Principles of Psychology*, New York: Holt.

Kintsch, W. (1974) *The Representation of Meaning in Memory*, Hillsdale, New Jersey: Erlbaum.

Leight, K.A. and Ellis, H.C. (1981) 'Emotional mood states, strategies, and state-dependency in memory', *Journal of Verbal Learning and Verbal Behavior* 20: 251–66.

Macintosh, N.J. (1975) 'A theory of attention', *Psychological Review* 82: 276–98.

Malpass, R.S. and Devine, P.G. (1981) 'Guided memory in eyewitness identification', *Journal of Applied Psychology* 66: 343–50.

Matzel, L.D., Schachtman, T.R. and Miller, R.R. (1985) 'Recovery of an overshadowed association achieved by extinction of the overshadowing stimulus', *Learning and Motivation* 16: 398–412.

Mensink, G.J. and Raaijmakers, J.G.W. (1988) 'A model for interference and forgetting', *Psychological Review* 95: 434–55.

—— (1989) *Journal of Mathematical Psychology* 33: 172–86.

Raaijmakers, J.G.W. and Shiffrin, R.M. (1980) 'SAM: A theory of probabilistic search of associative memory', in G.H. Bower (ed.) *The Psychology of Learning and Motivation: Advances in Research and Theory*, vol. 14, New York: Academic Press.

Richardson-Klavehn, A. and Bjork, R.A. (1988) 'Measures of memory', *Annual Review of Psychology* 39: 475–543.

Schank, R.C. and Abelson, R.P. (1977) *Scripts, Plans, Goals and Understanding*, Hillsdale, New Jersey: Erlbaum.

Shiffrin, R.M. (1970) 'Memory search', in D.A. Norman (ed.) *Models of Human Memory*, pp. 375–447, New York: Academic Press.

Smith, S. and Guthrie, E.R. (1927) *General Psychology in Terms of Behavior*, New York: D. Appleton.

Smith, S.M. (1979) 'Remembering in and out of context', *Journal of Experimental Psychology: Learning and Memory* 5: 460–71.

—— (1982) 'Enhancement of recall using multiple environmental contexts during learning', *Memory and Cognition* 10: 405–12.

—— (1984) 'A comparison of two techniques for reducing context-dependent forgetting', *Memory and Cognition* 12, 477–82.

—— (1985a) 'Background music and context-dependent memory', *American Journal of Psychology* 98: 591–603.

—— (1985b) 'Effects of number of study environments and learning instructions on free recall clustering and accuracy', *Bulletin of the Psychonomic Society* 23: 440–2.

—— (1986) 'Environmental context-dependent recognition memory using a short-term memory task for input', *Memory and Cognition* 14: 347–54.

—— (1988) 'Environmental context-dependent memory', in G.M. Davies and D.M. Thomson (eds) *Memory in Context: Context in Memory*, pp. 13–33, New York: Wiley.

Smith, S.M. and Rothkopf, E.Z. (1984) 'Contextual enrichment and distribution of practice in the classroom', *Cognition and Instruction* 1: 341–58.

Smith, S.M. and Sinha, A.K. (1987) 'Effects of brief immersion in a flotation tank on memory and cognition', Texas A&M University CSCS Technical Report no. 004.

Smith, S.M. and Vela, E. (1986) 'Outshining: The relative effectiveness of cues', presented at the annual meeting of the Psychonomic Society, New Orleans.

—— (in press) 'Environmental context-dependent eyewitness recognition', *Applied Cognitive Psychology*.

Smith, S.M., Glenberg, A.M. and Bjork, R.A. (1978) 'Environmental context and human memory', *Memory and Cognition* 6: 342–53.

Smith, S.M., Heath, F.R. and Vela, E. (1990) 'Environmental context-dependent homophone spelling', *American Journal of Psychology* 103: 229–42.

Stillman, R.C., Weingartner, H., Wyatt, R.J., Gillin, J.C. and Eich, J.E. (1974) 'State-dependent (dissociative) effects of marijuana on human memory', *Archives of General Psychiatry* 31: 81–5.

Thomson, D.M. and Davies, G.M. (1988) 'Introduction', in G.M. Davies and D.M. Thomson (eds) *Memory in Context: Context in Memory*, pp. 1–10, New York: Wiley.

Thorndyke, P.W. (1977) 'Cognitive structures in comprehension and memory of narrative discourse', *Cognitive Psychology* 9: 77–110.

Tulving, E. (1972) 'Episodic and semantic memory', in E. Tulving and W. Donaldson (eds) *Organization of Memory*, New York: Academic Press.

Tulving, E. and Thomson, D.M. (1973) 'Encoding specificity and retrieval processes in episodic memory', *Psychological Review* 80: 352–73.

Tulving, E. and Watkins, M.J. (1974) 'Structure of memory traces', *Psychological Review* 82: 261–75.

Tulving, E., Schacter, D.L. and Stark, H.A. (1982) 'Priming effects in word fragment completion are independent of recognition memory', *Journal of Experimental Psychology: Learning, Memory and Cognition* 8: 336–42.

Vela, E. (1991) 'Environmental context-dependent memory: A cue competition interpretation', presented at the annual meeting of the Midwestern Psychological Association, Chicago.

Vela, E. and Smith, S.M. (1992) 'A meta-analytic review of studies of environmental context-dependent memory effects', unpublished manuscript.

Watkins, O.C. and Watkins, M.J. (1970) 'Buildup of proactive inhibition: A cue overload effect', *Journal of Experimental Psychology: Human Learning and Memory* 1: 442–53.

Wright, D.L. and Shea, C.H. (1991) 'Contextual dependencies in motor skills', *Memory and Cognition* 19: 361–70.

7

CONNECTIONISM AND MEMORY

A.F. Collins and D.C. Hay

CONNECTIONISM AS A FRAMEWORK FOR COGNITION

Connectionism is a style of explanation, a framework for thinking about cognition; it is not a particular topic in memory research in the same way as autobiographical memory, working memory or prospective memory are topics. Frameworks can be viewed as more abstract than a particular theory or model of a cognitive process (Slack 1987). What a framework does is to provide a set of ideas that can be used in constructing a wide range of more specific theories or models. Several other ideas commonly used in cognitive psychology can be seen as frameworks. One example of this is the schema and related variants such as scripts and frames (Bartlett 1932; Minsky 1975; Schank and Abelson 1977). In this chapter we try to show the qualities of the connectionism approach that might make it an appealing framework for constructing models of memory. Frameworks are not open to the same kind of direct empirical test as models, so whilst a particular finding might be of difficulty for connectionism, it is unlikely to be sufficient to discard the whole approach. However, the popularity of a particular framework is likely to be affected by the empirical successes and failures of the models to which it gives rise.

As we shall see, the connectionism framework has become increasingly popular and influential in recent models of cognition. For someone interested in memory as a topic, this prompts the questions 'Why has it become so popular?' and 'What does connectionism offer to the study of memory?'. Before we look at some examples of connectionism and its areas of appeal in some detail, a few general comments addressing the second of these questions may be helpful.

Much cognitive-style research into memory has been conducted as though learning were a separate topic. Of course, this is not to say that there were not notable exceptions to such a generalization (Anderson 1983 is a classic example). Nevertheless, work which explicitly addresses both areas has been the exception rather than the norm. No doubt there are many reasons for this strange separation of learning and memory including the behaviourist connotation that lingered for so long in the term 'learning'. Against this background, perhaps the single most appealing aspect of connectionist models is that they have the capacity to learn. Because of this capacity, learning can become a key aspect of understanding whatever cognitive process is under consideration, rather than it being something to be explained separately or not at all (see e.g. the Rumelhart and McClelland 1986 model described later in this chapter). The term 'learning' implies the acquisition of new skills, including apparently qualitative change in how inputs are processed, rather than just accumulation of information, and this accords with the ability of connectionist nets to treat the same input in different ways according to the history of the net. The whole thrust of this work is to wean models of cognition away from their rather static, steady-state nature. In connectionism, the inter-dependency of learning and memory is not a forced relationship, instead it seems to emerge as an inevitable symbiosis.

For many years, cognitive psychology has produced models of memory that have paid little attention to the workings of the brain. This has been explicitly defended by a number of leading authorities who have argued that cognitive models provide a level of description that can be abstracted from the neural substrate and so need not pay much heed to the properties of that substrate or describe how neuro-physiology constrains functional models (Mehler *et al.* 1984). Similar arguments were made earlier by philosophers (Putnam 1960, 1967, but see Putnam 1988). In line with these arguments, work in cognition and neurophysiology could go along largely in parellel: there were models of the functional components of memory and there were physiological and biochemical models of memory with few atempts to integrate the two. Such parallelism was bolstered by at least two beliefs: translating functional models into neural models is essentially just a question of implementation, and the functional level captures insights that are unavailable (or at least very blurred) at the neural level. We have no quarrel with the idea that functional descriptions capture important insights which may be best – or even only – des-cribed at the functional level. However, it is all too easy to be sniffy about implementation: why shouldn't investigating how a functional model might be realized at the neural level offer fresh insights? For example, Allport (1985) points out that the standard functional components models have difficulty explaining why lesions to the brain most often result in a decline in performance on some cognitive tasks rather than the complete loss of a function. What is required to explain such degradation in performance, Allport argues, is a set of ideas about how neural and functional levels relate to one another. Connectionism provides such a set of ideas, and as we shall see later in this chapter, an appealing account of why, when the brain is damaged, one should frequently encounter degradation in performance rather than complete loss.

We believe that connectionism is a framework that facilitates communication between the functional and neural models and, in doing so, may itself provide insights that neither of these types of model would have done on their own. This hope for novel insights provides a criterion against which connectionism will be judged. However, connectionism does not only offer the potential for intervening between cognitive models and neural models of memory, it also provides techniques that are being used in a wide range of disciplines such as engineering, computing and biology. Thus it offers the promise of a kind of unified language for communicating with other disciplines and all the potential advantages that this brings.

Some of the more specific properties of the connectionist approach that should appeal to those interested in memory tend to go by rather technical names: distributed representations, graceful degradation, informational holism and constraint satisfaction. We believe that many of these are key issues for models of memory, but to explore them all here would be too great a diversion and would presume too much knowledge of what connectionism is. However, one example may help and we will return to it in more detail later in the chapter. Clark (1989) uses the term 'informational holism' to refer to the idea that one's idea about something is influenced by one's ideas about myriad other things, that is, there is a strong interdependence between ideas in memory. In this way, for example, the same word can take on different shades of meaning according to the context in which it is used. Likewise, the aspect of an episode that is remembered may vary according to the circumstances at recall or, more subtly, what is most salient about a memory may change over time depending on information elsewhere in the system. As we shall see, such interdependence and shades of 'meaning' are inevitable in connectionist frameworks where representations are extensively interlinked so that the activation in a particular part of the system is nearly always going to be affected by activations in other parts of the system and such influences are going to vary subtly from one occasion to another: on this view remembering an episode may never be quite the same twice. The idea that subtle differences in memory are an inevitable product of the framework adopted seems intuitively appealing and promises the kind of flexibility that seems such a feature of human memory. Of course, as with any such advantage, this flexibility also brings with it problems of how to recognize a memory as in some sense the same in different contexts (see Clark 1989; Fodor and Pylyshyn 1988; Rumelhart and McClelland 1986; Smolensky 1988 for various positions on this issue in relation to connectionism).

One final feature of the connectionist approach is that it requires models to be constructed and run on computers – hardly something unique to connectionism, but something which has considerable general advantages. There is not room to review these advantages in detail here particularly as they are themselves the subject of debate (see Boden 1977, 1988; Gardner 1985; Johnson-Laird 1990; Miller 1981; Pylyshyn 1984 for introductions). However, at the very least, implementing a model on a computer frequently forces the researcher to be specific and often requires them to confront issues which 'paper and pencil' models can fudge or simply avoid. This can not only highlight deficiencies in one's current theorizing but also throw into stronger relief the kinds of – often unmerited – assumptions that are implicit in an account. Getting a computer model to perform a particular task can actually be seen as a form of test of the model in the same way that constructing a prototype might be an important test of an engineering design. Modelling does not mean that the need for theory or other empirical work is removed nor, as we shall see, that models should not be constrained by empirical findings. Modelling does bring its own problems but, in the end, these may prove a price worth paying.

In sum, we argue that connectionism has much to offer the study of memory, but we do not argue that it can replace all existing frameworks, remove the need for empirical work, or be regarded as overcoming all of the problems already identified for computer models of cognition. Currently, connectionism is popular and, we believe, important, but we feel it is a new weapon in the armoury of those interested in memory and the question is where and when to apply it, not whether or not it should take over as a new paradigm for modellers of cognition.

RECOGNIZING A CONNECTIONIST MODEL

Much as the legendary phoenix rose from the ashes, the recent fashion for connectionist accounts in psychology represents the re-emergence of an area that had lain smouldering, if not dormant, since the middle part of this century. Connectionism is not new, nor are the views of mental processes with which it is consistent. However, acknowledging the current enthusiasm for such models begs the question of what is a connectionist model. We will begin with a description of the very general characteristics of connectionist models before going on to describe an example of such a model. We use the later example to illustrate some important properties of connectionist models which, we argue, are also important features of memory. We hope that readers familiar with such models will bear with us while we describe some of the general features before discussing their relevance to the study of memory in more depth.

Connectionism is an approach to modelling cognitive processes that considers the nature of the brain to be important and, in this sense, it is often referred to as *brain style computation* (Rumelhart 1989). This assumes that how the brain works and how it is organized are of relevance when constructing models of cognition and cannot simply be ignored. One example of a biological constraint considered to be important in connectionism is the slowness of communication via neurons – at least when compared to silicon chips. The slowness of nerve cells suggests that most cognitive processes must involve many operations occurring in parallel if they are to be completed in a reasonable time.

Detailed work on connectionist models frequently requires a good grasp of mathematics and linear algebra in particular. However, we hope to avoid use of equations as far as possible in this chapter. Nevertheless, some readers may find some points are easier to appreciate if they can see a concrete example of the operations being described. In Boxes 1 and 2 we provide a very brief set of such examples in the hope that they provide clarification and amplification for some, while they can be ignored by those less sure of their maths.

The concern with the nature of the brain is manifest in the two major components of any connectionist model: *units* and *connections* between units. At any one time, a unit has a level of activation. This level of activation can change over time and takes on a number of values according to particular restrictions being used in the model. The activation levels are expressed as numbers. So, for example, units may only be allowed to have an activation level of 0 or $+1$, whereas in other models they might have an activation value anywhere between 0 and $+1$. One can see how these units are rather like neurons and this is part of the reason for connectionist models frequently being described as 'neurally inspired'. Later in the chapter we will discuss what it means for concepts, memories, percepts, and so on to be expressed in the seemingly odd form of sets of activation levels. For now, we would just ask why such a scheme should be viewed as any more implausible as a way of expressing a model of memory than those which represent memories and processes using phrases like 'isa bird' or 'the schema for exams was selected'.

A unit in a network receives activation from other units via connections. Different amounts of activation can be transmitted and this depends upon two factors: the amount of activation going into the connection and the strength of the connection. The idea of different strengths of connection is at the heart of connectionism. Suppose that there are two units: u_i and u_j with a single link between them. If u_i is switched on, then it will pass activation to u_j. If the connection is a strong one, then the effect of u_i on the activation of u_j will be large; if the link is a weak one, then the effect of u_i on u_j will be smaller. Frequently, links in a network are bidirectional, that is, activation can pass from unit u_i to u_j and vice versa. Usually when talking about connectionist models, the strength of a connection is referred to as its *weight*. Weights can be positive or negative, and this is taken to be analogous to the excitatory or inhibitory effects that neurons can have on one another's activity levels (see Box 1 for examples). However, the activation level of a unit is not necessarily equal to the sum of all the inputs to it; rather, the final level of activation is some function of all those inputs and this function is referred to as the *activation rule* (see Box 1). Likewise, the output of a unit is not necessarily the same as its level of activation, but is a function of it computed by the *output function* (see Box 1).

The pattern of connections between units in a net and the weights of those connections constitutes the knowledge in the system (this is a rather abstract point and will become clearer when we consider an example of a model). A crucial point about weights is that they can be changed and so the knowledge in the system can be altered by experience. What this means is that the effect of one unit upon another need not be constant, but is sensitive to the patterns of activity encountered by the net. In some circumstances this alteration is a form of learning (though in others it can be a form of forgetting) and this capacity to

Box 1 The basics of a connectionist network

The basic model

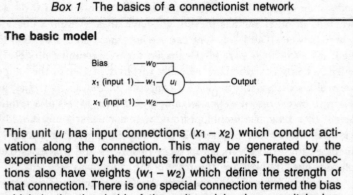

This unit u_i has input connections ($x_1 - x_2$) which conduct activation along the connection. This may be generated by the experimenter or by the outputs from other units. These connections also have weights ($w_1 - w_2$) which define the strength of that connection. There is one special connection termed the bias which is the threshold of the unit and is always switched or clamped on. The unit itself can be thought of as being responsible for the computational processes involved in determining whether or not to fire (i.e. send activation along the output connection). This is a simple two step process:

- calculate the overall input to the unit
- compare this to some threshold function

In the simplest system, calculation of the overall input is done by determining the *weighted sum* of the inputs. This *activation rule* is given by

$$\text{overall activation} = \sum_{i=1}^{n} w_i x_i$$

and is equivalent to

overall activation $= w_0 . x_0 + w_1 . x_1 + w_2 . x_2$

The first pair of values corresponds to the threshold of the unit which is usually denoted by θ. These have fixed values, $w_0 = -\theta$ and $x_0 = 1$. When multiplied these give a value of $-\theta$.

If the other input weights in the example were: $w_1 = 0.8$, $w_2 = 0.5$, and the values of the inputs were: $x_1 = 1$, $x_2 = 0$ then:

$$\begin{aligned}
\textbf{overall activation} &= -\theta + (0.8 \times 1) + (0.5 \times 0) \\
&= -\theta + 0.8 + 0.0 \\
&= 0.8 - \theta \\
&= \textbf{netinput} - \textbf{bias}
\end{aligned}$$

Thus, if the weighted sum from the inputs $x_1 - x_2$ (i.e. 0.8) exceeds the threshold value of θ, then the overall input is positive and the unit would send output activation along its output connection (in this case activation equal to 1). If the overall value is negative, then the weighted values of the inputs have failed to exceed the threshold and the unit remains dormant.

Box 1   Continued

Inputs and outputs

In the preceding example both the input and output activations took on discrete values. However, this need not be the case and these activations may take on one of a range of values (e.g. 0.0 to 1.0 or −1.0 to +1.0). In addition, the relationship between input and output activations need not be straightforward. In the previous example the output from the unit is either 1 or 0 depending on the level of the input activations. This may be expressed as.

Output activation = f_h (netinput − θ)

where f_h is the step function (known in mathematical parlance as the Heaviside function). This translates the comparison between the netinput and the threshold to either 1 or 0 depending on whether the comparison is positive or negative as shown below:

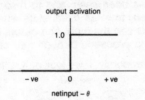

output activation

1.0

− ve   0   + ve

netinput − θ

More complex ouput functions are needed to meet certain constraints when networks are used to simulate learning. One of the most commonly used activation rules employs the *logistic function* to translate the comparison between the netinput and the threshold, and to produce a range of output activation levels. The mathematical equation of this function is:

$$\text{Output activation} = \frac{1}{1 + e^{\dfrac{-(\text{netinput} - \theta)}{T}}}$$

Graphically, this takes the form of a curve which depends on the value of T (known as the temperature). If the value of T is low, the curve looks similar to the step function and yields few output values, whereas high T values flatten the curve to produce a much wider range of output activations:

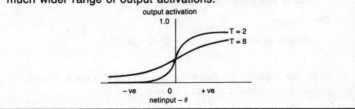

output activation

1.0

T = 2
T = 8

− ve   0   + ve

netinput − θ

Box 2   An example of learning in a connectionist network

One of the simplest methods of learning utilized in networks is a variant of that proposed in 1949 by Donald Hebb and is therefore referred to as *Hebbian Learning*. In our example we will consider a two-layer network with input units which receive external activation and an output layer.

The task of this

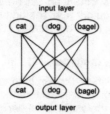

network is to respond cat when a cat has been *seen*, to respond dog when a dog has been *seen*, and to respond bagel when a bagel has been *seen*, from an initial state where the weights of the connections between the input and output units are random. This form of learning proceeds through four steps:

1. Set the weights randomly. If we look only at the cat output unit, we get:

2. Let the network *see* an object (i.e. present the input layer with an input activation pattern). If the object seen is a cat, then the input pattern would be $+1$, -1, -1. In this example, if an object is present, this is indicated by presenting the input unit with $+1$ and if an object is absent, presenting -1.
3. Get a *response* from the network (i.e. examine the output activations from the output layer). The function used here is that introduced in Box 1, namely:

    Output activation = (netinput)

    This yields:

    Output activation $= (0.05 - 0.01 - 0.02)$
    $= \underline{(0.02)}$

4. Alter the weights to reinforce correct identifications and to penalize *misidentifications*. The rule used is:

Box 2 Continued

$$W_{(new)} = W_{(old)} + \Delta W_{(input - output)}$$

where

$W_{(new)}$, $W_{(old)}$ are the new and the old weights of a connection between an input and output unit and where

$$\Delta W_{(input - output)} = \mathbf{lrate} \times a_{(input)} \times a_{(output)}$$

In this:

$\Delta W_{(input - output)}$ is the change in the weight between an input and an output unit;
lrate is the learning rate fixed by the experimenter and which allows faster or slower rates of learning;
$a_{(input)}$ is the activation of the input unit;
$a_{(output)}$ the activation of the output unit.

This has the effect of *strengthening* the weight on a connection if both the input and output activations have the *same sign* and of *weakening* the weight if the activations have *different* signs.

If the experimenter had fixed the learning rate to be 0.1 in our example, this would lead to the following weight changes:
For the connection between the cat input and output units

$$\Delta W_{(cat - cat)} = 0.01 \times + 1 \times 0.05 = \mathbf{\underline{0.005}}.$$

giving

$$W_{(cat\ new)} = 0.05 + 0.005 = \mathbf{\underline{0.055}}$$

for the dog input–cat output connection

$$\Delta W_{(dog - cat)} = 0.01 \times - 1 \times 0.01 = \mathbf{- 0.001}.$$

giving

$$W_{(cat\ new)} = 0.01 - 0.001 = \mathbf{\underline{0.009}}$$

for bagel input–cat output connection

$$\Delta W_{(dog - cat)} = 0.01 \times - 1 \times 0.02 = \mathbf{- 0.002}$$

giving

$$W_{(cat\ new)} = 0.02 - 0.002 = \mathbf{\underline{0.018}}$$

The same process occurs for all the connections between the input and the other output units and the network.

The network is repeatedly exposed to objects and training progresses in this fashion for any number of exposures the experimenter desires. At any time the network may be tested and the accuracy of the output assessed. There are many other forms of learning architectures employed, but the common feature of all of these is that learning is achieved by modifying the weights between units.

learn is another highly attractive view of connectionist models. In Box 2 we give a simple example of how the effect of one unit upon another changes with time according to a Hebbian learning rule.

We have now described the two basic components of connectionist models: units and connections. However, the operation of a network of units involves several other important factors. The structure of the model is one such factor and consists of the set of units used and the ways in which they are connected. Decisions about structure are made by the researcher in the light of theory and existing empirical research. The units may each represent a particular component such as a word, an attribute of a person, or a concept. Thus, for example, unit u_v might represent the word 'pig' so that when it is highly activated, this word is said to be accessed. Where there is such a simple one-to-one correspondence between units and the concepts used in our theories, the models are called *localist models*. However, in many connectionist models a particular unit does not stand for a particular concept and it is the pattern of activity over the set of units that corresponds to the main unit of analysis. These are known as *distributed models* (a common, though not synonymous, term for connectionism is parallel distributed processing or PDP). As it is the pattern of activity across units that is important, the same set of units can be used to represent a number of concepts. For example, the set of units in Figure 7.1 could represent the visual appearance of a particular 'cat' when in the state shown in Figure 7.1(a), whereas the state shown in Figure 7.1(b) could represent the visual appearance of a particular 'dog'. Obviously, these example patterns are highly simplified and in reality a large number of units would be needed to represent the visual appearance of different cats and dogs. The ability to represent a number of things over the same set of units is known as *superpositioning*. It should also be pointed out that the activity of an individual unit in a distributed system need not correspond to any particular feature of the concept – at least not as traditionally conceived (e.g. 'has four legs'). This leads to the activity of units in distributed systems being said to represent *microfeatures* (Rumelhart 1989) or *subsymbols* (Smolensky 1988).

The units in a net perform different functions. Broadly speaking, units can be classified as *input units, hidden units* or *output units*. What this means is that, for the cognitive system being considered, activity over the input units represents the information being presented to that system. Likewise, the activity over the output units is the system's response to the input – its answer if you like. In some models, input units are connected directly to output units. However, for technical reasons which we need not explore here (see Rumelhart

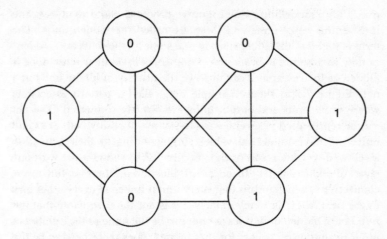

(a) Set of units showing connections between units and levels of activation of each unit. This pattern of activation could represent the visual appearance of a particular cat

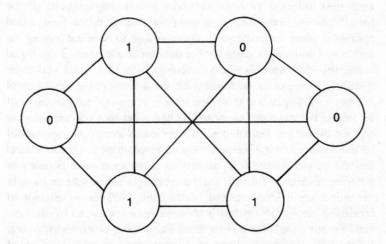

(b) Same set of units as (a) but with a different pattern of activation. This pattern could represent the visual appearance of a particular dog

Figure 7.1 A set of units showing how different patterns of activation and so different representations can be distributed across the same set of units.

207

et al. 1986), modelling many cognitive processes requires at least one intervening set of units and these are called the hidden units. The term is slightly misleading since in one sense all the units are 'hidden' as they correspond to brain processes, whilst in another sense none is hidden as the researcher can observe the activity of all the units in a net. Figure 7.2(a) shows a simple net, called a pattern associator, where input units and output units are directly connected. The net can be represented in several ways (note that in reality both links and units will have numerical values corresponding to their activation levels and weights respectively). Figure 7.2(b) shows a net with one layer of hidden units. In each net illustrated, there is full inter-connectivity, which means that every unit is linked to every other unit in the next layer; in many models this is not the case. Note that the number of hidden units does not have to be the same as the number of input or output units nor, for that matter, does there need to be the same number of input and output units.

Perhaps the most important and interesting aspect of connectionist models is the ability to learn. As has already been mentioned, this is achieved by modifying the weights in the network. Exactly how weights are modified becomes a very technical area and there are numerous different methods with new ones being invented all the time. However, a number of general points can be made. First, a distinction is often drawn between *supervised* and *unsupervised learning*. In supervised learning a pattern of activation is allocated to the input units; this then spreads via connections to hidden units and from them to the output units. Eventually, the activity of the output units reaches a stable pattern: this is the system's 'answer' for that particular input. For example, suppose one had a net that was supposed to convert the written form of a word to its sound form. The input could be the activity levels of certain units corresponding to certain letters, and the output could be the activity levels of units corresponding to different phonemes (in fact, such a scheme is too simple and would not work; see Seidenberg and McClelland 1989 for an attempt to tackle this issue). The system's output can be compared to what the ideal output should have been, the ideal answer being coded over a set of *teacher units*. So, in the present example the pattern of activity of the teacher units defines the correct pronunciation of the written word. Comparing the activity of the output units with this gives an indication of where the two patterns differ. This information can then be used to adjust the weights in the net in a way that makes those particular discrepancies less likely to occur next time that input pattern is

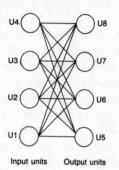

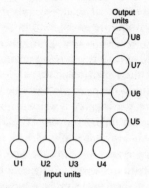

(a)   Input units   Output units

(where U1 represents unit 1, etc.)

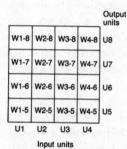

(where W1-5 represents the
weight of the connection running
(b)   from unit 1 to unit 5)

(a)   Three ways of representing a simple network of
two sets of units: input units and output units
(fully interconnected)

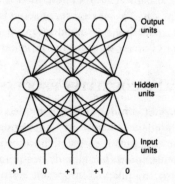

(b)   A simple network with input units, hidden units
and output units with full interconnectivity
between layers of units and an input pattern of
+1 0 +1 0 +1 being presented

Figure 7.2   Two simple networks of units (one without hidden units and
one with them).

presented to the net. The methods of adjusting weights in this way makes use of learning algorithms and two examples of such algorithms are given in Box 2.

Supervised learning as described above approximates to a real-world situation where a person is provided with input and can compare their own response with what the correct response should be. Pursuing the example described above, it would be a situation where the reader is given a written word and can compare their pronunciation with the correct one. Clearly many learning activities take place in this way. Equally clearly, however, much of our learning is unsupervised – we do not have the correct response against which to compare our own. Connectionist nets can learn without supervision where they are simply exposed to a series of input patterns and attempts to identify regularities in them, and many have advocated the need to develop this kind of model to explain the flexibility of many of our abilities (Grossberg 1987). However, as yet, unsupervised learning has not been applied widely to cognitive issues and the procedures become highly technical (see Carpenter and Grossberg 1991; Grossberg 1987; Kohonen 1984; Rumelhart and Zipser 1985 for examples).

In this brief introduction to connectionism we have tried to avoid too much use of mathematical equations. However, it should be apparent that the way in which such models operate is governed in many places by equations and the maths involved can get very technical indeed. Readers of this chapter who wish to pursue the basics in more detail but who do not feel ready or able to cope with detailed maths are recommended to consult sources described in the section on further reading (see pp. 230–2). Having spent some time on the basics, it is now worth considering how connectionism has already been applied to a number of issues in cognition in general.

CONNECTIONIST MODELS AND COGNITIVE PROCESSES

Connectionist models have been used to produce working models of a number of cognitive processes, and the purpose of this section is briefly to introduce some of these as a means of highlighting where some of the potential of connectionist models has already begun to be realized. In Table 7.1 we list some examples of important research where a connectionist model has been applied to some issues in cognition. This list is not meant to be comprehensive, but gives an idea of the types of issues tackled to date.

As can be judged from Table 7.1, it is probably fair to say that so far connectionism has had more impact on the modelling of 'lower' cognitive processes, such as speech perception, than in modelling the 'higher' cognitive processes, such as problem solving and reasoning. In part this may reflect what connectionism is and is not 'good at'. This is further compounded by the current tractability of these different research areas and the level of detail of the existing theory and empirical findings. The most pessimistic scenario is that connectionism is inherently unsuitable to tackling some of the problems of high-level cognition (see Barsalou 1993, for an excellent review of some of these limitations). However, one of the intriguing things about memory as a research area is that it manages to span much of the range from 'lower' to 'higher' cognitive processes. At one extreme there is concern with the idea of very short-term storage of sensory information, whilst at the other there is concern with huge and complex knowledge bases such as those involved in what is commonly referred to as semantic memory. It may be that how well connectionism copes with the different areas of memory research will reflect its applicability in modelling cognition in general. In the next section we present an influential connectionist model that was explicitly aimed at a set of issues in memory. We then use that as a springboard to discuss what connectionism offers to those interested in memory as cognitive process.

AN EXAMPLE OF A CONNECTIONIST MODEL

In this section we discuss in some detail one of the connectionist models designed with issues of memory as its main impetus. In trying to understand human memory, a central issue has been how memories for specific experiences and memories for general events coexist. For example, suppose one has been attending meetings of a particular committee on a regular basis for some time: while we may be able to remember a specific example of a meeting (the one where X and Y traded insults) we are also likely to be able to make general observations on what such meetings are like, who tends to make what kind of contributions, and so on (Linton 1978, 1982). McClelland and Rumelhart (1985) provide an example of a connectionist model which attempts to tackle the relationship between memory for individual instances and the apparent ability to make generalizations and to form general representations. Despite its simplicity, the model also

Table 7.1 Examples of connectionist models of cognitive processes

Authors	Topic
Bullock and Grossberg 1988	Models passive and active arm movements, reproduces many of the effects from the extensive literature on this aspect of human movement. For example, the model replicates Fitts' Law (a successful quantitative account of how movement time, distance moved and width of target are systematically related), which can be applied to movements such as those in dart throwing.
Burgess and Hitch, in press	Develops a model of the articulatory loop in working memory. The model makes some of the kinds of recall errors found in previous research on people and incorporates mechanisms for serial order and sensitivity to temporal context.
Burton, Bruce and Johnston 1990	Develops McClelland (1981) and shows how a localist model of face recognition can provide an implementation of earlier box-and-arrow models of the same process (Hay and Young 1982; Bruce and Young 1986). The implementation is able to mimic findings such as semantic priming effects.
Cohen, Dunbar and McClelland 1990	A distributed model that demonstrates the well-known Stroop effect. The authors argue that the way in which the model is implemented to reproduce the effect suggests a change in our views about the nature of automaticity in cognitive processes.
Dell 1986, 1988	Develops a connectionist model of speech production which not only reproduces some of the kinds of speech errors made by people but also makes predictions about factors affecting such errors. Dell shows that these predictions are supported when analysing the characteristics of naturally occurring and experimentally induced speech errors.
Farah and McClelland 1991	A model of semantic memory that attempts to implement the distinction between visual and functional knowledge. By lesioning the model, the authors show how damaging these different forms of knowledge can have differential effects on knowledge of living versus non-living things. The specific processing assumptions of the model have much in common with the cats–dogs–bagels model (McClelland and Rumelhart 1985).
Gluck and Bower 1988	A model that learns to diagnose diseases in hypothetical patients on the basis of symptom patterns. The model shows the same errors and biases in judgement as people given the same information. For a critique see Shanks (1990) and for a defence see Gluck and Bower (1990).

Authors	Topic
Hinton and Shallice 1991	Shows how by damaging a net designed to read words one can reproduce errors found in acquired dyslexia. Specifically, it can reproduce the semantic errors of deep dyslexics (such as reading yacht as 'boat'), something which previous models had had great difficulty explaining.
Linsker 1986a, b, c	A series of papers which give a connectionist account of how the visual cortex and some of its different functional cells might develop. The author describes how spatial-opponent and orientation-selective cells develop. The models use an unsupervised learning procedure. For an easier introduction see Quinlan (1991).
McClelland and Elman 1986	Describes a connectionist model of speech perception called TRACE which can reproduce many of the characteristics of speech perception, such as the ability to use lexical information to identify word boundaries and categorical perception of phonemes. For a detailed critique see Massaro (1988) and for a reply see McClelland (1991).
McClelland and Kawamoto 1986	A distributed model of sentence processing that learns such things as how to select the appropriate meaning of an ambiguous word (e.g. 'bat'), given information about linguistic context and how to represent verbs. See also Mikkullainen and Dyer (1991).
McClelland and Rumelhart 1981; Rumelhart and McClelland 1982	Describes a localist model for recognizing single words. The model reproduces several findings such as the word superiority effect (where letters in words are more likely to be correctly identified than letters in non-words). It also makes novel predictions about factors processing efficiency of different types of letter strings. For a critique see Quinlan (1991).
McClelland and Rumelhart 1985	A distributed model of memory that attempts to account for how general and specific memories can coexist. The model shows how prototypes can be learned from exposure to exemplars. It reproduces several general but important features of human memory, such as the ability to retrieve information from partial cues. For more detail see the present chapter and for a critique see Quinlan (1991).

(continued overleaf)

Authors	Topic
Rumelhart and McClelland 1986	A distributed model of memory that learns how to produce the correct past tense of English verbs from the present tense. As it learns, the model shows patterns of errors that are similar to those of children as they learn English. For a critique see Pinker and Prince (1988) and for developments see Plunkett and Marchman (1991).
Seidenberg and McClelland 1989	A connectionist model that learns to translate the written form of a word into its spoken form. The model simulates things like the regularity effect (where the sound forms of regular words are accessed more quickly than irregular ones) and differences in performance according to whether the task is lexical decision or naming. For a critique see Besner *et al.* (1990).
Tesauro and Sejnowski 1989	Describes a model that learns to play backgammon to an intermediate-advanced level after being trained on game positions evaluated by an expert. The high level nature of task raises new problems for implementing and training connectionist nets.

exhibits a number of links between connectionism and other connectionism and other central questions for those interested in memory.

In their attempts to construct a distributed model of memory that can represent both general and specific information, McClelland and Rumelhart (1985) constructed a model which attempted to learn the prototypical form of three kinds of objects: cats, dogs and bagels (a type of bread roll). Learning occurred by exposing the net to patterns of activity that were meant to represent individual instances of cats, dogs and bagels. Each instance consisted of information on the name of the thing encountered ('cat', 'dog' or 'bagel') and on the visual appearance. The kind of real-life situation to which the model might approximate is that of a young child who in his or her everyday wanderings keeps encountering objects which differ in their visual appearance, but which adults, in their all knowing way, insist on calling a 'cat', a 'dog' or a 'bagel'. Supervised learning or not, the world is a confusing place. In such situations there are two types of input to the system: a visual pattern which varies and an associated name which is fixed by someone who already knows the links between the visual pattern and its category name.

The structure of McClelland and Rumelhart's model is fairly

simple. There is a set of twenty-four units which form a module. Within this module, all the units are connected to all other units. In this particular model there is no distinction between input and output units and there are no hidden units (see Figure 7.3 for a schematic representation of the model). A particular unit, therefore, receives external input, fixed by the researcher and supposed to correspond to some form of processed sensory input, and internal inputs which come from all the other units in the module. The activity over units 1 to 8 is designated as representing name information and in the present example this name information represents the generic terms 'cat', 'dog' or 'bagel'. Activity over units 9 to 24 represents a visual pattern which is a variant of the prototypical visual form of each type of animal. Individual units can take on any activation value between -1 and $+1$. Weights between units can also take on negative or positive values.

It is assumed that activation takes time to spread. That is, upon presentation of a new input pattern, units do not immediately take on their final values. Instead, these have to be computed over a number of cycles; this way of slicing processing up into a series of discrete cycles is the way in which connectionist models attempt to represent the passing of time. In the cats–dogs–bagels model, the activation of a particular unit is a function of the external inputs and the internal inputs. Such inputs are determined by a number of factors: the activity of other units in the module, the weights on the connections between units, and an equation that determines how the sum of inputs relates to change in the particular units activation. There are also global parameters that lead to decay of activation in units and in the strength of links so that if there is no input to the system for some time, both the activations of units and the weights of links decrease. The effect of these decay functions is to mitigate the influence of more recent inputs to the system so that they do not swamp the effects of all previous inputs.

In response to a particular external input, the activations of units in the module will eventually reach a stable state after a number of cycles. Once this state is reached, a learning algorithm is invoked to alter the weights of the connections. Without going into detail, the aim of this algorithm – the delta rule – is to adjust weights so as to minimize the discrepancy between external and internal inputs to the units. Consider the case for a particular unit, j, where the activation from the external sources is greater than that from the internal sources. What the delta rule does in effect is to increase the weight of all links to the

Units 1–8 encode
name of the concept

Units 9–24 encode
visual appearance

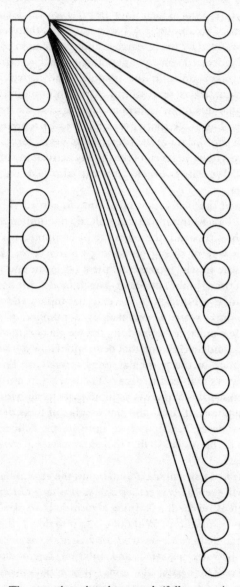

Figure 7.3 The cats–dogs–bagels network (full connections for just one
unit is shown for simplicity).

unit j where those links connect j to a unit that had a positive activation, and to decrease the strengths of links where the connecting units had a negative activation. If in most instances of a cat both units i and j are positively activated, the weight of the link between them also becomes more positive in a proportional way. If in most instances of a cat unit c is off while unit j is on, then the weight from c to j is reduced. These changes ensure that next time the net is presented with the same pattern of external input, the net's resulting pattern of activity is closer to the required pattern. The overall aim of the delta rule is to find a set of weights that allows there to be zero discrepancy between the external and internal inputs for all units and for all patterns. In many situations the delta rule has severe limitations when trying to achieve this aim (see Rumelhart *et al.* 1986a and Stone 1986 for technical discussions), but it does suffice in the current model.

In one simulation using the cats–dogs–bagels model, McClelland and Rumelhart trained the model on three sets of patterns corresponding to cats, dogs and bagels. Take the set of patterns for cats. On each learning trial, the input to the module would consist of a distortion of a prototypical visual pattern for a cat. This corresponds roughly to the real-life experiences of a young child encountering a number of slightly different cats: none of the cats is identical to the prototype (assuming such a prototype can be constructed), but each is more or less similar to it. The visual prototype for cat was represented by a 16-unit pattern (for more on how such patterns are thought to correspond to psychological concepts, see the next section):

$$+ + + - - + - - - + + - + - + -$$

A random distortion of this pattern, where the probability of the activation value of any one unit being reversed was .2, might look like:

$$+ - + - - - + - + - + + - - - + -$$

This particular visual pattern was accompanied by a similar distortion of the category name 'cat' which was represented over a further eight units:

$$+ - - + - + + +$$

McClelland and Rumelhart presented the module with 50 such patterns where each pattern was a distortion of the prototype for cat. In a similar fashion a further 50 learning trials were constructed for dog and 50 for bagel.

Once the learning phase was completed, McClelland and Rumelhart were finally in a position to see how the model behaved and whether it reflected any known characteristics of human memory. The most obvious achievement of the model was that it was able to extract three separate prototypes without ever being exposed to them. This was ascertained both by looking at the patterns of weights and by the strength of response of the module when presented with the prototype as input. In the latter case, the activation was greater than that to any other individual pattern (for similar data obtained in work with people see Posner *et al.* 1967; Posner and Keele 1968). Not only had the net captured regularities in inputs without the use of explicit rules, but it had also used the same set of units and connection weights to represent three different categories of information. As McClelland and Rumelhart remark, the importance of this success lies in the fact that the 'programmer' has not had to decide in advance which net to assign an instance to. Such an advantage is a little illusory, however, as of course there is an assumption that instances of cats, dogs and bagels somehow find their way to the same net, and unless one assumes that all such categories share the same net, the problem is simply pushed back. Another strength of the model is that given partial input, e.g. a visual pattern corresponding to a cat, it correctly retrieves the remaining information, in this case the appropriate category name (though the retrieval is not a perfect reproduction).

The cats–dogs–bagels model can do more than simply extract prototypes because it reflects patterns inherent in the inputs to which it is exposed. Consequently, on a training regime where there were repeated exemplars which were variations on the prototype for cat, at test the model was able both to extract the prototype *and* to retrieve the specific exemplars. This is an important observation as, in effect, it is claiming that a distributed model can represent specific and general information simultaneously in the same net. The ability to do this offers a reconciliation between models that rely on exemplars only and models that make use of prototypical style abstractions. McClelland and Rumelhart develop this theme by showing how the model can mimic repetition priming effects (that is, where having encountered a stimulus at time 1, responding to it when encountered again at time 2 is speeded up), effects of degree of similarity between primes and targets, and sensitivity of the system to the precise relationship between the specific exemplars and a prototype. While the model as described here does have considerable weaknesses, for a relatively small-scale and simple implementation its achievements are considerable and give some indication of the promise of connectionist models as a way of enhancing our understanding of memory. We will now discuss some of the more general advantages of such models.

CONNECTIONISM AND ISSUES IN MEMORY

Mental states as patterns of activity

McClelland and Rumelhart (1985) point out that the cats–dogs–bagels model reflects three key concepts in memory: mental states are patterns of activation, memories are traces and the retrieval of memories is the restoration of previous patterns of activity. In a connectionist account, mental states are different patterns of excitation over sets of units. In simulations such as the cats–dogs–bagels example the situation is sufficiently simplified for identical states to be reached many times. In everyday life, however, this is less likely: one sees the same dog from slightly different views, in different contexts and with differing prior mental states (consider a scenario where one had been bitten by a dog just the previous day). How such complexity will impinge on the activity of the module of units dealing with cats–dogs–bagels is an enormous question, but it raises the possibility that identical states of activity are the exception rather than the norm. Pushing this idea a little further, one can see that when viewed in this way the essence of connectionist systems as a form of memory is their sensitivity to context. Flexibility and context dependence fall out of connectionist models: context produces slight differences in activity patterns and the corresponding memory may be subtly different on different occasions (though, of course, these need not be so for the phenomenological experience). As Clark (1989) points out, the sensitivity of the models helps avoid the problems of the programmer having to anticipate contexts when constructing the system.

Not everyone sees the sensitivity of connectionist models to context as advantageous. Sterelny (1990) points out that variation is the enemy of the idea of concepts; if every time one encounters a cat it has to be qualified by the context in which it occurs ('cat as pet', 'cat as predator', 'cat as independent'), in what way does it make sense to think of there being a separable concept called 'cat' at all? He argues that it does not make sense to talk of a general concept 'cat' as being represented within a net if that concept can only be identified in the presence of other activity (context). These are not new worries, but they are persistent ones and we return to them later in the chapter.

Rumelhart and McClelland acknowledge that a key task for cognitive processes is to extract constancies despite variation in context. For them the problem of stimulus equivalence is the key: how is it that 'An A is an A is an A, no matter where it appears on the retina' (1986: 113)? This dilemma has similarities to the problem of the co-existence of general and specific memories, that is, how is it possible to reconcile claims for stimulus equivalence with claims for contextual dependence? Within the cognitive approach, connectionist models may hold out the best hope for such a reconciliation in that both equivalence and context sensitivity can emerge from such models.

Some readers may be troubled by the proposal that sets of activation levels, simply matrices of ones and zeros in some models, could ever correspond to 'meaningful' psychological concepts such as 'percepts' or 'words'. Although this raises a host of issues, we will confine ourselves to just a few remarks on why we do not feel this is a problem for connectionism. One argument is that the language used to describe processes, such as perception or memory retrieval, will contain concepts and terms which are not part of everyday language or even the everyday language of a psychologist. But this is surely not something new and has occurred many times in areas such as psycholinguistics, and the challenge is to see how, if at all, new terms map on to older ones. Sometimes, existing psychological concepts will *not* readily map on to the structure of connectionist models. For example, there is already some dispute about whether or not connectionist models of word recognition and pronunciation really need to incorporate anything that corresponds to the concept of a word (Besner *et al.* 1989; Seidenberg and McClelland 1989). Designing connectionist models may challenge both the need for and the adequacy of accepted psychological concepts, as we shall see later when we discuss the storage–retrieval distinction that is made in many theories of memory. The debate spreads even wider into considerations of whether descriptions of processes at the level of units in a connectionist model really give a more complete understanding of cognitive processes (see Smolensky 1988).

Sets of activation levels may seem a greatly impoverished framework for understanding cognition, and one which begs the serious question of how such activations do or do not correspond to the experience of having a particular memory or of understanding a particular word. Much of this difficulty may arise from the words 'experience' and 'understand' rather than from a scheme where concepts and memories are units with activation levels, and if this is so, connectionist models are simply inheriting the failings of other cognitive models, though perhaps in a more obvious way. For example, when one produces models of memory where the representations and processes are labelled by words, as in 'isa canary' or 'memory for last Thursday' or 'the schema for walks in the country is accessed', in what sense do these accounts explain what it is to 'experience' or 'understand' such concepts? Schemes for representation that are couched in words and rules may seem less weird and wonderful than matrices of zeros and ones, but it is doubtful that, as models, the latter are any less deficient as explanations of experience (though, of course, they may be worse as a medium for conveying some ideas about experience). Where the difference may lie is in the relation between the language we use to describe a model and its actual properties: in more traditional models the relationship is fairly transparent, whereas for connectionist models our everyday language may give only an approximate description (this leads into a philosophical nest of vipers; for those brave enough see Churchland and Sejnowski 1989 and Horgan and Woodward 1985 for differing views).

Memory traces

The second of Rumelhart and McClelland's key concepts is the idea that there is some form of trace of activity that is a memory and that in connectionist models the trace is encoded through a change in the strengths of connections between units. In a distributed representation, a number of traces can be represented over the same set of units and connections, and so superimposed on one another as in the cats–dogs–bagels model. While the pattern of activity is seen as the key in creating a trace, there is also the possibility that the location of the units that form the trace is important; it may be that the same pattern of activity over a different module of units would not correspond to the concept 'cat' (though how location as such could lead to a different mental state is a difficult question).

Memory as restoration of activation states

A feature of connectionist models is that memory traces can be activated according to content. As an example, imagine that John and Grace attend a party where they meet Bob who is a manager in a

221

local firm called TEG which manufactures electrical goods. His partner is a woman, Sue, who turns out to be John and Grace son's doctor and who cannot be at the party because she is on duty. The three people chat a while and discover that they have some common interests: eating out, jazz and good wine. At one point, Bob reveals that his greatest ambition is to play the trumpet like Miles Davis. Conversation flows and the evening passes well and they part agreeing that all four should meet up sometime soon. A few days later the phone rings at John and Grace's home, Grace answers it and the caller introduces himself: 'Hi, it's Bob – alias Miles Davis.' Immediately and apparently effortlessly, Grace is able to recall other details of the party encounter. This is an example of content addressable memory where information is retrieved from memory, not by some form of directed serial search (for example, of all the 'Bobs' that one knows) but the pattern recognition and completion. That is, the system has achieved some kind of recognition of the incoming pattern of activation as matching part of a previous pattern and this has been sufficient to reactivate other parts of the pattern; the incoming pattern for Bob together with Miles Davis has reinstated a pattern of activation including knowledge of events at the party.[1] A similar set of ideas has been developed in the encoding specificity principle (Tulving and Osler 1968; Tulving 1983). Encoding specificity assumes that a cue will only be successful in retrieving a memory if that cue was itself encoded as part of the trace (akin to part-whole retrieval). Retrieval itself is a matching process which involves direct access to information in the trace: that is, a cue will result in the retrieval of a memory if, and only if, information contained in that cue forms part of the memory trace concerned. A content addressable memory also means that one can get to the same piece of information from many directions, not all of which are easily specified in advance. For example, Bob may have introduced himself as 'It's Bob from TEG' and recall may have been just as rapid and easy. In the cats–dogs–bagels model, content addressability is illustrated by the ability of the model to reinstate correctly the activation pattern for the visual appearance of a dog given just the name as input pattern (and vice versa).

One of the fundamental characteristics of memory that is frequently referred to is its reconstructive nature (Bartlett 1932). That is, our recall of events is frequently not literal; rather, we construct memories of past events that contain inferences and these inferences may be indistinguishable from 'real' happenings. For example, one might assume that the host must have been at the party even though one did not actually see or speak to him. When remembering the party, the belief that he was there may be just as strong a part of one's memory as remembering the presence of someone to whom one did speak. The point of this is that in a connectionist model one of the general characteristics of such models – pattern completion – is also at the root of the reconstructive nature of remembering: inferencing becomes a form of pattern completion. What kind of information is incorporated into memories as a result of inferences, and how those inferences are or are not distinguished from other information, remains a major research area (for examples see Johnson and Raye 1981; Kolodner 1984; Loftus 1979; Neisser 1981; Schank 1982; Schank and Abelson 1977).

As Hinton *et al.* (1986) point out, in a distributed system there is no fundamental distinction between a genuine memory and a plausible inference. However, in everyday life we frequently *can* tell the difference between memories for events that happened and events that were imagined or planned but not executed (Johnson and Raye 1981). Johnson and Raye offer a number of principles that frequently allow one to distinguish between real events, such as locking the back door, and intentions, such as only planning to lock the door. For example, they argue that actual events are more intimately tied to when and where they occur. Implementing such disctinctions in a connectionist model would not seem to be beyond the scope of the framework, but the more general issue of how the system 'decides' which pattern of activity is and is not a 'real' memory remains problematic. A similar problem is that in everyday life we are able to distinguish inferences as just that and these can be marked in conversation ('Now you ask, I don't actually remember seeing him, I had just assumed he was at his own party'). The question becomes how on some occasions one recognizes something as an inference, whilst on others it simply becomes another, equally 'real', component of memory for an event.

Cross-talk, capture and analogy

Cross-talk occurs when, in an attempt to activate a particular memory trace, similarity to another trace may well lead to the alternative trace being reinstated rather than the 'intended' trace: one remembers the wrong thing. The phenomenon of 'cross-talk' is endemic in any reasonably large distributed system where a number of similar patterns have been learned. For example, if a pattern of activity over a set of units is shared by two concepts or memories, then on some occasions this may lead to the incorrect pattern being reinstated. The resulting errors resemble the kinds of errors encountered both in our everyday lives and in experimental work (McClelland 1986). Taken to extremes, such cross-talk might make a connectionist model so error prone that it is a poor model of the internal processes of human memory.

Reason and Mycielska (1982) describe a category of slips of action which exhibit capture. One example they give is of a woman who goes upstairs to her bedroom with the intention of changing out of her jeans into a dress but undresses completely instead. William James (1890) quoted similar stories of people whose actions became 'captured' by the environment in which they found themselves and so deviated from the original intentions. In these cases one plan for action is captured by a different plan at the point where the two are similar. Capture errors would be expected to emerge from distributed models of memory where a net for a planned action overlapped in parts with a net for a very familiar sequence; the activation of the less familiar plan might well trigger the more familiar and so more strongly weighted or consolidated action sequence (consolidation refers to a process invoked by McClelland and Rumelhart [1986] in their attempt to supply ideas of distributed memory to amnesia). Reintroducing the notions of context and the sensitivity of modules to the state of other modules might also contribute to explaining the occurrence of capture errors. As with cross-talk, no special set of requirements need be invoked to explain the existence of capture errors; indeed, they would seem to result from essentially the same mechanism.

Analogy is traditionally dealt with as a topic in 'thinking' rather than in memory. However, as should be apparent by now, such divisions are hard to maintain and this is especially so within connectionism. The essence of analogical thinking is the capacity to interpret one entity or event in terms of another. This requires a system which is able to pick out similarities on a host of possible dimensions (such as form and function). In a connectionist account of analogy, the extent to which two traces share subpatterns of activity will have some effect on the probability that one may trigger activation of the other – just as in cross-talk and capture. The idea is that the two traces may then be seen as having overlap on some dimension, one is reminiscent of the other, and so an analogy can be drawn between the two. On this basis, it would seem that in a connectionist scheme one cannot avoid analogies and it would not be surprising if such analogies were novel or non-obvious, so giving rise to creative insight. Clark (1989) describes how Kekule related having dreamt of a snake biting its own tail and from this suddenly realized how that shape could be analogous to the structure of benzene and so the benzene ring was discovered. Such an example may stretch the claim of connectionism as a basis for analogy rather far, but Clark's point is that the deceptive simplicity of connectionist accounts may offer profound insight into the mechanisms underlying the flexibility and creativity of our everyday thinking – the extreme represented by the example of Kekule relies on the mechanisms of everyday, 'commonsense' thought.

What remains as a huge problem for theories of analogy within a connectionist framework is accounting for how and why certain aspects of some object or event are seen as similar whilst others are not, for sorting out what is important from what is irrelevant. For the memory researcher interested in connectionism, it may not be possible to specify in advance what a net may extract as similarities and differences in input. This is an uneasy position for a researcher, and what it highlights is that in connectionist research the input on which a net is trained can be as important as the structure of the model. However, this section has highlighted how the same process, overlap in activation patterns, may underpin a wide diversity of observable behaviours.

In a connectionist model the mechanisms that underlie cross-talk are also the mechanisms that underpin many of the most impressive properties of connectionist models: analogical thinking and the ability to generalize (Clark 1989). The implication of this is that as connectionist models become larger and more complex, limiting cross-talk whilst allowing generalization and analogy will be a delicate balance. It is also clear that at some level cross-talk, capture and analogy are not identical phenomena, and it remains to be seen where their similarity ends and whether differences are best characterized at the cognitive level.

Graceful degradation

The rather elegant term 'graceful degradation' refers to a set of properties where the performance of a system does not crash completely in unfavourable circumstances but becomes slowly worse. Those ageing footballers amongst us know the feeling (though 'graceful' does seem to stretch a point). The kind of unfavourable circumstances may be external, such as the presence of distorted, partial or noisy inputs, or they may be of internal origin, such as loss of brain cells or disruption of neurotransmission by drugs. In his influential work on vision, Marr (1982) argued that resistance to unfavourable circumstances must be central to any plausible theory of a cognitive process. His central reason for this was the claim that input from the environment is typically imperfect: one rarely gets the same, perfect and full view of an object. In remembering it is almost certainly the same, with cues from the environment rarely being identical on different occasions and often not corresponding to the 'best possible cue' to a memory. The ability of memory processes to function adequately in unfavourable circumstances becomes a necessary property. Connectionist models show graceful degradation in most circumstances and so possess this property. For example, in the cats–dogs–bagels model, retrieval of the 'cat' pattern would still be largely correct even if the input was incomplete. Likewise, in a large distributed net, loss of some units need not lead to the complete loss of concepts in which they played a part. In his discussion of how connectionist models can be applied to aphasia, Allport (1985) points out that the differential loss of different classes of word, the increased confusability between similar items, and the partial retrieval of word meanings often found in aphasics are all compatible with damage to distributed representations. The interdependence of modules of units in a connectionist net suggests that one should rarely get loss of one function without *any* impairment to apparently separate functions, and this seems to be the case (Shallice 1988).

Biological plausibility

Here the term 'biological plausibility' does not refer to the idea of connectionist models as 'neurally inspired', something which is often claimed, but to the idea that the characteristics of connectionist models are just those that a biologically minded theorist might expect in a system attempting to make sense of its environment. This angle of approach encourages appreciation of the problems posed by the environment in which we live as a starting point for theorizing about cognition. Clark (1989) provides an excellent example of this approach. Starting from a slightly different point – the observation of human behaviour itself – Norman (1986) reviews a list of the kinds of components which he and some of his colleagues had previously argued to be essential when explaining human cognition (Norman and Bobrow 1975). The overlap between the set of characteristics produced by Clark and that produced by Norman and his colleagues is impressive. For both, human cognitive processes must be robust, relatively insensitive to missing or erroneous data, tolerant of ambiguity, flexible, with fast but not error-free processing. That two rather different approaches mesh so well with one another is encouraging and that they fit well with much that is claimed for connectionist models is even more encouraging. Clark concludes:

> Obviously, there is considerable and biologically attractive economy about all this. The use of one underlying algorithmic form [connectionism] to achieve so many high-level goals and the superpositional storage of data should appeal to a thrifty Mother Nature. . . . What makes PDP approaches biologically attractive is not merely their neurophysiological plausibility, as many seem to believe. They also begin to meet a series of more general constraints on any biologically and evolutionarily plausible model of human intelligence.
>
> (1989: 105)

Substitute 'memory' for 'intelligence' and this conclusion makes encouraging reading. Norman is equally upbeat:

> We argued for a set of essential properties. . . . Although these requirements seemed to us to be both necessary and sensible, supported by the evidence, a common complaint was that these were hand-waving speculation. . . . Well, the PDP mechanisms described in this book [McClelland and Rumelhart's 1986 volumes] have exactly the properties we required. Hurrah for our side.
>
> (1986: 537)

Temporal order and context

Many cues to memory are extended in time. Consider, for example, the familiar phenomenon of hearing a song that brings back a flood of particular memories. In such cases the cue is extended in time and it is something about the temporal pattern that can be essential to its power as a cue. Other more mundane problems also rely on the temporal sequencing – such as accessing the meaning of spoken words. Likewise, the essence of a memory may itself involve temporal order such as remembering a tune or, as is more common in experimental work, recalling a sequence of items. The problem for connectionist accounts is: how do they capture this change over time?

In trying to understand how connectionist accounts might deal with the problems of representing patterns of activity whose essential quality is that they change over time, Elman (1990) develops the idea of a dynamic memory which makes use of 'context units' (Jordan 1986). What this general structure means is that, at the end of each processing cycle, the pattern of activity in the hidden units is passed to the context units. The network developed by Elman clearly has the capacity for some kind of memory for temporal order, as have other nets (e.g. Amit *et al.* 1990; Burgess and Hitch 1992; Kleinfeld 1986). Elman demonstrates the ability of the net to learn a number of patterns that rely upon temporal order. For example, Elman presented the net with input which contained words but no cues to word boundaries – rather like hearing speech in an unfamiliar language or reading unfamiliar text without gaps (as was the case in some medieval texts). The point is that while there are predictable sequences within a word, the transitions between words are far less predictable. After training, the network's performance reflected this: the output of the system was good at predicting the next letter in the sequence provided that it was within a word. When the next letter was a new word, the prediction was far worse. In effect the model has learned something about word boundaries: it can almost be said to have learnt the idea of a word. This learning relies on using temporal context. Note that to achieve such a task the network must 'remember' further back than the immediately preceding letter (consider what should follow an 'i' that had been preceded by a 'p' and the necessity is clear).

Elman acknowledges that his model is far from a complete explanation of how the concept of a word may or may not be extracted. Certainly, cultural variations in what might constitute a word are important, as are many aspects of the conditions of use. However, the model does capture something of the notion that words are recognized in real time and that memory for the pattern affects interpretation of current input. More generally, Elman's model is an example of how connectionism can begin to capture something of the flavour of temporal order. In particular, it gives appropriate emphasis to the use of memory for previous associations to make predictions about future events – a function of memory which must be of fundamental importance.

Whilst Elman's model offers some interesting ideas about implementing temporal order in connectionist models, it does have a number of drawbacks as a general solution. For example, in recalling lists of words or letters in a short-term memory experiment, people frequently transpose items so that if the presented list were *d, a, s, t, r, p* a common error in recall would be *d, a, s, r, t, p* (Conrad 1964). Burgess and Hitch (1992) have attempted to develop a connectionist model of the articulatory loop in working memory which is where such ordering errors are thought to arise. The concept of working memory, and the articulatory loop in particular, has proved highly successful in accounting for a range of empirical findings (Baddeley 1986). However, Burgess and Hitch point out that it is difficult to see how ordering errors could occur using a solution such as Elman's. For example, how could transpositions occur? In the previous example, surely the early appearance of *r* at recall should encourage production of *p* as the next item rather than *t*? This and other difficulties led to a rather different proposal. Burgess and Hitch propose a variant on the use of context units which, added to a form of 'chaining together' of phonemes in a sequence, enables their model of the articulatory loop to reproduce many of the empirical phenomena attributed to such a mechanism. Rather than go into the details of the Burgess and Hitch model here, it is enough to note that the emergence of alternative connectionist accounts of related memory processes is a healthy sign.

Temporal order poses other problems for connectionist models. A number of papers have shown that recently presented patterns can interfere with previously learned ones to such an extent that the early patterns can no longer be retrieved – something which is clearly at odds with human behaviour (McCloskey and Cohen 1989; Ratcliff 1990). It remains to be seen whether such interference is a fundamental challenge to connectionist models or whether it can be solved by new techniques (Kruschke 1992; McClaren 1992).

CONCLUSION

In this chapter we have given a basic introduction to connectionism and tried to explain where its appeal lies for those interested in memory. As we see it, these general areas of appeal are: the provision of mechanisms for learning, performance after damage, the ability to deal with a number of constraints simultaneously, and biological plausibility. It is no surprise that such general characteristics are relevant to many other cognitive domains besides memory. However, what is less clear is whether or not these strengths are unique to connectionism. For example, supporters of production systems would claim that they can also deliver answers or insights in all of these areas (Anderson 1983). We have given a very positive picture of connectionism, but that is not to say that it does not face considerable technical, empirical and philosophical difficulties (see Barsalou 1993 for an excellent overview). It may be that connectionism and other approaches will need one another, with choice being dependent on factors such as the domain of explanation. What is certain, however, is that while connectionism might continue to provide models based on existing theories or empirical findings, if it is to fulfil its promise those models will need to continue to provide novel empirical predictions.

NOTE

1 Hinton, McClelland and Rumelhart (1986) point out that retrieval from a partial cue that is a set of features, such as 'Name is Bob, likes jazz and eating out', is easily achieved. However, retrieval based on relational information – such as the dreadful description 'Sue's husband' – is more problematic. Hinton *et al.* discuss some possible connectionist solutions to this based on the earlier work of Hinton (1981).

FURTHER READING

Introductions

Non-technical introductions to connectionism which still manage to convey an idea of the power and appeal of the approach are hard to come by. The following are some of the best that we have come across:

Allport (1985). Explores how the idea of distributed representations can enhance our understanding of aphasia. Captures in an excellent and non-technical way some of the most appealing characteristics of this style of explanation not only for those interested in language but also for those whose interest is in memory.

Bechtel and Abrahamsen (1991). Gives an overview of connectionism and is generally sympathetic to the approach.

McClelland, Rumelhart and the PDP Research Group (1986). The second of the seminal volumes by this group, it contains a number of important connectionist models of psychological processes and these give a good idea of how connectionism is used to tackle psychological issues. Some of the models do get quite technical, but the psychology is never too far away.

Quinlan (1991). Another general overview, but with more of a focus on psychological questions and a more critical tone than Bechtel and

Abrahamsen (1991). The great strength of much of Quinlan's book is that it approaches models from the point of view of a psychologist.

Rumelhart (1989). Written by one of the founders of the current wave of interest in connectionism, it gives an excellent account of the basic components of a connectionist model.

Rumelhart, McClelland and the PDP Research Group (1986). The first of the seminal volumes from this group. There are four chapters on the nature of connectionism, which are essential reading if a little technical in places. The remaining nine chapters look in some detail at technical aspects and are mainly of interest to those involved in research.

Critiques and defences

Barsalou (1993). While the body of this chapter develops a theory of concept representation based on symbols rather than connections, there is also an appendix which gives an excellent, though at times technical, overview of the main problems for connectionism.

Clark (1989). Primarily concerned with some of the philosophical issues raised by connectionism, though it also seeks to explore its relationship with biology. Introduces important ideas in a lively and clear way, whilst Clark also develops an interesting argument of his own. In general, he is enthusiastic about the promise of connectionism.

Fodor and McLaughlin (1990). Pursues many of the points made by Fodor and Pylyshyn (1988), but in a more accessible style.

Fodor and Pylyshyn (1988). Perhaps the major critique to date of the connectionist approach. Their argument is complex, but takes the radical view that in principle connectionism cannot offer anything of real interest to those interested in cognition.

Quinlan (1991). The final chapter gives a particularly good overview of criticisms of connectionism and connectionist models.

Smolensky (1988). One of the most detailed expositions of what is novel about the connectionist approach, to date this is as close as connectionism has come to a creed. For counters to its arguments see the peer commentaries of Fodor and Pylyshyn (1988) and Fodor and McLaughlin (1990).

Van Gelder (1990). Attempts to address the criticisms raised by both Fodor and Pylyshyn (1988) and Fodor and McLaughlin (1990).

More advanced readings

The following list is far from comprehensive, but guides the reader to some substantial sources. For examples of particular models see the works listed in Table 7.1.

Journal of Memory and Language (1988). Includes a special edition of the journal devoted to connectionism and contains a number of important papers, not all of which are sympathetic to it.

Levine (1991). A highly technical and mathematical book, but good for those who have a grasp of these subjects and wish to develop an in-depth understanding of these aspects.

McClelland, Rumelhart and the PDP Research Group (1986). See above under 'Introductions' for a description.

McClelland and Rumelhart (1989). A suite of programs with accompanying guide which take the reader through a number of the fundamentals, such as training hidden units, to use of the generalized delta rule. Versions for IBM PC compatibles and Apple Macintoshes. Not terribly user friendly, but does test one's understanding of basic concepts.

Rumelhart, McClelland and the PDP Research Group (1986). See above under 'Introductions' for a description.

REFERENCES

Allport, D.A. (1985) 'Distributed memory, modular subsystems and dysphasia', in S. Newman and R. Epstein (eds) *Current Perspectives in Dysphasia*, Edinburgh: Churchill Livingstone.

Amit, D.J., Sagi, D. and Usher, M. (1990) 'Architecture of attractor neural networks performing cognitive fast scanning', *Network* 14: 189–216.

Anderson, J.R. (1983) *The Architecture of Cognition*, Cambridge, Massachusetts: Harvard University Press.

Baddeley, A.D. (1986) *Working Memory*, Oxford: Oxford University Press.

Barsalou, L.W. (1993) 'Flexibility, structure, and linguistic vagary in concepts: manifestations of a compositional system of perceptual symbols', in A.F. Collins, S.E. Gathercole, M.A. Conway and P.E. Morris (eds) *Theories of Memory*, Hillsdale, New Jersey: Erlbaum.

Bartlett, F.C. (1932) *Remembering: A Study in Experimental and Social Psychology*, Cambridge: Cambridge University Press.

Bechtel, W. and Abrahamsen, H. (1991) *Connectionism and the Mind*, Oxford: Blackwell.

Besner, D., Twilley, L., McCann, R.S. and Seergobin, K. (1990) 'On the connection between connectionism and data: Are a few words necessary?' *Psychological Review* 97: 432–46.

Boden, M. (1977) *Artificial Intelligence and Natural Man*, Brighton: Harvester Press.

—— (1988) *Computer Models of the Mind: Computational Approaches in Theoretical Psychology*, Cambridge: Cambridge University Press.

Bruce, V. and Young, A.W. (1986) 'Understanding face recognition', *British Journal of Psychology* 77: 305–27.

Bullock, D. and Grossberg, S. (1988) 'Neural dynamics of planned arm movements: Emergent invariants and speed accuracy information during trajectory formation', *Psychological Review* 95: 49–90.

Burgess, N. and Hitch, G. (1992) 'Towards a network model of the articulatory loop', *Journal of Memory and Language* 31: 429–60.

Burton, A.M., Bruce, V. and Johnston, R.A. (1990) 'Understanding face recognition with an interactivation model', *British Journal of Psychology* 81: 361–80.

Carpenter, G. and Grossberg, S. (eds) *Pattern Recognition by Self-Organizing Neural Networks*, Cambridge, Massachusetts: MIT Press.

Churchland, P.S. and Sejnowski, T.J. (1989) 'Neural representation and neural computation', in N. Nadel, L. Cooper, P. Cullicover and R.

Harnish (eds) *Neural Connections, Mental Computations*, Cambridge, Massachusetts: MIT Press.

Clark, A. (1989) *Microcognition: Philosophy, Cognitive Science and Parallel Distributed Processing*, Cambridge, Massachusetts: MIT Press.

Cohen, J.D., Dunbar, K. and McClelland, J.L. (1990) 'On the control of automatic processes: a parallel distributed processing account of the Stroop effect', *Psychological Review* 97: 332–61.

Conrad, R. (1964) 'Acoustic confusions in immediate memory', *British Journal of Psychology* 55: 75–84.

Dell, G.S. (1986) 'A spreading activation theory of retrieval in sentence production', *Psychological Review* 93: 283–321.

—— (1988) 'The retrieval of phonological forms in production: Tests of predictions from a connectionist model', *Journal of Memory and Language* 27: 124–42.

Elman, J.L. (1990) 'Finding structure in time', *Cognitive Science* 14: 179–211.

Farah, M.J. and McClelland, J.L. (1991) 'A computational model of semantic memory impairment: Modality specificity and emergent category specificity', *Journal of Experimental Psychology: General* 120: 339–57.

Fodor, J.A. and McLaughlin, B.P. (1990) 'Connectionism and the problem of systematicity: Why Smolensky's solution doesn't work', *Cognition* 35: 183–204.

Fodor, J.A. and Pylyshyn, Z.W. (1988) 'Connectionism and cognitive architecture: A critical analysis', *Cognition* 28: 3–71.

Gardner, H. (1985) *'The Mind's New Science: A History of the Cognitive Revolution'*, New York: Basic Books.

Gluck, M.A. and Bower, G.H. (1988) 'From conditioning to category learning: an adaptive network model', *Journal of Experimental Psychology: General* 117: 227–47.

—— (1990) 'Component and pattern information in adaptive networks', *Journal of Experimental Psychology: General* 119: 101–4.

Grossberg, S. (1987) 'Competitive learning: from interactive activation to adaptive resonance', *Cognitive Science* 11: 23–63.

Hay, D.C. and Young, A.W. (1982) 'The human face', in A.W. Ellis (ed.) *Normality and Pathology in Cognitive Functions*, London: Academic Press.

Hinton, G.E. (1981) 'Implementing semantic networks in parallel hardware', in G.E. Hinton and J.A. Anderson (eds) *Parallel Models of Associative Memory*, Hillsdale, New Jersey: Erlbaum.

Hinton, G.E. and Shallice, T. (1991) 'Lesioning an attractor network: investigations of acquired dyslexia', *Psychological Review* 98: 74–95.

Hinton, G.E., McClelland, J.L. and Rumelhart, D.E. (1986) 'Distributed representations', in D.E. Rumelhart, J.L. McClelland and the PDP Research Group, *Parallel Distributed Processing: Explorations in the Microstructure of Cognition*, vol. 1, *Foundations*, Cambridge, Massachusetts: MIT Press.

Horgan, T. and Woodward, J. (1985) 'Folk psychology is here to stay', *The Philosophical Review* XCIV (2).

James, W. (1890) *Principles of Psychology*, vol. 1, New York: Holt.

Johnson, M.K. and Raye, C.L. (1981) 'Reality monitoring', *Psychological Review* 88: 67–85.

Johnson-Laird, P.N. (1990) *The Computer and the Mind: An Introduction to Cognitive Science*, London: Fontana.

Jordan, M.I. (1986) 'An introduction to linear algebra in parallel distributed processing', in D.E. Rumelhart, J.L. McClelland and the PDP Research Group, *Parallel Distributed Processing: Explorations in the Microstructure of Cognition*, vol. 1, *Foundations*, Cambridge, Massachusetts: MIT Press.

Kleinfeld, D. (1986) 'Sequential state generation by model neural networks', *Proceedings of the National Academy of Science USA* 83: 9469–73.

Kohonen, T. (1984) *Self-Organization and Associative Memory*, Berlin: Springer-Verlag.

Kolodner, J.L. (1984) 'Reconstructive memory: A computer model', *Cognitive Science* 7: 231–328.

Kruschke, J.K. (1992) 'ALCOVE: An exemplar-based connectionist model of category learning', *Psychological Review* 99: 22–44.

Levine, D.S. (1991) *Introduction to Neural and Cognitive Modelling*, Hillsdale, New Jersey: Erlbaum.

Linsker, R. (1986a) 'From basic network principles to neural architecture: Emergence of spatial-opponent cells', *Proceedings of the National Academy of Science USA* 83: 7508–12.

—— (1986b) 'From basic network principles to neural architecture: Emergence of orientation-selective cells', *Proceedings of the National Academy of Science USA* 83: 8390–4.

—— (1986c) 'From basic network principles to neural architecture: Emergence of orientation columns', *Proceedings of the National Academy of Science USA* 83: 8779–83.

Linton, M. (1978) 'Real-world memory after six years: An in vivo study of very long-term memory', in M.M. Gruneberg, P.E. Morris and R.N. Sykes (eds) *Practical Aspects of Memory*, London: Academic Press.

—— (1982) 'Transformations of memory in everyday life', in U. Neisser (ed.) *Memory Observed: Remembering in Natural Contexts*, London: Freeman.

Loftus, E.F. (1979) *Eyewitness Testimony*, Cambridge, Massachusetts: Harvard University Press.

McClaren, I.P.L. (1992) 'A solution to the sequential learning problem', paper given to meeting of the Experimental Psychology Society, University of York.

McClelland, J.L. (1986) 'The programmable blackboard model of reading', in J.L. McClelland, D.E. Rumelhart and the PDP Research Group, *Parallel Distributed Processing: Explorations in the Microstructure of Cognition*, vol. 2, *Psychological and Biological Models*, Cambridge, Massachusetts: MIT Press.

—— (1991) 'Stochastic interactive processes and the effect of context on perception', *Cognitive Psychology* 18: 1–86.

McClelland, J.L. and Elman, J.L. (1986) 'The TRACE model of speech perception', *Cognitive Psychology* 18: 1–86. (See also J.L. McClelland, D.E. Rumelhart and the PDP Research Group (1986) *Parallel Distributed Processing: Explorations in the Microstructure of Cognition*, vol. 2, *Psychological and Biological Models*, Cambridge, Massachusetts: MIT Press.)

McClelland, J.L. and Kawamoto, A.H. (1986) 'Mechanisms of sentence processing: assigning roles to constituents', in J.L. McClelland, D.E.

Rumelhart and the PDP Research Group, *Parallel Distributed Processing: Explorations in the Microstructure of Cognition*, vol. 2, *Psychological and Biological Models*, Cambridge, Massachusetts: MIT Press.

McClelland, J.L. and Rumelhart, D.E. (1981) 'An interactive activation account of context effects in letter perception', *Psychological Review* 88: 375–407.

—— (1985) 'Distributed memory and the representation of general and specific information', *Journal of Experimental Psychology: General* 114: 159–88. (See also J.L. McClelland, D.E. Rumelhart and the PDP Research Group (1986) *Parallel Distributed Processing: Explorations in the Microstructure of Cognition*, vol. 2, *Psychological and Biological Models*, Cambridge, Massachusetts: MIT Press.)

—— (1989) *Explorations in Parallel Distributed Processing: A Handbook of Models, Programs and Exercises*, London: MIT Press.

McClelland, J.L., Rumelhart, D.E. and Hinton, G.E. (1986a) 'The appeal of parallel distributed processing', in D.E. Rumelhart, J.L. McClelland and the PDP Research Group, *Parallel Distributed Processing: Explorations in the Microstructure of Cognition*, vol. 1, *Foundations*, Cambridge, Massachusetts: MIT Press.

McClelland, J.L., Rumelhart, D.E. and the PDP Research Group (1986b) *Parallel Distributed Processing: Explorations in the Microstructure of Cognition*, vol. 2, *Psychological and Biological Models*, Cambridge, Massachusetts: MIT Press.

McCloskey, M. and Cohen, N.J. (1989) 'Catastrophic interference in connectionist networks: The sequential learning problem', in G.H. Bower (ed.) *The Psychology of Learning and Motivation: Advances in Research and Theory*, vol. 24, San Diego: Academic Press.

Marr, D. (1982) *Vision*, San Francisco: Freeman.

Massaro, D.W. (1988) 'Some criticisms of connectionist models of human performance', *Journal of Memory and Language* 27: 213–34.

Massaro, D.W. and Cohen, M.M. (1991) 'Integration versus interactive activation: The joint influence of stimulus and context in perception', *Cognitive Psychology* 23: 558–614.

Mehler, J., Morton, J. and Jusczyk, P. (1984) 'On reducing language to biology', *Cognitive Neuropsychology* 1: 83–116.

Mikkulainen, R. and Dyer, M.G. (1991) 'Natural language processing with modular PDP networks and distributed lexicon', *Cognitive Science* 15: 343–99.

Miller, G.A. (1981) 'Trends and debates in cognitive psychology', *Cognition* 10: 215–25.

Minsky, M.L. (1975) 'A framework for representing knowledge', in P.H. Winston (ed.) *The Psychology of Computer Vision*, New York: McGraw-Hill.

Neisser, U. (1981) 'John Dean's memory: A case study', *Cognition* 9: 1–22.

Norman, D.A. (1986) 'Reflections on cognition and parallel distributed processing', in J.L. McClelland, D.E. Rumelhart and the PDP Research Group, *Parallel Distributed Processing: Explorations in the Microstructure of Cognition*, vol. 2, *Psychological and Biological Models*, Cambridge, Massachusetts: MIT Press.

Norman, D.A. and Bobrow, D.G. (1975) 'On data-limited and resource-limited processes', *Cognitive Psychology* 7: 44–64.

Pinker, S. and Prince, A. (1988) 'On language and connectionism – analysis of a parallel distributed processing model of language acquisition', *Cognition* 28: 73–193.

Plunkett, K. and Marchman, V. (1991) 'U-shaped learning and frequency effects in a multi-layered perceptron: Implications for child language acquisition', *Cognition* 38: 43–102.

Posner, M.I. and Keele, S. (1968) 'On the genesis of abstract ideas', *Journal of Experimental Psychology* 77: 353–63.

Posner, M.I., Goldsmith, R. and Welton, K.E., Jr (1967) 'Perceived distance and the classification of distorted patterns', *Journal of Experimental Psychology* 73: 28–38.

Putnam, H. (1960) 'Minds and machines', in S. Hook (ed.) *Dimensions of Mind*, New York: New York University Press.

—— (1967) 'Psychological predicates', in W. Capitan and D. Merill (eds) *Art, Mind and Religion*, Pittsburgh: University of Pittsburgh Press.

—— (1988) *Representation and Reality*, Cambridge, Massachusetts: MIT Press.

Pylyshyn, Z.W. (1984) *Computation and Cognition: Toward a Foundation for Cognitive Science*, Cambridge, Massachusetts: MIT Press.

Quinlan, P. (1991) *Connectionism and Psychology*, Hemel Hempstead: Harvester Wheatsheaf.

Ratcliff, R. (1990) 'Connectionist models of recognition memory: Constraints imposed by learning and forgetting problems', *Psychological Review* 97: 285–308.

Reason, J.T. and Mycielska, K. (1982) *Absent Minded? The Psychology of Mental Lapses and Everyday Errors*, Englewood Cliffs, New Jersey: Prentice-Hall.

Rumelhart, D.E. (1989) 'The architecture of mind: a connectionist approach', in M.I. Posner (ed.) *Foundations of Cognitive Science*, Cambridge, Massachusetts: MIT Press.

Rumelhart, D.E. and McClelland, J.L. (1982) 'An interactive activation model of context effects in letter perception: Part 2. The contextual enhancement effect and some tests and extensions of the model', *Psychological Review* 89: 60–94.

—— (1986) 'PDP models and general issues in cognitive science', in D.E. Rumelhart, J.L. McClelland and the PDP Research Group, *Parallel Distributed Processing: Explorations in the Microstructure of Cognition*, vol. 1, *Foundations*, Cambridge, Massachusetts: MIT Press.

Rumelhart, D.E. and Zipser, D. (1985) 'Feature discovery by competitive learning', *Cognitive Science* 9: 75–112.

Rumelhart, D.E., Hinton, G.E. and Williams, R.J. (1986a) 'Learning internal representations by error propagation', in D.E. Rumelhart, J.L. McClelland and the PDP Research Group, *Parallel Distributed Processing: Explorations in the Microstructure of Cognition*, vol. 1, *Foundations*, Cambridge, Massachusetts: MIT Press.

Rumelhart, D.E., McClelland, J.L. and the PDP Research Group (1986b) *Parallel Distributed Processing: Explorations in the Microstructure of Cognition*, vol. 1, *Foundations*, Cambridge, Massachusetts: MIT Press.

Schank, R.C. (1982) *Dynamic Memory: A Theory of Reminding and Learning in*

Computers and People, New York: Cambridge University Press.

Schank, R.C. and Abelson, R.P. (1977) *Scripts, Plans, Goals and Understanding: An Inquiry into Human Knowledge Structures*, Hillsdale, New Jersey: Erlbaum.

Seidenberg, M.S. and McClelland, J.L. (1989) 'A distributed, developmental model of word recognition and naming', *Psychological Review* 96: 523–68.

Shallice, T. (1988) *From Neuropsychology to Mental Structure*, Cambridge, Massachusetts: Cambridge University Press.

Shanks, D. (1990) 'Connectionism and human learning: Critique of Gluck and Bower (1988)', *Journal of Experimental Psychology: General* 119: 101–4.

Slack, J. (1987) 'Cognitive architecture', unit for course D309 Cognitive Psychology, Milton Keynes: Open University Press.

Smolensky, P. (1988) 'On the proper treatment of connectionism', *Behavioral and Brain Sciences* 11: 1–74.

Sterelny, K. (1990) *The Representational Theory of Mind*, Oxford: Blackwell.

Stone, G.O. (1986) 'An analysis of the delta rule and the learning of statistical associations', in D.E. Rumelhart, J.L. McClelland and the PDP Research Group, *Parallel Distributed Processing: Explorations in the Microstructure of Cognition*, vol. 1, *Foundations*, Cambridge, Massachusetts: MIT Press.

Tesauro, G. and Sejnowski, T.J. (1989) 'A parallel network that learns to play backgammon', *Artificial Intelligence* 39: 593–601.

Tulving, E. (1983) *Elements of Episodic Memory*, Oxford: Oxford University Press.

Tulving, E. and Osler, S. (1968) 'Effectiveness of retrieval cues in memory for words', *Journal of Experimental Psychology* 77: 357–90.

Van Gelder, T. (1990) 'Compositionality: A connectionist variation on a classical theme', *Cognitive Science* 14: 355–84.

8

THE COGNITIVE NEUROPSYCHOLOGY OF MEMORY

J. R. Hanley and A. W. Young

INTRODUCTION

The claim that we can gain important insights into the normal cognitive system from investigations of the impairments that can follow brain injury would be endorsed by virtually all contemporary neuropsychologists. Underlying the recent upsurge of interest in *cognitive* neuropsychology, however, is the belief that it is by *comparing* the precise nature of the different impairments from which carefully selected patients suffer that most progress will be made in advancing our understanding of the way in which the cognitive system is organized (Ellis and Young 1988; Shallice 1988). Consequently, influential theories in contemporary cognitive psychology in areas such as reading (Coltheart 1985), working memory (Baddeley 1992) and face processing (Young and Bruce 1991) are as strongly supported by findings from individual case studies of clinical patients as they are by experiments examining the performance of normal subjects under laboratory conditions.

Much of the research that has traditionally investigated the neuropsychology of memory, however, has been based upon the results of group studies rather than single cases. Instead of contrasting different patients with one another, researchers have tended to focus on the idea of a central amnesic syndrome. By comparing the mean scores of groups of amnesic patients with those of appropriately matched control groups, it is hoped that important information will emerge as to why, for instance, amnesic patients have such difficulties in remembering new information. The belief that such an approach will ultimately prove successful is usually based on the assumption that the symptoms associated with the amnesic syndrome are caused by one basic deficit which is common to all amnesic patients.

Here, we will prefer to highlight important *differences* in the forms of memory impairment that can be observed after brain injury. In our view such differences are of central theoretical importance, and point strongly toward the idea that, like cognitive abilities, memory results from the coordinate interaction of distinct functional components. In doing this, we do not seek to reject the more traditional approach in terms of the amnesic syndrome, but to set it in context by considering a much wider range of memory impairments. In the final part of the chapter, we will discuss some of the ways in which these findings might be interpreted. At that point, we will enter the debate between those who advocate a 'memory systems' framework (Schacter 1990; Tulving and Schacter 1990) and those who argue that while human memory may involve the use of many different encoding and retrieval *processes*, there is no need to postulate the existence of more than one memory *store* (Roediger 1990a, b; Roediger *et al.* 1990).

FORMS OF MEMORY IMPAIRMENT

Anterograde amnesia

Although the amnesic syndrome is associated with a number of different symptoms, perhaps the most important single feature is the severe difficulty that amnesic patients encounter when they attempt to recall or recognize events that have taken place since the time of their illness or accident. This inability to retain new memories is termed *anterograde* amnesia. The patient H.M., for instance, who became amnesic following surgery in 1953 to treat intractable epilepsy, will read the same magazine articles repeatedly, unaware that he has read them many times already (Scoville and Milner 1957). When his family moved house 10 months after his operation, H.M. was unable to find his way home and would return instead to his old house that was situated a few blocks away. H.M. will fail to recognize people that he has encountered recently, even neighbours who have visited his house regularly in the years following his operation (Milner 1966). His ability to remember the location of objects is also impaired; his mother apparently reported that he needed to be told where to find his lawnmower even though he mowed the lawn regularly, and may have even used the lawnmower during the previous day. This deficit was subsequently confirmed in formal testing sessions in which H.M. found it extremely difficult to remember the location of sixteen small objects presented in an array (Smith and

Milner 1981; Smith 1988). On formal tests of verbal memory, H.M. was able to retain a six-digit number in memory over a period of several minutes by actively rehearsing it in immediate memory. As soon as rehearsal was prevented by means of an interference test, however, his performance dropped virtually to zero (Milner 1966; Sidman *et al.* 1968). He failed to learn a seven-digit number even after twenty-five consecutive presentations (Drachman and Arbit 1966). Furthermore, Milner reports that:

> the retention deficit is not specific to any one kind of material, but is quite general, affecting stories, drawings, and numbers, and cutting across any distinction between verbal and perceptual material or between one sense modality and another.
> (Milner 1958: 254)

Despite the severity of his memory impairment, H.M.'s Wechsler IQ was as high as 117 when measured in 1962. Furthermore, while H.M.'s ability to recall information acquired pre-morbidly (particularly from the months leading up to his operation) is not completely normal, it is still vastly superior to his memory for more recent events. For instance, H.M. still recognizes environments that were familiar to him before his operation (Milner *et al.* 1968). Marslen-Wilson and Teuber (1975) report that H.M. performed within the normal range when asked to recognize faces that were famous before his operation in 1953. With more recent faces, however, his performance was very severely impaired indeed. Gabrieli *et al.* (1988) reported exactly the same pattern when H.M. was asked to recognize famous names. Similarly, patient N.A. (Cohen and Squire 1981), whose amnesia followed a fencing accident in 1960, outperformed all of the control subjects in identifying famous faces from the 1930s and 1940s, but was worse than any of the controls in recognizing faces that were famous in the 1970s.

Impaired recall of new memories

There is some evidence from group studies that patients with anterograde amnesia may be more severely impaired when their memory is tested by recall than it is on tests of recognition memory (Hirst *et al.* 1986). The technique that Hirst *et al.* used was to examine their amnesic patients' recall performance under circumstances in which recognition memory performance was equated with that of controls. For example, with presentation rates of 8 seconds per item, Hirst *et al.*'s amnesic patients performed as effectively on a recognition test as normal controls who had seen each item for only half a second. Even under these presentation conditions, however, the amnesics continued to perform significantly worse than controls on a test of recall.

Of course, the manipulations that were required in order to equate amnesic performance on the recognition test with that of controls were rather extreme. It is therefore clear that the ability of Hirst *et al.*'s amnesic subjects on tests of recognition memory was severely impaired. Is it, nevertheless, possible to observe *normal* performance on tests of recognition memory in the context of severely impaired recall in a single patient?

It is sometimes claimed that patients with frontal lobe lesions can exhibit normal recognition memory and impaired recall. Consistent with this, when Janowsky, Shimamura and Squire (1989) examined frontal patients as a group, they performed as well as matched controls on recognition tests, but were significantly worse at recall. However, the recall impairment that Janowsky *et al.* observed was relatively mild. For instance, the frontal patients' mean Wechsler Verbal MQ was as high as 100.7, whereas the Verbal MQ of a group of amnesic patients that Janowsky *et al.* also tested was only 73.6. Similarly, Huntington's disease patients have been shown to perform as badly as amnesics on tests of recall of words, but to perform significantly better than amnesics on tests of recognition memory (Butters *et al.* 1985). Nevertheless, the Huntington's disease patients still performed significantly worse than normal controls on the recognition test.

Recently, however, there have been reports of three patients with very severe recall problems in the absence of any apparent recognition memory deficit. These are patient H.W. (Moscovitch 1989), patient L.E. (Parkin *et al.* 1993), and patient R.O.B. (Hanley *et al.* 1994). All scored extremely poorly at learning unrelated verbal paired associates, and at recalling a short story from the Wechsler Memory test battery; patient R.O.B., for instance, had a Verbal MQ of only 66. Despite this, both R.O.B. and L.E. were at the 75th percentile on the Warrington (1984) recognition memory test for words, and H.W. performed in the normal range on the delayed recognition component of the California verbal learning test. On several occasions, R.O.B. has been asked to recall a list of words after a 30-second filled delay, but she has never been able to recall any of them. This occurs even when she has performed a semantic orienting task on them (cf. Craik and Tulving 1975), and even when she can subsequently remember around 80 per cent of them on a recognition test (Hanley *et al.* 1994).

A particularly striking recent case study by Delbecq-Derouesné, Beauvois and Shallice (1990) demonstrates that it is also possible to suffer from exactly the opposite type of impairment. Delbecq-Derouesné *et al.*'s patient, R.W., performs extremely poorly on recognition despite good performance on tests of recall. For instance, he was within the normal range for free recall of lists of words that he had recently learned, and for recall of prose passages that he had recently heard. The only unusual aspect of R.W.'s recall was that it was sometimes accompanied by an unusually high level of extralist intrusions. Despite good recall, however, R.W. produced severely impaired scores of only 34/50 on the Warrington recognition memory test for words, and only 32/50 on the equivalent test for faces. The performance of patients such as R.W. and R.O.B. shows that patients who are clearly *not* generally amnesic can nevertheless show amnesic-like levels of performance on certain types of memory test.

Material-specific memory loss

The operation which the amnesic patient H.M. underwent in an attempt to treat his epilepsy involved the surgical removal of the mesial parts of the temporal lobes in both the left and the right cerebral hemispheres. Since that time, if it is necessary to treat temporal lobe epilepsy surgically, the operation will only involve the hemisphere in which the epileptogenic lesion is lateralized. Although unilateral temporal lobectomy can occasionally produce a severe amnesia (Penfield and Milner 1958), it is more likely to lead to a milder impairment in which memory for *only certain types* of information is affected.

Milner (1958) reported that patients with left temporal lobe epilepsy did not have visual memory problems, but there was evidence of an impairment on verbal memory tasks. This deficit showed up most clearly on recall of prose passages, particularly when recall was tested after a delay. After left temporal lobectomy, Milner found that the verbal deficit that such patients experience became more severe. Even immediate recall of prose passages was now impaired. Milner summarized the deficits associated with left temporal lobe lesions: 'Quite consistently patients with such lesions show impairment on verbal memory tasks, regardless of how retention is being tested, whether by recognition, free recall, or rate of associative learning' (1967: 125).

Although Milner (1958) reported that patients with unilateral right hemisphere lesions showed no deficit on verbal memory tasks such as these, they were impaired on a series of visual memory tasks (Milner 1968). They made many mistakes when attempting to recognize photos of faces that they had been shown 2 minutes earlier, they were impaired at recognizing unfamiliar geometric shapes that had recently been presented to them, and they found it difficult to remember their way through a maze. Patients with left temporal lesions, by contrast, showed no impairment on any of these non-verbal memory tasks.

Subsequent work has provided further evidence for the differential involvement of the two hemispheres in memory tasks. Milner (1974, 1978) cites the work of her colleague Corsi which showed that patients with right temporal lesions had great difficulty in remembering where along a horizontal line a circle had been drawn. Left hemisphere patients performed normally at this task, but unlike the right hemisphere patients were impaired on the Peterson and Peterson (1959) interference paradigm where a consonant trigram has to be retained over a short interval in which rehearsal is prevented by backward counting. When learning supra-span sequences, left hemisphere patients had difficulty in remembering a series of digits. They had no difficulty, however, in reproducing the order in which the experimenter had tapped a set of blocks on a wooden board. Right hemisphere patients, by contrast, showed exactly the opposite pattern of impairment.

Loss of recent visual memory

In stark contrast to the case of H.M., Milner (1962) concluded that material-specific memory disorders are associated with deficits 'that are clinically rather trivial'. However, studies of individual patients with right hemisphere and bilateral lesions have shown that the consequences of visual memory loss can be very disabling. For example, Ross (1980) reported two patients whose verbal memory appeared to be intact, but who were unable to orient themselves in the environment in which they lived and who had severe difficulties in identifying faces of people that they had met.

One of the most interesting aspects of the results that Ross (1980) reported was that the visual memory problems that his patients experienced appeared to be most severe for the period following their illness. For instance, Ross' first case was unable to learn the layout of the neurology wing of the hospital in which he stayed for a month, yet his sister reported that he had no apparent problems orienting himself when he went to stay with his parents in the house in which he grew up. Ross' second case could recognize the faces of old acquaintances, but had severe problems in identifying the faces of people that he had met for the first time in the last few years. In neither case were the patient's visual memory problems completely confined to recent information, however. Case 1 had a general problem with recognizing faces, and Case 2 had difficulty in orienting himself in once familiar environments.

In 1990, we published a case study of patient E.L.D. (Hanley *et al.* 1990) whose severe visual memory problems do appear to be confined to information that she has encountered since the time of her illness (which occurred in 1985). On tests using photographs of celebrities that had become famous since 1985 (i.e. since her illness), E.L.D.'s recognition performance was severely impaired relative to controls. Her performance was as good as controls for faces that were famous before 1980, however, and her ability to recognize the *names* of people who had become famous since 1985 was completely normal. These problems in recognizing faces exactly parallel the pattern of impairment that she experiences in finding her way around. She is well oriented in her parent's house which she has known for many years, but has encountered severe difficulties in learning the layout of her new flat and in finding her way back to it after a day out shopping. It was therefore clear that E.L.D.'s loss of recent visual memories co-occurred with unimpaired verbal memory and with unimpaired retrieval of visual information acquired pre-morbidly; there was a circumscribed anterograde memory deficit.

On tests of episodic memory, E.L.D.'s recognition of unfamiliar faces was very poor (29/50 on the Warrington [1984] recognition memory test when tested most recently), but was excellent for words (49/50 on the Warrington test). Her episodic memory performance is equally poor for unfamiliar objects. One particularly striking finding, however, is that her ability to recognize *familiar* objects and faces on episodic memory tests appears to be unimpaired. This extends even to her ability to remember which view of a familiar face or object she had been exposed to recently. E.L.D.'s performance is in contrast to the pattern that emerged when the same materials were given to patients with Parkinson's disease. Although they also were good on the Warrington test for words and poor on the test for faces, these patients were as impaired on episodic memory tests for familiar faces as for unfamiliar faces (Dewick *et al.* 1991).

Retrograde amnesia

For patients such as H.M. or E.L.D., then, it is memory for events since their illness that is most severely disrupted. For other patients, however, the ability to retrieve information from the period prior to their illness or accident is also extremely limited. This impairment is known as *retrograde* amnesia. Retrograde amnesia has been studied extensively in patients with Korsakoff syndrome. Such patients appear to suffer from a retrograde amnesia that gets steadily worse in the period leading up to the start of their illness. Albert *et al.* (1979), for instance, found that Korsakoff patients remembered famous faces and events from early in their life much better than events and faces that were prominent in time periods that were closer to the onset of their illness.

There are, however, a number of issues that make the interpretation of this temporal gradient in the retrograde amnesia found in Korsakoff's syndrome rather controversial. For example, Korsakoff patients generally become severely ill as a result of a vitamin deficiency associated with many years of sustained alcohol abuse. Since the ability of alcoholics to register new information is relatively impaired (Parker and Noble 1977), it is possible that the increasingly poor memory that these patients show for the period leading up to their illness is actually a reflection of an anterograde amnesia that got steadily worse as their drinking and dietary habits deteriorated.

Some of these issues were addressed in Butters and Cermak's (1986) report of patient P.Z. P.Z. was a distinguished academic who developed Korsakoff's syndrome at the age of 65, shortly after publishing his autobiography. When Butters and Cermak subsequently tested him using material from this book, P.Z.'s retrograde amnesia showed a clear temporal gradient for both people and events. Since he was familiar enough with the most recent material to have written about it in his autobiography, it does not seem reasonable to attribute his subsequent inability to remember it to anterograde amnesia for events at the time.

It remains possible that poor registration of new information in the pre-morbid period plays *some* role in producing temporal gradients in Korsakoff's syndrome (Albert 1984). Nevertheless, there is growing evidence that patients whose amnesia has a clearly defined acute onset (e.g. patients who suffered from a cardiovascular accident or from anoxia) can also experience a retrograde amnesia that is characterized by a temporal gradient (Squire *et al.* 1989). Other patients, such as patient S.S., however, appear to suffer from a 'flat' retrograde amnesia that is equally severe for all time periods (Cermak and O'Connor 1983). S.S., who became amnesic following infection by the herpes simplex virus in 1971, is at least as poor at recognizing the faces of celebrities from the 1930s and 1940s as he is at recognizing faces from the 1960s. A similar pattern has been observed in a group of Alzheimer patients (Wilson *et al.* 1981) and in a group of patients suffering from Huntington's chorea (Albert *et al.* 1981). As Squire *et al.* (1989) acknowledge, the precise reasons for the differences in the patterns of retrograde amnesia that have been observed in these patients are not clear at the present time.

In most cases of retrograde amnesia, there is also an anterograde memory impairment. However, reports of patients who experience retrograde amnesia in the absence of anterograde amnesia exist, but are extremely rare. The patient described by Andrews *et al.* (1982) provides a particularly vivid example. Nevertheless, there has sometimes been a suspicion that this pattern of memory problems might have a psychogenic rather than an organic basis. The case of E.D., reported by Kapur *et al.* (1986), shows clear evidence of EEG abnormalities in the left temporal lobe, however.

Kapur and his colleagues report that, between 1977 and 1987, E.D. has suffered from at least thirty episodes of transient amnesia which can last from around 15 minutes to as long as several hours. Several papers have recently discussed the performance of patients in states of transient global amnesia (see Hodges 1991). It was, however, the pattern of performance that E.D. revealed when he had recovered from these episodes that Kapur *et al.* (1986) investigated, since E.D. appears to have been left with a severely impaired ability to remember information from the past. Formal testing has demonstrated that E.D. does not suffer from an anterograde amnesia. For example, Kapur *et al.* (1986) report that he had a memory quotient (MQ) of 120 on the Wechsler memory test when tested in 1984. When subsequently retested a few years later by Kapur *et al.* (1989), he had an MQ of 116. On tests of retrograde amnesia, however, the results of both studies indicated that E.D.'s ability to recognize famous faces, famous names, famous voices and famous scenes from past decades was extemely poor.

One interesting experiment that Kapur *et al.* (1986) carried out with E.D. involved asking him to remember incorrect occupations for names that he no longer found familiar. For example, he was taught (temporarily) that Tony Jacklin's career was in music and that Donny Osmond was a golfer. E.D. actually learnt incorrect name/ occupation pairings of this kind more rapidly than normal controls whose ability to learn the wrong occupations was presumably impaired by their ability to remember the correct occupations.

We have subsequently compared E.D.'s performance on this test with that of a post-encephalitic patient, B.D. (Hanley *et al.* 1989). B.D. is also severely impaired at recognizing people from their name, face and voice, although his impairment covers people that he knew before, as well as people that he has encountered since his illness. When asked to learn incorrect occupations to names of people that he no longer recognizes as familiar (e.g. Idi Amin = a gymnast; Olga Korbut = a politician), however, B.D. performs extremely badly. He does significantly better when he is asked to learn correct occupations to names that he no longer recognizes as familiar (e.g. Mark Spitz = a swimmer; Anna Ford = a newsreader). B.D. still seems to be able to achieve some form of access to information about these people from their names in a way that E.D. is not, despite B.D.'s initial complete lack of overt knowledge about who the people are. As a consequence, there may be a distinction to be drawn between impairments such as E.D.'s in which the memory records themselves appear to be lost, and those such as B.D.'s in which at least some information is preserved, but overt access is impaired.

Despite his poor memory for famous people and events from the past, Kapur *et al.* (1989) report that E.D.'s autobiographical memory is relatively well preserved. That is, E.D. can recall personal memories of events that happened to him in the past with reasonable levels of accuracy. De Renzi *et al.* (1987) report a similar dissociation in a 44-year-old post-encephalitic patient, L.P. Her ability to recognize famous people and past events was extremely limited. For instance, in response to the question 'What did Hitler do?', she replied, 'I really don't know'. On a questionnaire prepared in collaboration with her friends and relatives, however, L.P. was able to give full and accurate responses to questions about her personal history. This included information about her high school courses, her engagement and wedding, the birth of her children and her holidays. De Renzi *et al.* (1987) suggest that L.P. can recall events which had personal significance, but not similar events which had only public rather than personal importance. Thus, she could remember the death of a friend's daughter in a car accident, but not an incident that had gripped the whole of Italy, and that she had watched on television, in which desperate and ultimately unsuccessful attempts were made to save the life of a child who had fallen into a pit.

Although these cases show a dissociation between retrograde amnesia for personal and extra-personal events, most patients with retrograde amnesia are at least as impaired on tests of autobiographical memory as they are at remembering famous people and events (e.g. Warrington and McCarthy 1988). In very severe cases, patients such as S.S. (Cermak and O'Connor 1983) or K.C. (Tulving *et al.* 1988) seem unable to recall any specific event that has ever happened to them at any time in their lives. For instance, K.C. could not even remember the death of his brother by drowning, which happened when K.C. was in his early twenties. When he was asked to write a brief summary of his life, he did not respond at all, and stated that his 'mind is blank'. In contrast, S.S. did provide some rather general information when asked to describe events that had happened to him, but these accounts lacked the kind of specific detail that one would expect to find in a personal memory. Cermak and O'Connor therefore concluded that:

> SS had no episodic memory for any events in his life past or present. Recollections instead seem to be drawn entirely from a personal pool of generalised knowledge about himself.
>
> (1983: 230)

Confabulation

Some patients who have problems in remembering their past can provide vivid accounts of events that they claim took place earlier in their life, yet despite the fluency and the detail associated with these accounts, and despite the conviction with which the patients may attempt to defend them, they bear little relationship with reality. Such patients are demonstrating what Moscovitch (1989) has called 'honest lying' and are said to *confabulate*.

Confabulation occurs in a relatively small subset of patients with memory problems. It is usually only found in those who have suffered damage to the frontal lobes (Stuss *et al.* 1978). It can therefore be observed, perhaps in a milder form, in Korsakoff's syndrome, and is also common in patients who are in the early stages of recovery from operations performed to treat ruptured aneurysms of the anterior communicating artery (DeLuca and Cicerone 1991).

Some striking examples of confabulation have been described by Baddeley and Wilson (1986, 1988). Their procedure was based on that used by Robinson (1976) to investigate autobiographical memory in normal subjects. A series of words (e.g. happy, throw, dog, etc.) are presented one at a time, and the subject is asked to recollect a personally experienced incident that is related to each word. In response to the word 'letter', for example, patient R.J. said that he remembered sending a letter to an aunt when his younger brother Martin had been killed in a car accident. When asked how many brothers he now had, he replied, 'Martin and James'. Did he therefore once have two brothers called Martin? R.J. explained thus:

> We had actually in those days one Martin, then mother had another one and we called it Martin as well. I think she felt a bit sort of morbid so she called it Martin and so we had two I suppose, yes, or what would have been two.

In reality, of course, there was only one Martin and he had apparently never been in a serious accident. These confabulations were not maintained over time; when questioned in a later testing session, R.J. said that Martin had never been in an accident.

What makes a patient confabulate? Perhaps any prolonged attempt to retrieve elusive information will lead to the temporary activation of associations between concepts that in reality are unrelated. Like normal subjects, many amnesic patients can probably instantly reject these unlikely ideas as absurd. In the absence of any easy way of distinguishing fantasy from reality, the confabulator may, as Baddeley puts it, 'opt for the easy invention rather than the hazy and difficult truth' (1990: 318).

Loss of meaning

To what extent do patients' anterograde and retrograde memory impairments affect their knowledge of the meanings of words? Gabrieli *et al.*'s (1988) study of H.M. indicates that it is possible for patients to retain their vocabulary for words that were in use prior to the onset of their amnesia despite extreme difficulties in defining and making lexical decisions on words that have entered the language since that time. There is strong evidence, however, that several patients with retrograde amnesia have, in addition to their other memory problems, also lost semantic knowledge about the meanings of words that they once knew well (e.g. De Renzi *et al.* 1987; Hanley *et al.* 1989). De Renzi *et al.* s patient L.P., for instance, gave appropriate definitions for only 36/62 words; for example, she defined *lemon* as 'It is used by people who study or go to school . . . by children', and *violin* as 'I know it, it is used to colour a glass'.

Pioneering studies of patients with such semantic memory deficits have been carried out by Warrington and her colleagues. Typically, these are patients who have made a partial recovery from infection by the herpes simplex virus, which causes extensive damage that is usually centred around the temporal lobes. These patients usually show semantic memory impairments and poor performance on tests of episodic memory such as the Warrington (1984) recognition memory test (Warrington 1975). Much of Warrington's work has investigated cases with striking differences in the particular type of semantic information that is most affected.

McCarthy and Warrington (1988) showed that the modality of presentation can be highly significant. Their patient T.O.B. was able to define pictures of living things (94 per cent correct) even when he could not define the corresponding word (33 per cent correct). For instance, he responded 'lives in Africa, weighs a ton' to a *picture* of a rhinoceros and 'common for this country, on the Thames and canals' to a picture of a swan. In response to the corresponding *words*, however, T.O.B. responded 'totally new word' and 'another animal' respectively.

Warrington (1975) showed that, regardless of modality, the nature of the concept that the patient was asked to identify or define was also extremely important. Patient A.B. had particular problems in defining *concrete* words, being correct on only 24 per cent. Asked what a mosquito is, he responded, 'it sounds familiar'; to needle, 'I've forgotten'; to carrot, 'I must have known once.' By contrast, A.B achieved a score of 85 per cent with abstract words; responding, for instance, to supplication with 'making a serious request for help', and to arbiter with 'he is a man who tries to arbitrate – to produce a friendly solution'.

In subsequent work, Warrington and Shallice (1984) showed that impairment to concrete items can be even more specific in other patients. Patient J.B.R. defined 81 per cent of object names correctly, but only 19 per cent of animals and plant names, and he was also poor with foods. One might roughly characterize this as a difference between living and non-living things, but why should there be a difference of this kind? Warrington suggests that:

living things are comprehended in terms of attributes or sensory features differentiating them from other memories of the same class. This is also the case for foods. On the other hand, objects are comprehended not only in terms of sensory features but also in terms of function, and it is indeed more on the basis of functional differences that objects can be differentiated from members of the same class.

(1986: 5)

An alternative explanation of such living/non-living differences is that they reflect artefacts created by inappropriate selection of stimuli. According to Funnell and Sheridan (1992), the living and non-living things that have been selected for comparison have not always been properly matched for frequency, familiarity and visual complexity. They showed that a patient who initially appeared to show a selective deficit for living things no longer did so when the living and non-living stimuli were matched appropriately. A similar argument has been made by Stewart *et al.* (1992).

These demonstrations show that one needs to be very careful in selecting appropriate stimuli before concluding that a patient has a category-specific impairment. However, problems affecting living things can be found even in cases where this was done. For example, patient M.S. (Young *et al.* 1989) showed a differentially severe impairment to living things even with sets of word stimuli which were matched on typicality or familiarity and produced no living/non-living difference in the reaction times of normal controls. In addition, as Funnel and Sheridan noted, their argument cannot explain why patients such as V.E.R. and Y.O.T. (Warrington and McCarthy 1983, 1987) seem to have the opposite impairment to J.B.R. and perform better with living things than non-living things.

Much less controversial is the distinction that is now commonly made between patients such as J.B.R. in whom there is a loss of semantic knowledge, so that words and things lose their meaning, and *anomic* patients who appear to be simply unable to remember the actual word itself. Patient E.S.T. (Kay and Ellis 1987; Flude *et al.* 1989) is a particularly well-documented case of this kind. When asked to recognize photographs of famous faces, E.S.T. was able to distinguish familiar from unfamiliar people as accurately as normal controls. It was also clear that he knew who the famous person was on 30/40 trials (controls scored an average of 32/40). He was only able to put a name to 3 of the 40 people, however, whereas controls named an average of 26. Here is an example of what happened when E.S.T. was shown the photo of a celebrity:

> I know who he is. Dead. He's a   he's a   he's an American. He did his, he was getting his money, er, getting his money displaying how he could   on the   on the   on the   mm, not the TV   on the radio, er, not on the radio, on the, on the   again, I'm spelling the ruddy thing   f. fee, on the films. He's a great film, and he was, he was on the   cow, cow, er, the last time I saw him he was on the cow, one of the cow pictures.
>
> (Flude *et al.* 1989: 67)

Although E.S.T.'s word-finding problems make his description very tortuous, this account demonstrates that he knew exactly who the person was, but was unable to recall that his name was 'John Wayne'. It is also important to point out that E.S.T.'s problem with names is a retrieval problem. That is, although he cannot recall names, he has no difficulty in recognizing familiar names when they are spoken to him or when they are presented to him on cards.

Like patients with semantic memory impairments, anomic patients can also show very selective deficits (Goodglass *et al.* 1966). For instance, Semenza and Zettin (1988) have reported the case of patient P.C., who appears to have an anomia that is confined to proper names. Unlike E.S.T., P.C. has no problem with word finding in general, being able to provide the correct names for pictures of fruit, vegetables, body parts, colours, letters, transport, furniture and types of pasta. However, it took a year from the onset of his disease before he managed to relearn the names of his wife and son so as to be able to retrieve them consistently. Before that, the only name he could retrieve was his own. When given a set of 20 photographs of famous people to identify, P.C. named 0/20, despite being able to provide accurate biographical information for all 20.

Loss of knowledge of faces

We saw above (pp. 243–5) that the problems that E.L.D. (Hanley *et al.* 1990) encountered in recognizing faces were confined to the period following her illness. Prosopagnosic patients, however, are as severely impaired at recognizing faces of people that they once recognized without difficulty as they are at recognizing faces encountered for the first time in the period following their illness. Although in some cases prosopagnosia is caused by a perceptual deficit, many clinicians accept that there is also a form of prosopagnosia which is more properly considered an impairment of face memory (De Renzi *et al.* 1991; Hécaen 1981). These patients can show covert recognition effects which seem to parallel findings of preserved priming effects in amnesia (Bruyer 1991; Young and de Haan 1990).

An important question then becomes whether this memory impairment is specific to faces. Damasio and his colleagues believe that the visual memory impairment found in prosopagnosic patients is *not* confined to faces. According to Damasio, Tranel and Damasio, they are 'also impaired in the recognition of other unique stimuli – houses, cars, pets, articles of clothing . . . patients with face agnosia fail to recognize an exemplar as a unique individual' (1990: 93). Although this may be true for some prosopagnosic patients, such an account now appears unrealistic as a general explanation. Remarkably specific cases have been described by De Renzi and his colleagues (De Renzi 1986; De Renzi *et al.* 1991), whose patients had no difficulty in recognizing unique exemplars unless the category being tested was faces.

Loss of topographical knowledge

We saw above (pp. 243–5) that patients with loss of recent visual memory (Hanley *et al.* 1990; Ross 1980) often have difficulties both in recognizing faces and in finding their way around. This does not necessarily appear to be the case with prosopagnosic patients, however, who do not always suffer from topographical impairments (Levine *et al.* 1985; Farah *et al.* 1988). Levine *et al.*'s comprehensive review of the literature also makes it clear that topographical impairments do not necessarily co-occur with an impaired ability to recognize objects.

Patient L.H. (Levine *et al.* 1985; Farah *et al.* 1988) provides a clear example of a dissociation between topographical and face processing impairments. L.H. is unable to recognize faces following a car accident, failing even to identify his wife unless she wears something distinctive such as a ribbon in her hair. Yet L.H.'s *spatial* memory is remarkably well preserved. He has good knowledge of the relative relocation of the individual states of the USA, and can describe familiar routes in his native city of Boston without apparent difficulty. He can also travel around the city by himself without getting lost.

By contrast, another patient reported by Levine *et al.* (1985) frequently got lost in his own house and needed to be accompanied whenever he went out, but was not prosopagnosic. His ability to describe routes from his house to the shops was extremely poor, as was his knowledge of the location of cities in the USA. When he was sitting in a room in the hospital that he had inhabited for 2 months, he could not point to the location of his bed, the door or the window if he was blindfolded. It is therefore clear that this patient was suffering from a severe spatial memory impairment.

Nevertheless, it is not the case that all examples of topographical problems are due to an underlying impairment of spatial memory. As Levine *et al.* (1985) point out, there is evidence that patients with well-*preserved* spatial knowledge can none the less experience problems in finding their way around. Landis *et al.* (1986), for instance, described patients who can draw accurate maps of areas in which they get lost. Instead, their difficulties seem to be caused by an inability to recognize well-known environments and landmarks as familiar when they are looking at them. As Pallis' (1955) patient explained, 'My reason tells me I must be in a certain place and yet I don't recognise where I am.' These patients seem to lose their way because they are unable to integrate their perceptual experience with their apparently intact spatial knowledge.

Hence a difficulty in finding one's way around can be caused either by a primary problem in identifying buildings and other landmarks, or by the loss of knowledge of spatial layouts from memory. We have already argued that problems in recognizing faces can take different forms, and the same point seems to hold for problems in finding one's way around.

Working memory deficits

Earlier (see pp. 239–40) we noted that, despite his difficulty in learning new information, patient H.M. can maintain a six-digit sequence in memory by actively rehearsing it. However, Warrington and Shallice (1969) described patient K.F. who had a digit span of only two items. Tests on which K.F. did very badly involved the immediate *serial* recall of verbal materials (words, digits, letters). Nevertheless, K.F.'s long-term memory was not affected in any obvious way; he performed well at learning paired associates and at the free recall and recognition of verbal materials (exactly those tasks on which H.M. is so severely impaired).

Basso *et al.* (1982) and Vallar and Baddeley (1984) have made a detailed investigation of the serial recall performance of patient P.V.

who has an extremely low digit span and preserved long-term memory. Like K.F., and unlike normal subjects, P.V. performs better when the sequences are presented visually rather than auditorily. Normal subjects find serial recall more difficult when the stimuli are phonologically similar to one another and when their spoken duration increases. P.V., however, does not show a word length effect, and shows an effect of phonological similarity only when the stimuli are presented auditorily; there is no phonological similarity effect with visual presentation.

According to Vallar and Baddeley (1984), it is the 'articulatory loop' component of working memory that is defective in cases such as P.V. and K.F. Baddeley (1986) proposes that the articulatory loop comprises two distinct subcomponents: a phonological input store and an articulatory rehearsal mechanism. Since P.V.'s speech rate appears to be normal, Vallar and Baddeley argue that it is a defect of the phonological input store rather than an impairment to the process of articulation that is the cause of P.V.'s low memory span. This is consistent with Shallice and Warrington's (1974) view that an impaired 'auditory-verbal short-term store' was responsible for K.F.'s poor serial recall. It would appear that these patients can partially compensate for their phonological store deficit by using some alternative means of storage with visual presentation, but suffer when auditory presentation makes use of the articulatory loop unavoidable.

If, as Baddeley (1986) suggests, the articulatory loop is also associated with the recency effect in free recall, then patients like P.V. should show an impaired recency effect. This was confirmed by Vallar and Papagno (1986). With auditory presentation of a twelve-item list, P.V. showed no tendency to recall the last items first and did not recall items from the end of the list better than items earlier in the list. Even when she was instructed to recall the last items first, P.V. showed only a very mild recency effect. With visual presentation, however, P.V. showed a much stronger recency effect, particularly when she was instructed to recall from the end of the list. Vallar *et al.* (1991) reported that P.V. also showed a normal *long-term recency* effect. They used a task previously employed by Baddeley and Hitch (1977) in which subjects were asked to add a series of numbers following the presentation of each of the stimulus words. The results showed that P.V., like normal subjects, recalled the terminal items in the list significantly better than the early items. It therefore appears that the long-term recency effect and the short-term visual and auditory recency effects reflect the use of an ordinal retrieval strategy being applied to separate memory stores.

In addition to performing relatively well on serial recall with visual sequences, Basso *et al.* (1982) report that P.V. also performs well on the Corsi blocks task. On this task, the experimenter taps a set of blocks that are fixed on a small wooden board one at a time in a set order; the subject must then tap the blocks in the same order. P.V.'s intact performance of this task contrasts with E.L.D. (Hanley *et al.* 1991), who was impaired relative to controls on Corsi blocks despite excellent performance on tasks associated with the articulatory loop. The very different patterns of preserved and impaired performance that E.L.D. and P.V. show on tests of immediate memory are again consistent with the view that separate components of working memory are involved in the temporary storage of verbal and visuo-spatial material.

When Baddeley *et al.* (1988) investigated P.V.'s ability to learn *new* verbal information, they turned up an extremely interesting finding. Although her ability to learn verbal paired associates in her native Italian was perfectly normal, her ability to learn to associate Italian words with unfamiliar Russian vocabulary was severely impaired relative to controls, particularly when the materials were presented auditorily. What this suggests is that while a phonological short-term memory impairment may not cause a general impairment of new learning, it may severely disrupt the ability to learn unfamiliar verbal material such as new vocabulary. Similarly, the fact that patient E.L.D. had difficulty in learning unfamiliar faces and objects and was also impaired on the Corsi blocks test (Hanley *et al.* 1990; Hanley *et al.* 1991) is clearly consistent with the idea of an equivalent link in the case of visuo-spatial material. Finally, since neither P.V. nor E.L.D. encounters any problems in retrieving pre-morbidly familiar verbal and visuo-spatial information respectively, it would appear that the articulatory loop and visuo-spatial sketchpad are primarily input systems responsible for the processing of incoming information rather than for the retrieval of old memories.

DIFFERENT MEMORY STORES

In the final part of this chapter, we consider how different theoretical frameworks can (or cannot) accommodate the patterns of impairment that we have described. Our own preference is to view memory as resulting from the coordinated interaction of distinct functional components, and we think it is important to avoid reifying 'memory' into something divorced from the tasks an organism must carry out. The need to remember arises in many different circumstances in our everyday lives, and is integral to abilities that seem to have little to do with each other; why should remembering a face depend on the same system as remembering to go to the doctor's? Instead, there are strong biological and evolutionary grounds for thinking that different memory systems may have evolved for different purposes (Sherry and Schacter 1987).

Much of the evidence we have reviewed fits this general characterization very neatly. For example, the marked dissociations between impairments of working memory and impairments affecting long-term recall point strongly toward a 'separate systems' view; yet even here we can see the interdependence of these systems in findings that patients with working memory impairments do show long-term recall problems for certain types of new learning.

However, there are also many unresolved issues, and some areas of outright disagreement, which we will examine more closely.

The concept-driven versus data-driven distinction

According to Roediger and his colleagues (Blaxton 1989; Roediger 1990a, b), both encoding and retrieval tasks vary in the extent to which they involve concept-driven processing and data-driven processing. Consistent with Morris *et al.*'s (1977) notion of transfer-appropriate processing, Roediger believes that memory performance is dependent upon the overlap between the type of processing that was carried out at encoding and the type of processing that is required for the test of memory that is employed. For example, since a test of free recall makes heavy demands on subject-initiated retrieval strategies, it is said to involve concept-driven processing. Consequently, free recall performance will improve to the extent that a task that also involved extensive concept-driven processing (e.g. a semantic orienting task) was carried out at encoding. Conversely, a task such as perceptual identification involves data-driven processing and will benefit from an orienting task that required attention to the physical form of the stimulus.

Roediger (1990a, b) clearly sees the data-driven versus concept-driven distinction as an alternative to the view that memory involves the interaction of a large number of separate memory stores.

According to Roediger, dissociations are observed between different tasks not because they engage different memory stores, but because they involve a different balance between data-driven and concept-driven processing.

Unfortunately, though, Roediger's views are a lot less successful at explaining data from patients with memory impairments than they are at explaining data from normal subjects. The main problem concerns the performance of patients with anterograde amnesia on tests of *implicit* memory, in which performance is assessed by using an indirect measure which can show the influence of past experience without demanding that the subject knows that they are remembering something. For example, despite their impaired ability on tests of free recall and recognition memory, Warrington and Weiskrantz (1970) reported that a group of amnesic patients showed the same tendency as normal subjects to complete word stems and word fragments with words that they had recently been shown. Preserved performance by amnesic patients on these and other tests of implicit memory has been demonstrated many times since the publication of Warrington and Weiskrantz's work (for a review see Shimamura 1986).

One might attempt to explain this pattern of performance by claiming that amnesics are impaired at tasks which involve concept-driven processing, but are normal at tasks which require data-driven processing. As Roediger (1990a) acknowledges, it would therefore follow that amnesics should perform badly on implicit memory tasks that require concept-driven processing. This does not appear to be the case, however. Graf *et al.* (1985) showed that their group of amnesics produced as many items that they had recently seen as did control subjects in an implicit task that involved production of category members. In addition, Hamann (1990) reported that amnesic patients, just like normal controls, retrieved more targets on the category exemplar production task following a semantic than a non-semantic orienting task. Graf *et al.* (1984) also showed that their group of amnesics performed badly on an explicit task such as cued recall from word stems, even though this task is assumed to have a relatively high data-driven component.

How many stores?

It is not our wish to diminish the importance of the extremely interesting experimental demonstrations that Roediger and his associates have carried out. Nevertheless, we believe that it is essential to employ a rather more elaborate theoretical framework in which the existence of several different memory stores is postulated if one is to explain adequately the data from both brain-injured patients and normal subjects. The critical question then becomes: how many stores does one need?

Tulving (1972) drew a distinction between *episodic memory* which contains a record of personally experienced events that have happened to us, and *semantic memory* which contains our general knowledge of the world and is more abstract in form. He considered these as separate memory stores, and in 1985 added a third store called *procedural memory*. Procedural memory, according to Tulving (1985), is involved in tasks which do not require conscious awareness for the learning episode, such as memory for skills. Tulving also suggested that procedural memory is the source of priming, as revealed in tasks such as perceptual identification and word fragment completion.

More recently, however, Tulving and Schacter have instead suggested that priming is closely tied to the process of perceptual identification, and argue that 'it is an expression of a perceptual representation system that operates at a pre-semantic level' (1990: 301). The perceptual representation system (PRS) thus becomes a fourth separate memory system. Such a framework can provide a more adequate account of the pattern of performance that amnesic patients show on implicit and explicit tasks. Impaired performance on tasks such as recall and recognition can be explained in terms of a defective episodic memory. Preserved performance on perceptual learning and word-stem completion (Warrington and Weiskrantz 1968, 1970) and on skills tasks, such as pursuit rotor tracking (e.g. Brooks and Baddeley 1976), can be seen as reflecting unimpaired PRS and procedural memory systems respectively.

It follows from Tulving and Schacter's view that amnesic patients should still be able to acquire novel perceptual information if their impairment is confined to episodic memory. It is therefore consistent with recent evidence from Squire and his colleagues indicating that their amnesics show preserved priming for unfamiliar as well as for familiar stimuli. For instance, Haist *et al.* (1991) reported that amnesics showed equivalent repetition priming to control subjects on a test of perceptual identification regardless of whether the stimuli comprised words or non-words. Musen and Squire (1991) also showed equivalent priming of non-words in amnesics when the dependent variable was reading speed. Squire and McKee (1992) demonstrated that amnesics were just as likely as controls to state incorrectly that a non-famous name they had recently seen was that of a famous person. In this study, and in Haist *et al.* (1991), the amnesics' ability to remember explicitly that they had seen these items was significantly impaired.

Similar results have been obtained with non-verbal stimuli. Paller *et al.* (1992) showed that both amnesics and controls matched faces more quickly if they had seen them previously, regardless of whether they were faces of well-known or unknown people. Schacter *et al.* (1991) showed that amnesics, like controls, performed more accurately on an object decision test with unfamiliar objects that they had seen previously than with unfamiliar objects they had not seen earlier. Gabrieli *et al.* (1991) reported that, despite severely impaired explicit memory for new patterns, H.M. showed a tendency to complete a dot matrix with unfamiliar patterns that he had recently studied.

The distinction between PRS and episodic memory can therefore explain the dissociation between amnesics' poor explicit memory and good implicit memory for new information in terms of a damaged episodic memory in the context of a preserved PRS. What might at first sight seem to many cognitive neuropsychologists to be rather less attractive about Schacter (1990) and Tulving and Schacter's (1990) conceptualization of PRS is the way in which they refer to it as a single memory system. On the basis of the existence of dissociations between, for instance, prosopagnosia, object agnosia, alexia and topographical impairments, many cognitive neuropsychologists would prefer to decompose PRS into separate recognition systems for words, objects, faces, landmarks, etc. (e.g. Ellis and Young 1988).

However, Tulving and Schacter's position follows from a distinction made by Sherry and Schacter (1987) between memory *stores* which differ in terms of the type of information that they contain (e.g. faces, objects, words, etc.) and memory *systems* which differ in terms of their rules of operation (i.e. how they encode, retain or retrieve information). Sherry and Schacter believe it is possible that:

> information about faces is stored and retrieved by the faces module, information about space is stored and retrieved by the space module, but memory in each case operates in the same way.
>
> (1987: 440)

The principles by which these memory stores operate might be the same even though the different stores may represent information in 'neurologically distinct places'. Sherry and Schacter believe that multiple memory *systems*, by contrast, only exist when 'each module has its own acquisition, retention and retrieval processes and that the rules of operation of these processes differ across modules'. Whether the various perceptual modules operate 'in the same way' is not an issue that cognitive neuropsychologists have debated at any great length. It may therefore be the case that this difference between Tulving and Schacter (1990) and the more usual 'modular' position (e.g. Ellis and Young 1988) is essentially one of terminology rather than substance.

Episodic memory

If we accept that PRS consists of several modules, the next question concerns the extent to which episodic memory should also be conceptualized as comprising a number of distinct subsystems.

We believe that the evidence from Milner and her colleagues that was discussed above (see pp. 242–3), together with the studies of patients with recent visual memory loss that were also discussed earlier (see pp. 243–5), provide strong evidence for modularity. It seems likely that there is an episodic memory for verbal information that is primarily dependent on the left hemisphere, and an episodic memory for non-verbal material that primarily involves the right hemisphere. Patients with loss of recent visual memory have therefore suffered damage to the non-verbal episodic store, patients with material-specific memory disorders for verbal information have suffered damage to the verbal episodic store, and patients with anterograde amnesia have suffered damage to both episodic stores.

There is currently no reason to believe that any further decomposition of the episodic memory stores is necessary. One might speculate that there are separate verbal episodic memory stores for, say, visually presented material and auditorily presented material, since there appear to be separate lexicons or PRS stores for different modalities (Ellis and Young 1988). Equally, there might be separate non-verbal episodic stores for, say, faces and routes. There is, however, no strong evidence at present that patients with material-specific memory loss suffer from problems that are as specific as this. For instance, patients with loss of recent visual memory seem to have difficulty learning new faces, new objects and new routes (see pp. 243–5).

The supervisory system and working memory systems

We saw above (pp. 240–2) that there are patients who have difficulties in recalling new information, but who perform normally in tests of recognition memory. There is also a patient who performs normally in recall, but not in recognition (Delbecq-Derouesné *et al.* 1990). One possible explanation of this dissociation would be that separate episodic memory systems subserve performance on recall and recognition tests. Shallice and his colleagues have proposed an alternative explanation, however.

According to Shallice (1988), performance on tests of recall and recognition rely not merely on an intact episodic memory system, they also depend upon the normal functioning of a separate 'supervisory system'. The supervisory system plays a vitally important part in coordinating activity throughout the cognitive system, but Shallice believes that it also plays a key role in memory function. Specifically, it is involved with 'formulating the description of any memories that might be required and of verifying that any candidate memories that are retrieved are relevant' (1988: 378).

Patients with impaired recall but normal recognition would be seen as suffering from a difficulty in setting up effective retrieval strategies that would enable them to access information stored in episodic memory. A test of recognition memory, by contrast, depends much less on subject-initiated retrieval strategies. It depends on the presence of the appropriate information in episodic memory *and* upon the appropriate use of verification procedures. A recognition test could, therefore, be performed normally by a patient whose only deficit lay in formulating retrieval strategies.

Delbecq-Derouesné *et al.*'s (1990) patient R.W., who had difficulties with recognition but not with recall, would be seen as suffering from an impairment to the ability of the supervisory system to verify or reject candidate memories that are retrieved, despite intact episodic memory and normal retrieval strategies. Patient R.W. is also prone to confabulate (see pp. 248–9). According to Shallice (1988), patients who confabulate are also suffering from an inability to deal appropriately with information that reaches the supervisory system from episodic memory. As a consequence, they are unable to distinguish genuine episodic memories from irrelevant associations.

To summarize, a patient with a selective impairment of recall or of recognition can be seen as suffering from a disorder of the supervisory system, unlike an amnesic patient whose problems reflect a difficulty in registering new information in episodic memory. When the supervisory system is unable to formulate a retrieval strategy, the patient will have problems with recall; when the supervisory system is unable to verify candidate memories, the patient will have difficulties with recognition memory and will show evidence of confabulation. Finally, there is evidence that patients with memory impairments of this kind also show poor performance on the Wisconsin Card sorting test and other tasks that are associated with the normal functioning of the supervisory system (Shallice 1988).

It is also important to emphasise that the supervisory system is only one of several subsystems quite distinct from episodic and semantic memory that are responsible for the on-line processing and temporal storage of information within the cognitive system. We have seen (see pp. 254–6) that there is strong neuropsychological evidence for a dissociation between working memory and long-term episodic memory. Thus, there are patients with defective memory spans and reduced recency effects who perform normally on tests of episodic memory, and patients with anterograde amnesia who have normal memory spans and recency effects. This strongly supports the idea that temporary storage of information within the cognitive systems is the responsibility of specific working memory systems that are distinct from any episodic or semantic memory stores (Baddeley 1992). Within working memory, there is also neuropsychological evidence for a dissociation between an articulatory/phonological short-term store and a visuo-spatial short-term store.

Semantic memory

There is strong evidence that patients with semantic memory deficits should be distinguished from patients with deficits at the level of the PRS system such as prosopagnosics or alexics (see pp. 249–53). It is also clear that we should distinguish semantic memory systems from those that are concerned with word production. This follows from studies of anomic patients who have severe problems in retrieving word-forms despite having preserved access to the meanings of words that they cannot recall.

The extent to which semantic memory has a modular structure, however, remains one of the most controversial issues in contemporary cognitive neuropsychology. We saw earlier (see pp. 250–1) that there is, for instance, evidence for a dissociation between memory for abstract and concrete concepts, between memory for living and non-living concepts, and between memory for sensory/ visual information and functional/verbal information. As we saw, there are those who argue that category specificity is an artefact of the inappropriate selection of experimental stimuli, whilst others maintain that the dissociations that are observed in these patients reflect an underlying modular structure of semantic memory. The basis for modularity might lie in the nature of the concepts themselves (e.g. concrete versus abstract concepts) or it might reflect the different types of semantic features which represent individual concepts (e.g. sensory versus functional features). Others still (e.g. Shallice 1988) have pointed out that semantic memory might consist of one giant semantic net, and that the dissociations that are observed in patients might reflect the way in which particular types of concepts interact with modular perceptual systems and modular output systems. Much work will be needed to determine which of these approaches is going to turn out to be the most useful.

Episodic memory and semantic memory

The final question that we will consider is whether or not there is evidence from cognitive neuropsychology for a dissociation between episodic and semantic memory. We will discuss two relevant lines of evidence. These are the performance of patients with anterograde amnesia on tests of semantic memory, and the performance of patients with semantic memory impairments on tests of episodic memory.

As we have already noted, many patients with semantic memory impairments also have problems on episodic memory tasks (Warrington 1975). One exception to this pattern is patient E.D. (Kapur *et al.* 1986, 1989) who was discussed above (see pp. 245-8). E.D. was unable to remember many famous people or events from the past, so one must conclude that he had lost information from semantic memory. At the same time, however, his autobiographical memory did not appear to be impaired, which suggests that episodic memory for the same period was intact. De Renzi *et al.* (1987) pointed to a similar dissociation for their patient L.P. Such evidence is clearly consistent with a neuropsychological dissociation between episodic and semantic memory.

We have seen that there is very strong evidence that patients with severe deficits on tests of episodic memory can nevertheless learn new perceptual information, provided that indirect (implicit) tests are used. What of amnesics' semantic memory ability? We mentioned earlier (see pp. 258–61) evidence of normal performance by amnesics on the implicit task of category member generation, which would appear to tap semantic memory (Graf *et al.* 1985; Hamann 1990). If, however, their impairment is confined to episodic memory, then amnesics' ability to learn *new* semantic information should also be normal. Here, the evidence is rather less clear-cut. Tulving *et al.* (1991) investigated the ability of patient K.C., who apparently lacks the ability to retrieve any specific event that has ever happened to him (see p. 248), to learn new semantic facts. K.C. was presented with a series of pictures and three-word sentences, such as 'medicine-cured hiccup', next to a picture of a man in a hospital bed. K.C. received extensive training with these items over many separate testing sessions. Even when a year had elapsed since the final training session, however, K.C. continued to complete successfully a large number of the sentences in response to a cue which comprised part of the sentence. This occurred despite the fact that K.C. had no recollection of why he knew these 'facts'.

Tulving *et al.* (1991) argue that it is difficult to believe that K.C.'s defective episodic memory might be responsible for this new learning. In addition, they claim that since K.C.'s retention of these sentences was independent of their modality of presentation (modality of presentation has a critical effect on perceptual priming), PRS cannot be responsible either. Consequently, Tulving *et al.* (1991) conclude that K.C.'s semantic memory must be at least partially functional in contrast to his severely impaired episodic memory.

On the other hand, as we saw above (see pp. 249–52), Gabrieli *et al.* (1988) showed that the amnesic patient H.M. was unable to learn new vocabulary that they tried to teach him. Tulving *et al.* (1991) suggest that Gabrieli *et al.*'s (1988) learning conditions may have been such that they placed demands on H.M.'s defective episodic memory. However, Gabrieli *et al.* (1988) also showed that H.M. was unable to remember new vocabulary that had entered the language since his illness. Could this also be explained in terms of defective episodic memory? If one were to accept that performance on tasks thought to tap semantic memory may also involve episodic memory, then it would explain why there are no reports of patients who show fully preserved performance on standard tests of semantic memory in the presence of impaired episodic memory. It does, however, mean that a lot more work needs to be done to clarify the precise nature of the distinction between episodic and semantic memory!

The moral is perhaps that neuropsychologists should not expect to be able to answer questions such as the relationship between episodic and semantic memory without reference to the latest results and theorizing from within mainstream cognitive psychology. Neuropsychological research will not have a lasting impact on our understanding of human memory unless the results that it produces can be integrated with those from traditional experimental psychology. However, we hope that the data reviewed in this chapter are sufficiently powerful to have convinced you that this is happening, and that no serious student of human memory can afford to ignore them.

ACKNOWLEDGEMENT

Our work in this area has been funded by Economic and Social Research Council grant R000231922.

REFERENCES

Albert, M.S. (1984) 'Implications of different patterns of remote memory loss for the concept of consolidation', in H. Weingartner and E.S. Parker (eds) *Memory Consolidation*, Hillsdale, New Jersey: Erlbaum.

Albert, M.S., Butters, N. and Brandt, J. (1981) 'Development of remote memory loss in patients with Huntington's disease', *Journal of Clinical Neuropsychology* 3: 1–12.

Albert, M.S., Butters, N. and Levin, J. (1979) 'Temporal gradients in the retrograde amnesia of patients with alcoholic Korsakoff's disease', *Archives of Neurology* 36: 211–16.

Andrews, E., Poser, C.M. and Kessler, M. (1982) 'Retrograde amnesia for forty years', *Cortex* 18: 441–58.

Baddeley, A.D. (1986) *Working Memory*, Oxford: Clarendon Press.

—— (1990) *Human Memory: Theory and Practice*, London: Erlbaum.

—— (1992) 'Is working memory working?', *Quarterly Journal of Experimental Psychology* 44A: 1–31.

Baddeley, A.D. and Hitch, G.J. (1977) 'Recently re-examined', in S. Dornic (ed.) *Attention and Performance*, VI, Hillsdale, New Jersey: Erlbaum.

Baddeley, A.D. and Wilson, B. (1986) 'Amnesia, autobiographical memory and confabulation', in D.C. Rubin (ed.) *Autobiographical Memory*, Cambridge: Cambridge University Press.

—— 'Frontal amnesia and the dysexecutive syndrome', *Brain and Cognition* 7: 212–30.

Baddeley, A.D., Papagno, C. and Vallar, G. (1988) 'When long-term learning depends on short-term storage', *Journal of Memory and Language* 27: 586–95.

Basso, A., Spinnler, H., Vallar, G. and Zanabio, M.E. (1982) 'Left hemisphere damage and selective impairment of auditory short-term memory', *Neuropsychologia* 20: 263–74.

Blaxton, T.A. (1989) 'Investigating dissociations among memory measures:

Support for a transfer appropriate processing framework', *Journal of Experimental Psychology: Learning, Memory and Cognition* 15: 657–68.

Brooks, D.N. and Baddeley, A.D. (1976) 'What can amnesic patients learn?', *Neuropsychologia* 14: 111–22.

Bruyer, R. (1991) 'Covert face recognition in prosopagnosia: A review', *Brain and Cognition* 15: 223–35.

Butters, N. and Cermak, L.S. (1986) 'A case study of the forgetting of autobiographical knowledge: Implications for the study of retrograde amnesia', in D.C. Rubin (ed.) *Autobiographical Memory*, Cambridge: Cambridge University Press.

Butters, N., Wolfe, J., Martone, M. Granholm, E. and Cermak, L.S. (1985) 'Memory disorders associated with Huntington's disease: Verbal recall, verbal recognition and procedural memory', *Neuropsychologia* 23: 729–43.

Cermak, L.S. and O'Connor, M. (1983) 'The anterograde and retrograde retrieval ability of a patient with encephalitis', *Neuropsychologia* 21: 213–34.

Cohen, N.J. and Squire, L.S. (1981) 'Retrograde amnesia and remote memory impairment', *Neuropsychologia* 19: 337–56.

Coltheart, M. (1985) 'Cognitive neuropsychology and the study of reading', in M.I. Posner and O.S.M. Marin (eds) *Attention and Performance*, XI, Hillsdale, New Jersey: Erlbaum.

Craik, F.I.M. and Tulving, E. (1975) 'Depth of processing and the retention of words in episodic memory', *Journal of Experimental Psychology: General* 104: 268–94.

Damasio, A.R., Tranel, D. and Damasio, H. (1990) 'Face agnosia and the neural substrates of memory', *Annual Review of Neuroscience* 13: 89–109.

De Renzi, E. (1986) 'Current issues in prosopagnosia', in H.D. Ellis, M.A. Jeeves, F. Newcombe and A. Young (eds) *Aspects of Face Processing*, pp. 243–52, Dordrecht: Martinus Nijhoff.

De Renzi, E., Liotti, M. and Nichelli, P. (1987) 'Semantic amnesia with preservation of autobiographical memory: A case report', *Cortex* 23: 575–97.

De Renzi, E., Faglioni, P., Grossi, D. and Nichelli, P. (1991) 'Apperceptive and associative forms of prosopagnosia', *Cortex* 27: 213–21.

Delbecq-Derouesné, J., Beauvois, M.F. and Shallice, T. (1990) 'Preserved recall versus impaired recognition', *Brain* 113: 1045–74.

DeLuca, J. and Cicerone, K.D. (1991) 'Confabulation following aneurysm of the anterior communicating artery', *Cortex* 27: 417–23.

Dewick, H.C., Hanley, J.R., Davies, A.D.M., Playfer, J. and Turnbull, C. (1991) 'Perception and memory for faces in Parkinson's disease', *Neuropsychologia* 29: 785–802.

Drachman, D.A. and Arbit, J. (1966) 'Memory and the hippocampal complex', *Archives of Neurology* 15: 52–61.

Ellis, A.W. and Young, A.W. (1988) *Human Cognitive Neuropsychology*, Hove: Erlbaum.

Farah, M.J., Hammond, K.M., Levine, D.N. and Calvanio, R. (1988) 'Visual and spatial representations: Dissociable systems of representation', *Cognitive Psychology* 11: 60–72.

Flude, B.M., Ellis, A.W. and Kay, J. (1989) 'Face processing and name retrieval in an anomic aphasic: Names are stored separately from semantic information about familiar people', *Brain and Cognition* 20: 439–62.

Funnell, E. and Sheridan, J. (1992) 'Categories of knowledge? Unfamiliar aspects of living and non-living things', *Cognitive Neuropsychology* 9: 135–53.

Gabrieli, J.D.E., Cohen, N.J. and Corkin, S. (1988) 'The impaired learning of semantic knowledge following bilateral medial temporal-lobe resection', *Brain and Cognition* 7: 157–77.

Gabrieli, J.D.E., Milberg, W., Keane, M.M. and Corkin, S. (1990) 'Intact patterns of priming despite impaired memory', *Neuropsychologia* 28: 417–28.

Goodglass, H., Klein, B., Carey, P. and James, K.J. (1966) 'Specific semantic word categories in aphasia', *Cortex* 2: 74–89.

Graf, P., Shimamura, A.P. and Squire, L.R. (1985) 'Priming across modalities and priming across category labels: Extending the domain of preserved function in amnesia', *Journal of Experimental Psychology: Learning, Memory and Cognition* 11: 386–96.

Graf, P., Squire, L.R. and Mandler, G. (1984) 'The information that amnesics do not forget', *Journal of Experimental Psychology: Learning, Memory and Cognition* 10: 164–78.

Haist, F., Musen, G. and Squire, L.R. (1991) 'Intact priming of words and non-words in amnesia', *Psychobiology* 19: 275–85.

Hamann, S.B. (1990) 'Levels-of-processing effects in conceptually driven implicit tasks', *Journal of Experimental Psychology: Learning, Memory and Cognition* 16: 970–7.

Hanley, J.R., Pearson, N.A. and Young, A.W. (1990) 'Impaired memory for new visual forms', *Brain* 113: 1131–48.

Hanley, J.R., Young, A.W. and Pearson, N.A. (1989) 'Defective recognition of familiar people', *Cognitive Neuropsychology* 6: 179–210.

Hanley, J.R., Young, A.W. and Pearson, N.A. (1991) 'Impairment of the visuo-spatial sketch pad', *Quarterly Journal of Experimental Psychology* 43A: 101–25.

Hanley, J.R., Davies, A.D.M., Downes, J. and Mayes, A.R. (1994) 'Impaired recall of verbal material following rupture and repair of an anterior communicating artery aneurysm', *Cognitive Neuropsychology* 11.

Hécaen, H. (1981) 'The neuropsychology of face recognition', in G. Davies, H. Ellis and J. Shepherd (eds) *Perceiving and Remembering Faces*, pp. 39–54, London: Academic Press.

Hirst, W., Johnson, M.K., Kim, J.K., Phelps, E.A., Risse, C. and Volpe, B.T. (1986) 'Recognition and recall in amnesics', *Journal of Experimental Psychology: Learning, Memory and Cognition* 12: 445–51.

Hodges, J.R. (1991) *Transient Amnesia, Clinical and Neuropsychological Aspects*, London: Baillière Tindall.

Janowsky, J.S., Shimamura, A.P. and Squire, L.R. (1989) 'Memory and metamemory: Comparisons between patients with frontal lobe lesions and amnesic patients', *Psychobiology* 17: 3–11.

Kapur, N., Heath, P., Meudell, P. and Kennedy, P. (1986) 'Amnesia can facilitate performance: Evidence from a patient with dissociated retrograde amnesia', *Neuropsychologia* 24: 215–22.

Kapur, N., Young, A.W., Bateman, D. and Kennedy, P. (1989) 'Focal retrograde amnesia: A long-term clinical and neuropsychological follow up', *Cortex* 25: 387–402.

Kay, J. and Ellis, A.W. (1987) 'A cognitive neuropsychological case study of anomia', *Brain* 110: 613–29.

Landis, T., Cummings, J.L., Benson, D.F. and Palmer, E.P. (1986) 'Loss of topographic familiarity: An environmental agnosia', *Archives of Neurology* 43: 132–6.

Levine, D.N., Warach, J. and Farah, M. (1985) 'Two visual systems in mental imagery: Dissociation of what and where in imagery disorders due to bilateral posterior cerebral lesions', *Neurology* 35: 1010–18.

McCarthy, R.A. and Warrington, E.K. (1988) 'Evidence for modality specific meaning systems in the brain', *Nature* 334: 428–30.

Marslen-Wilson, W.D. and Teuber, H.L. (1975) 'Memory for remote events in anterograde amnesia: Recognition of public figures from photographs', *Neuropsychologia* 13: 353–64.

Milner, B. (1958) 'Psychological defects produced by temporal lobe excision', *Research Publications: Association for Research in Nervous and Mental Disease* 36: 244–57.

—— (1962) 'Laterality effects in audition', in V.B. Mountcastle (ed.) *Interhemispheric Relations and Cerebral Dominance*, Baltimore: Johns Hopkins Press.

—— (1966) 'Amnesia following operation on the temporal lobes', in C.W.M. Whitty and O.L. Zangwill (eds) *Amnesia*, London: Butterworths.

—— (1967) 'Brain mechanisms suggested by studies of temporal lobes', in C.H. Millikan and F.L. Darley (eds) *Brain Mechanisms Underlying Speech and Language*, New York: Grune & Stratton.

—— (1968) 'Alteration of perception and memory in man: Memory', in L. Weiskrantz (ed.) *Analysis of Behavioral Change*, New York: Harper & Row.

—— (1974) 'Hemispheric specialization: Scope and limits', in V.O. Schmitt and F.G. Worden (eds) *The Neurosciences: Third Study Program*, Cambridge, Massachusetts: MIT Press.

—— (1978) 'Clues to cerebral organization of memory', in P. Buser and A. Rougeul-Buser (eds) *Cerebral Correlates of Conscious Experience: INSERM Symposium no. 6*, Elsevier: North-Holland Biomedical Press.

Milner, B., Corkin, S. and Teuber, H.-L. (1968) 'Further analysis of the hippocampal amnesia syndrome: 14-year follow up study of H.M.', *Neuropsychologia* 6: 215–34.

Morris, C.D., Bransford, J.D. and Franks, J.J. (1977) 'Levels of processing versus transfer appropriate processing', *Journal of Verbal Learning and Verbal Behavior* 16: 519–33.

Moscovitch, M. (1989) 'Confabulation and the frontal lobes: Strategic versus associative retrieval in neuropsychological theories of memory', in H.L. Roediger and F.I.M. Craik (eds) *Varieties of Memory and Consciousness: Essays in Honor of Endel Tulving*, Hillsdale, New Jersey: Erlbaum.

Musen, G. and Squire, L.R. (1991) 'Normal acquisition of novel verbal information in amnesia', *Journal of Experimental Psychology: Learning, Memory and Cognition* 17: 1095–104.

Paller, K.A., Mayes, A.R., Thompson, K.M., Young, A.W., Roberts, J. and Meudell, P.R. (1992) *Brain and Cognition* 18: 46–59.

Pallis, C.A. (1955) 'Impaired identification of faces and places with agnosia for colours', *Journal of Neurology, Neurosurgery and Psychiatry* 18: 218–24.

Parker, E. and Noble, E. (1977) 'Alcohol consumption and cognitive functioning in social drinkers', *Journal of Studies on Alcohol* 38: 1224–32.

Parkin, A.J., Dunn, J.C., Lee, C., O'Hara, P.F. and Nussbaum, L. (1993) 'Neuropsychological sequelae of Wernicke's encephalopathy in a 20-year-old woman: Selective impairment of a frontal memory system', *Brain and Cognition* 21: 1–19.

Penfield, W. and Milner, B. (1958) 'The memory deficit caused by bilateral lesions in the hippocampal zone', *Archives of Neurology and Psychiatry* 79: 475–97.

Peterson, L.R. and Peterson, M.J. (1959) 'Short-term retention of individual verbal items', *Journal of Experimental Psychology* 58: 193–8.

Robinson, J.A. (1976) 'Sampling autobiographical memory', *Cognitive Psychology* 8: 578–95.

Roediger, H.L. (1990a) 'Implicit memory: Retention without remembering', *American Psychologist* 45: 1043–56.

—— (1990b) 'Implicit memory: A commentary', *Bulletin of the Psychonomic Society* 28: 1373–80.

Roediger, H.L., Rajaram, S. and Srinivas, K. (1990) 'Specifying criteria for postulating memory systems', in A. Diamond (ed.) *The Development and Neural Bases of Higher Cognitive Function*, New York: New York Academy of Sciences.

Ross, E.D. (1980) 'Sensory-specific and fractional disorders of recent memory in man: I. Isolated loss of visual recent memory', *Archives of Neurology* 37: 193–200.

Schacter, D.L. (1990) 'Perceptual representation systems and implicit memory: Towards a resolution of the multiple memory systems debate', in A. Diamond (ed.) *The Development and Neural Bases of Higher Cognitive Function*, New York: New York Academy of Sciences.

Schacter, D.L., Cooper, L.A., Tharan, M. and Rubens, A. (1991) 'Preserved priming of novel objects in patients with memory disorders', *Journal of Cognitive Neuroscience* 3: 118–31.

Scoville, W.B. and Milner, B. (1957) 'Loss of recent memory after bilateral hippocampal lesions', *Journal of Neurology, Neurosurgery and Psychiatry*, 20: 11–21.

Semenza, C. and Zettin, M. (1988) 'Generating proper names: A case of selective inability', *Cognitive Neuropsychology* 5: 711–21.

Shallice, T. (1988) *From Neuropsychology to Mental Structure*, Cambridge: Cambridge University Press.

Shallice, T. and Warrington, E.K. (1974) 'The dissociation between short-term retention of meaningful sounds and verbal material', *Neuropsychologia* 12: 553–5.

Sherry, D.F. and Schacter, D.L. (1987) 'The evolution of multiple memory systems', *Psychological Review* 94: 439–54.

Shimamura, A.P. (1986) 'Priming effects in amnesia: Evidence for a dissociable memory function', *Quarterly Journal of Experimental Psychology* 38A: 619–44.

Sidman, M., Stoddard, L.T. and Mohr, J.P. (1968) 'Some additional quantitative observations of immediate memory in a patient with bilateral hippocampal lesions', *Neuropsychologia* 6: 245–54.

Smith, M.L. (1988) 'Recall of spatial location by the amnesic patient H.M.', *Brain and Cognition* 7: 178–83.

Smith, M.L. and Milner, B. (1981) 'The role of the right hippocampus in the recall of spatial location', *Neuropsychologia* 19: 781–93.

Squire, L.R. and McKee, R. (1992) 'Influence of prior events on cognitive judgements in amnesia', *Journal of Experimental Psychology: Learning, Memory and Cognition* 18: 106–15.

Squire, L.R., Haist, F. and Shimamura, A.P. (1989) 'The neurology of memory: Quantitative assessment of retrograde amnesia in two groups of amnesic patients', *Journal of Neuroscience* 9: 828–39.

Stewart, F., Parkin, A.J. and Hunkin, N.M. (1992) 'Naming impairments following recovery from herpes simplex encephalitis', *Quarterly Journal of Experimental Psychology* 44A: 261–84.

Stuss, D.T., Alexander, M.P., Lieberman, A. and Levine, H. (1978) 'An extraordinary form of confabulation', *Neurology* 28: 1166–72.

Tulving, E. (1972) 'Episodic and semantic memory', in E. Tulving and W. Donaldson (eds) *The Organization of Memory*, New York: Academic Press.

—— (1985) 'How many memory systems are there?', *American Psychologist* 40: 385–98.

Tulving, E. and Schacter, D.L. (1990) 'Priming and human memory systems', *Science* 247: 301–6.

Tulving, E., Hayman, C.A.G. and Macdonald, C.A. (1991) 'Long-lasting perceptual priming and semantic learning in amnesia: A case experiment', *Journal of Experimental Psychology: Learning, Memory and Cognition* 17: 595–617.

Tulving, E., Schacter, D.L., McLachan, D.R. and Moscovitch, M. (1988) 'Priming of semantic autobiographical knowledge: A case study of amnesia', *Brain and Cognition* 8: 3–20.

Vallar, G. and Baddeley, A.D. (1984) 'Fractionation of working memory: Neuropsychological evidence for a phonological short-term store', *Journal of Verbal Learning and Verbal Behavior* 23: 151–61.

Vallar, G. and Papagno, C. (1986) 'Phonological store and the nature of the recency effect', *Brain and Cognition* 5: 428–42.

Vallar, G., Papagno, C. and Baddeley, A.D. (1991) 'Long-term recency effects and phonological short-term memory', *Cortex* 27: 323–6.

Warrington, E.K. (1975) 'The selective impairment of semantic memory', *Quarterly Journal of Experimental Psychology* 27: 635–57.

—— (1984) *Recognition Memory Test*, Windsor: NFER.

—— (1986) 'Memory for facts and memory for events', *British Journal of Clinical Psychology* 25: 1–12.

Warrington, E.K. and McCarthy, R.A. (1983) 'Category-specific access dysphasia', *Brain* 106: 859–78.

—— (1987) 'Categories of knowledge. Further fractionations and an attempted integration', *Brain* 111: 1273–96.

—— (1988) 'The fractionation of retrograde amnesia', *Brain and Cognition* 7: 184–200.

Warrington, E.K. and Shallice, T. (1969) 'The selective impairment of auditory short-term memory', *Brain* 92: 885–96.

—— (1984) 'Category-specific semantic impairments', *Brain* 107: 829–54.

Warrington, E.K. and Weiskrantz, L. (1968) 'New method of testing long-term retention with special reference to amnesic patients', *Nature* 277: 972–4.

—— (1970) 'Amnesic syndrome: Consolidation or retrieval', *Nature* 228: 628–30.

Wilson, R.S., Kaszniak, A.W. and Fox, J.H. (1981) 'Remote memory in senile dementia', *Cortex* 17: 41–8.

Young, A.W. and Bruce, V. (1991) 'Perceptual categories and the computation of "grandmother" ', *European Journal of Cognitive Psychology* 3: 5–49.

Young, A.W. and de Haan, E.H.F. (1990) 'Impairments of visual awareness', *Mind and Language* 5: 29–48.

Young, A.W., Newcombe, F., Hellawell, D. and de Haan, E.H.F. (1989) 'Implicit access to semantic information', *Brain and Cognition* 11: 186–209.

9

NATURALISTIC APPROACHES TO THE STUDY OF MEMORY

E. Winograd

It would be highly desirable if all the important questions about memory could be studied in the laboratory. The control and rigour of the laboratory speak for themselves. Indeed, any memory researcher who can read Ebbinghaus' (1885/1964) treatise showing that memory can be studied scientifically without a feeling of excitement is probably in the wrong field. The major legacy of Ebbinghaus, and the hallmark of laboratory research into memory, is that the target information is acquired under conditions established by the experimenter. Study time and its distribution, the type and amount of material studied, and the level of mastery are all controlled by the experimenter. When the investigator is not present at the encoding, this enormous advantage is lost. To many trained in the laboratory, studying memory for events without this kind of control induces dismay. Yet, in spite of the undeniable advantages of laboratory research, many contemporary memory researchers have ventured outside the laboratory. So much naturalistic memory research has been done that it has stimulated a heated controversy about method (see Banaji and Crowder 1989 for a critique of naturalistic memory research and the January 1991 issue of *American Psychologist* for responses).

The purpose of this chapter is not to debate the relative merits of different approaches to the study of memory, but to outline some methods that have been used to study memory in natural settings and discuss some interesting findings that have emerged. My position is that the phenomena of memory are so diverse that there is no single set of methods to be adopted to the exclusion of others. Diversity of method is called for when we consider the variety of phenomena there are to be explained. There is as little reason to believe that there is only one correct way to study memory as there is to believe that there

273

is only one correct way to study evolution. A major reason for enter-
taining a variety of methods is that following a single methodology
restricts the problems we choose to study. If a problem is interesting
but methodologically recalcitrant, it tends to be ignored in favour of a
different problem that is more easily studied in the laboratory. There
are a number of important and interesting phenomena of memory
that are very hard, perhaps impossible, to study in the traditional
memory laboratory. As a consequence, they tend to be overlooked.
Since there is no shortage of worthwhile problems amenable to traditional methods, the tendency is to continue with the methods we
know and trust. One result of this is that we study only certain kinds
of phenomena.

In this chapter, I will selectively review research on memory for
information not learned in a laboratory in order to demonstrate some
important aspects of the naturalistic, or ecological, approach to
memory. For related accounts, the interested reader might consult
Cohen (1989), Gruneberg and Morris (1992) and Winograd (1993).

RETENTION AND FORGETTING OVER LONG
INTERVALS

To most people, the proper study of memory is forgetting. Yet, after
100 years of study, there are great gaps in what we have learned from
laboratory research about forgetting over long periods of time. This is
because it is difficult to do experiments in which people acquire
information and then are tested on retention months and years later.
For many years, Ebbinghaus' (1885/1964) heroic effort with a single
subject, himself, was taken as representing the true course of forgetting. Ebbinghaus' function showed him to be a very leaky bucket,
forgetting at such a rapid rate that less than half the material he
mastered was retained only 2 hours later. When Peterson and Peterson
(1959) showed rapid forgetting in short-term memory over just 18
seconds, with a loss function mirroring Ebbinghaus', it appeared that
there was a universal forgetting curve. We now know that forgetting
curves are not necessarily of the leaky bucket variety and that the
passage of time may yield markedly different kinds of functions. This
area of study, more than any other, highlights the importance of
expanding our observational base.

The most dramatic departure from the laboratory forgetting curve
is to be found in the first of Harry Bahrick's landmark studies of
naturalistic memory. Bahrick *et al.* (1975) studied the retention of

names and faces of high school classmates over a 50-year period. Using each subject's own yearbook, the experimenters prepared customized tests. Recognition tests demanded that the subject choose the name (or face) of their classmate from among five names (or faces) of non-classmates. Matching required that the correct name and face be paired. In picture cueing, a face would be shown and name recall demanded. In free recall, subjects were asked to retrieve as many names of classmates as possible with no cues provided. The results are shown in Figure 9.1. The remarkable finding of this study is that, on tests of recognition and matching, no forgetting at all was observed during the first 35 years after graduation. So much for a leaky bucket view of forgetting.

How can we account for the remarkable durability of this information? One suggestion to be considered is that it is the nature of the remembered information, the memoria, that makes the difference. After all, Ebbinghaus and the Petersons studied memory for nonsense syllables, whereas Bahrick and his colleagues studied socially important memoria, namely, information about real people. This hypothesis has difficulty in accounting for another Bahrick (1984a) finding from a study of the memory of college teachers for the names and faces of their former students. In contrast with the outcome of the high school yearbook study, Bahrick found that professors do forget their students. The resulting function showed forgetting of former students by professors to be a declining logarithmic function of time, much like Ebbinghaus. Bahrick has argued that the stability of memory found in the high school yearbook study is due to the high degree of learning of high school classmates. The favourable conditions for acquisition were, first, the enormous degree of exposure to one's classmates over a minimum of 4 years of schooling (bear in mind that many of these classmates, in fact, knew each other before high school) and, second, the favourable spacing, or distribution, of practice. Encounters with one's classmates are spaced; one sees them daily, but not on the weekend or holidays, including long summer holidays. It is well known from laboratory research that distribution of practice promotes long-term retention (see Baddeley 1990). If Bahrick is correct, here is a case where principles discovered in the laboratory can aid our understanding of unusual findings encountered in nature. Bahrick argues that a professor's exposure to students for one academic semester is considerably more limited than one's exposure to high school classmates over 4 or more years. As a consequence, there is less resistance to forgetting.

275

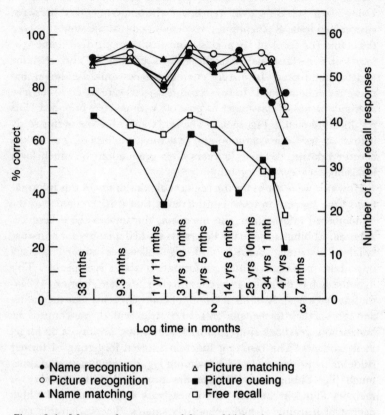

Figure 9.1 Memory for names and faces of high school classmates over 50 years (Bahrick *et al.* 1975).

Bahrick points out that the degree of learning hypothesis fits other long-term retention data obtained naturalistically. For example, Squire (1989) studied the retention of information about shows that appeared on American television for only one season and sunk without a trace, never appearing on reruns. He prepared recognition tests for the names of shows that appeared from 1 to 15 years ago (e.g. which of these was a TV show? Delvecchio, Street Scene, Peace and Justice, USAF). Over a period of 15 years, Squire found a continuous but gradual loss function that seems to represent an intermediate case between Ebbinghaus' rapid decay function and the plateau of retention over 35 years found by Bahrick *et al.* (see the top

276

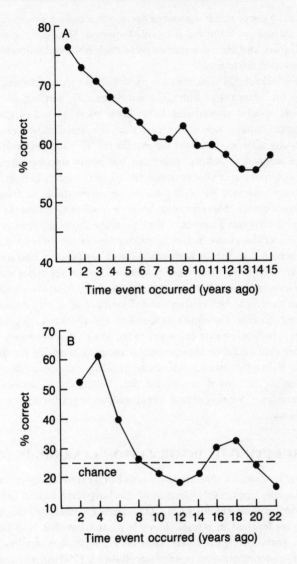

Figure 9.2 Memory for the names of television shows over 15 years
(Squire 1989).

panel of Figure 9.2). The observant reader may have noticed that, even in Bahrick *et al.*'s yearbook study, forgetting was found for the recall measures (see Figure 9.1). In naturalistic memory studies, as in

277

the laboratory, recall measures are more sensitive to changes occurring during the retention interval. However, the different patterns in the Squire and Bahrick studies were each obtained with measures of recognition memory.

Methodological concerns are as important in naturalistic research as in the laboratory. Since the conditions of learning are not controlled, special procedures have been used by investigators. For example, Squire was concerned that the association between how long ago a show originally appeared on TV and recognition of its name might not reflect forgetting but some uncontrolled artefact. Perhaps more recent shows are mentioned more often in the press and conversation; the effect might be attributable to frequency of exposure rather than recency. Another possibility is that the plausibility of the invented names of the distractor shows differed systematically across the years. Squire's control for these problems was to give the same test to junior high school students (see the bottom panel of Figure 9.2). Since they were not around when the older shows were on television, they should not yield the same function as adults. For shows that aired before they were 7 years of age, performance of the junior high school students (whose average age was 13.5 years) was at chance, indicating that exposure to the shows was necessary to obtain a score that could be interpreted as showing memory for the shows.

In Bahrick's work, statistical techniques, especially multiple regression, are used to control for the effects of factors such as rehearsal, i.e. looking at one's yearbook after graduation or attending reunions.

FORGETTING OF INFORMATION LEARNED IN SCHOOL

Recently, Bahrick and his associates have extended their research to the socially important question of the long-term fate of information acquired in formal education. It is commonly observed that we forget what we learned in school. Here is a question that is impossible to study with the rigour of the laboratory. Formal education does not occur under controlled conditions. Bahrick (1984b) investigated the retention of Spanish over intervals as long as 50 years and obtained still another unique forgetting curve (see Figure 9.3). Retention declined continuously for about 5 years following the last course in Spanish, but then stabilized for about 25 years. Whereas retention of information about high school classmates was stable at the level attained during acquisition, in this case stability was attained only

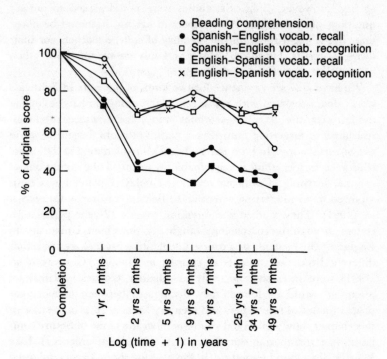

Figure 9.3 Retention of Spanish learned in school assessed by different testing methods (Bahrick 1984b).

after a period of forgetting. Bahrick proposes that information that survives the 5-year reign of terror has become immune to forgetting or is, in his words, in 'permastore'. Most interesting is the further finding that the proportion of Spanish that reached the safe haven of permastore was an increasing function of the two available measures of initial acquisition: number of years of study and grades earned in the courses. Those who had studied Spanish longer and earned higher grades showed the greatest resistance to forgetting. Although the conditions of acquisition were not controlled, reasonable estimates of learning were available from school records and these estimates predicted performance very well. This is pleasant news for teachers, of course, since it looks as if grading is fairer than students are usually willing to allow.

Students of ageing and memory might note that, in both the yearbook and Spanish experiments, there is a late drop associated with ageing. However, Bahrick's studies were not designed to answer questions about ageing. With respect to ageing, it should be noted that, in his experiment on the memory of college teachers for their former students, Bahrick (1984a) found only minor differences when he examined the effects of the teachers' ages.

We have now seen evidence for two kinds of plateaux in Bahrick's work, one associated with resistance to forgetting directly following the last exposure, as in the yearbook study, and one associated with resistance to forgetting only after a period of rapid forgetting, as in the Spanish study. In both cases, Bahrick's explanation is the same: resistance to forgetting is explainable in terms of the conditions of original learning. Confirmation of the delayed plateau has been reported in an interesting extension of Bahrick's work by Conway *et al.* (1991). They studied the retention over a 12-year period of a course in cognitive psychology taught by the Open University in England. The contents of a course in cognitive psychology are rather different from the contents of courses in Spanish. Conway *et al.* (1991) were interested not only in whether Bahrick's plateau of retention would be found; they distinguish between memory for proper names of researchers and memory for concepts (in the case of this chapter, how well would you remember the name of Squire compared to remembering the effects of distribution of practice?). Like Bahrick, they found forgetting, in this case for about 3 years, followed by a longer period of stability. In fact, this pattern was obtained for different kinds of information, although names were forgotten more quickly than concepts. Another interesting finding of Conway *et al.* (1991) is that the students' confidence in the accuracy of their knowledge continued to decline throughout the 12-year retention period, even during the lengthy period during which retention had stabilized. The authors offer the reasonable interpretation that the students subscribe to the belief that memory continues to decline as time goes by and their confidence ratings reflect this belief, even though they are not actually forgetting.

With respect to the predictive power of course grades on long-term retention, Conway *et al.* (1991) initially failed to find the strong association that Bahrick reported. But, in a further analysis of their data, they found that when course grades were separated into examination grades versus course-work grades, the marks on the course work were reliable predictors of retention, although performance on the final examination was not (Conway *et al.* 1992). Upon reflection, it is clear that the final grade in any course depends upon a varying mixture of papers, reports and examinations. The authors point out that, in the British system, examinations involve essays in which critical integration and evaluation are rewarded but 'staightforward regurgitation of learned material only attracts lower grades' (Conway *et al*. 1992: 384). Furthermore, they speculate that the type of high-level understanding expected in these essay examinations is forgotten more rapidly than the information that underlies it. Since objective tests were used to measure long-term retention, it is not surprising that performance on an essay examination did not predict later performance. In brief, then, both Bahrick and Conway, Cohen and Stanhope have found comparable retention curves for information acquired in formal education; these retention functions are characterized by forgetting for somewhere between 3 to 5 years, followed by a long period during which the remaining information is impervious to loss; and the level of stabilized knowledge attained is predictable from performance during acquisition of the knowledge.

It is not the case, however, that all information acquired through formal education is forgotten for a few years and then stabilizes. For mathematics, Bahrick and Hall (1991a) found that the retention of high school algebra showed two markedly different patterns. For those who had taken no further algebra courses, a classical decay function was obtained with no indication of any retention 50 years later. On the other hand, there was no indication of any forgetting at all during 50 years for those who continued the study of mathematics beyond calculus. It is clear that there is no single pattern of long-term retention to be found outside the laboratory.

The lesson of this overview of forgetting curves is that there is no single pattern of long-term retention, no universal forgetting curve, to be found when we venture outside the laboratory. Ebbinghaus' 'classical' forgetting curve is simply one number of a family of functions and it reflects particular learning conditions. Under other conditions, other forgetting functions are found, and some of these functions are notable for their resistance to forgetting over extremely long periods of time. It is unlikely that the existence of this diversity would be known had the observational base of our science not been broadened.

The determinants of retention need to be understood better for both theoretical and practical reasons. As a rich database accumulates, hypotheses about what Bahrick calls the 'maintenance of knowledge' will continue to be generated and tested. Educational institutions are interested not only in the acquisition of knowledge but also in its maintenance over time. Recent work by Bjork (1988) and Bahrick and Hall (1991b) has begun to deal with this important application of memory research.

REMOTE MEMORY IN AMNESIA

There are two major types of memory impairment associated with amnesia: anterograde and retrograde amnesia. Anterograde amnesia refers to difficulty in learning new information, whereas retrograde amnesia refers to difficulty in retrieving information that was previously learned. It is relatively easy to diagnose anterograde amnesia by means of tests requiring the learning of lists of words. Patients with anterograde problems have difficulty remembering more than an item or two from a list of ten words. Patients with retrograde amnesia have trouble remembering events that happened some time ago, and it is a challenging task to delineate their problem because we rarely have enough knowledge about an individual's past to ascertain whether or not one's inability to remember earlier events falls within the range of normal forgetting. One way to deal with this problem is to construct tests of dated general knowledge, that is, knowledge to which one can reasonably assume all members of the culture have had exposure and to which we can assign a date with some degree of confidence. We have already encountered an example in Squire's test of TV shows that appeared for only one season.

One approach to the problem of measuring remote memory using dated general cultural knowledge may be seen in a study by Marslen-Wilson and Teuber (1975). They were interested in the question of whether the world's most studied amnesic patient, H.M., who was born in 1926, manifested retrograde amnesia as well as a profound anterograde amnesia (Milner 1966). The dated materials they used were pictures of famous people, including statesmen, athletes and icons of popular culture. For example, if you were over 50 years of age and could identify a picture of Jimmy Carter, it is likely that the information was encoded during the 1970s. While it is possible that you saw a picture of Jimmy Carter for the first time only 2 weeks ago, we know with confidence the earliest time that the information was acquired. By taking people who became prominent during different decades, Marslen-Wilson and Teuber were able to make up an appropriate test for H.M. and control subjects of the same age and education (there were two groups of controls, one head-injured but non-amnesia and the other neither head-injured not amnesic).

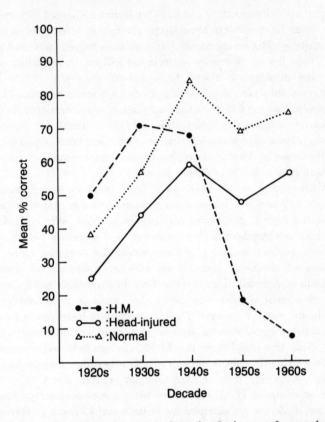

Figure 9.4 Memory for the names of people who became famous during different decades for the amnesic patient H.M. and two control groups (Marslen-Wilson and Teuber 1975).

The results for the famous faces memory test are shown in Figure 9.4. First note the functions for the control groups. In general, the more recent the decade during which the person came to prominence, the more likely it is that he or she is correctly identified. There is a slight irregularity such that faces from the 1940s are more recognizable than later faces; the authors attribute this to the great familiarity of war heroes such as Churchill and Eisenhower. Now compare the function that H.M. produces. He remembers faces prominent 30 years ago much better than faces that became famous within the most recent decade. Here is still another in our inventory of great forgetting curves: the inverse U-curve. In interpreting H.M.'s data, it

283

is important to know that the onset of his amnesia was on 1 September 1953, when he underwent brain surgery to relieve severe and intractable epilepsy. His severe anterograde amnesia began then, and it is likely that his performance reflects difficulties in encoding and retrieving information about the world subsequent to 1953. His retention of information acquired prior to 1950 seems normal. Thus, one interpretation of H.M.'s unusual pattern of remembering is that he did not acquire the information he fails to recall in a normal manner, rather than assuming that he at one time knew it and subsequently forgot it. That is to say, his unusual remote memory pattern probably reflects his anterograde amnesia.

An interesting recent study of H.M.'s memory shows that his inability to learn new information extends to words that have been introduced into English since his surgery in 1953. While H.M. is described as a regular television watcher, and therefore presumably has been exposed to many of these words, he does not know the meaning of charisma, jacuzzi, psychedelic, palimony or granola (Gabrielli et al. 1988). This is not a theoretically trivial finding, since it is not consistent with the theory that amnesia is a disorder of episodic memory (Tulving 1989). His inability to learn new words in general use suggests that his disorder extends to semantic memory as well. (While one could argue that H.M.'s failure to learn these words reflects a deficit in episode memory, it then becomes unclear how to distinguish episodic from semantic memory empirically.)

Let us compare H.M.'s memory with that of another profound amnesic, P.Z., as documented by Butters and Cermak (1986) in a remarkable study. P.Z. was a distinguished scientist who developed Korsakoff's syndrome in his sixties. This is a serious disorder associated with chronic alcoholism and marked by anterograde and retrograde amnesia. Butters and Cermak were able to construct a test of P.Z.'s memory based on a record of his own life as set forth in the autobiography he had written a few years before the onset of the disease. Rather than use a test of general knowledge, as Marslen-Wilson and Teuber were forced to, Butters and Cermak had available a rich source of information about P.Z.'s life as written by himself. All of the information in his autobiography could fairly be assumed to have been well encoded in his memory at the time that he wrote it. P.Z.'s recall of information from his autobiography is shown plotted by decade in Figure 9.5. Here is a perfect inverse forgetting function: the older the information the better P.Z. remembers it. Of the last 20 years, he remembers nothing. Different interpretations are possible, of course, of P.Z.'s distinctive pattern. One explanation would be that, with progressive alcoholism, more recent memories were less well encoded or more fragile, and therefore more susceptible to the trauma of Korsakoffism. A problem for this point of view is that all of the memories tested were encoded well enough to have been recorded in his autobiography. Also, his impairment stretches far back in time. Another interpretation is that memories continue to be consolidated long after their original encoding with more recent memories therefore less resistant to the trauma of Korsakoff's syndrome (see Butters and Cermak 1986 and Squire 1987 for discussions of retrograde amnesia). It is clear that any satisfactory theory of how memories are stored in the brain will have to account for the data of H.M. and P.Z. The richness of the data they provide is testimony to the diversity of memory phenomena awaiting study.

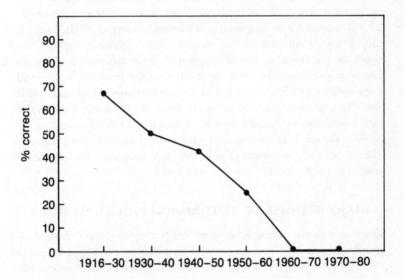

Figure 9.5 The amnesic patient P.Z.'s retrograde amnesia over six decades for information from his autobiography (Butters and Cermak 1986).

For our purposes, it needs to be emphasized that it is unlikely that such data would be obtained in the traditional laboratory. The information that is tested here was acquired in the course of everyday life and, even with the evidence of an autobiography, we know little about the conditions of acquisition. But we have a reasonable idea of the approximate age of the information that is being tested, and that suffices for the purposes of delineating the temporal distribution of the memories. The regularities of the obtained patterns are compelling evidence that control has been achieved over an important aspect of memory.

In all of the research surveyed so far, the researcher assumes the role of a memory detective and tries to figure out what happened some time ago. As in all detective work, the challenge is to construct a likely past on the basis of the evidence currently available. Bahrick and his colleagues used the evidence available from old yearbooks and class records. Squire probed available records of old TV broadcasts, while Marslen-Wilson and Teuber searched old magazines and newspapers for photographs and information about famous people. Butters and Cermak were extremely fortunate to have P.Z.'s autobiography available. What all of these investigators have in common is that their manipulations occur at the time of retrieval. This is a point I have discussed elsewhere (Winograd 1993). Laboratory research on memory is usually about learning because the conditions of learning can be controlled in the laboratory. Naturalistic studies of memory occur later on, they are retrieval studies and the conditions of learning have to be reconstructed. The trade-off is that the student of naturalistic memory is able to study a variety of rich questions. As Bahrick puts it, 'Naturalistic investigations rarely achieve the levels of control attainable in the laboratory, but they are able to explore phenomena that are not amenable to laboratory research' (1992: 113).

DIARY STUDIES OF AUTOBIOGRAPHICAL MEMORY

Elsewhere in this series, Robinson (1992) reviews studies of autobiographical memory. In much of the research on that topic, participants are provided with cue words and asked to describe the first episode from their lives that comes to mind. They are also asked to date the memory. While this procedure has provided investigators with a considerable amount of useful information about the nature and temporal distribution of memories that readily come to mind, we have no way of knowing to what extent the memories reflect events that actually occurred. Following the pioneering work of Linton (1975), some intrepid researchers have undertaken studies of autobiographical memory where a record is kept of selected events as they occur. These are usually known as diary studies and I will review some intriguing findings from this small literature.

One finding that reinforces a principle known from laboratory research has to do with cue distinctiveness. This principle states that the efficiency of a retrieval cue is inversely related to the number of associations it is part of; the more items associated with the cue, the less likely it is that a particular target will be successfully retrieved. Watkins and Watkins (1975) refer to this as the 'cue-overload effect'. In semantic memory, this principle refers to the longer time it takes to retrieve information to an overloaded cue and is referred to as 'the fan effect' (Anderson 1990). The optimal conditions for retrieval obtain when a cue is uniquely associated with the information it serves. It is noteworthy that classical mnemonic systems use one-to-one pairing of cue and target. (Although the same cues may be used repeatedly in different situations, their distinctiveness is preserved by being embedded in different contexts. In any given context, one-to-one pairing is the rule.) Classical interference phenomena such as retroactive and proactive interference may be seen as special cases of the cue distinctiveness principle. The interference condition in these experiments always has more information attached to the retrieval cue than does the control condition.

There are two studies of autobiographical memory that extend the cue distinctiveness principle to observations of everyday memory. The first is a heroic diary study by the Dutch psychologist Willem Wagenaar. At the end of each day for 6 years, he recorded descriptions of events that had occurred that day. He recorded the following aspects of each event: *who* was involved, *what* the event was, *where* it occurred and *when* it occurred. Wagenaar was interested in the relative potency of these different aspects of an event when presented as retrieval cues and, in his original article about this research, reported that *what* was the most potent cue, *who* and *where* were moderately effective, and *when* was the least effective cue by far (Wagenaar 1986). However, in 1988, Wagenaar reported a reanalysis of his data taking into account cue distinctiveness. When distinctiveness, or cue loading, was controlled for, it turned out that the differences in cue potency were largely eliminated.

I have plotted some of Wagenaar's (1988) reanalysed data in Figure 9.6 as a function of cue distinctiveness. This figure shows the probability of recalling the activity engaged in (*what*) to either the cue *who* or *where*. For both cues, it is apparent that the probability of recalling the nature of the event or activity declines as the number of

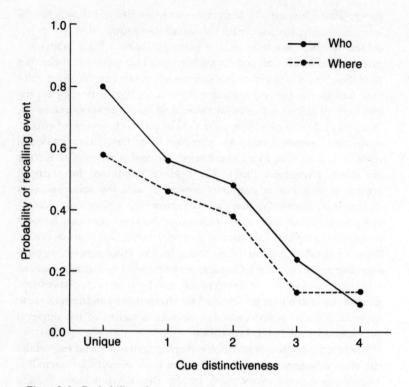

Figure 9.6 Probability of retrieving *what*, given cue of *who* or *where*, as a function of cue distinctiveness in diary corpus (adapted from Table 2 in Wagenaar 1988).

activities associated with that cue increases. To give an example, if you were asked what film you had seen at the Odeon versus what film you had seen at the Princess, and you regularly patronized the Odeon but had only been to the Princess twice, you would be more likely to recall a particular film you had seen at the Princess. While you would certainly remember more total films you had seen at the Odeon, the likelihood of recalling a target film would be greater if you had seen it at the Princess. Cue distinctiveness functions resembling Wagenaar's have been obtained in the laboratory by Earhard (1967) and Watkins and Watkins (1975).

A clever variation of the diary technique is to be found in Brewer's 'beeper' study (1988). The participants in Brewer's experiments were college students who wore a beeper on their person that was programmed to go off at irregular intervals. When it sounded, the wearer was instructed to record their activities, thoughts and feelings at the time. In agreement with Wagenaar's findings, the best predictor of later recall was distinctiveness (see Robinson 1992 for a fuller description of Brewer's research).

FLASHBULB MEMORIES AND DIARY STUDIES

A type of autobiographical memory that has attracted a great deal of interest is the vivid, detailed recall of a major event that seems to persist unchanged over many years. The paradigmatic case, at least for Americans, is remembering hearing the news of the assassination of President John F. Kennedy. In a famous article Brown and Kulik (1975) reported that, 12 years later, all of their informants could recite with unusual detail where they were, who they were with and how they heard the news of the assassination. What is remarkable is not that they remembered the historical facts about the slaying, but that they claimed to remember accurately their personal circumstances. Why should these memories be so powerful? Brown and Kulik's proposal that these are special memories that reflect the operation of a special mechanism has not gone unchallenged. Neisser (1982), for one, has argued that the claim that the memories are accurate was not verified and cited his own vivid, but inaccurate, memory of the attack on Pearl Harbour as a case of inaccurate flashbulb memories. More recently, Neisser and Harsch (1992) asked American undergraduates to report how they heard the news the day after the space shuttle *Challenger* exploded. Then, almost 3 years later, they retested the same informants to see if their memory remained intact. Contrary to the special mechanism hypothesis, over 40 per cent of their informants gave detailed accounts on the second occasion that clearly disagreed with their earlier accounts. One might counter these findings of inaccurate flashbulb memories by suggesting that the *Challenger* explosion was not that significant after all.

Fortunately, a recent diary study by the Danish psychologist Steen Larsen (1992) provides an interesting counterpart to Neisser and Harsch's work. Following a procedure similar to Wagenaar, Larsen recorded daily events for 6 months and cued his memory from 1 to 11 months later. It so happened that, during the period Larsen kept his diary, some truly major events occurred. Among them were the assassination of the Prime Minister of Sweden, Olaf Palme, and the Chernobyl nuclear disaster. Both of these were of great significance for Scandinavians; in fact, the Chernobyl nuclear cloud drifted toward Sweden and Denmark. In spite of the importance of these events, Larsen's recall was inaccurate for both events. Although he recalled hearing the news about Chernobyl on the radio in the morning while home alone, his diary shows that he heard the news 'at Pia's place just after work'. His recall of hearing the news about Palme was wrong as well. Interestingly, Larsen observes that his false memories are still so vivid that only the evidence of the diary convinces him that they are, in fact, not accurate. The Swedish psychologist Sven-Ake Christianson (1989) has also shown that memories of the Palme assassination can be inconsistent when the same people are asked to recall it twice.

These studies not only seriously undermine the assumption that flashbulb memories are necessarily accurate but also, more importantly, raise a general question about the accuracy of memory. This is not a new question, nor is it one that laboratory investigators have neglected, but research on autobiographical memory has served to focus attention on this fundamental question once more with a richer database (see Winograd, in press, for a discussion of memory accuracy). For a provocative theory of the sources of bias in autobiographical memory, we turn to the work of the social psychologist Michael Ross.

BIAS IN PERSONAL MEMORY

A question underlying research on memory is to what extent is memory accurate. Is distortion in remembering a rare event or is remembering intrinsically an unstable process? There are two research traditions, each on opposite sides of this issue. Traditional list learning researchers, the descendants of Ebbinghaus, rarely find errors (or 'intrusions') in the recall of their subjects, and their theories are constructed to explain accurate remembering. There is another tradition, however, whose patron saint is Bartlett (1932), that views memory as reconstructive rather than reproductive. From the viewpoint of constructive theories, remembering is driven as much by the current views and motives of the person remembering as it is by any record of past events. Researchers from both traditions have adhered to laboratory methods, differing primarily in the complexity of the materials learned by their subjects. Reproductive memory theorists teach their subjects lists of unrelated items, while reconstructive theorists tend to expose their subjects to sentences and stories. Meanwhile, a small body of social psychologists has been concerned with memory for more personal information acquired in the course of ordinary life. Recently, Ross (1989) has summarized some of this research and presented a theory of how people go about remembering information about themselves.

Imagine that you were asked about how much you weighed the summer before you began your university studies or to estimate how painful your last dental surgery was. Ross has reviewed the results of a large number of studies concerning people's memory for their past standing on such personal attributes, and found that when memory is not accurate, it is distorted to conform to present attitudes about the past. In particular, two principles seem to govern our interpretation of what we were like in the past. These principles are: (a) our present standing on the attribute in question, and (b) whether we believe that we are likely to have changed or not with respect to this attribute. So, if we are asked about how we used to feel about abortion some time ago, we would examine our current attitude, and if we believe that our attitudes are stable over time, we would be likely to remember that our past attitude was the same as our present attitude. Indeed, this is what seems to happen. Social psychologists (see Ross 1989) have shown that when attitudes change, people are likely to misrecall their earlier attitudes in just this way. Alternatively, if we believe that we have changed, then this view of ourselves governs personal recall, as when those who have taken self-improvement courses remember themselves as being worse than they really were, presumably in order to enhance perceived improvement. Therefore, we would expect those who have gone to a lot of trouble to lose weight to recall being even heavier than they actually were at the outset of their diet in line with their theory of having changed for the better. Since it is hard to argue with the present testimony of the scales, memory serves us by falsifying our earlier weight in line with our view of ourselves as an improved person. It is not the case, however, that the remembered past exists at the whim of the present. The research summarized by Ross shows that, on the whole, recall is highly accurate. However, when it is in error, the error is systematic.

Methodologically, this kind of research requires that there be a record of the earlier state of affairs so that the accuracy of recall can be established. In practice, this has meant that investigators have used medical records, questionnaire data and the like from a variety of settings in order to test their theories. As noted earlier, the student of memory in natural settings must be something of a detective, ferreting out reliable information about the past.

THE PROPER RELATIONSHIP BETWEEN LABORATORY AND NATURALISTIC RESEARCH ON MEMORY

When naturalistic findings converge with what we already know from laboratory research, it is tempting to conclude that we knew it all along, that the additional evidence is superfluous. I would argue that such convergence gives important generality to the laboratory finding. There are two possibilities in comparing across the two domains, one being convergence and the other divergence. When there is divergence, as is the case with some of Bahrick's studies of long-term retention, we clearly have learned something new. That is, although Bahrick interprets his findings with concepts drawn from laboratory-based theories, his retention curves, as we have seen, are new. When there is convergence, our confidence in the empirical basis of our science increases. Either way, we have made progress. Landauer (1991) has observed that the major contribution of naturalistic research lies in broadening our observational base and finding new phenomena overlooked by laboratory research. Perhaps such phenomena will be explainable in terms of the principles of learning and memory already known from the laboratory, in the way that Bahrick accounts for his unique retention curves in terms of degree of learning and distribution of practice. On the other hand, new kinds of explanations may be necessary. Interpretation of naturalistic memory phenomena in terms of function has been proposed by Bruce (1985) and others (see Baddeley 1988 and Neisser 1988), and this represents a new theoretical direction. When we broaden the observational base of a discipline, it is hard to foresee what the theoretical consequences will be. Of one thing, however, we can be certain: both the empirical and theoretical aspects of the science of memory will be enriched.

REFERENCES

Anderson, J.R. (1990) *Cognitive Psychology and its Implications*, San Francisco: Freeman.

Baddeley, A.D. (1988) 'But what the hell is it for?', in M.M. Gruneberg, P.E. Morris and R.N. Sykes (eds) *Practical Aspects of Memory: Current Research and Issues*, vol. 1, pp. 3–19, Chichester: Wiley.

—— (1990) *Human Memory*, Boston: Allyn & Bacon.

Bahrick, H.P. (1984a) 'Memory for people', in J.E. Harris and P.E. Morris (eds) *Everyday Memory, Actions and Absent Mindedness*, pp. 19–34, New York: Academic Press.

—— (1984b) 'Semantic memory in permastore: 50 years of memory for Spanish learned in school', *Journal of Experimental Psychology: General* 113: 1–29.

—— (1992) 'Stabilized memory of unrehearsed knowledge', *Journal of Experimental Psychology: General* 121: 112–13.

Bahrick, H.P. and Hall, L.K. (1991a) 'Lifetime maintenance of high school mathematics content', *Journal of Experimental Psychology: General* 120: 20–33.

—— (1991b) 'Preventive and corrective maintenance of access to knowledge', *Applied Cognitive Psychology* 5: 1–18.

Bahrick, H.P., Bahrick, P.O. and Wittlinger, R.P. (1975) 'Fifty years of memories for names and faces: A cross-sectional approach', *Journal of Experimental Psychology: General* 104: 54–75.

Banaji, M.R. and Crowder, R.G. (1989) 'The bankruptcy of everyday memory', *American Psychologist* 44: 1185–93.

Bartlett, F.C. (1932) *Remembering*, Cambridge: Cambridge University Press.

Bjork, R.A. (1988) 'Retrieval practice and the maintenance of knowledge', in M.M. Gruneberg, P.E. Morris and R.N. Sykes (eds) *Practical Aspects of Memory: Current Research and Issues*, vol. 1, pp. 396–401, New York: Wiley.

Brewer, W.F. (1988) 'Memory for randomly sampled autobiographical events', in U. Neisser and E. Winograd (eds) *Remembering Reconsidered: Ecological and Traditional Approaches to Memory*, pp. 21–90, Cambridge: Cambridge Univeristy Press.

Brown, R. and Kulik, J. (1975) 'Flashbulb memories', *Cognition* 5: 73–9.

Bruce, D. (1985) 'The how and why of ecological memory', *Journal of Experimental Psychology: General* 114: 78–90.

Butters, N. and Cermak, L.S. (1986) 'A case study of the forgetting of autobiographical knowledge: implications for the study of retrograde amnesia', in D.C. Rubin (ed.) *Autobiographical Memory*, pp. 253–72, Cambridge: Cambridge University Press.

Christianson, S.-A. (1989) 'Flashbulb memories: Special, but not so special', *Memory and Cognition* 17: 435–43.

Cohen, G. (1989) *Memory in the Real World*, Hillsdale, New Jersey: Erlbaum.

Conway, M.A., Cohen, G. and Stanhope, N. (1991) 'On the very long-term retention of knowledge acquired through formal education: twelve years of cognitive psychology', *Journal of Experimental Psychology: General* 120: 395–409.

—— (1992) 'Why is it that university grades do not predict very long-term retention?', *Journal of Experimental Psychology: General* 121: 382–4.

Earhard, M. (1967) 'Cued recall and free recall as a function of the number of items per cue', *Journal of Verbal Learning and Verbal Behavior* 6: 257–63.

Ebbinghaus, H. (1885/1964) *Memory: A Contribution to Experimental Psychology*, New York: Dover.

Gabrielli, J.D., Cohen, N.J. and Corkin, S. (1988) 'The impaired learning of semantic knowledge following bilateral medial temporal-lobe resection', *Brain and Cognition* 7: 157–77.

Gruneberg, M.M. and Morris, P.E. (1992) 'Applying memory research', in

M. Gruneberg and P. Morris (eds) *Aspects of Memory*, vol. 1, *The Practical Aspects*, pp. 1–17, London: Routledge, second edition.

Landauer, T.K. (1989) 'Some bad and some good reasons for studying memory and cognition in the wild', in L.W. Poon, D.C. Rubin and B.A. Wilson (eds) *Everyday Cognition in Adulthood and Late Life*, pp. 116–28, New York: Cambridge University Press.

Larsen, S.F. (1992) 'Potential flashbulbs: Memories of ordinary news as the baseline', in E. Winograd and U. Neisser (eds) *Affect and Accuracy in Recall: Studies of 'Flashbulb Memories'*, pp. 32–64, New York: Cambridge University Press.

Linton, M. (1975) 'Memory for real-world events', in D.A. Norman and D.E. Rumelhart (eds) *Explorations in Cognition*, pp. 376–404, San Francisco: Freeman.

Marslen-Wilson, W.D. and Teuber, H.L. (1975) 'Memory for remote events in anterograde amnesia: Recognition of public figures from news-photographs', *Neuropsychologia* 13: 353–64.

Milner, B. (1966) 'Amnesia following operation on the temporal lobes', in C.W.M. Whitty and O.L. Zangwill (eds) *Amnesia*, pp. 109–33, London: Butterworths.

Neisser, U. (1982) 'Snapshots or benchmarks', in U. Neisser (ed.) *Memory Observed*, pp. 43–8, San Francisco: Freeman.

—— (1988) 'Time present and time past', in M.M. Gruneberg, P.E. Morris and R.N. Sykes (eds) *Practical Aspects of Memory: Current Research and Issues*, vol. 2, pp. 545–60, Chichester: Wiley.

Neisser, U. and Harsch, N. (1992) 'Phantom flashbulbs: False recollections of hearing the news about *Challenger*', in E. Winograd and U. Neisser (eds) *Affect and Accuracy in Recall: Studies of 'Flashbulb Memories'*, pp. 9–31, New York: Cambridge University Press.

Peterson, L.R. and Peterson, M.J. (1959) 'Short-term retention of individual verbal items', *Journal of Experimental Psychology* 58: 193–8.

Robinson, J.A. (1992) 'Autobiographical memory', in M.M. Gruneberg and P.E. Morris (eds) *Aspects of Memory*, vol. 1, *The Practical Aspects*, pp. 223–51, London: Routledge, second edition.

Ross, M. (1989) 'Relation of implicit theories to the construction of personal histories', *Psychological Review* 96: 341–57.

Squire, L.R. (1987) *Memory and Brain*, New York: Oxford.

—— (1989) 'On the course of forgetting in very long-term memory', *Journal of Experimental Psychology: Learning, Memory and Cognition* 15: 241–5.

Tulving, E. (1989) 'Remembering and knowing the past', *American Scientist* 77: 361–7.

Wagenaar, W.A. (1986) 'My memory: A study of autobiographical memory over six years', *Cognitive Psychology* 18: 225–52.

—— (1988) 'People and places in my memory: A study of cue specificity and retrieval from autobiographical memory', in M.M. Gruneberg, P.E. Morris and R.N. Sykes (eds) *Practical Aspects of Memory: Current Research and Issues*, vol. 1, pp. 228–33, Chichester: Wiley.

Watkins, O.C. and Watkins, M.J. (1975) 'Buildup of proactive inhibition as a cue-overload effect', *Journal of Experimental Psychology* 104: 442–52.

Winograd, E. (1993) 'Memory in the laboratory and everyday memory: The case for both', in J.M. Puckett and H.W. Reese (eds) *Mechanisms of Every-day Cognition*, pp. 55–70, Hillsdale, New Jersey: Erlbaum.

—— (in press) 'Comments on the authenticity and utility of memories', in U. Neisser and R. Fivush (eds) *The Remembering Self: Construction and Accuracy in the Life Narrative*, New York: Cambridge University Press.

10

EXPERIMENTATION AND ITS DISCONTENTS

M.R. Banaji and R.G. Crowder

In this chapter, we address three issues: (a) the *generality* of a finding, its external validity and the centrality of internal validity, (b) *context*, in particular the claim that context is sometimes available in poorly controlled but not in well-controlled settings, and (c) the matter of *functionalism*. We regard the observations we offer, especially (a) and (b), to be among the most basic issues that confront any attempt at a systematic investigation of any aspect of mind and behaviour. In view of the sophistication of likely readers of this volume, we offer this discussion with some deference, intending our discussion most obviously for the neophyte to scientific psychology and, more ambitiously, for the teacher of scientific psychology.

We occasionally use memory as our target domain, although we view our comments as relevant to psychology in general. Whereas the issues we identify were brought to our attention by responses to an article we once wrote (Banaji and Crowder 1989), we shall not continue with individual rebuttals to those responses (see Banaji and Crowder 1991; Roediger 1991). Rather, we hope that these three issues will serve as new points of discussion for the thesis we originally wanted to stress about the value of the experimental method, in response to criticism of it in the name of 'real world' questions about memory.

We shall conclude (a) that the true generality of a finding is inextricably linked to the degree of the internal validity of the agencies (experimental or non-experimental) that produced the finding, (b) that the experimental setting *is* a real world context after all, and such settings, creatively contrived, can provide powerful examinations of contextual variables, and (c) that questions about function, although they are quite important, appear more often than not to be intractable and practically moot.

GENERALITY

Here we deal with a chronic troublemaker. In research methods courses, we teach that the primary reason to do an experiment is the ability it provides to manipulate a variable, to assign subjects to conditions randomly, and to control extraneous factors. Other methods such as surveys, case studies, naturalistic observation, etc. are useful and at times indispensable tools, but they rarely, if ever, can provide an explanation. They can describe and even predict, but experiments and quasi-experiments are the surest and most efficient way to explain a phenomenon. In theory, students appear to understand this without difficulty. However, recurring confusion about the value of experiments pops up in the most unexpected contexts. Perhaps this occurs because of a lack of understanding of what exactly is relinquished when alternatives are selected – even on the part of sophisticated experimenters themselves – and we conclude, therefore, that this point needs affirmation. An experiment is the least fallible guide to answers about causality. On this matter of causality, we specifically endorse Craik's (1952) conclusion that psychology ought to proceed *as if* the world were governed by a straightforward model of cause and effect.

The issue concerning generality cannot be discussed without raising a distinction between the internal and external validity of an experimental effect, a distinction first proposed by Campbell (1957). Internal validity was used to refer to the extent to which the research design permits a conclusion about the causal relationship between independent and dependent variables. External validity was used to refer to the extent to which the research findings from the sample can generalize to the population and settings specified in the hypothesis.

Often, these two types of validity are seen as contrasting or even reciprocal. For example, in a popular research methods text, Kidder and Judd state:

> Experimental designs and procedures maximize the internal validity of research – they enable the researcher to rule out most rival explanations or threats to internal validity. There is a tradeoff, however. *Experimenters maximize internal validity often at the expense of the external validity or generalizability of the results.* Do the findings extend beyond the laboratory? Can the experimenter talk about these phenomena in the world outside, or do they appear only in seemingly sterile conditions?
>
> (1986: 98, italics added)

The problem of generality, as we see it, stems not from what many think an experiment can do; rather, it may stem from what many think an experiment cannot do. This common representation of a trade-off between internal and external validity has perhaps obscured the obvious association and necessarily hierarchical relationship between them. Our point is this: when the internal validity of an experiment is threatened, so is its external validity or generalizability also threatened. In fact, Carlsmith *et al.* are especially clear about this:

> But of the two, internal validity is, of course, the more important, for if random or systematic error makes it impossible for the experimenter even to draw any conclusions from the experiment, the question of *generality* of these conclusions never arises.
>
> (1976: 85)

Often, the two types of validity are influenced by the same factors. For example, the experimental realism of the situation, important to *all* experimenters whether they are everyday memory specialists or not, is critical for both internal and external validity. If subjects know the purpose of the experiment – perhaps suspecting a surprise memory test – the internal validity of the experiment is compromised, but so is the external validity because the results would then be generalizable only to subjects who accurately knew the purpose of the experiment.

Thus, our earlier endorsement of scientific generality of research findings (Banaji and Crowder 1989) really sets a special premium on internal validity, the confidence that an experimental manipulation is unconfounded with unwelcome co-variation. Although influential commentators on quasi-experimental design and analysis tell us:

> Indeed, external validity and construct validity are so highly related that it was difficult for us to clarify some of the threats as belonging to one validity type or another
>
> (Cook and Campbell 1979: 82)

positing a trade-off between the two has led to the misguided belief that achieving a high degree of internal validity results in sacrificing external validity. A more reasonable attitude is that internal validity forms a necessary condition for external validity. But of course it is not a sufficient condition. Perhaps an experiment is assumed unjustifiably to generalize to a setting that is unlike the experimental one, such as remembering cards in poker playing, but unless it is an internally valid experiment, it makes no difference at all how close our experimental setting is to a target context such as poker playing; we have simply learned nothing.

An issue concerning generality often comes in the form of a general complaint about experimental method, that the artificiality of its setting makes it have little to do with the real context in which the phenomenon occurs. Perhaps this disenchantment derives from a naive optimism about what an experiment should deliver, resulting from amnesia for events in the emergence of scientific psychology (i.e. its divorce from philosophy on grounds of empiricism), coupled with sophisticated knowledge about how to 'do' an experiment. The successful debunking of one ostentatiously scientific approach to psychology, namely behaviourism, may have distracted some from the reasons why psychology remains a science.

A student attempting a first experiment in psychology must know that when a correctly designed experiment yields a relationship under specified conditions, our faith in the existence of that relationship is increased. Successive replications can allow still greater confidence that the finding is 'true' of the population identified by the sample, under the conditions identified by the test. But assuming that the relationship is true in any other sense is dangerous. Although the finding may well hold up under conditions other than those present in the experiment, that cannot be taken for granted. Yet it appears that a dissatisfaction with experiments often arises when conditions foreign to the experiment fail to provide confirmatory evidence for the thesis observed under the original conditions of the experiment. Experimenters should have realistic expectations of what precisely an experiment can do, and avoid the easy misunderstanding that an experiment is a general panacea, like the apocryphal advertisement for liquid that will 'clean your teeth and your driveway'.

Talking about generalizability reminds one of us of a well-intentioned graduate student who was troubled by what he considered the oppressive artificiality of much of experimental social psychology. Convinced that the study of person perception under controlled conditions could reveal nothing of importance about the process as it *really* operated, off he went to do a dissertation in a naturalistic setting, this one provided by the personnel department of a large company. After the usual painstaking data collection, vigorous analyses and articulate write-up, a member of the committee asked about the generality of the findings: the original purpose of removing the study from controlled conditions had been the belief in greater generality presumed for the supposedly real world setting. In the student's view, had this purpose been accomplished? The ensuing discussion was revealing. First, and not surprisingly, multiple factors present in the industrial environment had prevented random assignment to conditions, making it doubtful whether the findings were in fact interpretable or, more likely, the product of obvious confounds due to uncontrolled factors and imperfect random assignment. Second, in the opinion of the student himself, several of the conditions prevailing in this setting were so unique that it was unclear whether the findings obtained could generalize even to another branch of the same company in the same town!

This experience illustrates the second point we raised about generality, besides the primacy of internal validity: the generality of so-called real settings will result in findings that are themselves restricted to the specific set of conditions under which they are produced. A test in one worldly setting does not assure generalizability to another worldly setting. Students do not come knowing this intuitively, and we would hope that most learning exercises are less expensive than the above example would suggest. It appears that explicit awareness, through discussion and demonstration, of the tenuous nature of generalizing from one setting to another is necessary to teach it convincingly.

CONTEXT

The mention of experimental settings brings up a related point on which we should be clear: the psychology laboratory *is* an authentic real-world context, as Klatzky (1991) pointed out, and for many of us it is an everyday context. Even more to the point, for the subjects we test, it is usually a familiar context. We are on record as saying that a 'realistic' context is preferable to an 'artificial' context, provided there is an equal degree of experimental control in the two settings, and we continue to hold that tolerant position (although others have made persuasive arguments in defence of external *in*validity; see Mook 1983). It is an empirical question, when research is performed in one setting, to which other settings it might generalize. With almost infinite variety in the contexts in which we can perform experiments and even more contexts to which we might want our results to generalize, it would be foolish to suggest a priori principles of generalization from the former to the latter. But we can be sure that if the research is performed by sacrificing internal validity, it will not generalize to any other setting at all.

The distinction between the setting of a piece of research and the scientific utility of that research is underscored by the famous experiment of Godden and Baddeley (1975) on context effects in the acquisition and retrieval of word lists: subjects all wearing deep-sea diving gear received lists of words either underwater or on dry land. Half of each group was tested underwater and the other half on dry land. Performance was impressively better when the acquisition and testing contexts matched, whichever context it had been, compared to mismatched contexts. Now, in one sense, these are quite unusual and attractive non-laboratory contexts (and that is why we tend to tell undergraduates about this experiment in preference to more mundane studies showing virtually the same result). In another sense, the setting was highly artificial, for surely few if any human beings had ever previously received lists of words to remember while dressed in diving gear. But the reason for talking about it at all is of course that experimental control was perfectly achieved in the sense of independent groups, randomly assigned to treatments that were free of confounding factors. So, in this sense, the internal validity of the experiment was high. As it happens, the external validity of this research *to underwater learning* is also excellent, perhaps more so than if two different dry-land contexts had been used, but what is necessary for any generality of the study is its internal validity.

One legitimate model for scientific progress is to discover new contexts in which laws from previous research seem to be violated. (This did not occur, although we suppose it possibly might have, in the Godden and Baddeley study.) Many a time, serendipity, as well as careful observation, provides us with these new contexts. In the field of animal learning, such evolution occurred when observation of 'bait-shy' behaviour and the like seemed not to jibe with the then established temporal laws of learning. The scientific advance was made when Garcia and others (Barker *et al.* 1978; Garcia 1990; Garcia and Koelling 1966) showed in careful experiments that different temporal parameters govern classical conditioning, depending on an innate relationship between the stimuli and responses being used.

A similar episode has been initiated by Ceci and Bronfenbrenner (1985, 1991). These authors showed a difference between time-keeping behaviour of children in a home and a non-home (laboratory) setting. Children watched a clock with varying schedules when they were baking at home versus away from the home (we avoid the term

301

'laboratory' for the non-home situation from respect for Ceci and Bronfenbrenner's assumed intention to create two equally controlled environments). But, as Klatzky (1991) noted, there were several differences between the home and non-home (e.g. being watched by an unobtrusive experimenter versus being observed by an older sibling). In addition, home and non-home conditions surely differ in a number of uncontrollable ways (e.g. degree of relaxation). If this is the point to be made, it seems rather simplistic and unarguable: behaviour will differ when the conditions under which behaviour is observed also differ.

The natural evolution of the finding will be to examine a range of controlled settings that can provide a theoretical understanding of the differences between the two settings. Indications are that these authors accept such a mandate, e.g. in trying to determine whether the presence of a family member makes the difference (Ceci and Bronfenbrenner 1985). When the controlling factors are identified, we shall surely understand the target psychological processes better. As with bait-shyness, bringing the difference under scrutiny in the laboratory – gaining experimental control over the differences between what was called 'home' and 'laboratory' – will be the key to this progress.

We appreciate the point about context that motivates Ceci and Bronfenbrenner: a finding from a laboratory setting is sometimes glibly assumed to generalize to other settings. Their demonstration to the contrary is useful if the point to be made specifies the aspects of varying conditions under which behaviour variability is observed. This can be achieved by manipulating the pertinent variables under controlled conditions, as Klatzky (1991) suggested. Context effects can indeed be examined under controlled conditions, i.e. by producing a laboratory environment that is high in what social psychologists have called *mundane realism* (Carlsmith *et al.* 1976). To us, it is unclear that the home conditions are inherently superior to the non-home conditions. If the interest is in demonstrating behaviour in situations away from home, the particular non-home (laboratory) condition used by Ceci and Bronfenbrenner (1985) would actually be the more appropriate context. On the other hand, if there are influences that are present at home that interest these authors (and they wish to generalize to the home but not to non-home conditions), there are well-established ways of successfully conducting quasi-experiments in naturalistic settings (see Campbell and Stanley 1963; Cook and Campbell 1979).

Often, the context variables in one area of research are the primary independent variables in another. For example, the social features of an environment are sometimes considered important context variables by those whose dependent variables are cognitive in nature. For yet others, these same context variables are themselves of crucial interest. For example, Doise and Mugny (1984) have conducted experiments showing that intelligence as demonstrated by standard Piagetian tasks is inextricably linked to culture (socio-economic status) and features of the immediate situation. By systematically varying the presence or absence of others in the experimental situation, by creating cooperative ways of sharing knowledge, and by observing children from varying socio-economic backgrounds, they show, under controlled conditions, the importance of such variables on cognitive development. We applaud their concluding emphasis on the importance of experimentation in the study of issues often considered too complex and unique to the 'real world' to be brought under controlled observation. Often, the justification for conducting tests in the situation in which the behaviour naturally occurs (in the name of attention to context) is (a) a lack of creativity in making the laboratory a stage, and (b) a failure to grapple with explanation (rather than description) as the final goal.

Whatever one's interest in context, there are two pressing issues. First, an interest in context is orthogonal to the issue of controlled experimentation. In particular, context does not have to be examined only in naturalistic settings. Experiments on contextual variables have long been part of the history of research on memory. For example, studies of mood and memory (see Isen 1984; Singer and Salovey 1988), the influence of drug states on memory (see Birnbaum and Parker 1977; Eich 1980), and social factors in memory (see Fiske and Taylor 1991; Hastie *et al.* 1984) are examples of the study of contextual variables in memory that defy the claim that control has precluded an analysis of context. Second, the study of context, like the study of any other aspect of memory, must be driven theoretically.

FUNCTIONALISM

Bruce (1991) and Neisser (1991) have observed correctly that the life sciences may provide better models for the mandate of psychology than such sciences as chemistry. This might be true if only because the life sciences are concerned with living organisms and tend to be much younger than the physical sciences. We admit that our writing about a fictional 'Everyday Chemistry Movement' had rhetorical purposes (although we believe now as we did then that the rhetoric was on target).

Bruce (1991) is especially interested in evolutionary biology as an alternative model. We see three problems with the evolutionary biology model for a science of memory. First, as previously mentioned (Banaji and Crowder 1989), the pace of evolutionary change is many orders of magnitude too slow with humans to allow systematic observation of the evolution under study. The primary theoretical tool of evolutionary biology, i.e. the differential equation, which is not hampered by the slow rate of change and allows mechanisms about differing time-scales to be coupled, has not yet been applied usefully to memory. A related, second point is that the memory system does not, in principle, leave traces as palaeobiological forms do. Of course, memories themselves are traces in one way, but they are not unambiguous physical traces of *how the system operated* in some past time. So, even though we can study life-span development of memory, we cannot break free from that fixed constraint. Without fossils, carbon dating and related artefactual techniques, 'population thinking' in evolutionary biology would be stymied.

Biology, furthermore, has the possibility of choosing species with such a giddy reproductive rate – say fruit flies – that full experimental approaches to evolution are feasible. And experimental research from Mendel to Dobzhansky must surely be the foundation of evolutionary biology, as we are convinced it will be for psychology, whatever future directions our discipline might take. But, by experimental research, we are referring entirely to the criterion of controlled observation, the *sine qua non* of internal validity that we discussed earlier.

Finally, it can be argued that the correct approach is none the less to observe the functional significance of memory at a momentary slice of time, in order to place it in a proper evolutionary perspective. Baddeley (1988) asked what memory is 'good for' in yearning for answers within this perspective. Others have argued that everyday memory research can begin to look for adaptive rationalizations of observed memory behaviour (Neisser 1991). Indeed, concern with such questions of function was responsible for the character of American Functionalism as a historical movement within psychology (Boring 1929). We agree to the extent that a priority for psychology must be to see how individual, elementary behaviour principles articulate with others in larger, coordinated behavioural settings.

But such suggestions are in no sense causal explanations of the elementary behaviour principles in question: circularity is not the worst of the problems, because it is almost always possible to think of a reason for why a particular principle is, after all, 'for the better' in terms of evolution. For example, the facts of post-traumatic retrograde amnesia seem, at first, to be rather obviously maladaptive. For the preservation of the species, humans and other organisms should remember, if nothing else, what happened just moments before the traumatic incident (e.g. car crash, football skirmish, attack of the tiger). Knowing what happened just before the incident allows the organism to go on with its reproductive activities, even if little else. But the system works just the opposite: memories are typically spared, *except* for what was going on just before the trauma. We might thus conclude that evolution has given us a memory system 180 degrees out of phase with our environmental context.

But, faced with the same facts, others may well be able to see an evolutionary advantage to whatever produces retrograde amnesia. For example, other aspects of the system may make it advisable to work in exactly this way (i.e. to forget the traumatic event), even given the obvious costs. The absence of a system to resolve the validity of alternative explanations is the crucial problem here. The faith in functionalism reminds us of Sunday school arguments that God, in his wisdom, sometimes works in mysterious ways. The complacent reliance on faith in the final analysis is similar.

COMMENT

Our defence of controlled environments as the method of choice for theory testing should not be taken as innocence about the limitations of the experimental method and of science in general. What attracts us to the notion of a science of topics, such as memory, is the well-known ideology of the scientific revolution, in particular its tenets of anti-authoritarianism, anti-traditionalism and anti-revelationism. But, as Campbell (1986: 119) correctly pointed out, 'Sociologically, this is a difficult ideology to put into practice.' As attractive as the ideology of science may be, we are sometimes made painfully aware of the consequences of pseudo-science, with its trappings of controlled experimentation, impressive instruments, etc. In our own discipline, we have outrageous evidence for abuse in the name of the scientific method, in particular in theories espoused about race and gender (see Gould 1981; Fausto-Sterling 1985). Any field, and human memory is no exception, needs sociologists of knowledge who point out the multifarious ways in which the practice of science is 'seen as a product of cultural–evolutionary process on the part of a bounded belief-transmitting subsociety of many generations' (Campbell 1986: 120). But, as we have said before (Banaji and Crowder 1991), particular misuses of the experimental method do not provide a case for dispensing with a method that stands, at least at present, without competitors for the everyday theory testing that ensures the progress of normal psychological science.

CONCLUSION

We have suggested that internal validity is the single indispensable condition for the generalization of research to any conceivable context. Beyond that, generalization from the research setting to the desired setting of application is an important, but essentially tract-able, research agenda. Second, we have reaffirmed that the psychology laboratory is one among many such worldly settings, not different in kind from the others. Finally, we have indicated our respect for issues concerning how elementary principles of behaviour articulate with other elementary principles in observed human activity; however, we doubt that such evolutionary arguments can easily approach the status of explanatory principles.

ACKNOWLEDGEMENTS

We thank R. Bhaskar for comments. This writing of this chapter was supported in part by National Science Foundation grant DBC-9120987.

REFERENCES

Baddeley, A.D. (1988) 'But what the hell is it for?', in M.M. Gruneberg, P.E. Morris and R.N. Sykes (eds) *Practical Aspects of Memory: Current Research and Issues*, vol. 1, pp. 3–18, New York: Wiley.

Banaji, M.R. and Crowder, R.G. (1989) 'The bankruptcy of everyday memory', *American Psychologist* 44: 1185–93.

—— (1991) 'Some everyday thoughts on ecologically valid methods', *American Psychologist* 46: 78–9.

Barker, L.M., Best, M.R. and Domjan, M. (eds) (1978) *Learning Mechanisms in Food Selection*, Houston: Baylor University Press.

Birnbaum, I.M. and Parker, E.S. (eds) (1977) *Alcohol and Human Memory*, Hillsdale, New Jersey: Erlbaum.

Boring, E.G. (1929) *A History of Experimental Psychology*, New York: Appleton-Century.

Bruce, D. (1991) 'Mechanistic and functional explanations of memory', *American Psychologist* 46: 46–8.

Campbell, D.T. (1957) 'Factors relevant to the validity of experiments in social settings', *Psychological Bulletin* 54: 297–312.

—— (1986) 'Science's social system of validity-enhancing collective belief change and the problems of the social sciences', in D.W. Fiske and R.A. Schweder (eds) *Metatheory in Social Science: Pluralism and Subjectives*, pp. 108–35, Chicago: University of Chicago Press.

Campbell, D.T. and Stanley, J.C. (1963) *Experimental and Quasi-Experimental Designs for Research*, Chicago: Rand McNally.

Carlsmith, J.M., Ellsworth, P.C. and Aronson, E. (1976) *Methods of Research in Social Psychology*, Reading, Massachusetts: Addison-Wesley.

Ceci, S.J. and Bronfenbrenner, U. (1985) 'Don't forget to take the cupcakes out of the oven: Strategic time-monitoring, prospective memory and context', *Child Development* 56: 175–90.

—— (1991) 'On the demise of everyday memory', *American Psychologist* 46: 27–31.

Cook, T.D. and Campbell, D.T. (1979) *Quasi-Experimentation*, Chicago: Rand McNally.

Craik, K.J.W. (1952) *The Nature of Explanation*, Cambridge: Cambridge University Press.

Doise, W. and Mugny, G. (1984) *The Social Development of the Intellect*, vol. 10, New York: Pergamon Press.

Eich, J.E. (1980) 'The cue-dependent nature of state-dependent retrieval', *Memory and Cognition* 8: 157–73.

Fausto-Sterling, A. (1985) *Myths of Gender*, New York: Basic Books.

Fiske, S.T. and Taylor, S.E. (1991) *Social Cognition*, New York: McGraw-Hill, second edition.

Garcia, J. (1990) 'Learning without memory', *Journal of Cognitive Neuroscience* 2, 287–305.

Garcia, J. and Koelling, R.A. (1966) 'The relation of cue to consequence in avoidance learning', *Psychonomic Science* 4: 123–4.

Godden, D.R. and Baddeley, A.D. (1975) 'Context-dependent memory in two natural environments: On land and underwater', *British Journal of Psychology* 66: 325–31.

Gould, S.J. (1981) *The Mismeasure of Man*, New York: Norton.

Hastie, R., Park, B. and Weber, R. (1984) 'Social memory', in R.S. Wyer, Jr and T.K. Srull (eds) *Handbook of Social Cognition*, vol. 2, pp. 151–212, Hillsdale, New Jersey: Erlbaum.

Isen, A.M. (1984) 'Toward understanding the role of affect in cognition', in R.S. Wyer and T.K. Srull (eds) *Handbook of Social Cognition*, vol. 3, pp. 179–236, Hillsdale, New Jersey: Erlbaum.

Kiddler, L.H. and Judd, C.M. (1986) *Research Methods in Social Relations*, New York: Holt, Rinehart & Winston, fifth edition.

Klatzky, R.L. (1991) 'Let's be friends', *American Psychologist* 46: 43–5.

Mook, D.G. (1983) 'In defense of external invalidity', *American Psychologist* 38: 379–87.

Neisser, U. (1991) 'A case of misplaced nostalgia', *American Psychologist* 46: 34–6.

Roediger, H.L. (1991) 'They read an article?' *American Psychologist* 46: 37–40.

Singer, J.A. and Salovey, P. (1988) 'Mood and memory: Evaluating the network theory of affect', *Clinical Psychology Review* 8: 211–51.

INDEX

activity 215, 219–21
Albert, M.S. *et al.* 245
alexics 260, 263
Allport, D.A. 198, 226
amnesia 13, 282–6
analogy 223–5
Anderson, J.R. 229, 287; and
  Bower, G.H. 24, 40, 41, 168
Anderson, R.C. and Pearson, P.D.
  91, 98
Anisfeld, M. and Knapp, M.E.
  131
Aristotle 5, 7–9, 24
articulatory loop (later phonological
  loop q.v.) 52–3, 229
articulatory suppression 52, 55–6,
  58–9, 62
Ashcroft, M.A. and Kellas, G. 86
associationism 8, 11–12, 14, 20,
  22, 23, 24, 33, 41, 158–60;
  measuring long-term 149–56
asymmetric 175
Atkinson, R.C. and Shiffrin, R.M.
  22, 34, 50, 81, 85
autobiographical memory 12–13,
  37, 196, 248, 286–90
aviary metaphor 6–7
Ayer, A. J. 14

Baddeley, A.D. 22, 30, 34, 40, 42,
  53, 62, 69, 71, 73, 81, 174, 229,
  238, 275, 292; *et al.* 52, 55, 56,
  58, 63, 64, 68, 256; and Hitch,
  G.J. 24, 50, 52, 69, 255; and

Lieberman, K. 52, 65; and
  Warrington, E.K. 132; and
  Wilson, B. 249
Bahrick, H.P. 278–80; 292; *et al.*
  274–7
Baker-Ward, L. 86
Balsam, P.D. and Tomie, A. 170
Banaji, M.R. and Crowder, R.G.
  273, 296, 304, 306
Barclay, C.R. 85, 87
Barclay, J.R. *et al.* 39
Barker, L.M. *et al.* 301
Barnes, J.M. and Underwood, B.J.
  21
Barsalou, L.W. 146, 211
Bartlett, F.C. 17–20, 24, 41, 196,
  222
Basso, A. *et al.* 254, 256
Bebko, J. 89; and McKinnon, E.E.
  89
behaviourism 14–25
Belmont, J.M. and Butterfield,
  E.C. 86, 116; *et al.* 107
Berch, D.B. and Evans, R.C. 104
Berkeley, George 10
Besner, D. *et al.* 220
Besson, M. *et al.* 153, 154
Beuhring, T. and Kee, D.W. 88
Bilodeau, I.M. and Schlosberg, H.
  170
biological plausibility 226–7
Birnbaum, I.M. and Parker, E.S.
  303
Bisanz, G.L. *et al.* 104